# Praise for *Regress*

"The examples in the text are very applicable to various disciplines and very easy to understand and follow. Overall I would highly recommend this text to anyone in need of a manual on regression methods in JMP."

**Luis Rene Mateo**
**Research Statistician**


"I found *Regression Using JMP* by Freund, Littell, and Creighton to be well written and helpful. The chapter on collinearity is particularly useful as it explained the use of leverage plots to explore collinearity, in a clear, straightforward manner."

**Rob Gier**
**Medication Delivery**
**Baxter Healthcare Corporation**


"Although a non-statistician, I enjoyed the topics discussed and the almost 'one on one' feel in the verbiage. The book expanded my knowledge of JMP software as well as statistical concepts. Long-standing questions regarding the Stepwise Platform were resolved."

**James Thacker**
**TRIZ/DOE Engineering Mentor**


"*Regression Using JMP* is a well-written book for the intermediate-level statistician who wants to get more from the JMP program. This book offers a better blend of theory and mechanics than most software-oriented texts."

**Eric Hamann**
**Principal Biostatistician**
**Wyeth**


"I've been using JMP for about one year now. A couple months ago, I started to use JMP for regression analysis. I wished I had this book when I started. The explanation of the variable selection was terrific, and I know I will continue to use this book as a resource when I'm doing future analysis."

**Sharon Field, new JMP user**

# Regression Using JMP®

Rudolf Freund

Ramon Littell

Lee Creighton

The correct bibliographic citation for this manual is as follows: Freund, Rudolf J., Ramon C. Littell, and Lee Creighton. 2003. *Regression Using JMP*®. Cary, NC: SAS Institute Inc.

## Regression Using JMP®

Copyright © 2003 by SAS Institute Inc., Cary, NC, USA
Jointly co-published by SAS Institute and Wiley 2003.

SAS Institute Inc. ISBN 1-59047-160-1
John Wiley & Sons, Inc. ISBN 0-471-48307-9

All rights reserved. Printed in the United States of America. No part of this publication may be reproduced, stored in a retrieval system, or transmitted, in any form or by any means, electronic, mechanical, photocopying, or otherwise, without the prior written permission of the publisher, SAS Institute Inc.

**U.S. Government Restricted Rights Notice:** Use, duplication, or disclosure of this software and related documentation by the U.S. government is subject to the Agreement with SAS Institute and the restrictions set forth in FAR 52.227-19, Commercial Computer Software-Restricted Rights (June 1987).

SAS Institute Inc., SAS Campus Drive, Cary, North Carolina 27513.

1st printing, June 2003

SAS Publishing provides a complete selection of books and electronic products to help customers use SAS software to its fullest potential. For more information about our e-books, e-learning products, CDs, and hardcopy books, visit the SAS Publishing Web site at **support.sas.com/pubs** or call 1-800-727-3228.

SAS® and all other SAS Institute Inc. product or service names are registered trademarks or trademarks of SAS Institute Inc. in the USA and other countries. ® indicates USA registration.

IBM® and all other International Business Machines Corporation product or service names are registered trademarks or trademarks of International Business Machines Corporation in the USA and other countries.

Oracle® and all other Oracle Corporation product service names are registered trademarks of Oracle Corporation in the USA and other countries.

Other brand and product names are trademarks of their respective companies.

# Contents

Acknowledgments   v

Using This Book   vii

## 1 Regression Concepts   1

    1.1    What Is Regression?   1
    1.2    Statistical Background   13
    1.3    Terminology and Notation   15
    1.4    Regression with JMP   23

## 2 Regressions in JMP   25

    2.1    Introduction   25
    2.2    A Model with One Independent Variable   27
    2.3    A Model with Several Independent Variables   32
    2.4    Additional Results from Fit Model   36
    2.5    Further Examination of Model Parameters   50
    2.6    Plotting Observations   54
    2.7    Predicting to a Different Set of Data   63
    2.8    Exact Collinearity: Linear Dependency   67
    2.9    Summary   70

## 3 Observations   73

    3.1    Introduction   73
    3.2    Outlier Detection   74
    3.3    Specification Errors   91
    3.4    Heterogeneous Variances   96
    3.5    Summary   104

## 4 Collinearity: Detection and Remedial Measures   105

    4.1    Introduction   105
    4.2    Detecting Collinearity   107
    4.3    Model Restructuring   115

- 4.4 Variable Selection  125
- 4.5 Summary  136

## 5 Polynomial and Smoothing Models  139

- 5.1 Introduction  139
- 5.2 Polynomial Models with One Independent Variable  140
- 5.3 Polynomial Models with Several Variables  151
- 5.4 Response Surface Plots  156
- 5.5 A Three-Factor Response Surface Experiment  158
- 5.6 Smoothing Data  167
- 5.7 Summary  173

## 6 Special Applications of Linear Models  175

- 6.1 Introduction  175
- 6.2 Errors in Both Variables  176
- 6.3 Multiplicative Models  181
- 6.4 Spline Models  191
- 6.5 Indicator Variables  195
- 6.6 Binary Response Variable: Logistic Regression  203
- 6.7 Summary  214

## 7 Nonlinear Models  215

- 7.1 Introduction  215
- 7.2 Estimating the Exponential Decay Model  216
- 7.3 Fitting a Growth Curve with the Nonlinear Platform  229
- 7.4 Summary  236

## 8 Regression with JMP Scripting Language  237

- 8.1 Introduction  237
- 8.2 Performing a Simple Regression  237
- 8.3 Regression Matrices  241
- 8.4 Collinearity Diagnostics  242
- 8.5 Summary  246

References  247

Index  249

# Acknowledgments

We would like to acknowledge several people at SAS Institute whose efforts have contributed to the completion of this book. First of all, we are grateful to Jim Goodnight, who originally encouraged us to write the book. John Sall provided insight into the inner workings of JMP that proved invaluable.

Special thanks go to Dr. Mark Bailey, who meticulously read each chapter and made many suggestions that greatly enhanced the quality of the finished product. Duane Hayes, from SAS Technical Support, also reviewed the entire book through several stages and provided useful comments, as well as offering ideas for the JSL section of the text.

Jim Ashton, Jenny Kendall, Charles Lin, Eddie Routten, Warren Sarle, Mike Stockstill, Tonya Baker, John Sall, Bradley Jones, and Chuck Boiler also reviewed the text in various stages.

The work of several persons has influenced our writing. In particular, we acknowledge Walt Harvey of Ohio State University, Ron Hocking of Texas A&M University, Bill Saunders of SAS Institute, Shayle Searle of Cornell University, and Ann Lehman of SAS Institute.

Also important in the completion of this book was the SAS production team, including Julie Platt and Donna Faircloth.

Finally, we thank the students at Texas A&M University and the University of Florida whose research projects provided the ideas and data for many of the examples.

# Using This Book

## Purpose

Most statistical analyses are based on linear models, and most analyses of linear models can be performed by two JMP platforms: Fit Y by X and Fit Model. Unlike statistical packages that need different programs for each type of analysis, these procedures provide the power and flexibility for almost all linear model analyses.

To use these platforms properly, you should understand the statistics you need for the analysis and know how to instruct JMP to carry out the computations. *Regression Using JMP* was written to make it easier for you to use JMP in your data analysis problems. In this book, a wide variety of data is used to illustrate the basic kinds of regression models that can be analyzed with JMP.

## Audience

*Regression Using JMP* is intended to assist data analysts who use JMP software to perform data analysis using regression analysis. This book assumes you are familiar with basic JMP concepts such as entering data into a JMP table, and with standard operating system procedures like manipulating the mouse and accessing menus.

## Prerequisites

Although this book contains some explanation of statistical methods, it is not intended as a text for these methods. The reader should have a working knowledge of the statistical concepts discussed in this book.

# How to Use This Book

The following sections provide an overview of the information contained in this book and how it is organized.

# Organization

*Regression Using JMP* represents an introduction to regression analysis as performed by JMP. In addition to information about the customary Fit Y by X and Fit Model platforms found in all versions of JMP, this volume contains information about new features and capabilities of JMP Version 5. Here is a summary of the information contained in each chapter.

### Chapter 1, "Regression Concepts"

Chapter 1 presents an interactive introduction to regression, the terminology and notation used in regression analysis, and an overview of matrix notation.

### Chapter 2, "Regressions in JMP"

Chapter 2 introduces regression analysis, using both the Fit Y by X and Fit Model platforms with a single independent variable. The statistics in the output are discussed in detail. Next, a regression is performed using the same data but with several independent variables. Confidence limits are discussed in detail. The No Intercept option of the Fit Model dialog, which is controversial, is used and discussed. This option is also misused in an example to point out the dangers of forcing the regression response to pass through the origin when this situation is unreasonable or unlikely.

### Chapter 3, "Observations"

Chapter 3 discusses the assumptions behind regression analysis and illustrates how the data analyst assesses violations of assumptions. This chapter discusses outliers, or those observations that do not appear to fit the model; outliers can bias parameter estimates and make your regression analysis less useful. This chapter also discusses ways to identify the influence (or leverage) of specific observations. Studentized residuals are used to identify large residuals. Examples are shown using residuals that are plotted using the Overlay Plot platform. In addition, this chapter discusses ways to detect specification errors and assess the fit of the model, ways to check the distribution of the errors for nonnormality, ways to check for heteroscedasticity, or nonconstant variances of errors, and ways to detect correlation between errors.

### Chapter 4, "Collinearity: Detection and Remedial Measures"

Chapter 4 discusses the existence of collinearity (correlation among several independent variables). It contains measures you can use to detect collinearity and ways to alleviate the effects of it. Variance inflation factors are used to determine the variables involved. Multivariate techniques are used to study the structure of collinearity. Also presented in this chapter are discussions of principal components regression and variable selection, including stepwise regression techniques.

### Chapter 5, "Polynomial and Smoothing Models"

Chapter 5 gives examples of linear regression methods to estimate parameters of models that cannot be described by straight lines. The discussion of polynomial models, in which the dependent variable is related to functions of the powers of one or more independent variables, begins by using one independent variable. Then examples are given using several variables. Response surface plots are used to illustrate the nature of the estimated response curve.

### Chapter 6, "Special Applications of Linear Models"

Chapter 6 covers some special applications of the linear model, including orthogonal regression, log-linear (multiplicative) models, spline functions with known knots, and the use of indicator variables.

### Chapter 7, "Nonlinear Models"

Chapter 7 discusses special relationships that cannot be addressed by linear models or adaptations of linear models. Topics include the Nonlinear platform and fitting nonlinear growth curves.

### Chapter 8, "Regression with JMP Scripting Language"

Chapter 8 provides examples of how JMP can be customized to extend its built-in regression methods. Sample code is provided for doing simple regressions, displaying regression matrices, and performing collinearity diagnostics.

## Conventions

This book uses a number of conventions, including typographical conventions, syntax conventions, and conventions for presenting output.

## Typographical Conventions

This book uses several type styles. The following list summarizes style conventions:

**bold roman**   is used in headings, in text to indicate very important points, and in formulas to indicate matrices and vectors.

**bold Helvetica**   is used to refer to menu items and other control elements of JMP.

`monospace`   is used to show examples of programming code.

🖱   In addition, steps that are intended to be carried out on the computer are preceded by a mouse symbol, like the one shown here.

## Conventions for Output

All JMP analyses in the book were run on JMP Version 5.0 under the Macintosh OS X operating system. In most cases, generic output was produced (without operating system-specific title bars and menus). Because of differences in software versions, size options, and graphics devices, your graphics or numerical output may not be identical to what appears in this book, especially for the screen shots involving dialog boxes.

# Chapter 1  Regression Concepts

1.1 **What Is Regression?**  *1*
    1.1.1  *Seeing Regression*  *1*
    1.1.2  *A Physical Model of Regression*  *7*
    1.1.3  *Multiple Linear Regression*  *9*
    1.1.4  *Correlation*  *9*
    1.1.5  *Seeing Correlation*  *11*
1.2 **Statistical Background**  *13*
1.3 **Terminology and Notation**  *15*
    1.3.1  *Partitioning the Sums of Squares*  *16*
    1.3.2  *Hypothesis Testing*  *18*
    1.3.3  *Using the Generalized Inverse*  *21*
1.4 **Regression with JMP**  *23*

## 1.1 What Is Regression?

Multiple linear regression is a means to express the idea that a response variable, $y$, varies with a set of independent variables, $x_1, x_2, ..., x_m$. The variability that $y$ exhibits has two components: a systematic part and a random part. The systematic variation of $y$ is modeled as a function of the $x$ variables. This model relating $y$ to $x_1, x_2, ..., x_m$ is called the *regression equation*. The random part takes into account the fact that the model does not exactly describe the behavior of the response.

### 1.1.1 Seeing Regression

It is easiest to see the process of regression by looking at a single $x$ variable. In this example, the independent ($x$) variable is a person's height and the dependent ($y$) variable is a person's weight. The data are shown in Figure 1.1 and stored in the Small Class.jmp data file.

First, we explore the variables to get a sense of their distribution. Then, we illustrate regression by fitting a model of height to weight.

## 2  Regression Concepts

*Figure 1.1*
Small
Class.jmp
*Data Set*

| height | weight |
|---|---|
| 44 | 75 |
| 52 | 95 |
| 59 | 90 |
| 65 | 100 |
| 78 | 99 |
| 80 | 113 |

An excellent first step in any data analysis (one that is not expressly stated in each analysis of this book) is to examine the distribution of the *x* and *y* variables. Note that this step is not required in a regression analysis, but nevertheless is good practice. To duplicate the display shown here,

- Select **Analyze → Distribution**.
- Click on height in the list of columns.
- Click the **Y, Columns** button.
- Repeat these steps for the weight variable.
- Click **OK**.

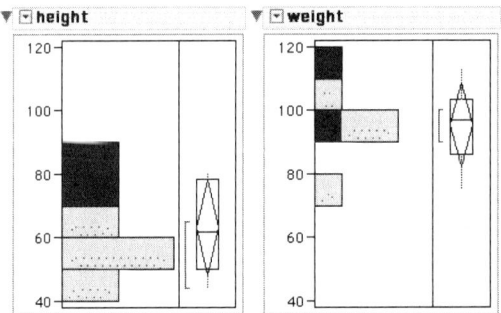

It is clear that the height values are generally less than the weight values. The box plots tell us that there are no outliers or unusual points. However, these unidimensional plots do not tell us much about the relationship between height and weight.

Remember that JMP is an interactive, exploratory tool and that in general, most plots and data are connected to each other. In the case of the two histograms, clicking on a histogram bar in one plot also highlights bars and points in the other plot. The example here shows the result when the two higher height bars are selected, revealing that these high values of height are associated with high values of weight. This fact is a good start in our exploration of the two variables.

It is now appropriate to get a bivariate plot of the two variables. In general, this is accomplished through the Fit Y by X platform, resulting in a graph similar to Figure 1.2.

*Figure 1.2*
*Graph of*
weight *by*
height

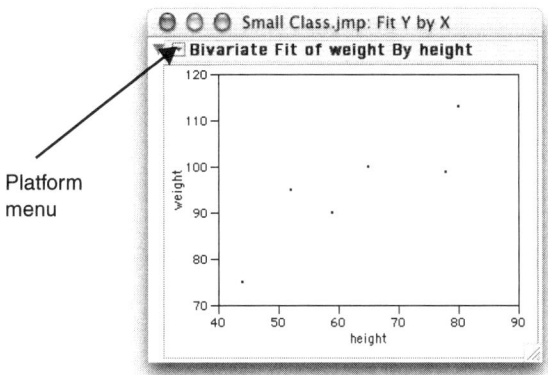

Platform menu

- Select **Analyze → Fit Y by X**.
- Select weight in the list of columns and click the **Y, Response** button.
- Select height in the list of columns and click the **X, Factor** button.
- Click **OK**.

We now see the relationship between weight and height. It appears that weight values increase with corresponding increases in height, and it appears that they increase in a linear way. Therefore, we fit a line to the data. The objective is to find a single line that best summarizes the data—to find a linear equation that predicts values of weight given values of height. To compute and draw this line,

- Select **Fit Line** from the platform menu on the title of the plot (see Figure 1.2).

JMP fits the regression and displays the output shown in Figure 1.3.

Most cases of simple linear regression are accomplished by repeating these steps.

For this introduction, the scatterplot has been coded into a script named demoLeastSquares.jsl. It is used as an illustration of the inner workings of the least-squares method. In practice, you complete the analysis as shown above. The script and accompanying activity are purely pedagogical.

**Figure 1.3**
*Regression Output*

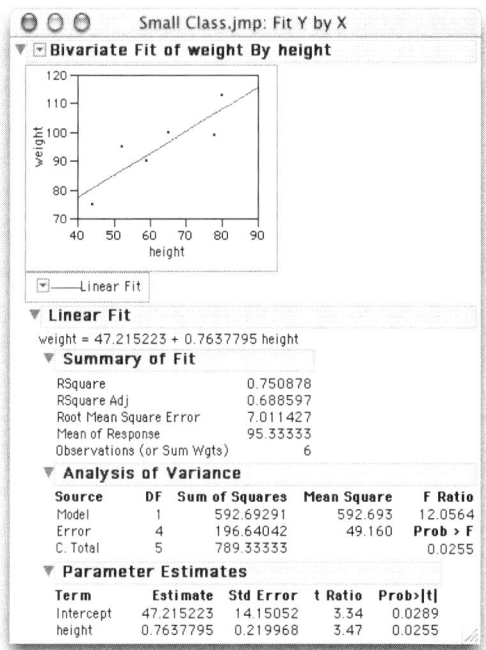

- Open the script demoLeastSquares.jsl, found in the Sample Scripts folder. Note that the Open dialog must show files of type JSL, so adjust the dialog to show Data Files, JMP Files, or All Readable documents.

- Select **Edit → Run Script**.

- When the script output appears, click the **Your Residuals** button (shown in Figure 1.5).

This button turns on a measurement for the accuracy of the linear model. The model itself is represented by an orange line. The distance from this line to each data point is called the *residual*, and it is represented by the dark blue vertical lines that connect the orange line to each data point. See Figure 1.4 for an explanation of the graph produced by the script.

The handles are used to move the model around so that it approximates the shape of the data. As you drag one handle, the other stays fixed. Obviously, many lines can be drawn through the data, each resulting in different residual values. The question is, of all the possible lines that can be drawn through the data, which is the best?

*Figure 1.4*
demoLeast
Squares
*Window*

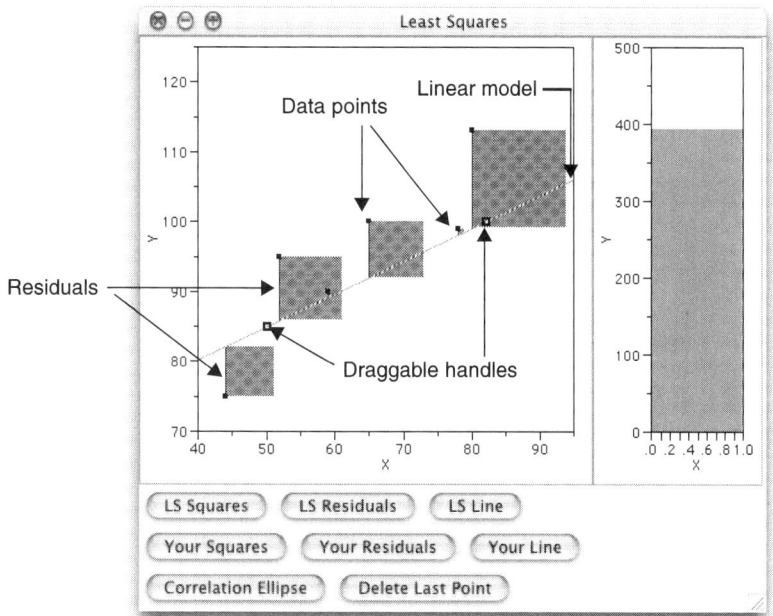

One logical criterion for a "best-fitting" line could be that it is the one where the sum of the residuals is the smallest number. Or, one could claim the best-fitting line is the one that has equal numbers of points above and below the line. Or, one could choose the line that minimizes the perpendicular distances from the points to the line.

In the least-squares method, the squares of the residuals are measured. Geometrically, this value of (residual)$^2$ can be represented as a square with the length of a side equal to the value of the residual.

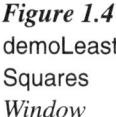 Click the **Your Squares** button to activate the squares of the residuals.

It is this quantity that is minimized. The line with the smallest sum of the squared residuals is used as the best fitting. Geometrically, this means that we seek the line that has the smallest area covered by the squares superimposed on the plot. As an aid to show the sum of the squared residuals, a "thermometer" is appended to the right of the graph (Figure 1.5). This thermometer displays the total area covered by the squared residuals.

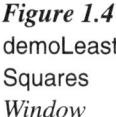 Drag the handles of the model to try to minimize the sum of the squared residuals.

**Figure 1.5**
*Squared Residuals*

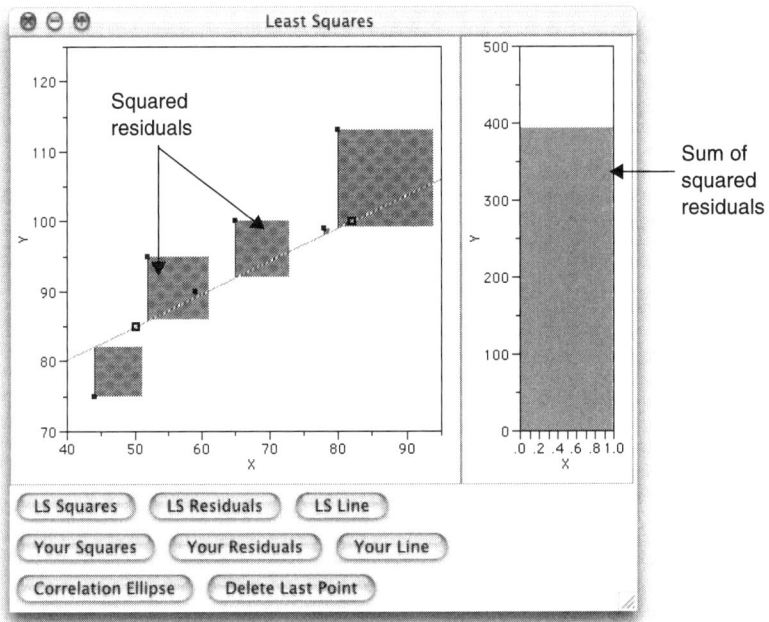

When you think the sum is at a minimum,

- Push the **LS Line** and **LS Squares** buttons.

The actual (calculated) least-squares line is superimposed upon the graph, along with the squares of its residuals. Additionally, a line is drawn on the thermometer representing the sum of the squared residuals from this line.

- Drag the handles so that the movable line corresponds exactly to the least-squares line.

Note that the sum of squares now corresponds to the least-squares sum (Figure 1.6). You should notice that as you dragged the handles onto the least-squares line, the sum of the squared residuals decreased until it matched the minimum sum of squares.

- Drag the handles so that the movable line moves off the least-squares line. Experiment with the line moving away from the least-squares line in all directions.

This illustrates the central concept of least-squares regression. The *least-squares line*, often called the *line of best fit*, is the one that *minimizes the sum of squares of the residuals*.

*Figure 1.6*
*Least-Squares Line*

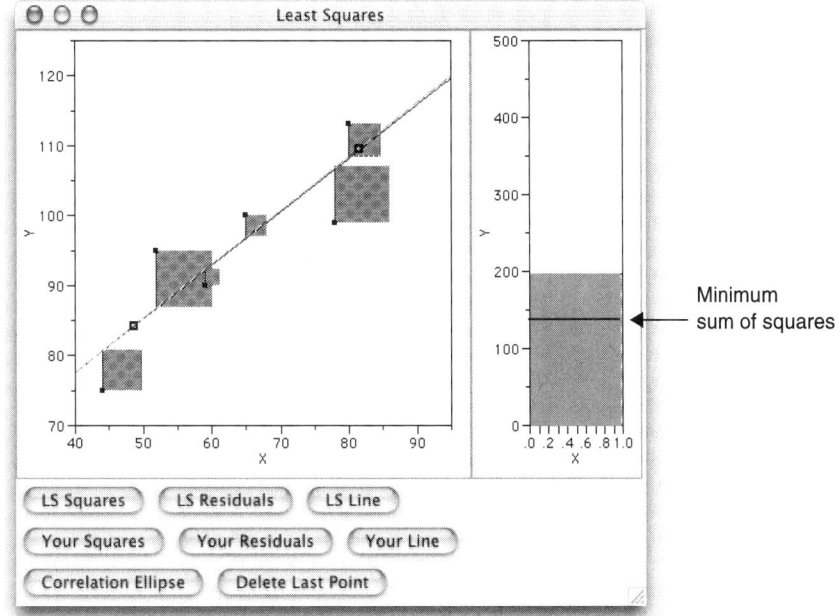

### 1.1.2 A Physical Model of Regression

The following explanation shows how fitting a least-squares line can be thought of in terms of a physical process. Specifically, it relates regression to properties of springs.

A well-known property of springs is that the force they exert is proportional to the distance they are stretched. Additionally, the energy in the spring is the integral of this force. Specifically, Hooke's law tells us that

$F=kx$

where

$F$ = force exerted by the spring

$k$ = spring constant measuring stiffness of the spring

$x$ = distance the spring is stretched.

## 8  Regression Concepts

For reasons that will become evident later, let the spring constant $k$ be represented by $1/\sigma$. Then, the energy in a spring with this value of $k$ is

$$E = \int \frac{1}{\sigma} x\, dx = \frac{x^2}{2\sigma}$$

Again consider the height/weight data shown in Figure 1.1.

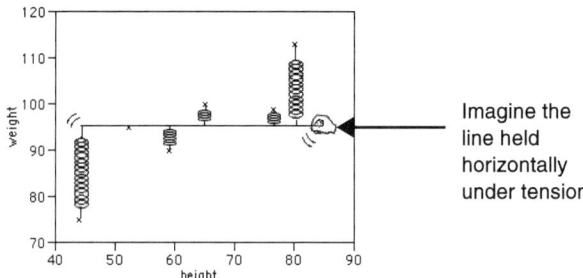

A graph of weight vs. height is shown here with a line drawn at the mean value of weight. Now, imagine hooking up springs, with one end on a data point and the other end on the mean line. If $x_i$ represents a data point and $\mu$ represents the value of the overall mean, then each spring is stretched a distance of $x_i - \mu$.

If the whole system were released, the mean line would rotate and shift to the point of minimum total energy in the system. Mathematically, where $\mu$ is the mean of $x$ and $\sigma$ is the standard deviation of $x$,

$$\sum_{i=1}^{n} \left(\frac{x_i - \mu}{\sigma}\right)^2 = \frac{1}{\sigma} \sum_{i=1}^{n} (x_i - \mu)^2$$

would be minimized. The constant on the outside of the sum would not come into play with a minimization, so in essence we would minimize

$$\sum_{i=1}^{n} (x_i - \mu)^2$$

This is exactly the expression that is minimized in least-squares fitting. So the physical system of springs is equivalent to fitting a least-squares line. The point where the line is balanced, rotationally and vertically, is the least-squares line.

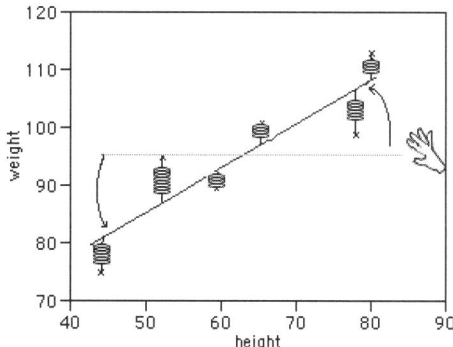

The reason $1/\sigma$ was chosen as the spring constant is that when $k = \sigma$, the expression to be minimized is also equivalent to the log-likelihood of the density of the normal distribution. In other words, the line given by maximizing the log-likelihood is also modeled by this same system.

### 1.1.3 Multiple Linear Regression

These ideas can be extended to regressions involving several $x$ variables. For two independent variables, the line becomes a plane, and the minimized springs and squares balance the plane in three dimensions.

Although not easy to visualize, the same idea extends to $n$ independent variables, with the same quantities being minimized.

### 1.1.4 Correlation

It is useful to measure the strength of the relationship between two (or more) variables. Two variables $x$ and $y$ are related if they tend to vary together—if they co-relate. So any measure of correlation should reflect whether they vary together or not. The measure should have a high value when this correlation is strong and a low value when the correlation is weak.

The rules of correlation mimic those of integer multiplication. Factors that are the same (either both positive or both negative) yield a positive product. Similarly, factors that are different yield a negative product. This is similar to our desired measure of correlation, so multiplication of the values of $x$ and $y$ is used in the correlation measure. Of course, $x$ and $y$ might be measured on different scales, so standardized values are used instead of actual values.

The corresponding (standardized) values for each pair are multiplied together, and a weighted average of these products is computed. Stated mathematically,

$$r = \frac{\left(\frac{x_1-\bar{x}}{s_x}\right)\left(\frac{y_1-\bar{y}}{s_y}\right) + \left(\frac{x_2-\bar{x}}{s_x}\right)\left(\frac{y_2-\bar{y}}{s_y}\right) + \ldots + \left(\frac{x_n-\bar{x}}{s_x}\right)\left(\frac{y_n-\bar{y}}{s_y}\right)}{n-1}$$

This quantity, termed the *correlation coefficient* and abbreviated $r$, measures linear correlation in two variables. A similar quantity, known as the coefficient of determination and abbreviated $R^2$, is used in measuring correlation in multiple regression. In fact, $r^2 = R^2$ for the case of simple regression.

Thinking about this formula reveals some properties of $r$.

- Switching the roles of $x$ and $y$ in the regression does not change the value of $r$, since multiplication is commutative. This does *not* mean that one can do something similar with the coefficients in regression. Although switching $x$ and $y$ values does not influence correlation, it does affect the regression equation.

- Changing the units of $x$ or $y$ does not change the correlation, since standardized scores are used.

- The correlation coefficient is sensitive to outliers, since it is based on the mean and standard deviation.

An interesting property of $r$ is that it can be calculated through regression of the standardized variables. Figure 1.7 shows the result of a least-squares regression of standardized values of **weight** on standardized values of **height**. When the variables are standardized, note that the slope of the regression line and the correlation coefficient are equal.

Finally, it should be noted that there are other (equivalent) formulas for computing the correlation coefficient $r$.

*Figure 1.7
Standardized
Regression*

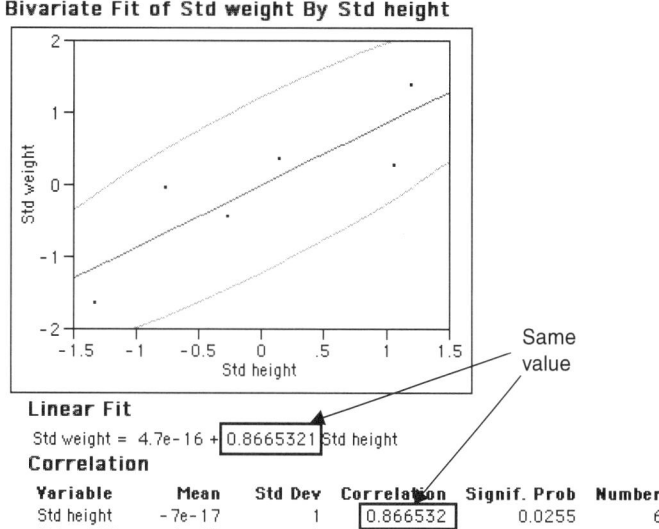

$$r = \frac{\sum(x-\bar{x})(y-\bar{y})}{\sqrt{(x-\bar{x})^2}\sqrt{(y-\bar{y})^2}}$$

shows the relationship among the sum of the cross-products (in the numerator) and a standardization measure (in the denominator) in a similar way to the discussion above.

$$r = \hat{\beta}\frac{s_x}{s_y}$$

shows the relationship between *r* and the slope of the regression of *y* on *x*. If the standard deviations of *y* and *x* are equivalent (as they are when both variables were standardized above), then *r* is equal to the slope of the regression line.

### 1.1.5 Seeing Correlation

The demoLeastSquares script used above can also demonstrate correlation.

If there are lines and squares still showing on the plot,

- Click the buttons at the bottom of the screen to toggle all lines and squares off.

- Click the **LS Line** button to turn on the least-squares line.

Now, overlay a correlation ellipse and a label of the correlation coefficient.

🖱 Click the **Correlation Ellipse** button.

The display now appears as in Figure 1.8.

*Figure 1.8*
*Correlation Ellipse*

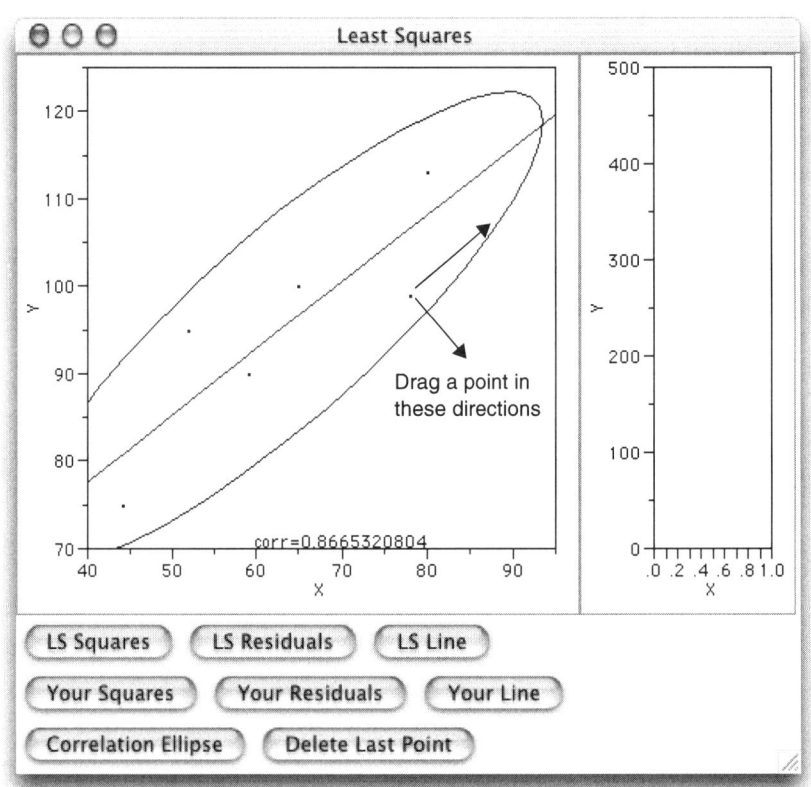

🖱 Drag one of the points in directions parallel to the least-squares line.

Notice that the line does not move much and that the correlation does not change much.

🖱 Drag one of the points in directions perpendicular to the least-squares line.

In this case, both the correlation and least-squares line change drastically. This demonstrates the effect of outliers on the correlation—and why the correlation should always be interpreted in conjunction with a graphical display of the data.

Similarly, points can be added to the plot close to the existing least-squares line with little effect, but single outliers can be added with great effect.

- 🖱 Click near and away from the regression line to add points and see their effect.

## 1.2 Statistical Background

This section presents the rigorous definitions of many concepts involved in regression. A background in linear algebra is necessary to follow the discussion. However, it is not necessary to know all of this material to be able to use and interpret the results from JMP. Return to this section as a reference when regression methods are studied in detail.

Formally, multiple linear regression fits a response variable $y$ to a function of regressor variables and parameters. The general linear regression model has the form

$$y = \beta_0 + \beta_1 x_1 + \ldots + \beta_m x_m + \varepsilon$$

where

$y$ is the response, or dependent, variable

$\beta_0, \beta_1, \ldots, \beta_m$ are unknown parameters

$x_1, x_2, \ldots, x_m$ are the regressor, or independent, variables

$\varepsilon$ is a random error term.

*Least squares* is a technique used to estimate the parameters. The goal is to find estimates of the parameters $\beta_0, \beta_1, \ldots, \beta_m$ that minimize the sum of the squared differences between the actual $y$ values and the values of $y$ predicted by the equation. These estimates are called the *least-squares estimates* and the quantity minimized is called the *error sum of squares*.

Typically, you use regression analysis to do the following:

- ❏ obtain the least-squares estimates of the parameters
- ❏ estimate the variance of the error term
- ❏ estimate the standard error of the parameter estimates

- test hypotheses about the parameters
- calculate predicted values using the estimated equation
- evaluate the fit or lack of fit of the model.

The classical linear model assumes that the responses, *y*, are sampled from several populations. These populations are determined by the corresponding values of $x_1, x_2, ..., x_m$. As the investigator, you select the values of the *x*'s; they are not random. However, the response values are random. You select the values of the *x*'s to meet your experimental needs, carry out the experiment with the set values of the *x*'s, and measure the responses. Often, though, you cannot control the actual values of the independent variables. In these cases, you should at least be able to assume that they are fixed with respect to the response variable.

In addition, you must assume the following:

1. The form of the model is correct; that is, all important independent variables are included and the functional form is appropriate.
2. The expected values of the errors (from the mean) are zero.
3. The variances of the errors (and thus the response variable) are constant across observations.
4. The errors are uncorrelated.
5. For hypothesis testing, the errors are normally distributed.

Not all regression models are necessarily linear in their parameters. For example, the model

$$y = \beta_1 e^{\beta_2 x} + \varepsilon$$

is not linear in the parameter $\beta_2$. Specifically, the term $e^{\beta_2 x}$ is not a linear function of $\beta_2$. This particular nonlinear model, called the *exponential growth* or *decay* model, is used to represent increase (growth) or decrease (decay) over time (*t*) of many types of responses such as population size or radiation counts. Chapter 7, "Nonlinear Models," is devoted to analyses appropriate for this type of model.

Additionally, the random error may not be normally distributed. If this is the case, the least squares technique is not necessarily the appropriate method for estimating the parameters. One such model, the logistic regression model, is presented in the section "Binary Response Variable: Logistic Regression" on page 203.

## 1.3 Terminology and Notation

The principle of least squares is applied to a set of $n$ observed values of $y$ and the associated $x_j$ to obtain estimates $\hat{\beta}_0, \hat{\beta}_1, ..., \hat{\beta}_m$ of the respective parameters $\beta_0, \beta_1, ..., \beta_m$. These estimates are then used to construct the fitted model, or estimating equation

$$\hat{y} = \hat{\beta}_0 + \hat{\beta}_1 x_1 + ... + \hat{\beta}_m x_m$$

Many regression computations are illustrated conveniently in matrix notation. Let $y_i$, $x_{ij}$, and $\varepsilon_i$ denote the values of $y$, $x_j$, and $\varepsilon$, respectively, in the $i$th observation. The **Y** vector, the **X** matrix, and the **ε** vector can be defined as follows:

$$\mathbf{Y} = \begin{bmatrix} y_1 \\ \cdot \\ \cdot \\ \cdot \\ y_m \end{bmatrix}, \quad \mathbf{X} = \begin{bmatrix} 1 & x_{11} & \cdots & x_{1m} \\ \cdot & \cdot & & \cdot \\ \cdot & \cdot & & \cdot \\ \cdot & \cdot & & \cdot \\ 1 & x_{n1} & \cdots & x_{nm} \end{bmatrix}, \quad \boldsymbol{\varepsilon} = \begin{bmatrix} \varepsilon_1 \\ \cdot \\ \cdot \\ \cdot \\ \varepsilon_m \end{bmatrix}$$

Then the model in matrix notation is

$$\mathbf{Y} = \mathbf{X}\boldsymbol{\beta} + \boldsymbol{\varepsilon}$$

where $\beta' = (\beta_0\ \beta_1\ ...\ \beta_m)$ is the parameter vector.

The vector of least-squares estimates is

$$\hat{\boldsymbol{\beta}}' = \begin{bmatrix} \hat{\beta}_0 \\ \hat{\beta}_1 \\ \cdot \\ \cdot \\ \cdot \\ \hat{\beta}_m \end{bmatrix}$$

and is obtained by solving the set of normal equations

$$\mathbf{X'X}\hat{\boldsymbol{\beta}} = \mathbf{X'Y}$$

Assuming that **X'X** is of full rank (nonsingular), there is a unique solution to the normal equations given by

## 16  Regression Concepts

$$\hat{\beta} = (X'X)^{-1}X'Y$$

The matrix $(X'X)^{-1}$ is very useful in regression analysis and is often denoted as follows:

$$(X'X)^{-1} = C = \begin{bmatrix} c_{00} & c_{01} & \cdots & c_{0m} \\ c_{10} & c_{11} & \cdots & c_{1m} \\ \vdots & & & \vdots \\ c_{m1} & c_{m2} & \cdots & c_{mn} \end{bmatrix}$$

### 1.3.1 Partitioning the Sums of Squares

A basic identity results from least squares, specifically,

$$\sum (y - \bar{y})^2 = \sum (\hat{y} - \bar{y})^2 + \sum (y - \hat{y})^2$$

This identity shows that the total sum of squared deviations from the mean,

$$\sum (y - \bar{y})^2$$

is equal to the sum of squared differences between the mean and the predicted values,

$$\sum (\hat{y} - \bar{y})^2$$

plus the sum of squared deviations from the observed $y$'s to the regression line,

$$\sum (y - \hat{y})^2$$

These two parts are called the regression (or model) sum of squares and the residual (or error) sum of squares. Thus,

Corrected Total SS = Model SS + Residual SS

Corrected total SS always has the same value for a given set of data, regardless of the model that is used; however, partitioning into model SS and residual SS depends on the model. Generally, the addition of a new $x$ variable to a model increases the model SS and, correspondingly, reduces the residual SS. The residual, or error, sum of squares is computed as follows:

$$\begin{aligned}\text{Residual SS} &= \mathbf{Y}'(\mathbf{I} - \mathbf{X}(\mathbf{X}'\mathbf{X})^{-1}\mathbf{X}')\mathbf{Y}\\ &= \mathbf{Y}'\mathbf{Y} - \mathbf{Y}'\mathbf{X}(\mathbf{X}'\mathbf{X})^{-1}\mathbf{X}'\mathbf{Y}\\ &= \mathbf{Y}'\mathbf{Y} - \hat{\boldsymbol{\beta}}'\mathbf{X}'\mathbf{Y}\end{aligned}$$

The error, or residual, mean square

$$s^2 = \text{MSE} = (\text{Residual SS}) / (n - m - 1)$$

is an unbiased estimate of $\sigma^2$, the variance of the $\varepsilon$'s.

Sums of squares, including the various sums of squares computed by any regression procedure such as the **Fit Y by X** and **Fit Model** commands, can be expressed conceptually as the difference between the regression sums of squares for two models, called *complete* (unrestricted) and *reduced* (restricted) models, respectively. This approach relates a given SS to the comparison of two regression models.

For example, denote as $SS_1$ the regression sum of squares for a complete model with $m = 5$ variables:

$$y = \beta_0 + \beta_1 x_1 + \beta_2 x_2 + \beta_3 x_3 + \beta_4 x_4 + \beta_5 x_5 + \varepsilon$$

Denote the regression sum of squares for a reduced model not containing $x_4$ and $x_5$ as $SS_2$:

$$y = \beta_0 + \beta_1 x_1 + \beta_2 x_2 + \beta_3 x_3 + \varepsilon$$

Reduction notation can be used to represent the difference between regression sums of squares for the two models:

$$R(\beta_4, \beta_5 \mid \beta_0, \beta_1, \beta_2, \beta_3) = \text{Model SS}_1 - \text{Model SS}_2$$

The difference or reduction in error $R(\beta_4, \beta_5 \mid \beta_0, \beta_1, \beta_2, \beta_3)$ indicates the increase in regression sums of squares due to the addition of $\beta_4$ and $\beta_5$ to the reduced model. It follows that

$$R(\beta_4, \beta_5 \mid \beta_0, \beta_1, \beta_2, \beta_3) = \text{Residual SS}_2 - \text{Residual SS}_1$$

which is the decrease in error sum of squares due to the addition of $\beta_4$ and $\beta_5$ to the reduced model. The expression

$$R(\beta_4, \beta_5 \mid \beta_0, \beta_1, \beta_2, \beta_3)$$

is also commonly referred to in the following ways:

- the sums of squares due to $\beta_4$ and $\beta_5$ (or $x_4$ and $x_5$) adjusted for $\beta_0, \beta_1, \beta_2, \beta_3$ (or the intercept and $x_1, x_2, x_3$)
- the sums of squares due to fitting $x_4$ and $x_5$ after fitting the intercept and $x_1, x_2, x_3$
- the effects of $x_4$ and $x_5$ above and beyond (or partialing) the effects of the intercept and $x_1, x_2, x_3$.

## 1.3.2 Hypothesis Testing

Inferences about model parameters are highly dependent on the other parameters in the model under consideration. Therefore, in hypothesis testing, it is important to emphasize the parameters for which inferences have been adjusted. For example, $R(\beta_3 \mid \beta_0, \beta_1, \beta_2)$ and $R(\beta_3 \mid \beta_0, \beta_1)$ may measure entirely different concepts. Similarly, a test of $H_0: \beta_3 = 0$ may have one result for the model

$$y = \beta_0 + \beta_1 x_1 + \beta_3 x_3 + \varepsilon$$

and another for the model

$$y = \beta_0 + \beta_1 x_1 + \beta_2 x_2 + \beta_3 x_3 + \varepsilon$$

Differences reflect actual dependencies among variables in the model rather than inconsistencies in statistical methodology.

Statistical inferences can also be made in terms of linear functions of the parameters of the form

$$H_0: \mathbf{L}\boldsymbol{\beta}: l_0\beta_0 + l_1\beta_1 + \ldots + l_m\beta_m = 0$$

where the $l_i$ are arbitrary constants chosen to correspond to a specified hypothesis. Such functions are estimated by the corresponding linear function

$$\mathbf{L}\boldsymbol{\beta} = l_0\beta_0 + l_1\beta_1 + \ldots + l_m\beta_m$$

of the least-squares estimates $\hat{\boldsymbol{\beta}}$. The variance of $\mathbf{L}\hat{\boldsymbol{\beta}}$ is

$$V(\mathbf{L}\hat{\boldsymbol{\beta}}) = (\mathbf{L}(\mathbf{X}'\mathbf{X})^{-1}\mathbf{L}')\sigma^2$$

A $t$ test or $F$ test is used to test $H_0: (\mathbf{L}\boldsymbol{\beta}) = 0$. The denominator is usually the residual mean square (MSE). Because the variance of the estimated function is based on statistics computed for the entire model, the test of the hypothesis is made in the presence of all model parameters. Confidence intervals can be constructed to correspond to these tests, which can be generalized to simultaneous tests of several linear functions.

Simultaneous inference about a set of linear functions $\mathbf{L}_1\beta, ..., \mathbf{L}_k\beta$ is performed in a related manner. For notational convenience, let $\mathbf{L}$ denote the matrix whose rows are $\mathbf{L}_1, ..., \mathbf{L}_k$:

$$\mathbf{L} = \begin{bmatrix} \mathbf{L}_1 \\ \cdot \\ \cdot \\ \cdot \\ \mathbf{L}_k \end{bmatrix}$$

Then the sum of squares

$$SS(\mathbf{L}\beta = 0) = (\mathbf{L}\beta)'(\mathbf{L}(\mathbf{X'X})^{-1}\mathbf{L'})(\mathbf{L}\beta)$$

is associated with the null hypothesis

$$H_0: \mathbf{L}_1\beta = ... = \mathbf{L}_k\beta = 0$$

A test of $H_0$ is provided by the $F$ statistic

$$F = (SS(\mathbf{L}\beta = 0) / k) / MSE$$

Three common types of statistical inferences follow:

1. A test that all parameters ($\beta_1, \beta_2, ..., \beta_m$) are zero. The test compares the fit of the complete model to that using only the mean:

    $$F = (\text{Model SS} / m) / MSE$$

    where

    $$\text{Model SS} = R(\beta_0, \beta_1, ..., \beta_m \mid \beta_0)$$

    The $F$ statistic has $(m, n - m - 1)$ degrees of freedom.
    Note that $R(\beta_0, \beta_1, ..., \beta_m)$ is rarely used. For more information on no-intercept models, see the section "Regression through the Origin" on page 44.

2. A test that the parameters in a subset are zero. The problem is to compare the fit of the complete model

$$y = \beta_0 + \beta_1 x_1 + \ldots + \beta_g x_g + \beta_{g+1} x_{g+1} + \ldots + \beta_m x_m + \varepsilon$$

to the fit of the reduced model

$$y = \beta_0 + \beta_1 x_1 + \ldots + \beta_g x_g + \varepsilon$$

An $F$ statistic is used to perform the test

$$F = (R(\beta_{g+1}, \ldots, \beta_m \mid \beta_0, \beta_1, \ldots, \beta_g) / (m - g))\text{MSE}$$

Note that an arbitrary reordering of variables produces a test for any desired subset of parameters. If the subset contains only one parameter, $\beta_m$, the test is

$$F = (R(\beta_m \mid \beta_0, \beta_1, \ldots, \beta_{m-1}) / 1) / \text{MSE} = (\text{partial SS due to } \beta_m) / \text{MSE}$$

which is equivalent to the $t$ test

$$t = \frac{\hat{\beta}_m}{s_{\hat{\beta}_m}} = \frac{\hat{\beta}_m}{\sqrt{c_{mm}\text{MSE}}}$$

The corresponding $(1 - \alpha)$ confidence interval about $\beta_m$ is

$$\beta_m \pm t_{\alpha/2} \sqrt{c_{mm}\text{MSE}}$$

3. Estimation of a subpopulation mean corresponding to a specific $x$. For a given set of $x$ values described by a vector $\mathbf{x}$, denote the population mean by $\mu_x$. The estimated population mean is

$$\mu_x = \beta_0 + \beta_1 x_1 + \ldots + \beta_m x_m = \mathbf{x}\beta$$

The vector $\mathbf{x}$ is constant; hence, the variance of the estimate $\hat{\mu}_\mathbf{x}$ is

$$V(\hat{\mu}_x) = \mathbf{x}'(\mathbf{X}'\mathbf{X})^{-1}\mathbf{x}\sigma^2$$

This equation is useful for computing confidence intervals. A related inference concerns a future single value of $y$ corresponding to a specified $x$. The relevant variance estimate is

$$V(\hat{y}_x) = (1 + \mathbf{x}'(\mathbf{X}'\mathbf{X})^{-1}\mathbf{x})\sigma^2$$

## 1.3.3 Using the Generalized Inverse

Many applications of regression procedures involve an $\mathbf{X'X}$ matrix that is not of full rank and has no unique inverse. Fit Model and Fit Y by X compute a generalized inverse $(\mathbf{X'X})^-$ and use it to compute a regression estimate

$$\mathbf{b} = (\mathbf{X'X})^- \mathbf{X'Y}$$

A generalized inverse of a matrix $\mathbf{A}$ is any matrix $\mathbf{G}$ such that $\mathbf{AGA} = \mathbf{A}$. Note that this also identifies the inverse of a full-rank matrix.

If $\mathbf{X'X}$ is not of full rank, then an infinite number of generalized inverses exist. Different generalized inverses lead to different solutions to the normal equations that have different expected values; that is, $E(\mathbf{b}) = (\mathbf{X'X})^- \mathbf{X'Y}\boldsymbol{\beta}$ depends on the particular generalized inverse used to obtain $\mathbf{b}$. Therefore, it is important to understand what is being estimated by the solution.

Fortunately, not all computations in regression analysis depend on the particular solution obtained. For example, the error sum of squares is invariant with respect to $(\mathbf{X'X})^-$ and is given by

$$\text{SSE} = \mathbf{Y'}(1 - \mathbf{X}(\mathbf{X'X})^-\mathbf{X'})\mathbf{Y}$$

Hence, the model sum of squares also does not depend on the particular generalized inverse obtained.

The generalized inverse has played a major role in the presentation of the theory of linear statistical models, notably in the work of Graybill (1976) and Searle (1971). In a theoretical setting, it is often possible, and even desirable, to avoid specifying a particular generalized inverse. To apply the generalized inverse to statistical data using computer programs, a generalized inverse must actually be calculated. Therefore, it is necessary to declare the specific generalized inverse being computed. For example, consider an $\mathbf{X'X}$ matrix of rank $k$ that can be partitioned as

$$\mathbf{X'X} = \begin{bmatrix} \mathbf{A}_{11} & \mathbf{A}_{12} \\ \mathbf{A}_{21} & \mathbf{A}_{22} \end{bmatrix}$$

where $\mathbf{A}_{11}$ is $k \times k$ and of rank $k$. Then $A_{11}^{-1}$ exists, and a generalized inverse of $\mathbf{X'X}$ is

$$(\mathbf{X'X})^- = \begin{bmatrix} A_{11} & \varphi_{12} \\ \varphi_{21} & \varphi_{22} \end{bmatrix}$$

where each $\varphi_{ij}$ is a matrix of zeros of the same dimension as $\mathbf{A}_{ij}$.

This approach to obtaining a generalized inverse, the method used by Fit Model and Fit Y by X, can be extended indefinitely by partitioning a singular matrix into several sets of matrices as illustrated above. Note that the resulting solution to the normal equations, $\mathbf{b} = (\mathbf{X'X})^-\mathbf{X'Y}$, has zeros in the positions corresponding to the rows filled with zeros in $(\mathbf{X'X})^-$. This is the solution printed by these procedures, and it is regarded as providing a biased estimate of $\mathbf{b}$.

However, because $\mathbf{b}$ is not unique, a linear function, $\mathbf{Lb}$, and its variance are generally not unique either. However, a class of linear functions called *estimable functions* exists, and they have the following properties:

- The vector $\mathbf{L}$ is a linear combination of rows of $\mathbf{X}$.

- $\mathbf{Lb}$ and its variance are invariant through all possible generalized inverses. In other words, $\mathbf{Lb}$ is unique and is an unbiased estimate of $\mathbf{L\beta}$.

Analogous to the full-rank case, the variance of an estimable function $\mathbf{Lb}$ is given by

$$V(\mathbf{Lb}) = (\mathbf{L}(\mathbf{X'X})^-\mathbf{L'})\sigma^2$$

This expression is used for statistical inference. For example, a test of $H_0$: $\mathbf{L\beta} = 0$ is given by the $t$ test

$$t = \frac{\mathbf{Lb}}{\sqrt{\mathbf{L}(\mathbf{X'X})^-\mathbf{L'}\mathrm{MSE}}}$$

Simultaneous inferences on a set of estimable functions are performed in an analogous manner.

## 1.4 Regression with JMP

This section reviews the following JMP platforms that are useful in regression analysis.

> **Note** The two platforms for most regression analyses are Fit Y by X and Fit Model.

| | |
|---|---|
| Fit Y by X | fits general linear models of two variables. Its capabilities include simple regression, analysis of variance, contingency table analysis, and logistic regression. In addition, the regression portion allows for orthogonal fits that take variation in $x$ variables into account and for the fitting of cubic splines. |
| Fit Model | fits general linear models. In addition to many other analyses, Fit Model can perform simple, multiple, polynomial, and weighted regression, as well as analysis of variance and analysis of covariance. It is also used for logistic regression and stepwise regression, and for the analysis of response surface models. |
| Distribution | provides univariate statistics. Although it does not compute regressions itself, it is an essential platform for in-depth regression analyses. It is useful for preliminary analyses of variables, as well as for plotting residuals to assess their distribution (shape). |
| Multivariate | analyzes multivariate data, providing several types of correlations and three different methods of principal components. |
| Survival | fits univariate and regression models to failure-time data that may be right-, left-, or interval-censored. These types of models are commonly used in survival analysis. |
| Nonlinear | fits nonlinear regression models. The iterative method is a modified Gauss-Newton. |
| PLS | analyzes data with Partial Least Squares. |
| Neural Net | is used for prediction when the form of the model is not important. |

Finally, if a regression method cannot be performed by any of the platforms above, JMP provides a scripting language with extensive matrix abilities that can be used.

# Chapter 2  Regressions in JMP

2.1  *Introduction*  25
2.2  *A Model with One Independent Variable*  27
2.3  *A Model with Several Independent Variables*  32
2.4  *Additional Results from Fit Model*  36
    2.4.1  *Predicted Values and Confidence Intervals*  37
    2.4.2  *Sequential and Partial: Two Types of Sums of Squares*  41
    2.4.3  *Standardized Coefficients*  43
    2.4.4  *Regression through the Origin*  44
2.5  *Further Examination of Model Parameters*  50
    2.5.1  *Tests for Subsets and Linear Functions of Parameters*  50
    2.5.2  *Changing the Model*  53
2.6  *Plotting Observations*  54
    2.6.1  *Interactive Methods*  55
    2.6.2  *Regression with Deleted Observations*  58
    2.6.3  *Deleting Effects*  60
2.7  *Predicting to a Different Set of Data*  63
2.8  *Exact Collinearity: Linear Dependency*  67
2.9  *Summary*  70

## 2.1  Introduction

As indicated in "Regression with JMP" on page 23, Fit Y by X and Fit Model are the primary JMP platforms for performing the computations for a statistical analysis of data based on a linear regression model. Both commands are found on the Analyze menu.

This chapter provides instructions on the use of both platforms for performing regression analysis. Included are instructions for employing some of the more frequently used options, altering data sets for further analysis, and utilizing the interactive features available in each platform. Subsequent chapters deal with procedures for more specialized analyses and models.

The data for the example in this chapter concern factors considered to be influential in determining the cost of providing air service. The goal is to develop a model for estimating the cost per passenger mile so that the major factors in determining that cost can be isolated. The source of the data is a Civil Aeronautics Board report, "Aircraft Operation Costs and Performance Report," from August 1972.

The variables are

| | |
|---|---|
| Cost | cost per passenger mile (cents) |
| Use | average hours per day the aircraft is used |
| Length | average length of nonstop legs of flights (1000 miles) |
| Seats | average number of seats per aircraft (100 seats) |
| Load | average load factor (% of seats occupied by passengers). |

Data have been collected for 33 US airlines with average nonstop lengths of flights greater than 800 miles.

- Open the JMP data file air.jmp.

An additional indicator variable, Type, has been constructed. This variable has a value of zero for airlines with Length<1200 miles, and a value of unity for airlines with Length≥1200 miles. This variable is constructed in the data table with the JMP formula

$$\text{If} \begin{pmatrix} Length >= 1.2 \Rightarrow 1 \\ else \qquad\quad \Rightarrow 0 \end{pmatrix}$$

which assigns the value one if (Length>=1.2) is true and zero otherwise. To see this formula, access the JMP Formula Editor.

- Right-click (Control-click on the Macintosh) on the column name (Type) and select **Formula** from the menu that appears.

This variable is used in "Predicting to a Different Set of Data" on page 63. The data appear in Figure 2.1.

*Figure 2.1*
*Airline Cost Data*

| Load | Use | Length | Seats | Type | Cost |
|---|---|---|---|---|---|
| 0.591 | 7.87 | 1.79 | 0.1375 | 1 | 2.258 |
| 0.488 | 9.5 | 2.515 | 0.3546 | 1 | 2.275 |
| 0.412 | 7.91 | 1.35 | 0.192 | 1 | 2.341 |
| 0.397 | 13.3 | 3.607 | 0.339 | 1 | 2.357 |
| 0.582 | 8.48 | 1.963 | 0.1381 | 1 | 2.363 |
| 0.466 | 9.38 | 1.123 | 0.1481 | 0 | 2.404 |
| 0.535 | 10.8 | 1.576 | 0.1361 | 1 | 2.425 |
| 0.434 | 8.36 | 1.912 | 0.3148 | 1 | 2.711 |
| 0.439 | 8.43 | 1.584 | 0.1607 | 1 | 2.743 |
| 0.417 | 8.83 | 2.377 | 0.3287 | 1 | 2.78 |
| 0.4 | 8.42 | 1.495 | 0.3597 | 1 | 2.833 |
| 0.41 | 9.62 | 0.84 | 0.139 | 0 | 2.846 |
| 0.478 | 8.71 | 1.392 | 0.1148 | 1 | 2.906 |
| 0.495 | 8.44 | 0.871 | 0.1186 | 0 | 2.954 |
| 0.476 | 8.91 | 0.961 | 0.1236 | 0 | 2.962 |
| 0.539 | 6.84 | 1.008 | 0.115 | 0 | 2.971 |
| 0.409 | 9 | 0.845 | 0.139 | 0 | 3.044 |
| 0.381 | 10.2 | 1.692 | 0.3007 | 1 | 3.096 |
| 0.486 | 8.29 | 0.877 | 0.106 | 0 | 3.14 |
| 0.287 | 8.09 | 1.528 | 0.3522 | 1 | 3.306 |
| 0.504 | 9.47 | 1.408 | 0.1345 | 1 | 3.306 |
| 0.455 | 7.7 | 1.236 | 0.1221 | 1 | 3.311 |
| 0.405 | 9.57 | 0.863 | 0.139 | 0 | 3.313 |
| 0.422 | 8.35 | 1.031 | 0.1365 | 0 | 3.392 |
| 0.476 | 7.27 | 1.416 | 0.1145 | 1 | 3.437 |
| 0.426 | 7.52 | 0.975 | 0.2025 | 0 | 3.462 |
| 0.349 | 9.56 | 2.189 | 0.3279 | 1 | 3.527 |
| 0.394 | 7.94 | 0.949 | 0.1488 | 0 | 3.689 |
| 0.452 | 7.55 | 1.164 | 0.127 | 0 | 3.76 |
| 0.425 | 10.6 | 2.78 | 0.1282 | 1 | 3.856 |
| 0.362 | 10.8 | 1.518 | 0.1356 | 1 | 3.959 |
| 0.541 | 6.31 | 0.823 | 0.0943 | 0 | 4.024 |
| 0.378 | 5.65 | 0.821 | 0.129 | 0 | 4.737 |

## 2.2 A Model with One Independent Variable

A regression with a single independent variable is known as a *simple linear regression* model. Since such a model is easy to visualize, it is presented here to introduce several aspects of regression analysis you can perform with JMP. This model is illustrated using the single variable Load, the average load factor, to estimate the cost per passenger mile, Cost. In terms of the example, the model is

$$\text{Cost} = \beta_0 + \beta_1(\text{Load}) + \varepsilon$$

In this model, $\beta_1$ is the effect on the cost per passenger mile of a one-unit (percentage point) increase in the load factor. For this example, you expect this coefficient to be negative. The coefficient $\beta_0$, the intercept, is the cost per passenger mile if the load factor is zero. Since a zero load factor is not possible, the value of this coefficient is not useful, but the term is needed to fully specify the regression line. The term ε represents the random error and accounts for variation in costs due to factors other than variation in Load.

In the case of a regression with one independent variable, it is instructive to plot the observed variables. As with most analyses in JMP, the plot appears with the analysis. You can produce such a plot with the following steps:

- Select **Analyze → Fit Y by X**.
- Select **Cost** and click the **Y, Response** button.
- Select **Load** and click the **X, Factor** button.
- Click **OK**.

Figure 2.2 shows the resulting plot.

*Figure 2.2*
*Bivariate plot of* Cost *against* Load

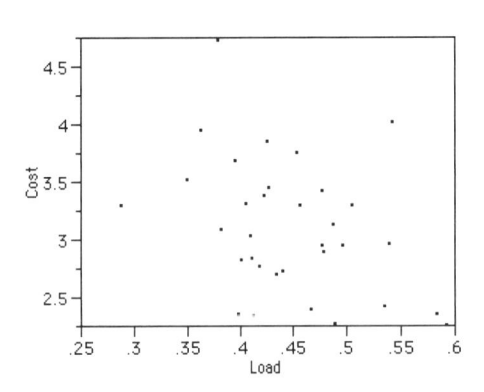

The plot shows the expected tendency for lower costs (Cost) with higher load factors (Load). However, the relationship is not very strong. This suggests that there may be other factors affecting Cost, as you will see in "A Model with Several Independent Variables" on page 32.

Since there may be a linear relationship between these two variables, the next step in analyzing these data is to fit a line to them. To do so,

- Click on the platform pop-up menu (the triangle in the upper-left corner of the plot).
- Select **Fit Line** from the menu that appears.

This tells JMP to plot a regression line on the data and display appropriate statistical tables.

# A Model with One Independent Variable

The Fit Y by X platform automatically assumes that the intercept is to be estimated (to fit a line with the intercept constrained to be zero, see "Regression through the Origin" on page 44). Fit Y by X produces ordinary least-squares estimates of the parameters ($\beta_0$ and $\beta_1$ in this example), which are optimal if the errors are independent and have equal variances. Methods for checking these assumptions and some suggestions for alternate methodologies are presented in Chapter 3, "Observations."

The output from the fit appears in Figure 2.3. The number arrows in Figure 2.3 have been added to key the descriptions that follow.

*Figure 2.3*
*Results for Regression with One Independent Variable*

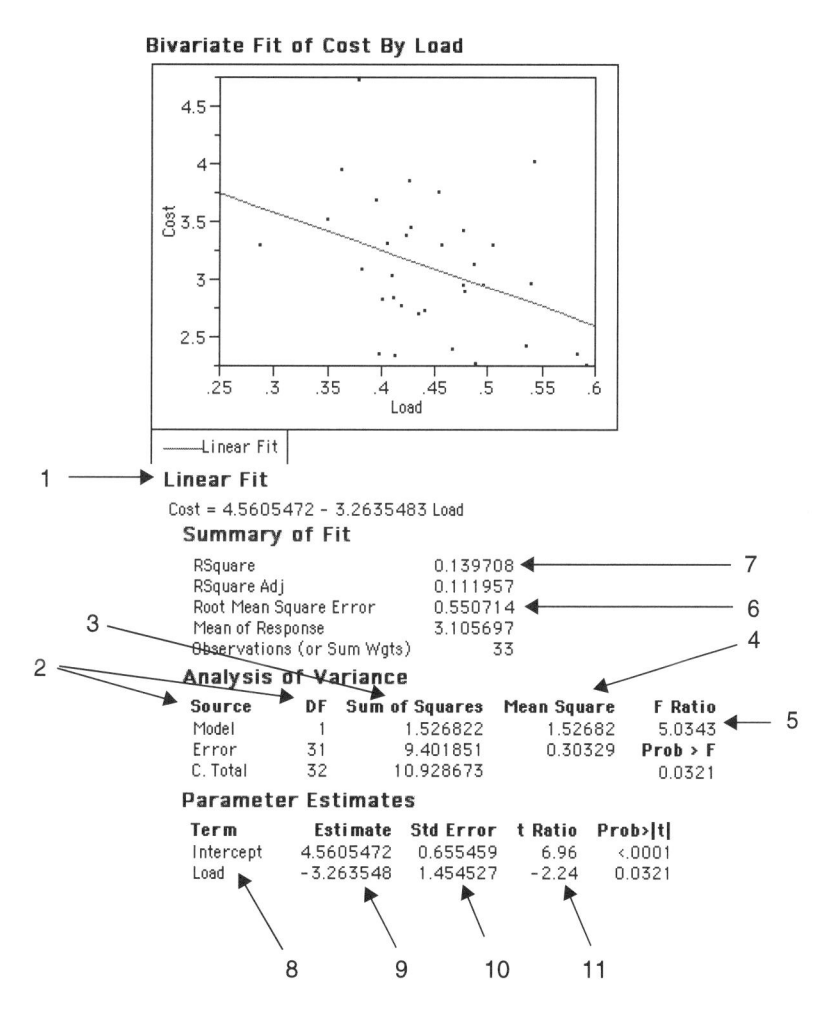

**Bivariate Fit of Cost By Load**

1 → **Linear Fit**
Cost = 4.5605472 − 3.2635483 Load

**Summary of Fit**

| | |
|---|---|
| RSquare | 0.139708 ← 7 |
| RSquare Adj | 0.111957 |
| Root Mean Square Error | 0.550714 ← 6 |
| Mean of Response | 3.105697 |
| Observations (or Sum Wgts) | 33 |

3 → (Observations)
2 → (Source, DF, Sum of Squares)
4 → (Mean Square)

**Analysis of Variance**

| Source | DF | Sum of Squares | Mean Square | F Ratio |
|---|---|---|---|---|
| Model | 1 | 1.526822 | 1.52682 | 5.0343 ← 5 |
| Error | 31 | 9.401851 | 0.30329 | Prob > F |
| C. Total | 32 | 10.928673 | | 0.0321 |

**Parameter Estimates**

| Term | Estimate | Std Error | t Ratio | Prob>|t| |
|---|---|---|---|---|
| Intercept | 4.5605472 | 0.655459 | 6.96 | <.0001 |
| Load | −3.263548 | 1.454527 | −2.24 | 0.0321 |

8 ↑    9 ↑    10 ↑    11 ↑

**29**

1. The uppermost outline bar identifies the model. Since Fit Y by X can fit many models in one report (see "Changing the Model" on page 53), each model is labeled by its type of fit. To change this name,

    🖰 Double-click in the outline and type the new name.

    The estimated equation is directly under this line.

2. These two columns give the sources of variation and degrees of freedom associated with the sums of squares discussed in number 3 below.

3. The regression sum of squares (called **Model**, see "Partitioning the Sums of Squares" on page 16) is 1.5268, and the residual sum of squares (called **Error**) is 9.4019. The sum of these two is the **C. Total** of 10.9287, the corrected total sum of squares. This illustrates the basic identity in regression analysis that **C. Total** SS=**Model** SS+**Error** SS, which says that variation among the observed values of the dependent variable can be attributed to two sources: (1) variation due to changes in the independent variable and (2) variation not due to changes in the independent variable. If the model is correctly specified, this latter variation is *random variation*.

4. Mean squares are computed by dividing the sums of squares by their respective degrees of freedom. The mean square for error is an unbiased estimate of $\sigma^2$, the variance of $\varepsilon$, if the model has been correctly specified.

5. The value of the *F* statistic, 5.034, is the ratio of the model mean square divided by the error mean square. For the general multiple regression case, it is used to test the composite hypothesis that all coefficients except the intercept are zero. In this case, the hypothesis is $\beta_1 = 0$. The *p* value (which follows the *F* statistic) of 0.0321 indicates that there is about a 0.032 chance of obtaining an *F* value this large or larger if, in fact, $\beta_1 = 0$. Thus, there is reasonable evidence to state that $\beta_1 \neq 0$.

6. **Root Mean Square Error** = 0.5507 is the square root of the error mean square. It estimates the standard deviation of $\varepsilon$. **Mean of Response** = 3.106 is the mean of Cost.

7. **RSquare** = 0.1397 is the square of the multiple correlation coefficient. For a one-variable regression it is equivalent to the square of the correlation between the dependent and independent variables. Equivalently, since the predicted values are a linear function of the independent variable, it is also the square of the correlation between the dependent variable and its predicted values. Finally, it is also the ratio of **Model** SS divided by **C. Total** SS, and thereby represents the fraction of total variation in the values of Cost explained by, or due to, the linear relationship to Load (see number 3 above). **RSquare Adj** is an alternative to **RSquare**, which is discussed in "A Model with Several Independent Variables" on page 32.

8. The **Term** column identifies the regression coefficients. The label **Intercept** identifies $\beta_0$, and the other coefficients are identified by their respective variable names. In this case, the only coefficient is that for Load.

9. The values in the **Estimate** column are the estimated coefficients. The estimate of the intercept, $\beta_0$, is 4.561, and the estimate of the coefficient, $\beta_1$, is −3.264. These give the fitted model

$$\widehat{\text{Cost}} = 4.561 - (3.26355)\text{Load}$$

where the caret (^) over Cost indicates that it is an estimated value. This expression can be used to estimate the average cost per passenger mile for a given average load factor. The coefficient, $\beta_1 = -3.264$, shows that on the average, the cost is decreased by 3.264 cents for each unit increase in the average load factor. Following sections show how to print and plot such estimates and their standard errors and confidence intervals.

10. The estimated standard errors of the coefficient estimates are given in the Std Error column. These are 0.655 and 1.454, respectively, and may be used to construct confidence intervals for these model parameters. For example, a 95% confidence interval for $\beta_1$ is computed as

$$(-3.26355) \pm (2.042 \times 1.45453)$$

where 2.042 is the 0.05 level two-tail value of the *t* distribution for 30 degrees of freedom (used to approximate 31 degrees of freedom needed here). The resulting interval is from −6.235 to −0.293. Thus, with 95% confidence, you can state that the interval (−6.235, −0.293) includes the true change in cost due to a one-percentage-point increase in Load.

In JMP, these confidence interval columns are initially hidden.

To make JMP produce these confidence limits,

- Right-click on the Parameter Estimates column.
- Select Columns → Lower 95% from the menu that appears.
- Repeat for the Upper 95% confidence interval.

11. The *t* statistics, used for testing the individual null hypotheses that each coefficient is zero, are given in the column labeled t Ratio. These quantities are simply the parameter estimates divided by their standard errors. The next column, labeled Prob> | t |, gives the *p* value for the two-tailed test. For example, the *p* value of 0.0321 for Load states that if you reject $H_0$: (Load=0), there is a 0.0321 chance of erroneous rejection. Note that for this one variable model, this is the same chance as that for the *F* test of the model. Because the intercept has no practical value in this example, the *p* value for this parameter is not useful.

## 2.3 A Model with Several Independent Variables

The same example is used throughout this chapter for illustrating regression in a model with several independent variables. This section presents the results obtained from a model for relating cost per passenger mile to all the variables in the data except for Type (see Figure 2.1).

As you will see later, examining relationships among individual pairs of variables is not often useful in establishing the basis for a multiple regression model. Nevertheless, you may want to examine pairwise correlations among all variables in the model to compare to the results obtained by using all variables simultaneously in a regression model. In addition, you may want to have some information about the nature of the variables in the model. The correlations as well as some simple statistics are obtained using the Multivariate platform.

- Select **Analyze** → **Multivariate Methods** → **Multivariate**.

- Highlight all the variables in the column selection list except for Type.

- Click **OK**.

The output from these commands appears in Figure 2.4.

The upper portion of the report shows the correlation coefficients for each pair of variables. Scatterplots appear as a matrix in the lower portion of the output. Each row and each column correspond to a variable in the analysis. 95% confidence ellipses also appear on each scatterplot of the grid.

Note that the Multivariate platform omits rows that contain a missing value for any variable. If all the values of a column are missing, the variable is dropped from the analysis.

JMP can compute pairwise correlations as well.

- From the Multivariate platform pop-up menu, select **Pairwise Correlations**.

The pairwise correlation report is shown in Figure 2.5.

Examining the correlations, you can, for example, see that the estimated correlation between Load and Seats is −0.4949.

The correlations between the dependent variable, Cost, and the four independent variables are of particular interest. All of these correlations have a high enough magnitude (that is, absolute value) to suggest that each of these factors could be useful by itself in estimating the cost of providing air service.

In terms of the example, the model for estimating Cost using the four cost factors is

*A Model with Several Independent Variables* 33

*Figure 2.4*
*Correlations among Airline Cost Variables*

**Multivariate**

**Correlations**

|  | Load | Use | Length | Seats | Cost |
|---|---|---|---|---|---|
| Load | 1.0000 | -0.2054 | -0.0872 | -0.4949 | -0.3738 |
| Use | -0.2054 | 1.0000 | 0.6284 | 0.3244 | -0.3720 |
| Length | -0.0872 | 0.6284 | 1.0000 | 0.6071 | -0.3508 |
| Seats | -0.4949 | 0.3244 | 0.6071 | 1.0000 | -0.2976 |
| Cost | -0.3738 | -0.3720 | -0.3508 | -0.2976 | 1.0000 |

**Scatterplot Matrix**

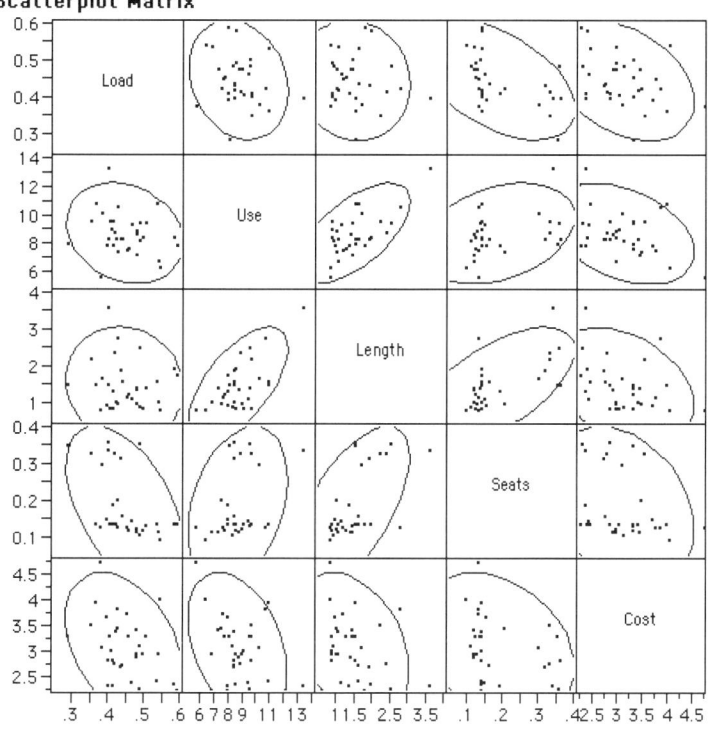

*Figure 2.5*
*Pairwise Correlations*

**Pairwise Correlations**

| Variable | by Variable | Correlation | Count | Signif Prob | -.8 -.6 -.4 -.2 0 .2 .4 .6 .8 |
|---|---|---|---|---|---|
| Use | Load | -0.2054 | 33 | 0.2515 |  |
| Length | Load | -0.0872 | 33 | 0.6295 |  |
| Length | Use | 0.6284 | 33 | 0.0001 |  |
| Seats | Load | -0.4949 | 33 | 0.0034 |  |
| Seats | Use | 0.3244 | 33 | 0.0655 |  |
| Seats | Length | 0.6071 | 33 | 0.0002 |  |
| Cost | Load | -0.3738 | 33 | 0.0321 |  |
| Cost | Use | -0.3720 | 33 | 0.0330 |  |
| Cost | Length | -0.3508 | 33 | 0.0453 |  |
| Cost | Seats | -0.2976 | 33 | 0.0926 |  |

$$\text{Cost} = \beta_0 + \beta_1(\text{Load}) + \beta_2(\text{Use}) + \beta_3(\text{Length}) + \beta_4(\text{Seats}) + \varepsilon$$

To fit this model,

- Select **Analyze** → **Fit Model**.
- Select **Cost** and click the **Y** button.
- Select each of other variables in the order Load, Use, Length, Seats in the model, and click the **Add** button after each variable is selected.
- Select **Minimal Report** from the **Emphasis** drop-down menu.

**Minimal Report** is an *emphasis* choice in the Fit Model dialog. These emphasis choices do not alter the fit in any way, but rather select certain combinations of initial output. The **Minimal Report** emphasis shows only text reports and serves as a basic form of output to which other results and graphs can be appended. The other two emphases, **Effect Leverage** and **Effect Screening**, are generally more useful once the basic concepts of regression are in place. For this chapter, **Minimal Report** is used to focus attention on certain portions of standard regression output.

- Click **Run Model**.

The results appear in Figure 2.6.

The Analysis of Variance portion of the output, as in Figure 2.6, contains the partitioning of the sums of squares and the corresponding *F* ratio. Other items in the output associated with the numbered arrows are explained as follows:

1. The *F* value of 10.556 is used to test the null hypothesis $H_0: \beta_1 = \beta_2 = \beta_3 = \beta_4 = 0$. The associated *p* value, shown as < 0.0001 under **Prob > F**, leads to the rejection of this hypothesis and indicates that at least one of the coefficients is not zero.

2. **RSquare** = 0.6013 tells you that a major portion of the variation of Cost is explained by variation in the independent variables in the model. Note that this $R^2$ value is much larger than that for Load alone (see Figure 2.3). The statistic **RSquare Adj** = 0.5443 is an alternative to $R^2$ that is adjusted for the number of parameters in the model according to the formula

$$\text{Adjusted } R^2 = 1 - (1 - R^2)\frac{n-1}{n-m-1}$$

where *n* is the number of observations in the data set and *m* is the number of regression parameters in the model excluding the intercept.

Alternatively, $R^2$ and adjusted $R^2$ can be defined as

*Figure 2.6*
*Fit Model*
*Results*

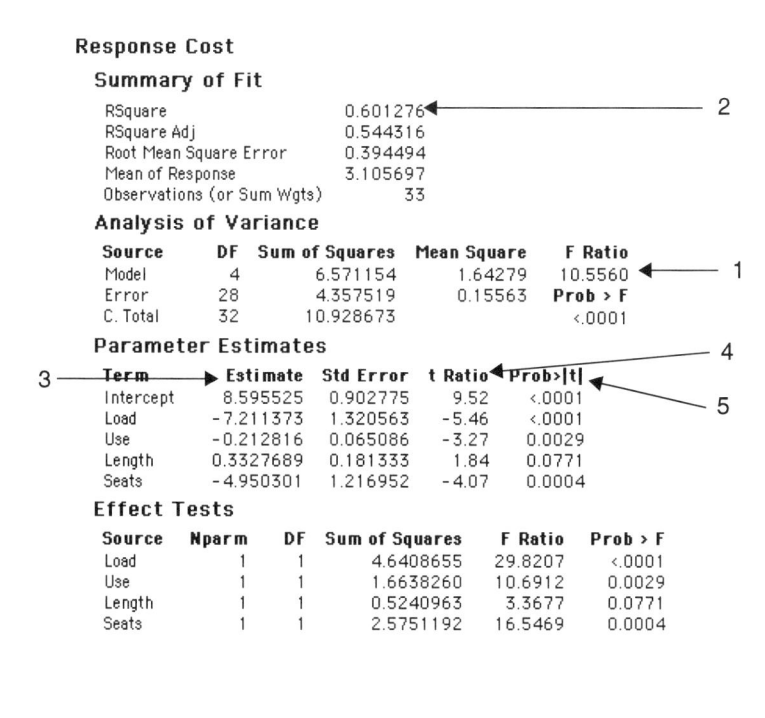

**Response Cost**
**Summary of Fit**

| | |
|---|---|
| RSquare | 0.601276 | ← 2
| RSquare Adj | 0.544316 |
| Root Mean Square Error | 0.394494 |
| Mean of Response | 3.105697 |
| Observations (or Sum Wgts) | 33 |

**Analysis of Variance**

| Source | DF | Sum of Squares | Mean Square | F Ratio |
|---|---|---|---|---|
| Model | 4 | 6.571154 | 1.64279 | 10.5560 | ← 1
| Error | 28 | 4.357519 | 0.15563 | Prob > F |
| C. Total | 32 | 10.928673 | | <.0001 |

**Parameter Estimates**                                  ← 4

| Term → | Estimate | Std Error | t Ratio ← | Prob>|t| |
|---|---|---|---|---|
| Intercept | 8.595525 | 0.902775 | 9.52 | <.0001 | ← 5
| Load | -7.211373 | 1.320563 | -5.46 | <.0001 |
| Use | -0.212816 | 0.065086 | -3.27 | 0.0029 |
| Length | 0.3327689 | 0.181333 | 1.84 | 0.0771 |
| Seats | -4.950301 | 1.216952 | -4.07 | 0.0004 |

(3 → Term)

**Effect Tests**

| Source | Nparm | DF | Sum of Squares | F Ratio | Prob > F |
|---|---|---|---|---|---|
| Load | 1 | 1 | 4.6408655 | 29.8207 | <.0001 |
| Use | 1 | 1 | 1.6638260 | 10.6912 | 0.0029 |
| Length | 1 | 1 | 0.5240963 | 3.3677 | 0.0771 |
| Seats | 1 | 1 | 2.5751192 | 16.5469 | 0.0004 |

$$R^2 = 1 - \frac{SS(\text{Error})}{SS(\text{Model})} \qquad \text{Adjusted } R^2 = 1 - \frac{MS(\text{Error})}{MS(\text{Model})}$$

This adjustment provides for measuring the reduction in the mean square (rather than sum of squares) due to the regression. It is used to overcome an objection to $R^2$ as a measure of goodness of fit of the model, namely that $R^2$ can be driven to one (suggesting a perfect fit) simply by adding superfluous variables to the model with no real improvement in the fit. This is not the case with *adjusted* $R^2$, which tends to stabilize to a certain value when an adequate set of variables is included in the model. When $m/n$ is small, say, less than 0.05, the adjustment almost vanishes. This adjustment is also purported by some authors (Rawlings 1988, Section 7.5) to permit the comparison of regression models based on different sets of data, although its value for this purpose is not uniformly agreed upon. Adjusted $R^2$ can have values less than zero.

3. Rounding the values of the parameter estimates provides the equation for the fitted model

Cost = 8.596 − (7.211)(Load) − (0.213)(Use) + (0.333)(Length) − (4.950)(Seats)

Thus, for example, a one-unit (percent) increase in the average load factor, Load, is associated with a decreased cost of 7.211 cents per passenger mile, holding all other factors constant. This is quite a difference from the coefficient of the bivariate model discussed earlier, which showed a decrease of a little more than three cents per passenger mile.

4. The estimated standard errors of the parameter estimates are useful for constructing confidence intervals as illustrated in "A Model with One Independent Variable" on page 27. Remember, however, to use the degrees of freedom for MSE.

5. The $t$ statistics are used for testing hypotheses about the individual parameters. It is important that you clearly understand the interpretation of these tests. This statistic can be explained in terms of comparing the fit of full and reduced models ("Partitioning the Sums of Squares" on page 16). The full model for all of these tests contains all the variables listed in the **Effects** portion of the Fit Model dialog (those that were added using the **Add** button). The reduced model contains all these variables except the one being tested. Thus the $t$ statistic of $-5.461$ for testing the null hypothesis that $\beta_1 = 0$ (there is no effect due to Load) is actually testing whether the full four-variable model fits the data better than the reduced three-variable model containing only Use, Length, and Seats. In other words, the test indicates whether there is variation in Cost due to Load that is not due to Use, Length, and Seats. The $p$ value for this test is $< 0.0001$, indicating quite clearly that there is an effect due to Load. By contrast, the corresponding $p$ value for Load in the regression where it is the only variable was only 0.0321. Note that for Use and Seats, the $p$ value for the parameter in the multiple variable model is smaller than that for the corresponding correlation (see Figure 2.4), while for Length the reverse is true. This type of phenomenon is the result of correlations among the independent variables. This correlation is more fully discussed in the presentation of partial and sequential sums of squares (see "Sequential and Partial: Two Types of Sums of Squares" on page 41) and in even greater detail in "Regressions in JMP" on page 25.

## 2.4 Additional Results from Fit Model

This section presents a number of options that produce additional results and modify the regression model. Although these options provide useful results, not all are useful for all analyses and should only be requested if needed.

### 2.4.1 Predicted Values and Confidence Intervals

One of the most common objectives of regression analysis is to compute predicted values

$$\hat{y} = \hat{\beta}_0 + \hat{\beta}_1 x_1 + \ldots + \hat{\beta}_m x_m$$

as well as their standard errors for some selected values of $x_1, \ldots, x_m$.

To produce both the predicted values and confidence intervals, use the drop-down menu of the Fit Model report (Figure 2.7).

*Figure 2.7*
*Fit Model Drop-Down Menu*

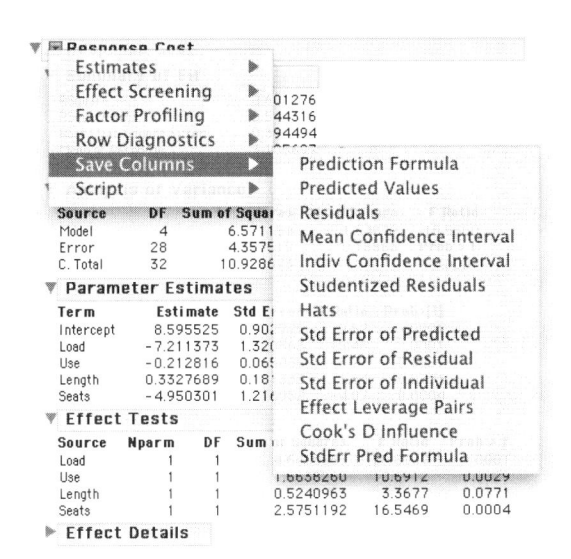

⤺ Select **Save Columns** → **Prediction Formula**.

This adds a column to the data table with the prediction equation as a formula (corresponding to the Pred Formula Cost column in Figure 2.8). Since this formula is evaluated for all rows of the data table, you can add rows to the data table and their prediction is automatically computed. If you only want the values (without the formula being stored), select **Save Columns** → **Predicted Values**, corresponding to the Predicted Cost column in Figure 2.8. Note that the Predicted Cost column does not have a formula indicator beside its name in the columns panel, indicating that the values are raw data. Adding more rows to the data table creates missing values in this column.

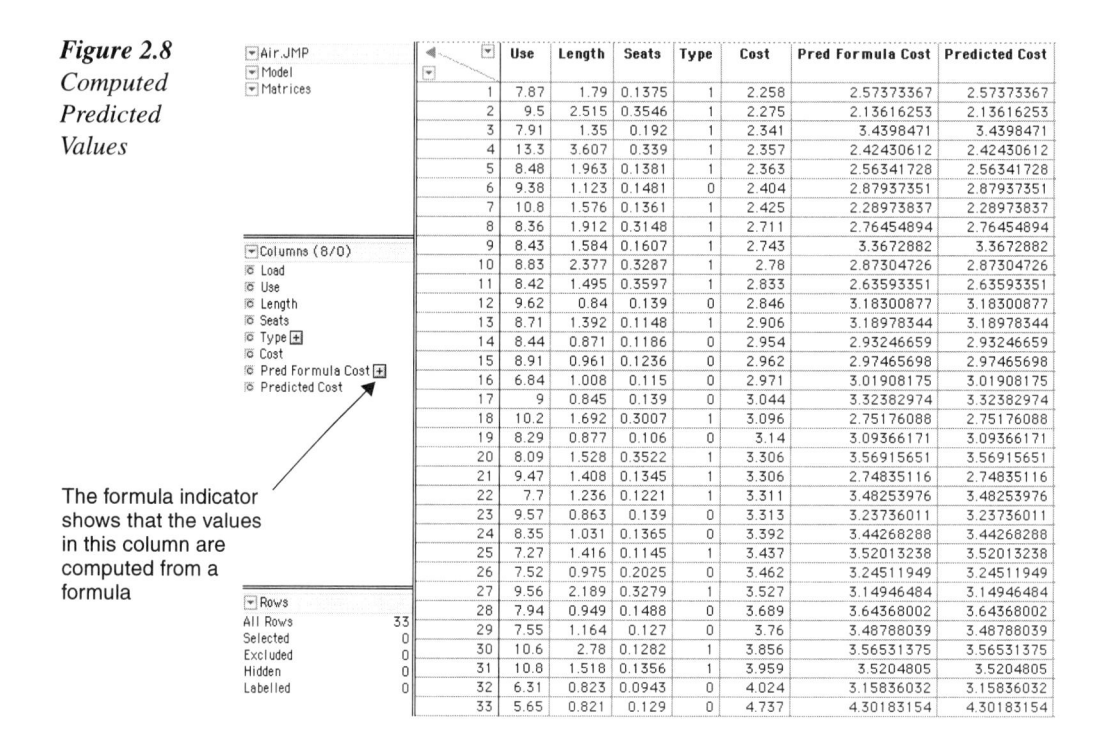

**Figure 2.8**
*Computed Predicted Values*

| | Use | Length | Seats | Type | Cost | Pred Formula Cost | Predicted Cost |
|---|---|---|---|---|---|---|---|
| 1 | 7.87 | 1.79 | 0.1375 | 1 | 2.258 | 2.57373367 | 2.57373367 |
| 2 | 9.5 | 2.515 | 0.3546 | 1 | 2.275 | 2.13616253 | 2.13616253 |
| 3 | 7.91 | 1.35 | 0.192 | 1 | 2.341 | 3.4398471 | 3.4398471 |
| 4 | 13.3 | 3.607 | 0.339 | 1 | 2.357 | 2.42430612 | 2.42430612 |
| 5 | 8.48 | 1.963 | 0.1381 | 1 | 2.363 | 2.56341728 | 2.56341728 |
| 6 | 9.38 | 1.123 | 0.1481 | 0 | 2.404 | 2.87937351 | 2.87937351 |
| 7 | 10.8 | 1.576 | 0.1361 | 1 | 2.425 | 2.28973837 | 2.28973837 |
| 8 | 8.36 | 1.912 | 0.3148 | 1 | 2.711 | 2.76454894 | 2.76454894 |
| 9 | 8.43 | 1.584 | 0.1607 | 1 | 2.743 | 3.3672882 | 3.3672882 |
| 10 | 8.83 | 2.377 | 0.3287 | 1 | 2.78 | 2.87304726 | 2.87304726 |
| 11 | 8.42 | 1.495 | 0.3597 | 0 | 2.833 | 2.63593351 | 2.63593351 |
| 12 | 9.62 | 0.84 | 0.139 | 0 | 2.846 | 3.18300877 | 3.18300877 |
| 13 | 8.71 | 1.392 | 0.1148 | 1 | 2.906 | 3.18978344 | 3.18978344 |
| 14 | 8.44 | 0.871 | 0.1186 | 0 | 2.954 | 2.93246659 | 2.93246659 |
| 15 | 8.91 | 0.961 | 0.1236 | 0 | 2.962 | 2.97465698 | 2.97465698 |
| 16 | 6.84 | 1.008 | 0.115 | 0 | 2.971 | 3.01908175 | 3.01908175 |
| 17 | 9 | 0.845 | 0.139 | 0 | 3.044 | 3.32382974 | 3.32382974 |
| 18 | 10.2 | 1.692 | 0.3007 | 1 | 3.096 | 2.75176088 | 2.75176088 |
| 19 | 8.29 | 0.877 | 0.106 | 0 | 3.14 | 3.09366171 | 3.09366171 |
| 20 | 8.09 | 1.528 | 0.3522 | 1 | 3.306 | 3.56915651 | 3.56915651 |
| 21 | 9.47 | 1.408 | 0.1345 | 1 | 3.306 | 2.74835116 | 2.74835116 |
| 22 | 7.7 | 1.236 | 0.1221 | 1 | 3.311 | 3.48253976 | 3.48253976 |
| 23 | 9.57 | 0.863 | 0.139 | 0 | 3.313 | 3.23736011 | 3.23736011 |
| 24 | 8.35 | 1.031 | 0.1365 | 0 | 3.392 | 3.44268288 | 3.44268288 |
| 25 | 7.27 | 1.416 | 0.1145 | 1 | 3.437 | 3.52013238 | 3.52013238 |
| 26 | 7.52 | 0.975 | 0.2025 | 0 | 3.462 | 3.24511949 | 3.24511949 |
| 27 | 9.56 | 2.189 | 0.3279 | 1 | 3.527 | 3.14946484 | 3.14946484 |
| 28 | 7.94 | 0.949 | 0.1488 | 0 | 3.689 | 3.64368002 | 3.64368002 |
| 29 | 7.55 | 1.164 | 0.127 | 0 | 3.76 | 3.48788039 | 3.48788039 |
| 30 | 10.6 | 2.78 | 0.1282 | 1 | 3.856 | 3.56531375 | 3.56531375 |
| 31 | 10.8 | 1.518 | 0.1356 | 1 | 3.959 | 3.5204805 | 3.5204805 |
| 32 | 6.31 | 0.823 | 0.0943 | 0 | 4.024 | 3.15836032 | 3.15836032 |
| 33 | 5.65 | 0.821 | 0.129 | 0 | 4.737 | 4.30183154 | 4.30183154 |

The formula indicator shows that the values in this column are computed from a formula

The results of these actions on the data table are shown in Figure 2.8. The formula stored in the Pred Formula Cost column appears in Figure 2.9.

**Figure 2.9**
*Prediction Formula Stored in Column*

8.59552504974981
+-7.2113732478228*Load
+-0.2128157231492*Use
+0.33276893156182*Length
+-4.9503013730156*Seats

Note that the column Pred Formula Cost has the formula symbol beside it, to designate that the column contains a formula.

To compute the upper and lower 95% confidence limits for the expected value (conditional mean) for each observation,

⌐ Select **Save Columns** → **Mean Confidence Interval**.

New columns are then created in the data table that hold the confidence intervals. Computation of these limits requires the standard errors of the predicted values, which can also be saved to the data table.

- Select **Save Columns → Std Error of Predicted**.

These errors are computed according to the formula

$$\text{Std Error Mean Predicted} = ((x'(X'X)^{-1} x)*MSE)^{1/2}$$

where **x** is a row vector of the design matrix **X** corresponding to a single observation and MSE is the error mean square. This error is equal to the square root of the variance of $\hat{y}$ given in "Partitioning the Sums of Squares" on page 16. The upper and lower 95% confidence limits are then calculated by

$$\hat{y} \pm t \cdot (\text{Std Error Mean Predicted})$$

where $t$ is the 0.05 level tabulated $t$ value with degrees of freedom equal to those of the error mean square. For example, for observation 1, for which Load = 0.591 and the actual Cost is 2.258, the predicted value is 2.573 and the 95% confidence limits are the interval (2.20, 2.94).

JMP can also compute the 95% prediction interval for a single observation. The formula for this is similar to that of the confidence interval for the mean, except that the variance of the predicted value is larger than that of the interval of the mean by the value of the residual mean square.

$$\text{Std Error Individual} = ((1 + x'(X'X)^{-1} x)*MSE)^{1/2}$$

- Select **Save Columns → Indiv Confidence Interval**.

The interpretation of the mean and individual confidence statistics are sometimes confused. Specifically, Mean Confidence Interval yields a confidence interval for the subpopulation mean and Indiv Confidence Interval yields a prediction interval for a single unit to be drawn at random from that subpopulation. The Indiv Confidence Interval limits are always wider than the Mean Confidence Interval limits because the mean limits need to accommodate only the variability in the predicted value, whereas the individual limits must accommodate the variability in the predicted value as well as the variability in the future value of $y$. This is true even though the same predicted value $\hat{y}$ is used as the point estimate of the subpopulation mean as well as the predictor of the future value.

To draw an analogy, suppose you walk into a roomful of people and are challenged to

1. guess the average weight of all the people in the room, and
2. guess the weight of one particular person to be chosen at random.

You make a visual estimate of, say, 150 lbs. You would guess the average weight to be 150 lbs., and you would also guess the weight of the mystery person to be 150 lbs. But you would have more confidence in your guess of the average weight for the entire roomful than in your guess of the weight of the mystery person.

In the airline cost data, the 95% confidence interval for the mean of the first airline is from 2.20 to 2.94 cents. This means that you can state with 95% confidence that these limits include the true mean cost per passenger mile of the hypothetical population of airlines having the characteristics of that airline. On the other hand, the Indiv Confidence Interval option for this airline provides the interval from 1.68 to 3.46 cents. This means that there is a 95% probability that a single airline chosen from that population of airlines will have a cost that is within those limits.

The following guidelines are offered to assist in deciding whether to use **Mean Confidence Interval** or **Indiv Confidence Interval**:

❑ Use **Mean Confidence Interval** if you want the limits to show the region that should contain the population regression curve.

❑ Use **Indiv Confidence Interval** if you want the limits to show the region that should contain (almost all of) the population of all possible observations.

The confidence coefficients for Mean Confidence Interval and Indiv Confidence Interval are valid on a single-point basis.

Residuals are produced in a fashion similar to saving the prediction formula.

🖑 Select **Save Columns → Residuals**

to add a column Residuals Cost to the data table.

When assessing the goodness of fit of a model, it is sometimes useful to scan this column of values for relatively large values (see Chapter 3, "Observations"). Large values show cases where the model does not closely predict the observed value. A plot of these residuals, displayed by default in other emphases of the Fit Model platform, can be obtained in this report.

🖑 Select **Row Diagnostics → Plot Residual by Predicted**. (See Figure 2.10.)

*Figure 2.10
Residual by
Predicted Plot*

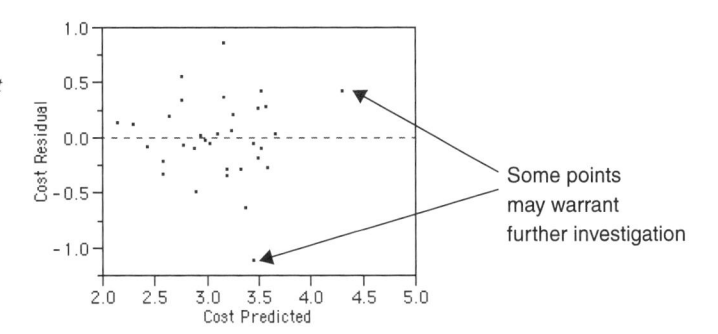

Some points may warrant further investigation

## 2.4.2 Sequential and Partial: Two Types of Sums of Squares

JMP can compute two types of sums of squares associated with the estimated coefficients in the model. These types are referred to as *sequential* and *partial* sums of squares.

Partial sums of squares are automatically produced in the Fit Model platform. They are found in the Effect Tests portion of the output. (See Figure 2.11.)

*Figure 2.11
Effect Tests
with Partial
Sums of
Squares*

**Effect Tests**

| Source | Nparm | DF | Sum of Squares | F Ratio | Prob > F |
|---|---|---|---|---|---|
| Load | 1 | 1 | 4.6408655 | 29.8207 | <.0001 |
| Use | 1 | 1 | 1.6638260 | 10.6912 | 0.0029 |
| Length | 1 | 1 | 0.5240963 | 3.3677 | 0.0771 |
| Seats | 1 | 1 | 2.5751192 | 16.5469 | 0.0004 |

To obtain sequential sums of squares,

- Select **Estimates** → **Sequential Tests** (Figure 2.12).

*Figure 2.12
Sequential
Tests with
Sequential
Sums of
Squares*

**Sequential (Type 1) Tests**

| Source | Nparm | DF | Seq SS | F Ratio | Prob > F |
|---|---|---|---|---|---|
| Load | 1 | 1 | 1.5268221 | 9.8109 | 0.0040 |
| Use | 1 | 1 | 2.2975672 | 14.7634 | 0.0006 |
| Length | 1 | 1 | 0.1716456 | 1.1029 | 0.3026 |
| Seats | 1 | 1 | 2.5751192 | 16.5469 | 0.0004 |

The interpretation of these sums of squares is based on the material in "Partitioning the Sums of Squares" on page 16. In particular, the following concepts are useful in understanding the different types of sums of squares:

- partitioning of sums of squares
- complete and reduced models
- reduction notation.

The sequential sums of squares (called Type I in SAS) represent a partitioning of the model sum of squares into component sums of squares due to each variable as it is added sequentially to the model in the order prescribed in the Fit Model dialog box. This is why the order in which terms were added to the Fit Model dialog matters.

The sequential SS for Intercept is simply $(\Sigma y)^2 / n$, which is commonly called the *correction for the mean*. The sequential SS for Load (1.5268) is the model SS for a regression equation containing only Load and the intercept. This is easily verified as the Model SS in Figure 2.3. The sequential SS for Use (2.2976) is the reduction in the error SS due to adding Use to a model that already contains Load and the intercept. Since Model SS + Error SS = Total SS, this is also the increase in the model SS due to the addition of Use to the model containing Load.

Equivalent interpretations hold for the sequential SS for Length and Seats. In general terms, the sequential SS for any particular variable is the reduction in error SS due to adding that variable to a model that already contains all the variables preceding that variable in the model.

Note that the sum of the sequential SS is the overall model SS:

$$6.5711 = 1.5268 + 2.2976 + 0.1716 + 2.5751$$

This equation shows the sequential partitioning of the model SS into sequential components corresponding to the variables as they are added to the model in the order given. In other words, the sequential sums of squares are order dependent; if the variables in the Fit Model dialog are given in different order, the sequential sums of squares will change.

The partial sums of squares for a variable (called Type III in SAS) are the reduction in error SS due to adding that variable to the model that already contains all the other variables in the model list. For a given variable, the partial SS is equivalent to the sequential SS for that variable if it were the last variable in the model list. This result is easily verified by the fact that both types of sums of squares for Seats, which is the last variable in the list, are the same. The partial sums of squares, therefore, do not depend on the order in which the independent variables are listed in the Fit Model dialog. Furthermore, they do not yield a partitioning of the model SS unless the independent variables are mutually uncorrelated.

Reduction notation (see "Partitioning the Sums of Squares" on page 16) provides a convenient device to determine the complete and reduced models that are compared if the corresponding one degree of freedom sum of squares is used as the numerator for an $F$ test. In reduction notation the two types of sums of squares are shown in Table 2.1.

*Table 2.1* Sum of Squares in R Notation

| Parameter | Sequential | Partial |
|---|---|---|
| Load | R(Load\|Intercept) | R(Load\|Intercept, Use,Length,Seats) |
| Use | R(Use\|Intercept,Load) | R(Use\|Intercept, Load,Length,Seats) |
| Length | R(Length\|Intercept, Load,Use) | R(Length\|Intercept, Load,Use,Seats) |
| Seats | R(Seats\|Intercept, Load,Use,Length) | R(Seats\|Intercept, Load,Use,Length) |

$F$ tests derived by dividing the partial SS by the error mean square are equivalent to the $t$ tests for the parameters provided in the computer output. In fact, the partial $F$ statistic is equal to the square of the $t$ statistic.

Tests derived from the sequential SS are convenient to use in model building in those cases where there is a predetermined order for selecting variables. Not only does each sequential SS provide a test for the improvement in the fit of the model when the corresponding term is added to the model, but the additivity of the sums of squares can be used to assess the significance of a model containing, say, the first $k < m$ terms.

Unlike corresponding SAS GLM output, JMP provides $F$ tests for both types of sums of squares.

### 2.4.3 Standardized Coefficients

JMP produces the set of standardized regression coefficients, although they are initially hidden in the Fit Model report. To make them visible,

- Right-click (Control-click on the Macintosh) in the body of the parameter estimates table.
- Select **Columns → Std Beta**.

Figure 2.13 shows the parameter estimates table augmented with the standardized parameter estimates.

*Figure 2.13 Standardized Coefficients*

**Parameter Estimates**

| Term | Estimate | Std Error | t Ratio | Prob>\|t\| | Std Beta |
|---|---|---|---|---|---|
| Intercept | 8.595525 | 0.902775 | 9.52 | <.0001 | 0 |
| Load | -7.211373 | 1.320563 | -5.46 | <.0001 | -0.82592 |
| Use | -0.212816 | 0.065086 | -3.27 | 0.0029 | -0.52768 |
| Length | 0.3327689 | 0.181333 | 1.84 | 0.0771 | 0.370112 |
| Seats | -4.950301 | 1.216952 | -4.07 | 0.0004 | -0.75983 |

These coefficients, labeled Std Beta, are the estimates that would be obtained if all variables in the model were standardized to zero mean and unit variance prior to performing the regression computations. Each coefficient indicates the number of standard deviation changes in the dependent variable associated with a standard deviation change in the independent variable, holding all other variables constant. In other words, the magnitudes of the standardized coefficients are not affected by the scales of measurement of the various model variables and thus may be useful in ascertaining the relative importance of the effects of independent variables not affected by the scales of measurement. For example, Load is of more importance (larger effect) than Length (smallest effect).

### 2.4.4 Regression through the Origin

The Fit Model dialog has a check box labeled No Intercept (see Figure 2.14) that forces the regression response to pass through the origin; that is, the estimated value of the dependent variable is zero when all independent variables have the value zero. An example of this requirement occurs in some growth models where the response (say, weight) must be zero at the beginning—that is, when time is zero. In many applications this requirement is not reasonable, especially when this condition does not or cannot actually occur. If this option is used in such situations, the results of the regression analysis are often grossly misleading. Moreover, even when the conditions implied by the No Intercept option are reasonable, the results of the analysis have some features that may mislead the unwary practitioner.

The No Intercept option is illustrated with the airline data. This example demonstrates the uselessness of this option when it is not justified, since in this example zero values of the variables in the model cannot occur.

*Figure 2.14*
No Intercept *Option*

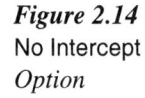

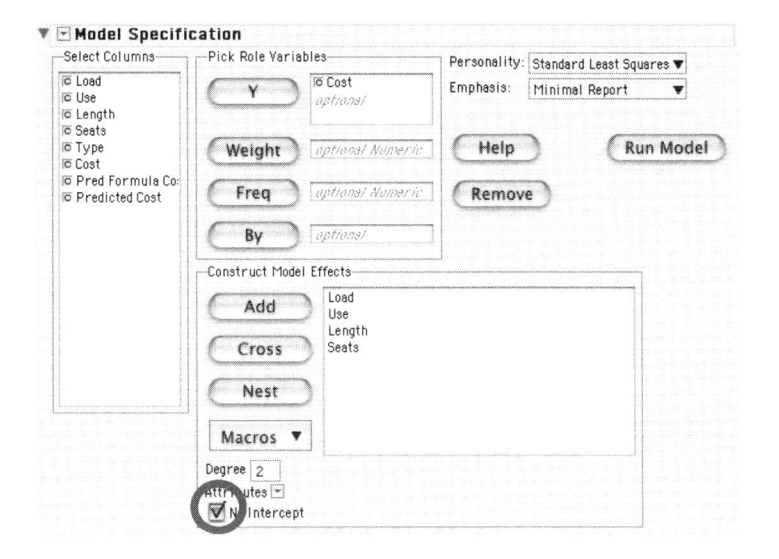

- If the previous Fit Model window is still open, bring it to the front using the Window menu. Otherwise, select **Analyze** → **Fit Model** and fill it in as shown in Figure 2.14.

- Make sure the **No Intercept** check box is selected.

- Select **Minimal Report** from the **Emphasis** drop-down list.

- Click **Run Model**.

The results are shown in Figure 2.15.

The overall partitioning of the sum of squares certainly suggests a well-fitting model. In fact, the model $F$ statistic is much larger than those for the model with the intercept (see Figure 2.6). However, closer examination of the results shows that the error sum of squares for the no-intercept model is actually larger than the *total* sum of squares for the model with intercept.

This apparent contradiction can be explained by remembering what the $F$ statistic represents. When fitting a model with an intercept, total SS is the corrected or centered sum of squares for the response variable, which can be interpreted as the error SS for the model

$$y = \mu + \varepsilon$$

The model SS shows the reduction from the sum of squares due to fitting the regression model. In this example (Figure 2.6),

***Figure 2.15***
*Results of Fit Model with No Intercept Option*

```
Response Cost
Summary of Fit
RSquare                                  .
RSquare Adj                              .
Root Mean Square Error          0.797962
Mean of Response                3.105697
Observations (or Sum Wgts)            33

Analysis of Variance
Source     DF   Sum of Squares   Mean Square   F Ratio
Model       4       310.75979       77.6899   122.0114
Error      29        18.46555        0.6367   Prob > F
C. Total   33       329.22534                   <.0001
Tested against reduced model: Y=0

Parameter Estimates
Term                Estimate   Std Error   t Ratio   Prob>|t|
Intercept Zeroed           0           0         .          .
Load               3.6320233    1.352173      2.69     0.0118
Use                0.2210246    0.094009      2.35     0.0257
Length            -0.578061    0.311597     -1.86     0.0738
Seats              1.9573264    1.976324      0.99     0.3302

Effect Tests
Source   Nparm   DF   Sum of Squares   F Ratio   Prob > F
Load         1    1        4.5940627    7.2149     0.0118
Use          1    1        3.5196957    5.5277     0.0257
Length       1    1        2.1914143    3.4416     0.0738
Seats        1    1        0.6245607    0.9809     0.3302
```

Total SS = 10.92867, Model SS = 6.57115, $R^2 = 0.6013$

However, when you are fitting a model without an intercept, total SS is the uncorrected or raw sum of squares, which can be interpreted as the error SS for fitting the model

$$y = 0 + \varepsilon$$

This is obviously a very poor model. The model SS, then, is the reduction from the sum of squares due to fitting the regression model. In this example,

Total SS = 329.22534, Model SS = 310.75979

which would yield an $R^2$ of 0.9439. Thus, the error sum of squares for the no-intercept model is much larger than that for the model with intercept (18.46555 versus 4.35782). Furthermore, both total and error degrees of freedom are larger by one in the no-intercept model since one less parameter has been estimated.

This is one of the reasons that $R^2$ has a missing (.) value in the no-intercept report. Since

$$R^2 = \frac{\text{Model SS}}{\text{Total SS}}$$

and, since these two sums of squares are computed from vastly different models, the $R^2$ for the no-intercept model is meaningless and therefore reported as missing. In other words, the $R^2$ from a no-intercept model is in no way comparable to the $R^2$ from a model with an intercept. It is useless for most of the purposes for which $R^2$ is computed in the first place, so it is omitted in no-intercept model reports.

Looking further you can also see that the coefficient estimates for the no-intercept model bear no resemblance to those of the intercept model because you have really fitted two entirely different models.

Finally, a property of the residuals is not true with the no-intercept model. In the model with the intercept, the residuals should sum to zero (or very close to it). This is not true with the no-intercept model. To see this,

- Select **Save Columns → Residuals** for the model with the intercept.
- Select **Save Columns → Residuals** for the model without the intercept.

This results in two columns added to the air data table. To find the sum of these columns, use the Distribution platform.

- Select **Analyze → Distribution**.
- Click on both residual columns and click the **Y, Columns** button.
- Click **OK**.

When the report appears,

- Select **Display Options → More Moments** for both variables in the report.

The sum is now displayed in the Moments section of the report. It is easy to see that the model with the intercept is quite close to zero (0.0000000000000024), while the model without an intercept is not (0.049). The results are shown in Figure 2.16.

A rather simple example is used to illustrate the fact that the use of a no-intercept model can result in misleading results even in cases where the true intercept is near zero. This example uses the Fit Y by X platform to illustrate the use of the **Fit Special** command. Eight data points are generated using the model $y = x$, with a normally distributed error having zero mean and unit variance. Figure 2.17 shows the data, stored in the No Intercept Data.jmp file.

Fit Y by X is used for models with and without intercept as follows:

- Select **Analyze → Fit Y by X**.
- Assign X as the X variable and Y as the Y variable.

**48** *Regressions in JMP*

***Figure 2.16***
*Distributions of Residuals*

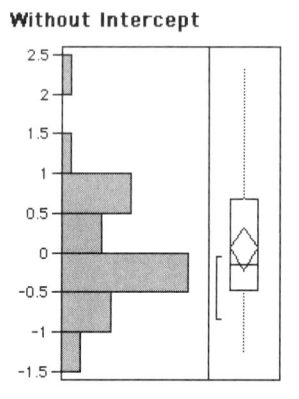

**Without Intercept**

| Quantiles | | |
|---|---|---|
| 100.0% | maximum | 2.337 |
| 99.5% | | 2.337 |
| 97.5% | | 2.337 |
| 90.0% | | 0.923 |
| 75.0% | quartile | 0.683 |
| 50.0% | median | -0.141 |
| 25.0% | quartile | -0.469 |
| 10.0% | | -0.852 |
| 2.5% | | -1.261 |
| 0.5% | | -1.261 |
| 0.0% | minimum | -1.261 |

**Moments**

| | |
|---|---|
| Mean | 0.0497371 |
| Std Dev | 0.7579561 |
| Std Err Mean | 0.1319432 |
| upper 95% Mean | 0.3184966 |
| lower 95% Mean | -0.219022 |
| N | 33 |

**With Intercept**

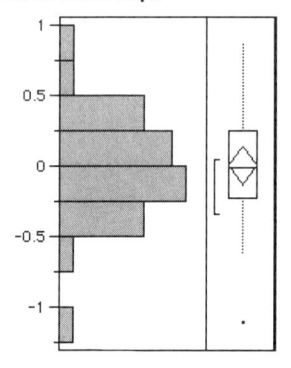

| Quantiles | | |
|---|---|---|
| 100.0% | maximum | 0.866 |
| 99.5% | | 0.866 |
| 97.5% | | 0.866 |
| 90.0% | | 0.437 |
| 75.0% | quartile | 0.245 |
| 50.0% | median | -0.013 |
| 25.0% | quartile | -0.232 |
| 10.0% | | -0.420 |
| 2.5% | | -1.099 |
| 0.5% | | -1.099 |
| 0.0% | minimum | -1.099 |

**Moments**

| | |
|---|---|
| Mean | -2.4e-16 |
| Std Dev | 0.3690155 |
| Std Err Mean | 0.0642374 |
| upper 95% Mean | 0.1308472 |
| lower 95% Mean | -0.130847 |
| N | 33 |

***Figure 2.17***
*No-Intercept Data*

| X | Y |
|---|---|
| 1 | -0.35 |
| 2 | 2.79 |
| 3 | 1.81 |
| 4 | 2 |
| 5 | 3.88 |
| 6 | 6.79 |
| 7 | 7.67 |
| 8 | 6.79 |

🖰 Click **OK**.

When the scatterplot appears,

🖰 Select **Fit Line** from the platform pop-up menu located in the upper-left corner of the report.

## Additional Results from Fit Model 49

This command fits a regular linear model, including an intercept. To fit a model without an intercept,

- Select **Fit Special** from the platform pop-up menu.

- Check the box beside **Constrain intercept to** and make sure there is a zero entered as the constraint.

- Click **OK**.

The results of these analyses appear in Figure 2.18. The reports were listed horizontally by right-clicking (control-click on Macintosh) on the disclosure icon next to Bivariate Fit of Y by X and selecting **Horizontal** from the menu that appears.

**Figure 2.18** *Results of Fit Y by X*

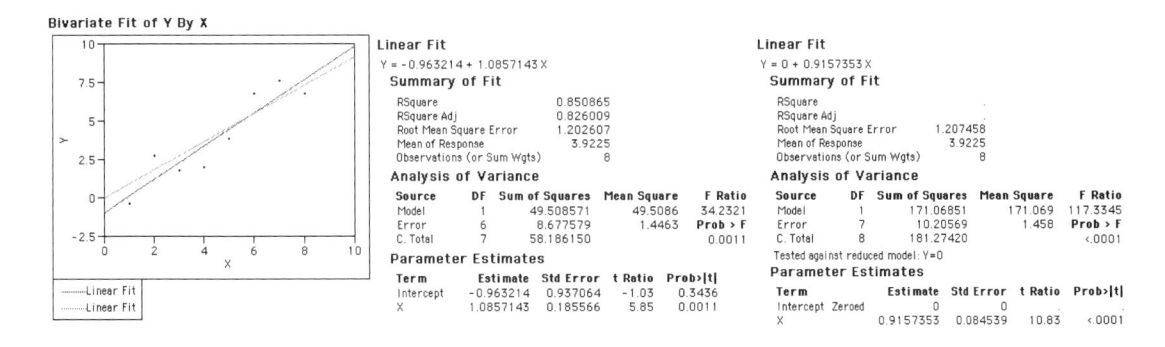

You can see immediately that the model *F* values are much larger for the no-intercept model, whereas the residual mean squares are almost identical. Actually, both models have estimated very similar regression lines since the estimated intercept (−0.963) is sufficiently close to zero that a hypothesis test of a zero intercept cannot be rejected ($p = 0.3436$). However, the residual mean square of the no-intercept model is still somewhat larger and the sum of residuals for the no-intercept model is −1.586, even though the intercept is quite close to zero.

The difference between the test statistics for the models is based on which null hypothesis is tested in each case. Remember that the test for the model is based on the difference between the error and total sum of squares. The error sum of squares measures the variability from the estimated regression, while the total sum of squares measures the variability from the model specified by the null hypothesis.

In the model with an intercept, the null hypothesis $H_0: \beta_1 = 0$ specifies the model

$$y = \beta_0 + \varepsilon = \mu + \varepsilon$$

Here $\mu$ is estimated by the sample mean. Therefore, the test for the model compares the variation from the regression to the variation from the sample mean.

In the no-intercept model, the null hypothesis $H_0: \beta_1 = 0$ specifies the model $y = \varepsilon$, that is, a regression where the mean response is zero for all observations. The test for this model then compares the variation from the regression to the variation from $y = 0$. Obviously, unless the mean of the response variable is close to zero, the variation from the mean is smaller than the variation from zero, and hence the apparent contradiction.

You can readily make this comparison from the above example. Since the true intercept is indeed zero, the error sums of squares are not very different (8.68 with intercept, 10.21 without intercept) but the total sums of squares are much larger for the no-intercept model (181.27 for no intercept, 58.19 with intercept).

## 2.5 Further Examination of Model Parameters

In addition to testing the statistical significance of the model and the individual parameters, you can investigate other properties of the model. Specifically, you can

- ❏ test hypotheses on any linear function(s) of the parameters. This is performed by the **Custom Test** option described in the following section, "Tests for Subsets and Linear Functions of Parameters."

- ❏ change the model by adding or deleting variables. This can be done by specifying a new model or, interactively, by using the original Fit Model dialog as described in the section "Changing the Model" on page 53. Additional model selection methods are presented in Chapter 4, "Collinearity: Detection and Remedial Measures."

### 2.5.1 Tests for Subsets and Linear Functions of Parameters

The *t* tests on the parameters in the minimal Fit Model output (see Figure 2.6) provide the tests of hypotheses that individual regression coefficients are zero. "Sequential and Partial: Two Types of Sums of Squares" on page 41 indicates that the sequential sums of squares may be used to test whether certain subsets of coefficients are zero. This section shows how the Custom Test command can be used to test the hypothesis that one or more linear functions of parameters are equal to zero.

One or more custom tests may be run in a single Fit Model report. These statements may be entered interactively. In general, after running a model, select **Estimates → Custom Test** to begin the testing.

The tests can be interpreted in terms of comparing complete with reduced or restricted models in the manner described in previous sections. The complete model for all tests specified by a custom test is the model containing all variables specified in the Fit Model dialog. The reduced model is derived from the complete model by imposing the restrictions implied by the equations specified in the Custom Test dialog. For this example the following tests are examined:

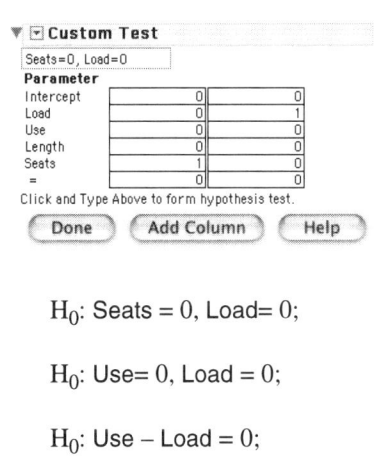

$H_0$: Seats = 0, Load= 0;

$H_0$: Use= 0, Load = 0;

$H_0$: Use − Load = 0;

To enter the first test,

- Select **Estimates → Custom Test**.

- In the text box that appears just below the outline title, label the test as Seats=0, Load=0.

- Enter a 1 beside Seats.

- Click the **Add Column** button.

- Enter a 1 beside Load.

- Click **Done**.

To enter the second test, use a method almost identical to the first.

## 52 Regressions in JMP

```
▼ ☐ Custom Test
  Use - Load = 0
  Parameter
  Intercept        0
  Load            -1
  Use              1
  Length           0
  Seats            0
  =                0
  Click and Type Above to form hypothesis test.
  [ Done ]  [ Add Column ]  [ Help ]
```

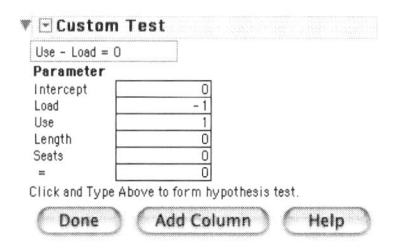

- Select **Estimates → Custom Test**.
- In the text box that appears just below the outline title, label the test as Use=0, Load=0.
- Enter a 1 beside Use. Click the **Add Column** button.
- Enter a 1 beside Load.
- Click **Done**.

To enter the third test,

- Select **Estimates → Custom Test**.
- Enter a 1 beside Use and a –1 beside Load.
- Click **Done**.

The first test command tests the hypothesis that coefficients for both Seats and Load are zero. This test compares the full model with one containing only Use and Length. The second test command tests the hypothesis that coefficients for both Use and Load are zero. This test compares the full model with the one containing only Length and Seats. The third test command tests the hypothesis that the difference between the coefficients for Use and Load is zero. This is equivalent to the test that the coefficient for Use is equal to the coefficient for Load. (This particular test has no practical interpretation in this example and is used for illustration only.) The results of these custom tests appear in Figure 2.19.

---

**Note**  If there are linear dependencies or inconsistencies among the equations of a custom test, JMP prints a message that the test is not an estimable contrast.

---

For each indicated custom test, a partial sum of squares is computed with degrees of freedom equal to the number of columns in the custom test. A mean square is then computed that forms the numerator of an $F$ statistic. The denominator of this

**Figure 2.19**
*Output from Custom Tests*

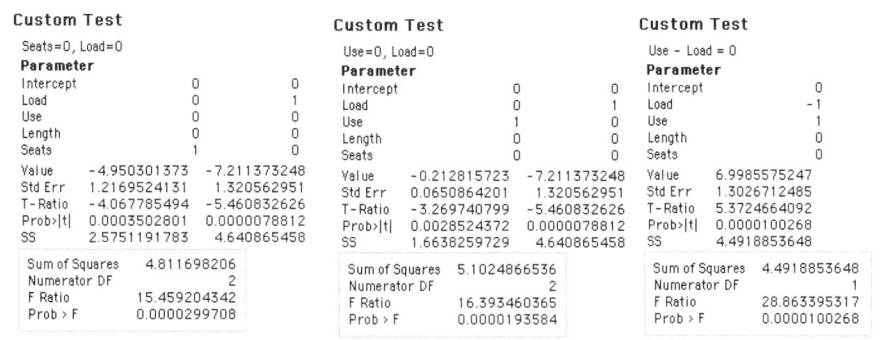

```
Custom Test
Seats=0, Load=0
Parameter
Intercept         0            0
Load              0            1
Use               0            0
Length            0            0
Seats             1            0
Value      -4.950301373  -7.211373248
Std Err     1.2169524131   1.320562951
T-Ratio    -4.067785494  -5.460832626
Prob>|t|    0.0003502801  0.0000078812
SS          2.5751191783  4.640865458

Sum of Squares    4.811698206
Numerator DF              2
F Ratio          15.459204342
Prob > F          0.0000299708
```

```
Custom Test
Use=0, Load=0
Parameter
Intercept         0            0
Load              0            1
Use               1            0
Length            0            0
Seats             0            0
Value      -0.212815723  -7.211373248
Std Err     0.0650864201   1.320562951
T-Ratio    -3.269740799  -5.460832626
Prob>|t|    0.0028524372  0.0000078812
SS          1.6638259729  4.640865458

Sum of Squares    5.1024866536
Numerator DF              2
F Ratio          16.393460365
Prob > F          0.0000193584
```

```
Custom Test
Use - Load = 0
Parameter
Intercept         0
Load             -1
Use               1
Length            0
Seats             0
Value       6.9985575247
Std Err     1.3026712485
T-Ratio     5.3724664092
Prob>|t|    0.0000100268
SS          4.4918853648

Sum of Squares    4.4918853648
Numerator DF              1
F Ratio          28.863395317
Prob > F          0.0000100268
```

statistic is the error mean square for the full model. The values of the two sums of squares, the degrees of freedom, the *F* ratio, and its *p* value are in the output.

It is important to note that each test is performed independently rather than simultaneously with the other tests. Therefore, the results of the various tests are usually not independent of each other. Also, in making multiple hypothesis tests, you run an increased risk of making an experiment-wise Type I error—that is, declaring a test significant when it is really only significant by chance.

### 2.5.2 Changing the Model

Figure 2.6 on page 35 shows that the tests for the coefficient for **Length** and **Use** resulted in *p* values that were larger than those for **Load** and **Seats**. You may be interested in examining a model that omits these two variables from the model.

In JMP, the Fit Model dialog does not disappear after a model is run for this very reason. The same dialog can be used to add or delete effects from the model, then have the model rerun. If you already closed the original Fit Model dialog, you can re-create the original Fit Model dialog by selecting **Script → Redo Analysis**.

Assuming that you have the Fit Model dialog used in the original four-variable model for the airline cost data, you can delete variables **Length** and **Use** as follows.

- Highlight the effect(s) to delete in the Construct Model Effects list.
- Click the **Remove** button.

Alternatively, simply double-click on a variable name to remove it from the model.

After running the model, Figure 2.20 is produced.

**Figure 2.20**
*Model with Two Effects*

**Response Cost**

**Summary of Fit**

| | |
|---|---|
| RSquare | 0.44811 |
| RSquare Adj | 0.411318 |
| Root Mean Square Error | 0.448383 |
| Mean of Response | 3.105697 |
| Observations (or Sum Wgts) | 33 |

**Analysis of Variance**

| Source | DF | Sum of Squares | Mean Square | F Ratio |
|---|---|---|---|---|
| Model | 2 | 4.897250 | 2.44862 | 12.1793 |
| Error | 30 | 6.031423 | 0.20105 | Prob > F |
| C. Total | 32 | 10.928673 | | 0.0001 |

**Parameter Estimates**

| Term | Estimate | Std Error | t Ratio | Prob>|t| |
|---|---|---|---|---|
| Intercept | 6.5559962 | 0.722714 | 9.07 | <.0001 |
| Load | -6.025141 | 1.362856 | -4.42 | 0.0001 |
| Seats | -4.163687 | 1.016915 | -4.09 | 0.0003 |

**Effect Tests**

| Source | Nparm | DF | Sum of Squares | F Ratio | Prob > F |
|---|---|---|---|---|---|
| Load | 1 | 1 | 3.9294608 | 19.5449 | 0.0001 |
| Seats | 1 | 1 | 3.3704278 | 16.7643 | 0.0003 |

Alternatively, you could build this model from scratch with a new Fit Model request.

## 2.6 Plotting Observations

JMP produces many plots and graphs by default. For example, the Fit Y by X command (when used on two continuous variables) always produces a scatterplot. Fit Model produces leverage plots (see "Leverage Plots" on page 110) when **Effect Leverage** is chosen as the **Emphasis**.

However, JMP also allows you to plot results of a regression using its **Overlay Plot** command. For example, you can

❑ produce plots involving the predicted and residual values, or the confidence or prediction limits

❑ examine the distribution of residuals

❑ compare predicted and residual values for different models

❑ see how the estimated regression model is affected by deleting selected observations

There are two ways to accomplish most of these tasks:

❑ by manipulating the rows of the data table and producing scatterplots of variables involved in the regression. For example, you may delete observations and add or delete variables from the model (as described in "Further Examination of Model Parameters" on page 50). The use of such methods is presented in "Changing the Model" on page 53.

❑ by augmenting the data table to contain variables such as the predicted and residual values, which can be used in other JMP procedures.

## 2.6.1 Interactive Methods

While executing either Fit Y by X or Fit Model, you can obtain a scatterplot of residuals. Fit Model contains the added ability to plot residuals against rows or against predicted values. Both commands are illustrated here.

In Fit Y by X,

- Click on the drop-down menu next to the name of the model below the plot (for example, "Linear Fit").

- Select **Plot Residuals** from the menu that appears.

In Fit Model,

- Click on the platform pop-up menu in the top-left corner of the report.

- Select **Row Diagnostics → Plot Residual by Row** or **Row Diagnostics → Plot Residual by Predicted**.

Both plots from Fit Model are shown in Figure 2.21.

It is also usually useful to examine a plot of actual values of the dependent variable against the predicted values from the model. To produce the plot,

- Select **Row Diagnostics → Plot Actual by Predicted**.

This plot, shown in Figure 2.22, is discussed in detail in the section "Leverage Plots" on page 110.

The default plotting symbol is a small dot. It is possible to change the type of marker based on the type of airline.

- Select **Rows → Color or Mark by Column**.

In the window that opens,

- Select the Type variable in the variable list.

**Figure 2.21**
*Interactive Residual Plots*

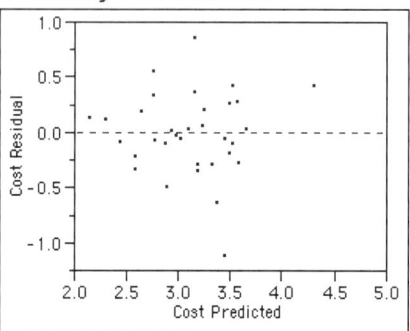

**Residual by Predicted Plot**

**Residual by Row Plot**

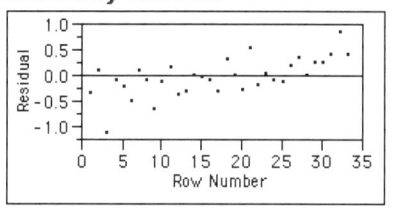

**Figure 2.22**
*Actual by Predicted Plot*

**Actual by Predicted Plot**

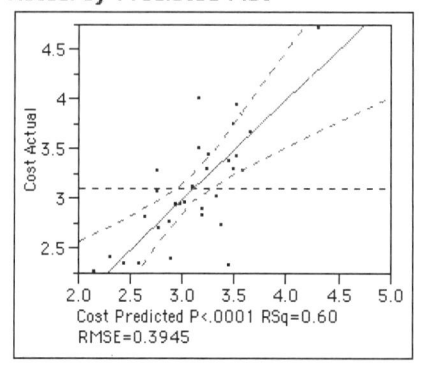

- Check the boxes for both **Set Color by Value** and **Set Marker by Value**.
- Click **OK**.

Newly colored and marked reports are shown in Figure 2.23.

It is questionable whether these residuals are sufficiently random. Using Type to determine the plotting symbol shows further interesting patterns—for example,

*Figure 2.23
Residuals
after Marking
and Coloring*

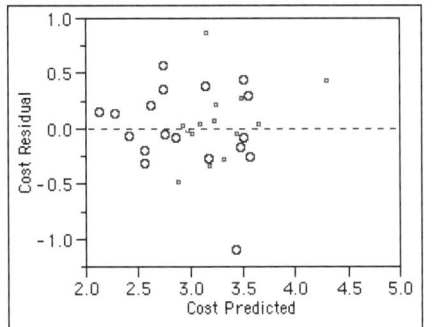

**Residual by Predicted Plot**

**Residual by Row Plot**

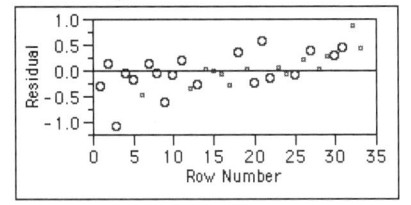

that both types of flights have increasing residuals when plotted by row number, or that the large residuals are not confined to a single flight type.

Why would such a trend exist? To investigate this, request an overlay plot of all the variables as follows.

- Select **Graph → Overlay Plot**.
- Add all the variables in the **Y** role.

Since nothing is given in the **X** role, the values are plotted by row number.

- Click **OK**.

When the overlay plot appears,

- Select **Overlay** from the platform menu to uncheck the option. This produces separate overlay plots for each variable.
- Also, select **Separate Axes** to give each plot its own set of axes.

Notice the plot for Cost, as shown in Figure 2.24.

In this case, the data set is sorted by increasing values of Cost. Our model obviously has higher residuals for higher values of Cost, a fact that should be considered when judging the effectiveness of the model and its use in prediction.

**Figure 2.24**
Plot of Cost by Row Number

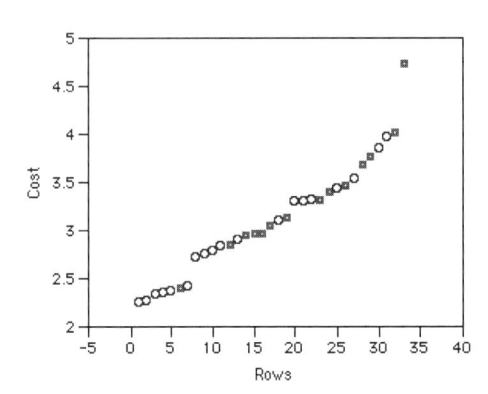

The data have two airlines with Cost values exceeding 4.0. You can change the above plots with a highlighting of the residuals for these two airlines with the following statements.

- In the **Rows** menu, select **Row Selection** → **Select Where**.
- In the dialog that appears, select the variable Cost.
- In the drop-down list below the variables list, select **is greater than**.
- Type 4 in the box next to this condition.
- Select **OK**.

These two points highlight in the plots. They can be marked with a special marker as well.

- Select **Rows** → **Markers**.
- Select the **X** marker from the palette that appears.

The results are shown in Figure 2.25.

### 2.6.2 Regression with Deleted Observations

Sometimes it is useful to see what happens to an estimated regression if some observations are deleted. You can estimate the regression model without using the data from airlines with Cost > 4.0 as follows:

- Use **Rows** → **Row Selection** → **Select Where** to select all rows where Cost is greater than 4. Make sure **Clear Current Selection** is checked in the

**Figure 2.25**
*Specially Marked Residual Plots*

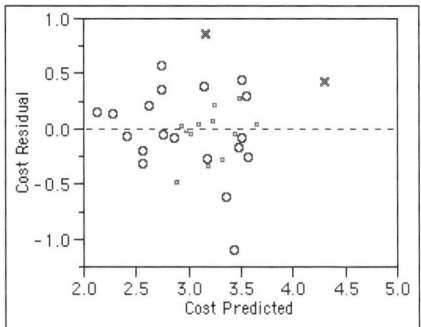

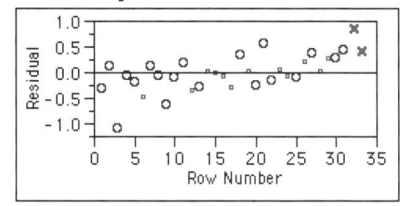

Select Where dialog, in case there were points still selected from the previous steps.

- Select **Rows → Exclude**.

The Exclude command removes points from future analyses.

The regression with the excluded rows can be run using the same Fit Model dialog as the original regression.

- Click **Run Model** to run the model with the excluded points removed from the calculations.

If you have deleted some of the original variables from the Fit Model dialog, they can be re-added at this point. Figure 2.26 shows the results.

You can see that the regression estimates are not changed much by the deletion of these observations (as compared to Figure 2.6 on page 35). Residual plots for this regression, using the same procedures as above, can be produced, but are not shown here.

**Figure 2.26**
*Deleting Observations with the Exclude Command*

**Response Cost**

**Summary of Fit**

| | |
|---|---|
| RSquare | 0.574281 |
| RSquare Adj | 0.508786 |
| Root Mean Square Error | 0.3437 |
| Mean of Response | 3.023452 |
| Observations (or Sum Wgts) | 31 |

**Analysis of Variance**

| Source | DF | Sum of Squares | Mean Square | F Ratio |
|---|---|---|---|---|
| Model | 4 | 4.1431785 | 1.03579 | 8.7683 |
| Error | 26 | 3.0713712 | 0.11813 | Prob > F |
| C. Total | 30 | 7.2145497 | | 0.0001 |

**Parameter Estimates**

| Term | Estimate | Std Error | t Ratio | Prob>|t| |
|---|---|---|---|---|
| Intercept | 7.6526035 | 0.922781 | 8.29 | <.0001 |
| Load | -6.908211 | 1.257658 | -5.49 | <.0001 |
| Use | -0.12506 | 0.065477 | -1.91 | 0.0672 |
| Length | 0.2576629 | 0.163441 | 1.58 | 0.1270 |
| Seats | -4.423997 | 1.10141 | -4.02 | 0.0004 |

**Effect Tests**

| Source | Nparm | DF | Sum of Squares | F Ratio | Prob > F |
|---|---|---|---|---|---|
| Load | 1 | 1 | 3.5642249 | 30.1721 | <.0001 |
| Use | 1 | 1 | 0.4309442 | 3.6481 | 0.0672 |
| Length | 1 | 1 | 0.2935896 | 2.4853 | 0.1270 |
| Seats | 1 | 1 | 1.9058566 | 16.1336 | 0.0004 |

## 2.6.3 Deleting Effects

You can overlay plots from different regressions with the **Overlay Plot** command. For example, you can examine the effect of deleting the **Seats** variable on the residual plots given in Figure 2.21. First, you must return to the original full model. If it is not available, use the Fit Model dialog.

- Select **Analyze → Fit Model**.

- Add Cost as the Y variable.

- Add Load, Use, Length, and Seats as the model effects.

- Click **Run Model**.

Now, save the residuals from this model in the data table.

- Select **Save Columns → Residuals** from the platform pop-up menu.

This creates a column called Residuals Cost. Since there will be more residuals from other models, it may be smart to rename this column to reflect its contents.

- In the data table, click once on the column header of Residuals Cost.

When a column header is highlighted like this, simply begin typing to change its name.

- Change the name of the column to Full Model Residuals.
- Click **OK**.

You may want to plot these residuals against their predicted values, so save the predicted values to the data table as well.

- Select **Save Columns** → **Predicted Values** from the platform pop-up menu.

Next, remove the variable Seats from the model.

- In the Fit Model dialog, remove the variable Seats.
- Click **Run Model**.

Now, save these residuals to the data table.

- Select **Save Columns** → **Residuals** from the platform pop-up menu.
- Once the name of the column is saved, change it to Reduced Model Residuals.

Now, produce a plot of residuals by row number.

- Select **Graph** → **Overlay Plot**.
- Select both columns of residuals and click the **Y** button.
- Click **OK**.

Since there was no *X* variable selected, the Overlay Plot platform plots by row number.

To add a reference line at *y*=0,

- Double-click the *y*-axis.
- In the Axis Specification dialog that appears, click the **Add Ref Line** button to add a line at 0 (the default).

In addition, the plot in Figure 2.27 has the Separate Axes option in effect.

Another way to look at these differences emphasizes the effect that each row has on the regression.

- Select the **Range Plot** option from the platform drop-down menu.

This produces the plot shown in Figure 2.28. Note that some rows have vastly different residuals for the two models.

**62** *Regressions in JMP*

***Figure 2.27***
*Residuals by Row Number*

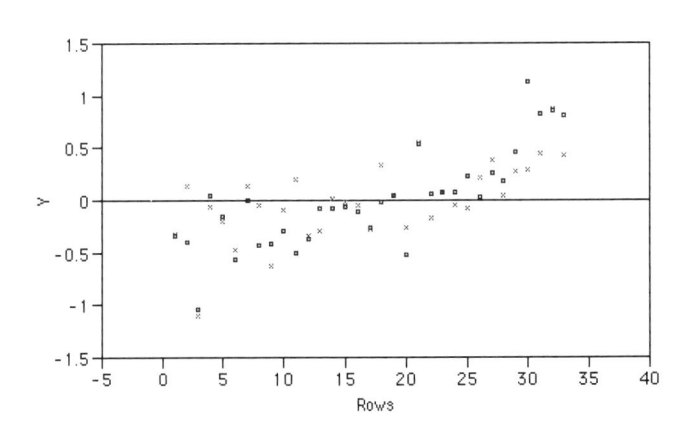

***Figure 2.28***
*Residuals by Row Number Range Plot*

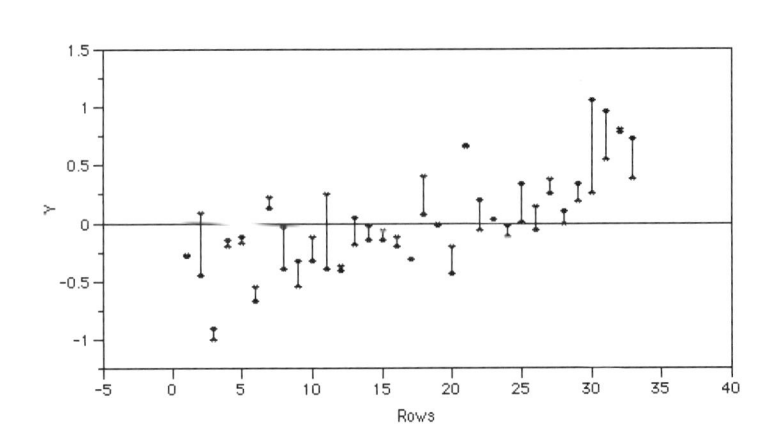

Similar techniques produce an overlay plot of residuals by (full model) predicted values.

- Select **Graph → Overlay Plot**.
- Select both columns of residuals and click the **Y** button.

- Select the column of predicted values and click the **X** button.
- Click **OK**.
- Add a horizontal line at Y = 0.

See Figure 2.29 for the results of these changes.

*Figure 2.29*
*Residuals by Predicted Values*

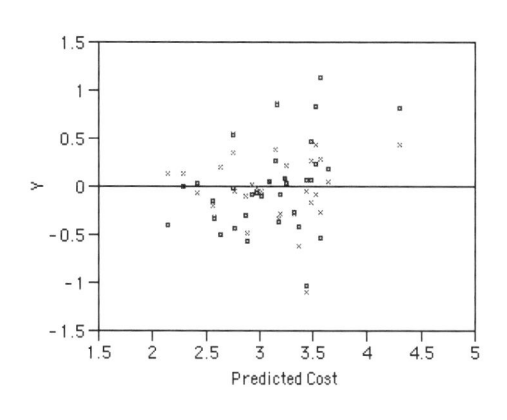

You may quickly produce two separate plots of the full model and reduced model residuals by deselecting Overlay Plot from the platform pop-up menu (Figure 2.30).

## 2.7 Predicting to a Different Set of Data

A regression equation estimated from one set of data can be used to predict values of the dependent variable using the same model for another set of similar data. This type of prediction has been used, for example, to settle charges of pay discrimination against minorities. An equation relating pay to factors such as education, performance, and tenure is estimated using data for nonminority employees, usually white males. This equation predicts what the pay rate should be for all employees in the absence of discrimination or other factors. If this equation predicts substantially higher salaries for minority employees than they are actually being paid, there is cause to suspect pay discrimination.

***Figure 2.30***
*Separated
Residual Plots*

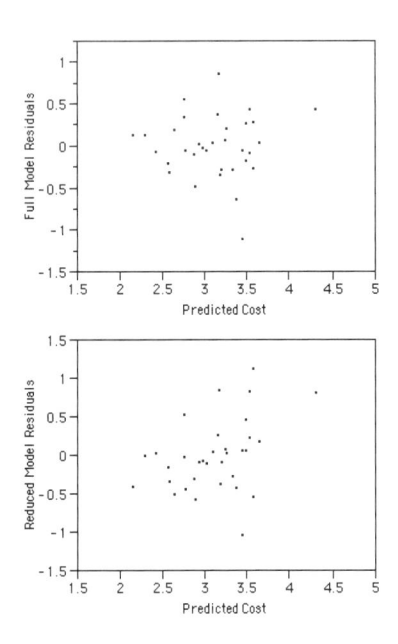

This feature may also be used for cross-validation, where a data set is split randomly into two parts and the effectiveness of a statistical procedure used on one of the data sets is determined by finding how well it works on the other.

This type of analysis is illustrated with the airline cost data. The variable Type was created to divide the airlines into two groups: the short-haul lines with Length<1200 miles and the long-haul lines with Length≥1200 miles. This assumes that we have some knowledge about airline flights that tells us that 1200 is a worthwhile place to divide the data. In this case, however, the choice of 1200 is arbitrary and for illustration only. Use prior knowledge of your own data when you divide them like this. Your mileage may vary.

One way to ascertain if there are differences in the cost structures between these two types is to see how well the cost equation for short-haul lines estimates costs for the long-haul lines.

First, clear the row states from the previous work.

- Select **Rows → Clear Row States**.

Then, exclude the data for long-haul lines.

- Select **Rows → Row Selection → Select Where**.

- Select **Type** in the variable list.
- Make sure the condition below the variable list is set to **equals**. Type a 1 into the box next to the condition.
- Click **OK**.
- Select **Rows** → **Exclude/Unexclude**.

Next,

- Use **Analyze** → **Fit Model** to fit a model of Cost with the effects Load, Use, Length, and Seats.

Fit model results are shown in Figure 2.31.

*Figure 2.31 Regression for Short-Haul Airlines*

**Response Cost**

**Summary of Fit**

| | |
|---|---|
| RSquare | 0.885997 |
| RSquare Adj | 0.83533 |
| Root Mean Square Error | 0.23639 |
| Mean of Response | 3.335571 |
| Observations (or Sum Wgts) | 14 |

**Analysis of Variance**

| Source | DF | Sum of Squares | Mean Square | F Ratio |
|---|---|---|---|---|
| Model | 4 | 3.9085755 | 0.977144 | 17.4864 |
| Error | 9 | 0.5029220 | 0.055880 | Prob > F |
| C. Total | 13 | 4.4114974 | | 0.0003 |

**Parameter Estimates**

| Term | Estimate | Std Error | t Ratio | Prob>|t| |
|---|---|---|---|---|
| Intercept | 10.700037 | 1.116851 | 9.58 | <.0001 |
| Load | -6.7204 | 1.652185 | -4.07 | 0.0028 |
| Use | -0.413886 | 0.055847 | -7.41 | <.0001 |
| Length | -0.273706 | 0.652351 | -0.42 | 0.6846 |
| Seats | -5.49132 | 3.459248 | -1.59 | 0.1469 |

**Effect Tests**

| Source | Nparm | DF | Sum of Squares | F Ratio | Prob > F |
|---|---|---|---|---|---|
| Load | 1 | 1 | 0.9245510 | 16.5452 | 0.0028 |
| Use | 1 | 1 | 3.0692070 | 54.9248 | <.0001 |
| Length | 1 | 1 | 0.0098370 | 0.1760 | 0.6846 |
| Seats | 1 | 1 | 0.1408148 | 2.5199 | 0.1469 |

- Verify that there are only 14 observations in the model (listed under Summary of Fit).

Note that the coefficients are somewhat different from those estimated from the entire data set (Figure 2.6). The most striking difference is that the effect of the number of seats per plane (Seats) is not statistically significant ($p = 0.1469$).

This is probably because short-haul lines do not have a wide assortment of airplane sizes.

Save the prediction formula for this model back to the data set.

- Select **Save Columns → Prediction Formula** from the platform pop-up menu.

Note in the data table that the prediction formula computes predicted values for excluded values as well as the variables used in the regression. We now need to compute the value of the residual for each row.

- Double-click to the right of the last column in the data table to create a new column.
- Name the column Residuals and press Enter.
- Right-click (control-click on the Macintosh) on the new column header and select Formula from the menu that appears.

This brings up the Formula Editor for the column.

- Click on the Cost column in the variables list.
- Click on the – (subtraction) key in the formula keypad.
- Click on the Pred Formula Cost column in the variables list.

The formula should appear as in Figure 2.32.

- Click **OK**.

So that you can see a difference between the residuals for the two levels of Type, color and mark the columns based on their Type value.

- Select **Rows → Clear Row States** so that all the rows will show on the upcoming plot.
- Select **Rows → Color or Mark by Column**.

In the dialog that appears,

- Select Type from the variables list.
- Make sure **Set Color by Value** and **Set Marker by Value** are both checked.
- Click **OK**.

Now, produce plots to see the residuals.

- Select **Graph → Overlay Plot**.

**Figure 2.32**
*Formula Editor Window*

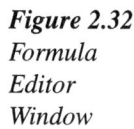

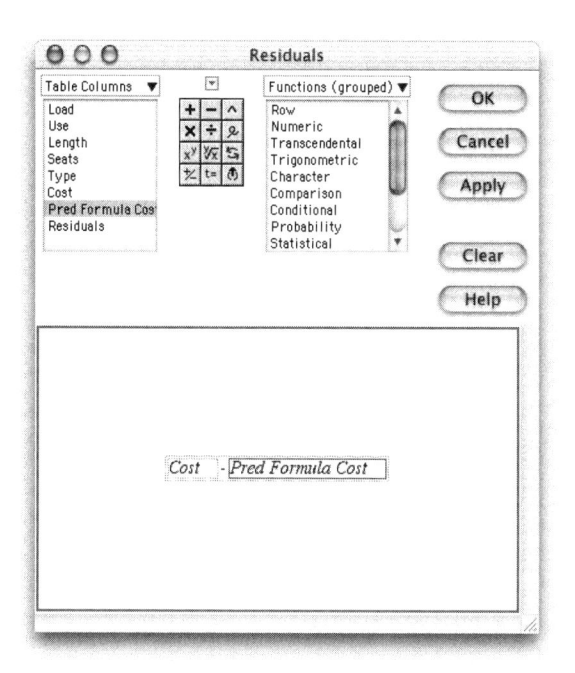

⟵ Assign the predicted values to **X** and the residuals to **Y**.

⟵ Click **OK**.

This produces the plot shown in Figure 2.33.

You can see that the cost equation of the short-haul lines does not accurately predict costs of the long-haul lines. In fact, it appears that this equation underpredicts the costs for the long-haul lines.

## 2.8 Exact Collinearity: Linear Dependency

Linear dependency occurs when exact linear relationships exist among the independent variables. More precisely, a linear dependency exists when one or more columns of the **X** matrix can be expressed as a linear combination of other columns. This means that the **X'X** matrix is singular and cannot be inverted in the usual sense to obtain parameter estimates. JMP is programmed to detect the existence of exact collinearity and, if it exists, uses a generalized inverse (see "Using the Generalized Inverse" on page 21) to compute *parameter estimates*.

*Figure 2.33*
*Residuals Plot*

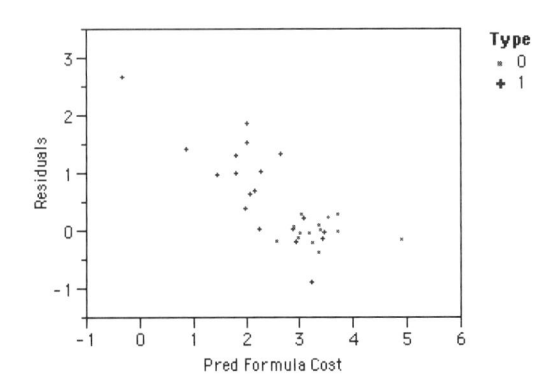

The words *parameter estimates* are stressed to emphasize that care must be exercised to determine exactly what parameters are being estimated. More technically, the generalized inverse approach yields only one of many possible solutions to the normal equations.

JMP computations with an exact linear dependency are illustrated with an alternate model of the airline cost data.

First, open Log Air.JMP, a JMP data set with additional variables, which were created as follows:

Pass represents the average number of passengers per flight, and is defined as

Pass = Load*Seats

The addition of this variable does not create a linear dependency, since Pass is defined with a multiplicative relationship. To convert this multiplicative relationship to a linear one, all variables have been converted to logarithms. (The logarithmic model is discussed in some detail in "Multiplicative Models" on page 181.) The conversion was completed in each case by the use of a formula in the additional JMP columns. The resulting columns are named Log Load, Log Use, and so on.

Because Pass = Load*Seats, then log(Pass) = log(Load) + log(Seats), which constitutes an exact collinearity. In this model, then,

Log Pass = Log Load + Log Seats

## Exact Collinearity: Linear Dependency

Now run a model using all five variables:

- Select **Analyze → Fit Model**.
- Designate Log Cost as **Y**.
- Designate Log Load, Log Use, Log Length, Log Seats, and Log Pass as effects in the model.
- Select **Minimal Report** from the **Emphasis** drop-down list.
- Click **Run Model**.

The results appear in Figure 2.34.

*Figure 2.34*
*Exact Collinearity*

```
Response log Cost
  Singularity Details
    log Load = - log Seats + log Pass
  Summary of Fit
    RSquare                         0.638501
    RSquare Adj                     0.586859
    Root Mean Square Error          0.11917
    Mean of Response                1.116472
    Observations (or Sum Wgts)           33
  Analysis of Variance
    Source     DF   Sum of Squares   Mean Square   F Ratio
    Model       4        0.7023352      0.175584   12.3638
    Error      28        0.3976392      0.014201   Prob > F
    C. Total   32        1.0999744                  <.0001
  Parameter Estimates
    Term              Estimate   Std Error   t Ratio   Prob>|t|
    Intercept         0.638787    0.390103      1.64     0.1127
    log Load  Biased -1.033775    0.180116     -5.74    <.0001
    log Use          -0.467788    0.158401     -2.95     0.0063
    log Length        0.1108091   0.08473       1.31     0.2016
    log Seats Biased -0.337168    0.080831     -4.17     0.0003
    log Pass  Zeroed  0           0              .         .
  Effect Tests
    Source      Nparm   DF   Sum of Squares    F Ratio   Prob > F
    log Load      1      0       0.00000000        .         .     LostDFs
    log Use       1      1       0.12385432     8.7213    0.0063
    log Length    1      1       0.02428908     1.7103    0.2016
    log Seats     1      0       0.00000000        .         .     LostDFs
    log Pass      1      0       0.00000000        .         .     LostDFs
```

The existence of collinearity is indicated by the Biased and Zeroed parameter estimates and the LostDFs in the Effect Tests section. The exact nature of the collinearity is given at the top of the report in the Singularity Details, which show

Log Load = –Log Seats + Log Pass

The parameter estimates that are printed are equivalent to those that are obtained if Log Pass were not included in the model. In general, the parameter estimates are those that would be obtained if any variable that is a linear function of variables that precede it in the Fit Model effects list were deleted. These deleted variables are indicated with **Zeroed** under the DF heading and 0 under the Parameter Estimate heading. Other variables involved in the linear dependencies are indicated with **Biased** under the DF heading. These estimates are in fact unbiased estimates of the parameters of the model that does not include the zeroed variable(s), but they are biased estimates for other models.

The bias can readily be seen by using a model with the independent variables listed in a different order. For example,

- In the Fit Model dialog, remove all the effects and enter them in the order

    Log Pass
    Log Load
    Log Use
    Log Length
    Log Seats

- Click **Run Model**.

As shown in Figure 2.35, Log Seats is designated with **Zeroed** and Log Pass and Log Load with **Biased** under the DF heading. We are therefore fairly certain that all the variables are not needed in the analysis. A reasonable solution would be to delete one of the variables involved in the collinearity and reanalyze the data.

Due to roundoff error, determining when exact linear dependency occurs is somewhat arbitrary. In JMP the matrix inversion procedure computes successive tolerance values. A tolerance of zero signifies an exact collinearity, but since roundoff errors essentially preclude the computing of exact zero values, a tolerance of $10^{-7}$ is used to indicate exact collinearity.

## 2.9 Summary

The purpose of this chapter has been to provide instruction on how to use JMP to perform a regression analysis. This included

❑ estimating the model equation and error variance

❑ providing predicted values and their standard errors

*Figure 2.35
Rearranged
Model Output*

**Response log Cost**
**Singularity Details**
log Pass = log Load + log Seats
**Summary of Fit**

| | |
|---|---|
| RSquare | 0.638501 |
| RSquare Adj | 0.586859 |
| Root Mean Square Error | 0.11917 |
| Mean of Response | 1.116472 |
| Observations (or Sum Wgts) | 33 |

**Analysis of Variance**

| Source | DF | Sum of Squares | Mean Square | F Ratio |
|---|---|---|---|---|
| Model | 4 | 0.7023352 | 0.175584 | 12.3638 |
| Error | 28 | 0.3976392 | 0.014201 | Prob > F |
| C. Total | 32 | 1.0999744 | | <.0001 |

**Parameter Estimates**

| Term | | Estimate | Std Error | t Ratio | Prob>|t| |
|---|---|---|---|---|---|
| Intercept | | 0.638787 | 0.390103 | 1.64 | 0.1127 |
| log Pass | Biased | -0.337168 | 0.080831 | -4.17 | 0.0003 |
| log Load | Biased | -0.696607 | 0.144145 | -4.83 | <.0001 |
| log Use | | -0.467788 | 0.158401 | -2.95 | 0.0063 |
| log Length | | 0.1108091 | 0.08473 | 1.31 | 0.2016 |
| log Seats | Zeroed | 0 | 0 | | |

**Effect Tests**

| Source | Nparm | DF | Sum of Squares | F Ratio | Prob > F | |
|---|---|---|---|---|---|---|
| log Pass | 1 | 0 | 0.00000000 | . | . | LostDFs |
| log Load | 1 | 0 | 0.00000000 | . | . | LostDFs |
| log Use | 1 | 1 | 0.12385432 | 8.7213 | 0.0063 | |
| log Length | 1 | 1 | 0.02428908 | 1.7103 | 0.2016 | |
| log Seats | 1 | 0 | 0.00000000 | . | . | LostDFs |

❏ making inferences on the regression parameters

❏ checking the residuals and providing plots to check the fit of the model

❏ making modifications of the model

❏ checking results when some observations have been deleted

❏ finding how well the model may fit an equivalent data set

Some of the analyses outlined above can be performed in different ways. They also do not exhaust all of the possible analyses that can be performed with JMP.

You are now ready to further investigate how well the data fit the model (see Chapter 3, "Observations") and the suitability of the variables you have chosen for your model (see Chapter 4, "Collinearity: Detection and Remedial Measures"). Later chapters expand the variety of regression models you can analyze with JMP.

# Chapter 3  Observations

3.1  *Introduction*  73

3.2  *Outlier Detection*  74

    3.2.1  *Univariate and Bivariate Investigations*  76

    3.2.2  *Residuals and Studentized Residuals*  80

    3.2.3  *Influence Statistics*  85

3.3  *Specification Errors*  91

3.4  *Heterogeneous Variances*  96

    3.4.1  *Weighted Least Squares*  100

3.5  *Summary*  104

## 3.1  Introduction

In the linear model

$$Y = X\beta + \varepsilon$$

the elements of the vector $\varepsilon$ are the differences between the observed values of the $y$'s and those expected from the model. These elements comprise the *error term* of the model and are specified to be a set of independently and normally distributed random variables with mean zero and variance $\sigma^2$. This error term represents natural variation in the data, but it can also be interpreted as the cumulative effect of factors not specified in the model. Often this variation results in errors that, for practical purposes, behave as specified in which case the use of linear model methodology may be appropriate. However, this is not always the case and, if the assumptions are violated, the resulting analysis may provide results of questionable validity.

Violations of this assumption can occur in many ways. The most frequent occurrences may be categorized as follows:

❑   The data may contain *outliers*, or unusual observations that do not reasonably fit the model.

- A *specification error* occurs when the specified model does not contain all of the necessary parameters. This includes the situations where only linear terms have been specified and the true relationships are curvilinear.

- The *distribution* of the errors may be distinctly nonnormal; it may be severely skewed or heavy-tailed.

- The errors may exhibit *heteroscedasticity*—that is, the variances are not the same for all observations.

- The errors may be *correlated*, a phenomenon usually found in time series data, but is not restricted to such situations.

Violations of the assumptions underlying the random errors are often not so severe as to invalidate the analysis, but this condition is not guaranteed. Therefore, it is useful to examine the data for possible violations and, if violations are found, to employ remedial measures.

Most methods of detecting violations of assumptions are based on the analysis of the estimated errors, which are the *residuals*:

$$\varepsilon = y - X\beta$$

However, other statistics may be used. This chapter presents some tools available in JMP to detect such violations. Some of these tools involve the estimated residuals, while others are concerned with the behavior of the independent variables. Alternative analysis methodologies that may be employed if assumptions fail are also presented. It must, however, be emphasized that the coverage is not exhaustive, especially with respect to alternative methodologies (Belsley et al. 1980).

## 3.2 Outlier Detection

Observations that do not appear to fit the model, often called *outliers*, can be quite troublesome since they can bias parameter estimates and make the resulting analysis less useful. For this reason it is important to examine the results of a statistical analysis to ascertain if there are observations that have the potential of causing the analysis to provide misleading results. *This is especially important in regression analyses where the lack of structure of the independent variables makes detection and identification of outliers more difficult.*

It is important to note that observations that may cause misleading results may be unusual with respect to the independent variables, the dependent variable, or both, and that each of these conditions may create different types of results. Furthermore, the identification of unusual observations alone does not provide directions as to what to do with such observations. Any action must be consistent with the purpose of the analysis and conform to good statistical practice.

The following example comes from a study of manpower needs for operating a U.S. Navy Bachelor Officers Quarters (BOQ.jmp) (Myers 1990). The observations are records from 25 establishments. The response variable represents the monthly man hours (MANH) required to operate each establishment. The independent variables are

| OCCUP | average daily occupancy |
| CHECKIN | monthly average number of check-ins |
| HOURS | weekly hours of service desk operation |
| COMMON | square feet of common use area |
| WINGS | number of building wings |
| CAP | operational berthing capacity |
| ROOMS | number of rooms. |

The data appear in Figure 3.1.

*Figure 3.1*
*BOQ Data*

| OCCUP | CHECKIN | HOURS | COMMON | WINGS | CAP | ROOMS | MANH |
|---|---|---|---|---|---|---|---|
| 2 | 4 | 4 | 1.26 | 1 | 6 | 6 | 180.23 |
| 3 | 1.58 | 40 | 1.25 | 1 | 5 | 5 | 182.61 |
| 5.3 | 1.67 | 42.5 | 7.79 | 3 | 25 | 25 | 199.92 |
| 7 | 2.37 | 168 | 1 | 1 | 7 | 8 | 284.55 |
| 16.5 | 8.25 | 168 | 1.12 | 2 | 19 | 19 | 267.38 |
| 16.6 | 23.78 | 40 | 1 | 1 | 13 | 13 | 164.38 |
| 25.89 | 3 | 40 | 0 | 3 | 36 | 36 | 999.09 |
| 31.92 | 40.08 | 168 | 5.52 | 6 | 47 | 47 | 931.84 |
| 39.63 | 50.86 | 40 | 27.37 | 10 | 77 | 77 | 944.21 |
| 44.42 | 159.75 | 168 | 0.6 | 18 | 48 | 48 | 1103.24 |
| 54.58 | 207.08 | 168 | 7.77 | 6 | 66 | 66 | 1387.82 |
| 56.63 | 373.42 | 168 | 6.03 | 4 | 36 | 37 | 1489.5 |
| 95 | 368 | 168 | 30.26 | 9 | 292 | 196 | 1845.89 |
| 96.67 | 206.67 | 168 | 17.86 | 14 | 120 | 120 | 1891.7 |
| 96.83 | 677.33 | 168 | 20.31 | 10 | 302 | 210 | 1880.84 |
| 97.33 | 255.08 | 168 | 19 | 6 | 165 | 130 | 2268.06 |
| 102.33 | 288.83 | 168 | 21.01 | 14 | 131 | 131 | 3036.63 |
| 110.24 | 410 | 168 | 20.05 | 12 | 115 | 115 | 2628.32 |
| 113.88 | 981 | 168 | 24.48 | 6 | 166 | 179 | 3559.92 |
| 134.32 | 145.82 | 168 | 25.99 | 12 | 192 | 192 | 2227.76 |
| 149.58 | 233.83 | 168 | 31.07 | 14 | 185 | 202 | 3115.29 |
| 188.74 | 937 | 168 | 45.44 | 26 | 237 | 237 | 4804.24 |
| 274.92 | 695.25 | 168 | 46.63 | 58 | 363 | 363 | 5539.98 |
| 384.5 | 1473.66 | 168 | 7.36 | 24 | 540 | 453 | 8266.77 |
| 811.08 | 714.33 | 168 | 22.76 | 17 | 242 | 242 | 3534.49 |

### 3.2.1 Univariate and Bivariate Investigations

It is always reasonable to examine graphical displays of these data to look for patterns and to check for clerical errors. JMP is an ideal tool for these initial investigations.

- Select **Analyze → Distribution**.
- Add all the variables as **Y, Columns**.
- Click **OK**.

*Figure 3.2 Histograms of BOQ Variables with Mouse Pointer Showing One of the Outliers*

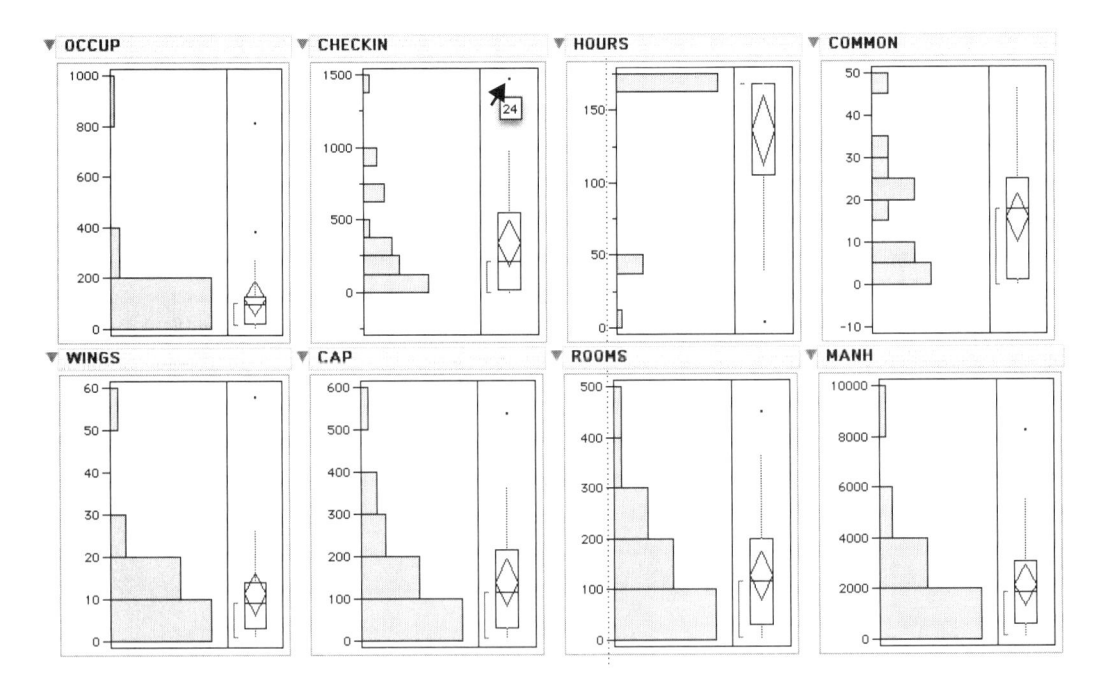

Note that the outlier box plots (Figure 3.2) reveal a few univariate outliers. This is not necessarily a bad thing, nor is it an indication that information was miskeyed into the data table. However, it may be useful to identify these rows and keep them in mind in the analyses to come.

- Move the mouse pointer over each of the outliers in the box plots and let the pointer hover over them for a moment.

JMP shows a tool tip that labels the row as in the data table. In this case, there is no special label column identified, so the row number of the data point is presented as the label. For these data, the univariate outliers are rows 1, 23, 24, and 25.

Now, investigate the data in pairs.

- Select **Analyze → Multivariate Methods → Multivariate**.
- Enter all the variables as **Y, Columns**.
- Click **OK**.

*Figure 3.3*
*Scatterplot Matrix for BOQ Data with Mouse Pointer Showing One of the Outliers*

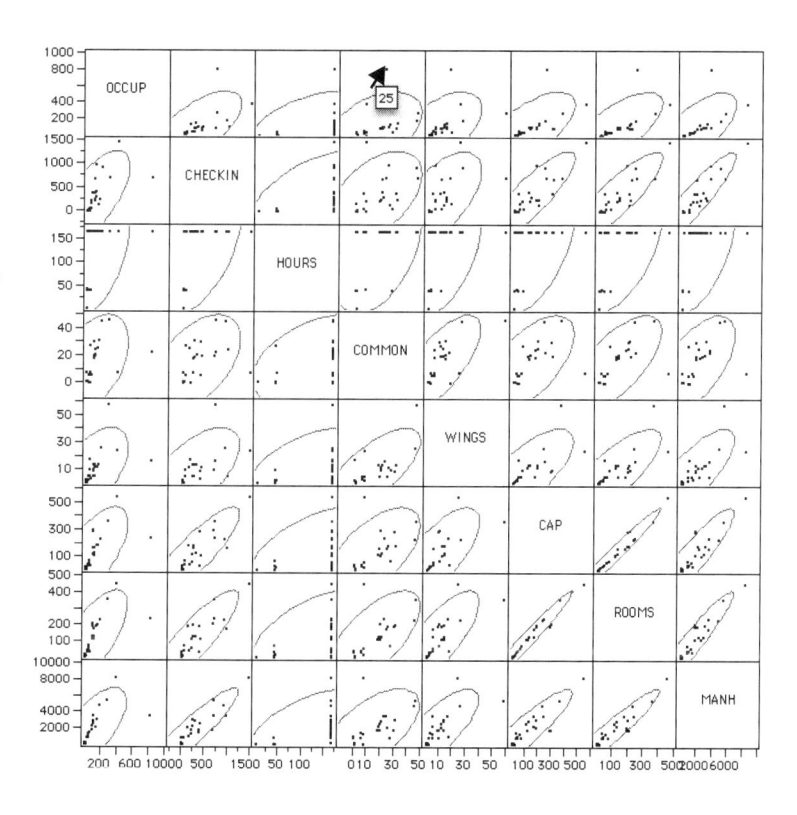

There are a few bivariate outliers as well, as seen in Figure 3.3.

- Again, move the mouse pointer over the outliers to reveal their identities.

Rows 23, 24, and 25 again appear to be the culprits.

It is also possible to search for outliers in higher dimensions. In this case, we are looking at eight variables, so the Multivariate platform can report on eight-dimensional outliers.

- From the platform pop-up menu, select **Outlier Analysis**.

This returns an analysis showing the Mahalanobis distance (a sort of covariance-adjusted distance) of each point from the centroid of the distribution. When computing the Mahalanobis distance for each point, the point itself is included in the computation. For strong outliers, this can affect the outlier computation itself, so some analysts prefer to exclude each point from its own outlier computation. To exclude the point from the distance computation,

- Select **Jackknife Distances** from the platform pop-up menu.

The output for the standard and jackknife distances are shown in Figure 3.4.

*Figure 3.4*
*Outlier Analysis Plot*

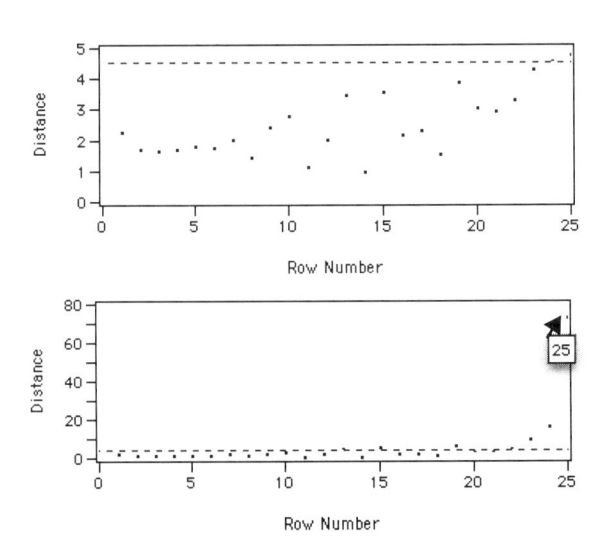

These reports show row 25 as a moderate outlier in the standard distance calculation, and rows 23, 24, and (especially) 25 in the jackknife calculations.

Again, these plots do not necessarily show evidence of mistakes in the design or input of the data. They only provide information that certain points are in some sense extreme.

Now, we are ready to perform the regression. Use the following steps:

- Select **Analyze → Fit Model**.
- Select MANH in the variables list and click the **Y** button.
- Select the rest of the variables and click the **Add** button.

Note that Shift-clicking allows selection of many variables at once.

- Click on the first variable in a list, hold down the Shift key, and click on the last variable in the list.
- Select **Minimal Report** from the **Emphasis** drop-down list.
- Click **Run Model**.

The results appear in Figure 3.5.

*Figure 3.5 Regression for BOQ Data*

**Response MANH**

**Summary of Fit**

| | |
|---|---|
| RSquare | 0.961258 |
| RSquare Adj | 0.945305 |
| Root Mean Square Error | 455.1673 |
| Mean of Response | 2109.386 |
| Observations (or Sum Wgts) | 25 |

**Analysis of Variance**

| Source | DF | Sum of Squares | Mean Square | F Ratio |
|---|---|---|---|---|
| Model | 7 | 87387188 | 12483884 | 60.2570 |
| Error | 17 | 3522013 | 207177.24 | Prob > F |
| C. Total | 24 | 90909201 | | <.0001 |

**Parameter Estimates**

| Term | Estimate | Std Error | t Ratio | Prob>\|t\| |
|---|---|---|---|---|
| Intercept | 134.9679 | 237.8143 | 0.57 | 0.5778 |
| OCCUP | -1.283767 | 0.804691 | -1.60 | 0.1291 |
| CHECKIN | 1.8035097 | 0.516236 | 3.49 | 0.0028 |
| HOURS | 0.6691502 | 1.846399 | 0.36 | 0.7215 |
| COMMON | -21.42263 | 10.1716 | -2.11 | 0.0504 |
| WINGS | 5.6192263 | 14.74609 | 0.38 | 0.7079 |
| CAP | -14.48025 | 4.220177 | -3.43 | 0.0032 |
| ROOMS | 29.324751 | 6.365904 | 4.61 | 0.0003 |

**Effect Tests**

| Source | Nparm | DF | Sum of Squares | F Ratio | Prob > F |
|---|---|---|---|---|---|
| OCCUP | 1 | 1 | 527297.9 | 2.5452 | 0.1291 |
| CHECKIN | 1 | 1 | 2528612.7 | 12.2051 | 0.0028 |
| HOURS | 1 | 1 | 27210.6 | 0.1313 | 0.7215 |
| COMMON | 1 | 1 | 918986.5 | 4.4358 | 0.0504 |
| WINGS | 1 | 1 | 30084.4 | 0.1452 | 0.7079 |
| CAP | 1 | 1 | 2439117.8 | 11.7731 | 0.0032 |
| ROOMS | 1 | 1 | 4396333.1 | 21.2202 | 0.0003 |

The test for the model is certainly significant. However, only three of the coefficients appear to be important, and among these, the effect of **CAP** has an illogical sign. Such results are typical when collinearity exists, which is the topic of Chapter 4, "Collinearity: Detection and Remedial Measures." For now, the focus is on finding unusual observations.

### 3.2.2 Residuals and Studentized Residuals

The traditional tool for detecting outliers (as well as specification error; see "Specification Errors" on page 91) consists of examining the residuals.

JMP provides a quick way to see plots of the residuals.

- From the platform pop-up menu, select **Row Diagnostics → Plot Residual by Predicted**.

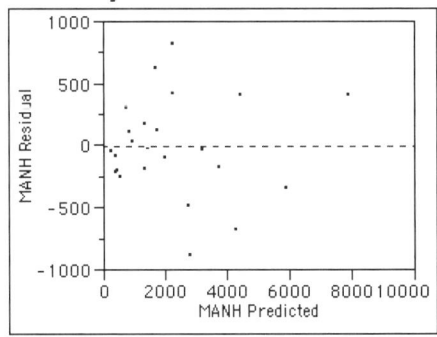

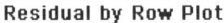

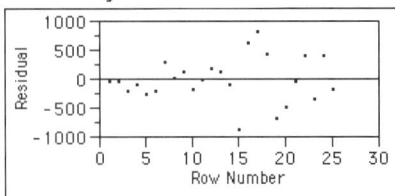

- Also select **Row Diagnostics → Plot Residual by Row**.

These plots appear in Figure 3.6.

*Figure 3.6*
*Residual Plots*

A difficulty with residuals is that they are not all estimated with the same precision. However, you can compute standard errors of residuals, and when the residuals are divided by these standard errors, you will obtain standardized or *studentized* residuals. These studentized residuals follow Student's *t* distribution. For error degrees of freedom exceeding 10, in this case 17, values from the *t* distribution greater than 2.5 are relatively rare. Thus, studentized residuals exceeding this value provide a convenient vehicle for identifying unusually large residuals.

These residuals, as well as other statistics used for detecting violations of assumptions, are provided by JMP in the **Save Columns** section of the platform pop-up menu. There are also some useful commands in the **Row Diagnostics** section. Once obtained, they can be analyzed further with JMP's exploratory tools.

For this example,

- From the platform pop-up menu, select **Save Columns → Studentized Residuals**.

This adds a column to the data table, as shown in Figure 3.7.

*Figure 3.7*
*Studentized Residuals*

| MANH | Studentized Resid MANH |
|---|---|
| 180.23 | -0.0759 |
| 182.61 | -0.0748 |
| 199.92 | -0.4302 |
| 284.55 | -0.1815 |
| 267.38 | -0.5821 |
| 164.38 | -0.4705 |
| 999.09 | 0.7630 |
| 931.84 | 0.0942 |
| 944.21 | 0.3335 |
| 1103.24 | -0.4832 |
| 1387.82 | -0.0230 |
| 1489.5 | 0.4534 |
| 1845.89 | 0.4406 |
| 1891.7 | -0.1872 |
| 1880.84 | -2.4013 |
| 2268.06 | 1.4929 |
| 3036.63 | 1.8833 |
| 2628.32 | 1.0070 |
| 3559.92 | -2.1973 |
| 2227.76 | -1.3018 |
| 3115.29 | -0.0557 |
| 4804.24 | 1.2357 |
| 5539.98 | -1.5360 |
| 8266.77 | 2.5803 |
| 3534.49 | -3.2779 |

Other useful outlier statistics are the predicted values, the residuals plotted in Figure 3.6, the standard error of the residuals, and Cook's $D$ statistic.

- From the platform pop-up menu, select **Save Columns → Prediction Formula**.
- From the platform pop-up menu, select **Save Columns → Residuals**.
- From the platform pop-up menu, select **Save Columns → Std Error of Residual**.
- From the platform pop-up menu, select **Save Columns → Cook's D Influence**.

These statistics are identified by column headings that reflect the statistic and the variable being predicted. Looking at these columns, you can verify that the studentized residuals are the residuals divided by their standard errors.

It is useful to have a plot of the studentized residuals by row number. The Overlay Plot command is ideal for this task.

- Select **Graph → Overlay Plot**.
- Select Studentized Resid MANH from the variables list and click the **Y** button.
- Click **OK**.

Since no $X$ variable was specified, the Overlay Plot command uses the row number on the horizontal axis. This series of commands can be repeated to get plots of StdErr Resid MANH, Residual MANH, and Cook's D Influence MANH. All four plots appear in Figure 3.8.

The reference lines at $Y = 0$ and the dotted lines at $Y = 2.5$ (in the studentized residual plot) were added by double-clicking on the plot's $Y$-axis and adding the lines in the dialog that appears.

Observation 25, also noticed in our initial exploration, is of particular interest. Note that the residual of −160.3 is not excessively large compared with the other residuals or the residual standard deviation (root mean square error in Figure 3.5) of 455. But the standard error of the residual, 48.896, is by far the smallest, thus producing the largest studentized residual among all observations. Its Cook's $D$ clearly shows this as an influential point. You can also see that observations 15 and 17 have the largest residuals, while observations 24 and 25 have the largest studentized residuals, both of which exceed 2.5 in magnitude.

It may be instructive to see both residuals and studentized residuals plotted against the predicted values. As shown above, JMP provides residual by predicted plots as part of the regression report, but they can also be plotted using the JMP Overlay Plot platform.

*Figure 3.8* Studentized Residual Plot

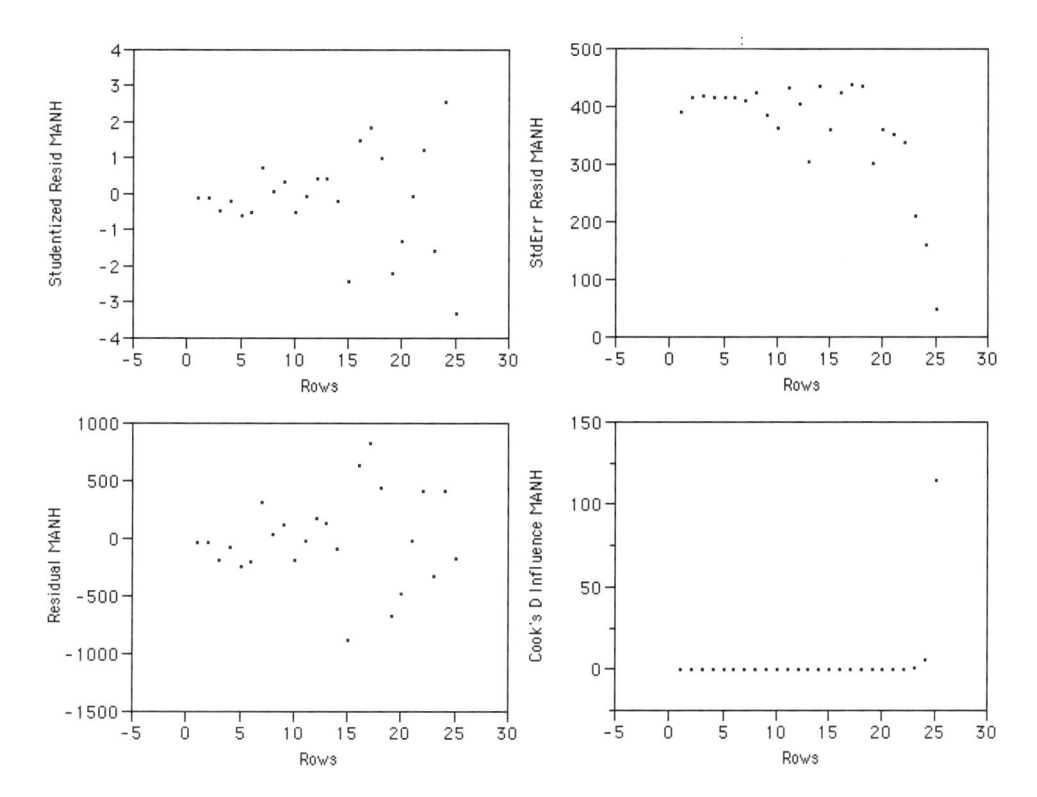

- Select **Graph → Overlay Plot**.
- Assign Residual MANH and Studentized Resid MANH to the **Y** role.
- Assign Pred Formula MANH to the **X** role.
- Click **OK**.

The plots appear with both sets of residuals on the same graph. To separate them,

- Select **Overlay** from the platform pop-up menu to deselect it.

It also might be helpful to place a reference line at $Y = 0$.

- Double-click on the *Y*-axis of the top plot.
- In the Axis Specification dialog that appears, click the **Add Ref Line** button to add a reference line at the default value of 0.

**84** *Observations*

- Repeat for the *Y*-axis of the lower graph.
- Select **Separate Axes** from the platform pop-up menu to add a separate *X*-axis to each plot.

This results in the two plots shown in Figure 3.9.

*Figure 3.9*
*Residual Plots*

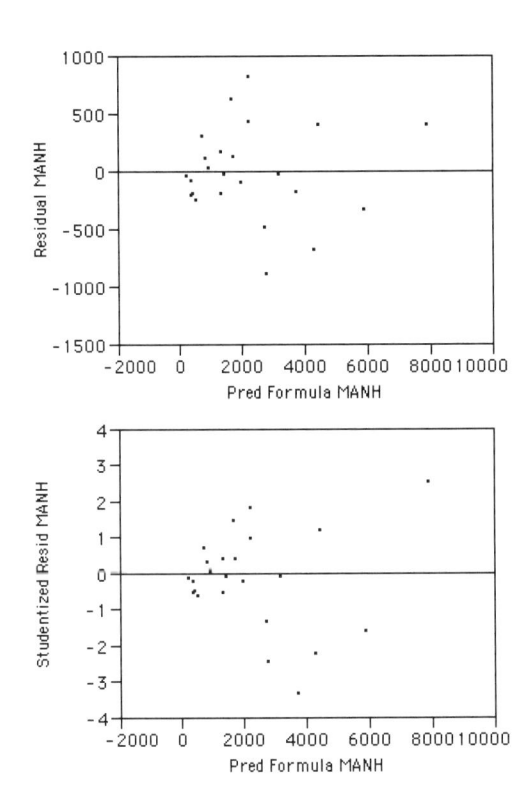

You can see that the pattern of the studentized residuals differs somewhat from that of the actual residuals (look, for example, at predicted values around 4000), and although a number of studentized residuals exceed 2.5 in magnitude, none clearly stands out. The studentized residuals do, however, emphasize that the magnitudes of residuals increase with larger predicted values. This may be an indicator of heterogeneous variances, which are discussed in "Heterogeneous Variances" on page 96.

### 3.2.3 Influence Statistics

Outliers are sometimes not readily detected by an examination of residuals because the least-squares estimation procedure tends to pull the estimated regression response towards observations that have extreme values in either *x* or *y* dimensions. The estimated residuals for such observations may therefore not be especially large, thus hindering the search for outliers. You may be able to overcome this difficulty by asking what would happen to various estimates and statistics if the observation in question were not used in the estimation of the regression equation used to calculate the statistics. This is similar to the jackknife distances computer earlier.

Such statistics are annotated by the subscript (*i*) to indicate that they are computed by omitting (subtracting) the *i*th observation. For example, $s_{(i)}^2$ is the residual mean square obtained when all but the *i*th observation are used to estimate the regression. Statistics of this type are said to determine the potential *influence* of a particular observation; hence they are called *influence statistics*.

The basic influence statistic is the *hat diagonal*. The hat diagonal, abbreviated *h* in JMP tables, represents the diagonal elements of the hat matrix

$$\mathbf{h} = \mathbf{X}(\mathbf{X}'\mathbf{X})^{-1}\mathbf{X}$$

The form of this matrix comes directly from the formula for predicting *Y*. Recall that

$$\hat{\mathbf{Y}} = \mathbf{X}\hat{\beta}$$

where $\hat{\beta}$ is the vector of least-squares estimates. These estimates were computed with the formula

$$\hat{\beta} = [(\mathbf{X}'\mathbf{X})^{-1}\mathbf{X}'\mathbf{Y}]$$

So, by substituting this into the equation for $\hat{\mathbf{Y}}$, we can state

$$\hat{\mathbf{Y}} = \mathbf{X}(\mathbf{X}'\mathbf{X})^{-1}\mathbf{X}'\mathbf{Y}$$

$$\hat{\mathbf{Y}} = \mathbf{h}\mathbf{Y}$$

where *h* is the hat matrix shown above.

The individual values, often denoted $h_i$, indicate the *leverage* of each observation, which is a standardized measure of how far an observation is from the center of the space of *x*-values. Observations with high leverages, which are indicated by large $h_i$, have the potential of being influential, especially if they are also outliers in *y*. The sum of $h_i$ is $(p + 1)$, where *p* is the number of independent variables;

hence the mean value of $h_i$ is approximately $(p + 1)/n$, where $n$ is the number of observations in the data set. Therefore, observations with values of $h_i$ exceeding twice this value may be considered as having high leverage.

The hat diagonal values can be saved to the data table.

- From the pop-up menu at the top of the regression report, select **Save Columns → Hats**.

This produces a column h MANH in the data table.

As shown earlier, JMP also generates the Cook's $D$ statistic when requested. Cook's $D$ measures the shift in the vector of regression coefficients when a particular object is omitted. It is computed as

$$D_i = \frac{(\hat{\beta}_{(i)} - \hat{\beta})'(\mathbf{X'X})(\hat{\beta}_{(i)} - \hat{\beta})}{p's^2}$$

where $\beta_{(i)}$ represents the matrix of regression coefficients with the point dropped from the model, $\beta$ is the matrix of regression coefficients from the full data set, $p'$ is the number of parameters in the model, and $s^2$ is the estimated variance of the regression. To obtain the Cook's $D$ statistic,

- From the pop-up menu at the top of the regression report, select **Save Columns → Cook's D Influence**.

Other regression diagnostics not built in can be computed from the quantities that JMP computes. Several of these have been computed for this regression and are stored in the data table BOQ Regression Diagnostics.jmp (Figure 3.10).

The formulas for these statistics take some time and care to key in manually. However, it is important to remember that you can drag and drop formulas (or pieces of formulas) from one Formula Editor window to another. You are encouraged to copy and modify these formulas in your own data tables.

The first computation necessary for these diagnostics is an estimate of the regression standard deviation for each point dropped from the model, named s(i) in the BOQ Regression Diagnostics table. According to Belsley, Kuh, and Welsch (1980),

$$s^2_{(i)} = \frac{(n-p)}{n-p-1}s^2 - \frac{e_i^2}{(n-p-1)(1-h_i)}$$

where $n$ is the number of observations in the data set, $p$ is the number of estimated parameters, $e$ is the vector of residuals, and $h$ is the hat matrix. For this data table, assuming the residuals from the model are stored in a column Residual

*Figure 3.10 Regression Diagnostics Data*

| MANH | Predicted MANH | s(i) | Residual MANH | RSTUDENT | h MANH | COVRATIO | DFFITS | Studentized Resid MANH |
|---|---|---|---|---|---|---|---|---|
| 180.230 | 209.985 | 469.096 | -29.755 | -0.074 | 0.257 | 2.181 | -0.043 | -0.076 |
| 182.610 | 213.796 | 469.098 | -31.186 | -0.073 | 0.161 | 1.930 | -0.032 | -0.075 |
| 199.920 | 380.703 | 466.615 | -180.783 | -0.420 | 0.147 | 1.745 | -0.175 | -0.430 |
| 284.550 | 360.106 | 468.721 | -75.556 | -0.176 | 0.163 | 1.911 | -0.078 | -0.181 |
| 267.380 | 510.373 | 464.476 | -242.993 | -0.570 | 0.159 | 1.644 | -0.248 | -0.582 |
| 164.380 | 360.486 | 466.111 | -196.106 | -0.459 | 0.161 | 1.744 | -0.202 | -0.470 |
| 999.090 | 685.167 | 461.073 | 313.923 | 0.753 | 0.183 | 1.504 | 0.356 | 0.763 |
| 931.840 | 891.846 | 469.053 | 39.994 | 0.091 | 0.130 | 1.858 | 0.035 | 0.094 |
| 944.210 | 815.466 | 467.638 | 128.744 | 0.325 | 0.281 | 2.143 | 0.203 | 0.334 |
| 1103.240 | 1279.299 | 465.943 | -176.059 | -0.472 | 0.359 | 2.269 | -0.353 | -0.483 |
| 1387.820 | 1397.786 | 469.168 | -9.966 | -0.022 | 0.097 | 1.798 | -0.007 | -0.023 |
| 1489.500 | 1305.177 | 466.330 | 184.323 | 0.443 | 0.202 | 1.847 | 0.223 | 0.453 |
| 1845.890 | 1710.861 | 466.489 | 135.029 | 0.430 | 0.547 | 3.269 | 0.472 | 0.441 |
| 1891.700 | 1973.416 | 468.692 | -81.716 | -0.182 | 0.080 | 1.737 | -0.054 | -0.187 |
| 1880.840 | 2750.910 | 381.397 | -870.070 | -2.866 | 0.366 | 0.093 | -2.179 | -2.401 |
| 2268.060 | 1632.137 | 437.343 | 635.923 | 1.554 | 0.124 | 0.603 | 0.585 | 1.493 |
| 3036.630 | 2210.134 | 417.372 | 826.496 | 2.054 | 0.070 | 0.269 | 0.565 | 1.883 |
| 2628.320 | 2190.326 | 454.968 | 437.994 | 1.007 | 0.087 | 1.087 | 0.311 | 1.007 |
| 3559.920 | 4225.131 | 397.002 | -665.211 | -2.519 | 0.558 | 0.254 | -2.828 | -2.197 |
| 2227.760 | 2698.738 | 445.175 | -470.978 | -1.331 | 0.368 | 1.110 | -1.016 | -1.302 |
| 3115.290 | 3134.895 | 469.133 | -19.605 | -0.054 | 0.402 | 2.714 | -0.044 | -0.056 |
| 4804.240 | 4385.778 | 447.608 | 418.462 | 1.257 | 0.446 | 1.382 | 1.129 | 1.236 |
| 5539.980 | 5863.874 | 435.405 | -323.894 | -1.606 | 0.785 | 2.290 | -3.071 | -1.536 |
| 8266.770 | 7853.505 | 365.947 | 413.265 | 3.209 | 0.876 | 0.246 | 8.537 | 2.580 |
| 3534.490 | 3694.766 | 284.604 | -160.276 | -5.242 | 0.988 | 0.047 | -48.518 | -3.278 |

MANH and the corresponding hat matrix values in h MANH, the dropped-point standard deviation can be computed using the formula

$$\sqrt{\frac{(NRow()-7)*\frac{Col\ Sum\left(Residual\ MANH^2\right)}{17} - \left(\frac{Residual\ MANH^2}{(1-h\ MANH)}\right)}{(NRow()-7-1)}}$$

Given this value, several other diagnostic measures are easily computed.

RSTUDENT is another version of studentized residuals, where the residuals are divided by a standard error that uses $s_{(i)}^2$ rather than $s^2$ as the estimate of $\sigma^2$. It is thus a more sensitive studentized residual than the studentized residual statistic. If there are no outliers, these statistics should obey a $t$ distribution with $(n - m - 2)$ degrees of freedom, and therefore the criterion for large is the same as for the studentized residual. Belsley, Kuh, and Welch give the following formula for RSTUDENT.

$$e_i^* = \frac{e_i}{s_{(i)}\sqrt{1-h_i}}$$

This is implemented in JMP for this example with the formula

$$\frac{\text{Residual MANH}}{s(i)*\sqrt{1 - h\ \text{MANH}}}$$

COVRATIO indicates the change in the precision of the estimates of the set of partial regression coefficients resulting from the deletion of an observation. This precision is measured by the *generalized variance*, which is computed $(s^2)|(\mathbf{X'X})^{-1}|$. The COVRATIO statistic is the ratio of the generalized variance without the *i*th observation and the generalized variance using all observations; that is,

$$\text{COVRATIO} = \frac{s_{(i)}^2 |(\mathbf{X'X})_{(i)}^{-1}|}{s^2 |(\mathbf{X'X})^{-1}|}$$

In other words, COVRATIO values exceeding unity indicate that the inclusion of the observation results in increased precision, while values less than unity indicate decreased precision. Belsley, Kuh, and Welsch suggest that deviations from unity may be considered large if they exceed $3(m + 1)/n$. They also give an equivalent formula for COVRATIO as

$$\text{COVRATIO} = \frac{1}{\left[\dfrac{n-p-1}{n-p} + \dfrac{e_i}{n-p}\right]^2 (1 - h_i)}$$

which is the formulation used in the **BOQ Diagnostics** table.

$$\frac{1}{\left[\dfrac{(\text{NRow}()-8-1)}{(\text{NRow}()-8)} + \dfrac{\text{RSTUDENT}^2}{(\text{NRow}()-8)}\right]^8 * (1 - h\ \text{MANH})}$$

DFFITS measures the difference between predicted value for the *i*th observation obtained by the equation estimated by all observations and the equation estimated from all observations except the *i*th. The difference is standardized, using the residual variance estimate from all *other* observations, $s_i^2$. This statistic is a prime indicator of influence. Belsley, Kuh, and Welsch (1980, p. 28) suggest that DFFITS values exceeding $2[(m + 1)/n]^{1/2}$ in absolute value provide a convenient criterion for identifying influential observations. The formula for computing DFFITS is

$$\text{DFFITS}_i = \left[\frac{h_i}{1 - h_i}\right]^{\frac{1}{2}} \frac{e_i}{s_i \sqrt{1 - h_i}}$$

Cook's *D* is the DFFITS statistic, scaled and squared to make extreme values stand out more clearly. However, the estimated error variance obtained by using all observations is used for standardization.

Another useful statistic is the PRESS. It can be added to the regression report.

- Select **Row Diagnostics** → **Press**.

The PRESS sum of squares is the difference between the sum of squares of residuals obtained by estimating the equation normally and the sum of squares excluding an observation. The sum of residuals should be zero and the sum of squares should be the same as the error SS in the regression output; if they are not, severe roundoff has occurred. The sum of squares of the PRESS statistic should be compared to the error SS. When it is appreciably larger than the error SS, as it is here, there is reason to suspect that some influential observations or outliers exist.

The influence statistics now appear to focus more on observations 24 and 25, with 25 being very pronounced in its DFFITS statistic.

A clearer picture is provided by interactive plots.

- Select **Graph** → **Overlay Plot**.
- Assign Studentized Residuals MANH, h MANH, COVRATIO, Studentized Residuals, Residuals, and DFFITS as Y variables.
- Assign Pred Formula MANH as the X value.
- Click **OK**.
- When the overlay plot appears, select **Overlay** from the platform drop-down menu.

This produces six plots instead of one.

- Add a reference line at $Y = 0$ on plots by double-clicking the $Y$-axis and clicking the **Add Ref Line** button from the dialog that appears.

This produces the plots shown in Figure 3.11.

You can see that the statistics for row 25 are all large according to the guidelines outlined above, although none is appreciably larger than the next largest. However, the DFFITS statistic certainly appears to indicate a problem with that observation. The DFFITS statistic is also quite large for observation 24, and in this case the cause appears to be in the COMMON variable, although the evidence is not very clear-cut.

What to do now is not strictly a statistical problem. Discarding observations simply because they do not fit is bad statistical practice. You should first examine the data for obvious discrepancies by various other interactive plots. In addition, you

*Figure 3.11* Interactive Plots for Influence Statistics

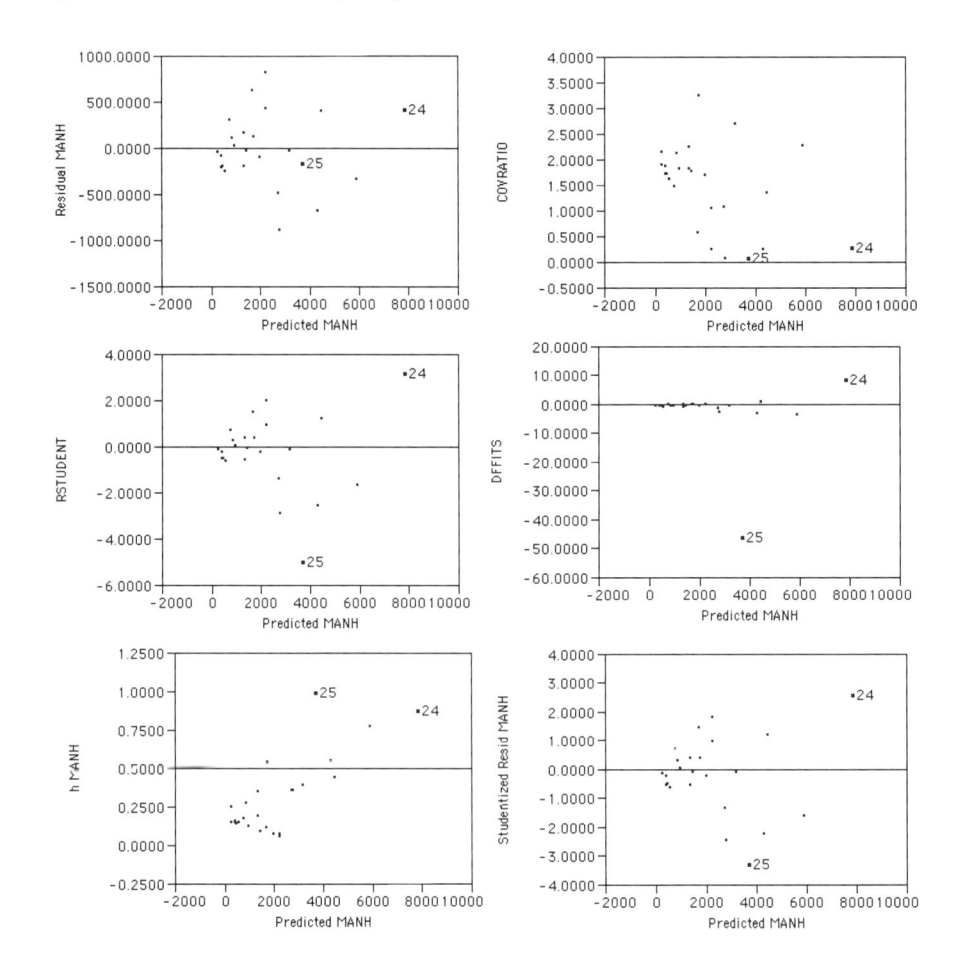

can further examine the various statistics with the Distribution platform or other descriptive procedures. In this example, looking at observation 25, and focusing on the OCCUP variable, it becomes obvious that this value is impossible: how can average occupancy be 811 with a capacity of only 242? Observation 24 has a very high CHECKIN rate along with a very small COMMON area and high MANH requirements.

Normally, an obvious error such as that in observation 25 would be investigated and probably corrected. Observation 24 is, however, probably correct and should be left alone.

Although it is not necessarily the correct procedure, you can eliminate observation 25 from the data set and redo the regression. This can be done in three ways:

- by physically eliminating observation 25 from the data table and running the model again
- by assigning the dependent variable (MANH) a missing value in observation 25, which you can do in the data table, and then running the model again
- by excluding the point in the data table.

This final option is employed here.

- Click on observation 25 in the data table.
- Select **Rows → Exclude/Unexclude**.
- Select the Fit Model window from the previous model.
- Click **Run Model**.

The changes in the estimated regression relationship are quite marked (see Figure 3.12). The residual mean square has decreased considerably, and the coefficient for OCCUP has become highly significant, while those for CAP and ROOMS are not. Therefore, as indicated by the influence statistics, observation 25 did indeed influence the estimated regression.

Before continuing, it is important to point out that these statistics often do not provide clear evidence of outliers or influential observations. The different statistics are not all designed to detect the same type of data anomalies; hence, they may provide apparently contradictory results. Furthermore, they may fail entirely, especially if there are several outliers. In other words, these statistics are only tools to aid in outlier detection; they do not replace careful data monitoring.

## 3.3 Specification Errors

Specification error is defined as the result of an incorrectly specified model, and it often results in biased estimates of parameters. Specification errors may be detected by examining the residuals from a fitted equation. However, it is not normally useful to use statistics designed to identify single outliers to detect specification errors, because specification errors are usually evidenced by patterns involving groups of residuals. A common pattern is for the residuals to suggest a curvilinear relationship, although other patterns such as bunching or cycling are possible.

**Figure 3.12**
*Excluding Observation 25*

```
Response MANH
   Summary of Fit
   RSquare                         0.985405
   RSquare Adj                     0.979019
   Root Mean Square Error          284.6035
   Mean of Response                2050.007
   Observations (or Sum Wgts)            24
   Analysis of Variance
   Source    DF   Sum of Squares   Mean Square    F Ratio
   Model      7         87497673      12499668   154.3185
   Error     16          1295987      80999.171  Prob > F
   C. Total  23         88793659                   <.0001
   Parameter Estimates
   Term        Estimate    Std Error   t Ratio   Prob>|t|
   Intercept  171.47336    148.8617      1.15     0.2663
   OCCUP       21.045622     4.289049    4.91     0.0002
   CHECKIN      1.4263228    0.33071     4.31     0.0005
   HOURS       -0.089268     1.163532   -0.08     0.9398
   COMMON       7.6503311    8.438352    0.91     0.3781
   WINGS       -5.30231      9.452761   -0.56     0.5826
   CAP         -4.074748     3.30195    -1.23     0.2350
   ROOMS        0.3319106    6.813987    0.05     0.9618
   Effect Tests
   Source   Nparm   DF   Sum of Squares   F Ratio   Prob > F
   OCCUP       1     1        1950212.8   24.0769    0.0002
   CHECKIN     1     1        1506682.9   18.6012    0.0005
   HOURS       1     1             476.8   0.0059    0.9398
   COMMON      1     1           66577.2   0.8219    0.3781
   WINGS       1     1           25485.5   0.3146    0.5826
   CAP         1     1          123350.5   1.5229    0.2350
   ROOMS       1     1             192.2   0.0024    0.9618
```

The following example (Irrigation.jmp) consists of data collected to determine the effect of certain variables on the efficiency of irrigation. The dependent variable is the percent of water percolation (Percolation), and the independent variables are

| | |
|---|---|
| Ratio | the ratio between irrigation time and advance time |
| Infiltration | the exponent of time in the infiltration equation, a calculated value |
| Lost | the percentage of water lost to deep percolation |
| Advance | the exponent of time in the water advance equation, a calculated value. |

The data appear in Figure 3.13.

Perform the regression analysis as follows:

🖱 Select **Analyze → Fit Model**.

## Figure 3.13
*Irrigation Data*

| Percolation | Ratio | Infiltration | Lost | Advance |
|---|---|---|---|---|
| 37.75 | 0.77 | 0.427 | 29.100 | 0.582 |
| 34.83 | 0.97 | 0.427 | 29.100 | 0.698 |
| 33.75 | 1.15 | 0.309 | 20.900 | 0.519 |
| 30.6  | 1.27 | 0.309 | 20.900 | 0.685 |
| 30.26 | 1.27 | 0.427 | 29.100 | 0.880 |
| 29.05 | 1.51 | 0.309 | 20.900 | 0.800 |
| 25.76 | 1.67 | 0.343 | 21.270 | 0.564 |
| 26.26 | 1.87 | 0.309 | 20.900 | 0.836 |
| 25.75 | 2.25 | 0.309 | 20.900 | 0.841 |
| 17.16 | 2.32 | 0.397 | 26.530 | 0.596 |
| 14.73 | 2.34 | 0.343 | 21.270 | 0.750 |
| 19.04 | 2.39 | 0.427 | 29.100 | 0.600 |
| 13.16 | 2.71 | 0.397 | 25.450 | 0.747 |
| 18.03 | 2.82 | 0.427 | 29.100 | 0.730 |
| 14.46 | 3.17 | 0.397 | 26.530 | 0.436 |
| 12.96 | 3.35 | 0.397 | 26.530 | 0.760 |
| 16.8  | 3.64 | 0.343 | 21.270 | 0.699 |
| 13.72 | 3.69 | 0.387 | 26.530 | 0.600 |
| 14.56 | 3.73 | 0.397 | 25.450 | 0.701 |
| 12.71 | 3.78 | 0.387 | 25.450 | 0.680 |
| 9.06  | 4.97 | 0.397 | 26.530 | 0.772 |
| 9.52  | 6.86 | 0.397 | 26.530 | 0.840 |

- Assign Percolation as the Y variable.
- Assign Ratio, Infiltration, Lost, and Advance as the effects in the model.
- Select **Minimal Report** from the **Emphasis** drop-down list.
- Click **Run Model**.

The results appear in Figure 3.14.

The regression is certainly statistically significant. The variable Ratio appears to be very important, and Infiltration and Lost contribute marginally, while Advance appears to have little effect.

The residuals from the regression of the irrigation data are obtained easily.

- Select **Row Diagnostics** → **Plot Residual by Predicted** in the platform pop-up menu.

A curved pattern in the residuals is evident (see Figure 3.15). This suggests that a curvilinear component, probably a quadratic term in one or more variables, should be included in the model. Unless there is some prior knowledge to suggest which variable(s) should have the added quadratic, you can use *partial regression residual plots* for this purpose. JMP refers to these plots as leverage plots, which are fully explained in "Leverage Plots" on page 110.

The estimate of the partial regression coefficient $\beta_i$ can be defined as the coefficient of the simple linear regression of the residuals of $y$ and $x_i$, respectively, from the regressions involving all other independent variables in the model (Ryan

***Figure 3.14***
*Irrigation Data Results*

**Response Percolation**

**Summary of Fit**

| | |
|---|---|
| RSquare | 0.792521 |
| RSquare Adj | 0.743703 |
| Root Mean Square Error | 4.474678 |
| Mean of Response | 20.90545 |
| Observations (or Sum Wgts) | 22 |

**Analysis of Variance**

| Source | DF | Sum of Squares | Mean Square | F Ratio |
|---|---|---|---|---|
| Model | 4 | 1300.1983 | 325.050 | 16.2340 |
| Error | 17 | 340.3867 | 20.023 | Prob > F |
| C. Total | 21 | 1640.5849 | | <.0001 |

**Parameter Estimates**

| Term | Estimate | Std Error | t Ratio | Prob>|t| |
|---|---|---|---|---|
| Intercept | 40.558255 | 11.34545 | 3.57 | 0.0023 |
| Ratio | -4.820525 | 0.742962 | -6.49 | <.0001 |
| Infiltration | -209.311 | 100.9311 | -2.07 | 0.0536 |
| Lost | 2.7548259 | 1.356384 | 2.03 | 0.0582 |
| Advance | 4.285067 | 8.82268 | 0.49 | 0.6334 |

**Effect Tests**

| Source | Nparm | DF | Sum of Squares | F Ratio | Prob > F |
|---|---|---|---|---|---|
| Ratio | 1 | 1 | 842.90502 | 42.0974 | <.0001 |
| Infiltration | 1 | 1 | 86.11088 | 4.3007 | 0.0536 |
| Lost | 1 | 1 | 82.59363 | 4.1250 | 0.0582 |
| Advance | 1 | 1 | 4.72322 | 0.2359 | 0.6334 |

***Figure 3.15***
*Residuals for Irrigation Regression*

**Residual by Predicted Plot**

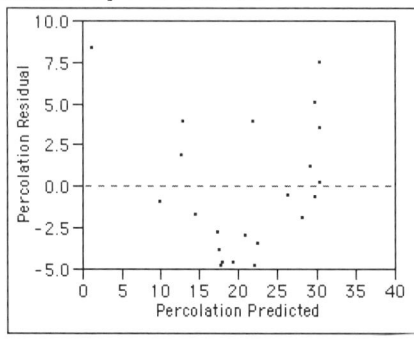

1997, Section 5.5). A plot of these residuals thus shows the data for estimating that coefficient. If, in this example, such a plot shows a curved pattern, there may be a need for curvilinear terms.

These plots are also quite useful for determining influential points. For that reason, JMP refers to them as *leverage plots*. They are so useful, in fact, that they are generally included in standard JMP Fit Model reports, and are often the first plot examined in any analysis. To see the Effect Leverage version of the report for this model,

- Return to the Fit Model dialog that generated the regression report.
- Change the **Emphasis** from **Minimal Report** to **Effect Leverage**.
- Click **Run Model**.

A new model report appears with leverage plots for the whole model and each effect. Note, however, that leverage plots are always available, regardless of the report that you start with, by selecting **Row Diagnostics → Plot Effect Leverage**.

Figure 3.16 shows leverage plots for the variables Ratio and Infiltration. The others are not shown to save space. The plot involving Ratio shows a strong linear trend ($p < 0.0001$) as well as a suggestion of a slight upward curved pattern, suggesting that this variable requires the addition of the quadratic term. The plot involving Infiltration shows the rather weak negative relationship implied by the $p$ value of 0.0536. None of the other leverage plots reveal anything of interest.

*Figure 3.16* *Leverage Plots*

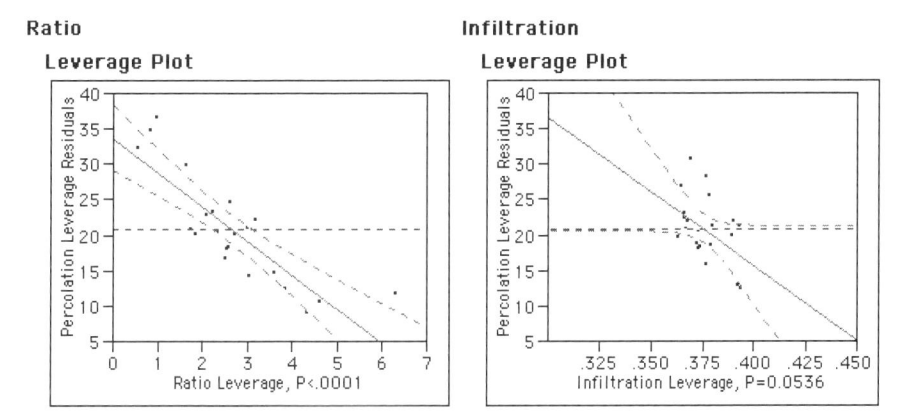

To add a quadratic term to the model,

- Return to the Fit Model dialog that generated the report.
- Select **Ratio** in the variable list.
- Also select **Ratio** in the Effects list.
- Click the **Cross** button.

Ratio*Ratio now appears in the Effects list.

96    Observations

⌐ Click **Run Model**.

The results appear in Figure 3.17.

*Figure 3.17*
*Quadratic*
*Regression for*
*Irrigation*
*Data*

**Response Percolation**
**Summary of Fit**

| | |
|---|---|
| RSquare | 0.933775 |
| RSquare Adj | 0.913079 |
| Root Mean Square Error | 2.605863 |
| Mean of Response | 20.90545 |
| Observations (or Sum Wgts) | 22 |

**Analysis of Variance**

| Source | DF | Sum of Squares | Mean Square | F Ratio |
|---|---|---|---|---|
| Model | 5 | 1531.9366 | 306.387 | 45.1198 |
| Error | 16 | 108.6484 | 6.791 | Prob > F |
| C. Total | 21 | 1640.5849 | | <.0001 |

**Parameter Estimates**

| Term | Estimate | Std Error | t Ratio | Prob>\|t\| |
|---|---|---|---|---|
| Intercept | 44.809701 | 6.64707 | 6.74 | <.0001 |
| Ratio | -6.754958 | 0.544843 | -12.40 | <.0001 |
| Infiltration | -108.203 | 61.27321 | -1.77 | 0.0965 |
| Lost | 1.3086441 | 0.827785 | 1.58 | 0.1335 |
| Advance | -0.517066 | 5.203299 | -0.10 | 0.9221 |
| (Ratio-2.65909)*(Ratio-2.65909) | 1.1848242 | 0.202818 | 5.84 | <.0001 |

**Effect Tests**

| Source | Nparm | DF | Sum of Squares | F Ratio | Prob > F |
|---|---|---|---|---|---|
| Ratio | 1 | 1 | 1043.7710 | 153.7099 | <.0001 |
| Infiltration | 1 | 1 | 21.1758 | 3.1184 | 0.0965 |
| Lost | 1 | 1 | 16.9712 | 2.4992 | 0.1335 |
| Advance | 1 | 1 | 0.0671 | 0.0099 | 0.9221 |
| Ratio*Ratio | 1 | 1 | 231.7383 | 34.1267 | <.0001 |

Comparing these results with those of Figure 3.14, you can see that the residual mean square has been halved. In other words, a better-fitting equation has been developed. The relationship is one where Percolation decreases with Ratio, but the rate of decrease diminishes with increasing values of Ratio. The other variables remain statistically insignificant. Therefore, you may want to consider variable selection (see Chapter 4).

## 3.4 Heterogeneous Variances

A fundamental assumption underlying linear regression analyses is that all random errors (the $e_i$) have the same variance. Outliers may be considered a special case of unequal variances since such observations may be considered to have very large variances.

Violations of the equal variance assumption are usually detected by residual plots that may reveal groupings of observations with large residuals suggesting larger variances. Some of the other outlier detection statistics may also be helpful, especially when the violation occurs in only a small number of observations.

In many applications there is a recognizable pattern for the magnitudes of the variances. The most common of these is an increase in variation for larger values of the response variable. For such cases, the use of a transformation of the dependent variable is in order (Steel and Torrie 1980, Section 9.16). The most popular of these, especially in regression, is the logarithmic transformation discussed in Chapter 6, "Special Applications of Linear Models."

If the use of transformations is not appropriate, it is sometimes useful to alter the estimation procedure by either modifying the least-squares method or implementing a different estimation principle. A discussion of some alternatives, including additional references, is given in Myers (1990, Section 7.7). An illustration of one of these special methods, using iteratively reweighted least squares, is shown in the *JMP Statistics and Graphics Guide*.

Because the effects of heterogeneous variances are subtle, the effects and remedial methods for this condition are illustrated with a very simple and somewhat pathological example. The data consist of records of sales prices of a set of investment-grade diamonds, and are to be used to estimate the relationship of the sales price (Price, in $1000) to the weight (Carats) of the diamonds. The data, stored in Diamonds.jmp, appear in Figure 3.18.

- Select **Analyze → Fit Y by X**.
- Assign Carats to X and Price to Y.
- Click **OK**.

The corresponding plot appears in Figure 3.19.

The plot clearly reveals the large variation of prices for larger diamonds. It is difficult to ascertain if the most expensive diamond is an outlier or if the plot simply reflects the much higher variability of prices for larger stones. The plot also suggests an upward curving response, and hence it is appropriate to specify a quadratic regression.

- Select **Fit Polynomial → 2, quadratic** from the platform menu at the top left of the report.

The results appear in Figure 3.20.

**Figure 3.18**
*Diamonds Data*

| | CARATS | COLOR | CLA |
|---|---|---|---|
| 1 | 1.9 | H | A |
| 2 | 1.35 | F | D |
| 3 | 1.46 | G | C |
| 4 | 1.03 | G | C |
| 5 | 1.66 | E | F |
| 6 | 0.91 | G | F |
| 7 | 0.68 | G | F |
| 8 | 1.92 | D | B |
| 9 | 1.25 | D | F |
| 10 | 1.36 | E | E |
| 11 | 0.73 | G | E |
| 12 | 1.41 | H | A |
| 13 | 1.29 | E | A |
| 14 | 0.5 | H | D |
| 15 | 0.77 | G | E |
| 16 | 0.79 | G | E |
| 17 | 0.6 | G | E |
| 18 | 0.63 | G | F |
| 19 | 0.79 | G | E |
| 20 | 0.53 | I | B |
| 21 | 0.52 | G | E |
| 22 | 0.54 | G | E |
| 23 | 1.02 | D | C |
| 24 | 1.02 | G | C |
| 25 | 1.06 | F | D |

**Figure 3.19**
*Plot of Diamond Prices*

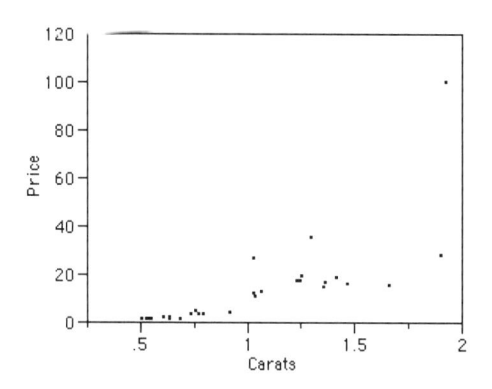

As expected, the regression is certainly significant. The estimated equation is

Price = −17.34068 + 26.435056 Carats + 28.439561 (Carats−1.003)$^2$

The coefficient for (Carats)$^2$ is statistically significant, confirming the upward curve of the relationship of price to carats. The pattern of residuals is informative.

*Figure 3.20*
*Diamond Data, Ordinary Least Squares*

**Bivariate Fit of Price By Carats**

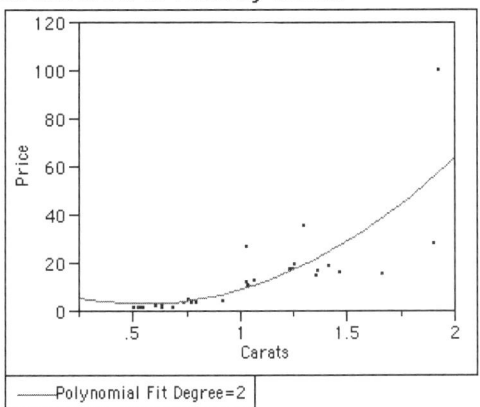

——— Polynomial Fit Degree=2

**Polynomial Fit Degree=2**

Price = -17.34068 + 26.435056 Carats + 28.439561 (Carats-1.003)^2

**Summary of Fit**

| | |
|---|---|
| RSquare | 0.615276 |
| RSquare Adj | 0.586778 |
| Root Mean Square Error | 12.10588 |
| Mean of Response | 13.86623 |
| Observations (or Sum Wgts) | 30 |

**Analysis of Variance**

| Source | DF | Sum of Squares | Mean Square | F Ratio |
|---|---|---|---|---|
| Model | 2 | 6328.150 | 3164.08 | 21.5901 |
| Error | 27 | 3956.915 | 146.55 | Prob > F |
| C. Total | 29 | 10285.065 | | <.0001 |

**Parameter Estimates**

| Term | Estimate | Std Error | t Ratio | Prob>|t| |
|---|---|---|---|---|
| Intercept | -17.34068 | 6.002206 | -2.89 | 0.0075 |
| Carats | 26.435056 | 6.353865 | 4.16 | 0.0003 |
| (Carats-1.003)^2 | 28.439561 | 12.88434 | 2.21 | 0.0360 |

🖱 Click on the pop-up menu beside **Polynomial Fit Degree=2**.

🖱 Select **Plot Residuals**.

These residuals (shown in Figure 3.21) clearly indicate the increasing price variation for the larger diamonds and suggest that these values may be unduly influencing the estimated regression relationship.

Another result of the equal variance assumption can be seen by observing the widths of the prediction intervals.

🖱 From the pop-up menu beside **Polynomial Fit Degree=2**, select **Confid Curves Indiv.**

**Figure 3.21**
*Residuals for Diamonds Regression*

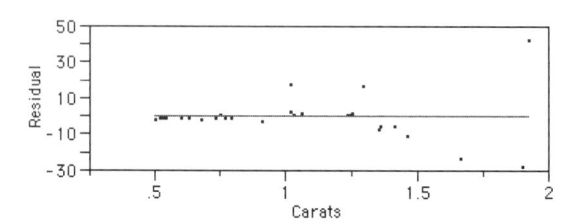

⊕ Click and drag on the axis to adjust it to appear as in Figure 3.22.

**Figure 3.22**
*Confidence Curves*

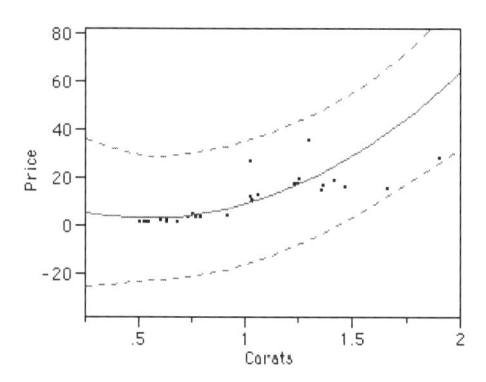

The prediction intervals do not vary much between the small and large diamonds. The assumption of heterogeneous variances is clearly violated, so information from these intervals is not realistic.

### 3.4.1 Weighted Least Squares

One principle that may be used to reduce the influence of highly variable observations is that of weighted least squares, which is a direct application of generalized least squares (Myers 1990, Section 7.1). The estimated parameters obtained by this method are those that minimize the weighted residual sum of squares,

$$\sum w_i(y_1 - \beta_0 - \beta_1 x_1 - \ldots - \beta_m x_m)^2$$

where the $w_i$ are a set of nonnegative weights assigned to the individual observations. Observations with small weights contribute less to the sum of squares and thus provide less influence to the estimation parameters, and vice versa for observations with larger weights. Thus, it is logical to assign small weights to observations whose large variances make them more unreliable, and likewise to assign larger weights to observations with smaller variances. It can, in fact, be shown that best linear unbiased estimates are obtained if the weights are inversely proportional to the variances of the individual errors.

The variances of the residuals, however, are not usually known. Multiple observations, or replicates, may be used to estimate this variance (Myers 1990, Section 7.1), or if true replicates are not available, near replicates (Rawlings 1988, Section 11.5.2) may be used. However, these are all estimated variances, and both of the above references warn that the use of weights based on poor estimates of variances may be counterproductive.

Alternately, knowledge about the distribution of residuals may provide a basis for determining weights. It is well known that prices tend to vary by proportions. This relation implies that standard deviations are proportional to means; hence the variances are proportional to the squares of means. In sample data, the means are not known, but estimated means based on an unweighted regression can be used for this purpose.

- From the pop-up menu beside **Polynomial Fit Degree=2**, select **Save Predicteds**.

This command saves predicted values for the ordinary regression model. These will be used to compute the weights in a weighted regression.

- Add a column to the data table called weight.

- Right-click (Control-click on the Macintosh) and select Formula from the resulting menu.

- Enter the formula

$$\frac{1}{\textit{Predicted Price}^2}$$

- Select **Fit Y by X**.

- Click the **Recall** button to again assign Price as Y and Carats as X.

- Select the new weight column in the variables list and click the **Weight** button.

- Click **OK**.

- When the **Fit Y by X** report appears, select **Fit Polynomial → 2, quadratic** from the platform menu.

The results of the weighted regression appear in Figure 3.23.

*Figure 3.23*
*Weighted*
*Regression*

**Bivariate Fit of Price By Carats**
Weight: weight

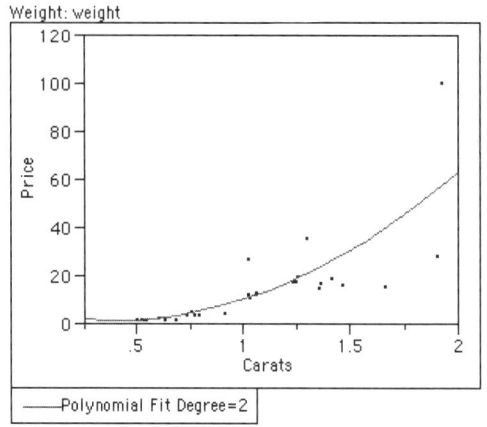

**Polynomial Fit Degree=2**

Price = -4.787584 + 11.952615 Carats + 23.978563 (Carats-0.64008)^2

### Summary of Fit

| | |
|---|---|
| RSquare | 0.712141 |
| RSquare Adj | 0.690818 |
| Root Mean Square Error | 0.461859 |
| Mean of Response | 3.44598 |
| Observations (or Sum Wgts) | 1.235845 |

### Analysis of Variance

| Source | DF | Sum of Squares | Mean Square | F Ratio |
|---|---|---|---|---|
| Model | 2 | 14.248505 | 7.12425 | 33.3979 |
| Error | 27 | 5.759481 | 0.21331 | Prob > F |
| C. Total | 29 | 20.007986 | | <.0001 |

### Parameter Estimates

| Term | Estimate | Std Error | t Ratio | Prob>|t| |
|---|---|---|---|---|
| Intercept | -4.787584 | 2.35544 | -2.03 | 0.0520 |
| Carats | 11.952615 | 3.833676 | 3.12 | 0.0043 |
| (Carats-0.64008)^2 | 23.978563 | 7.967855 | 3.01 | 0.0056 |

A comparison of the results with those of the unweighted least-squares regression (see Figure 3.20) shows the effect of weighting. Since sums of squares reflect the weights, they (and the statistics based on them) cannot be compared with results of the unweighted analysis. However, the $R^2$ statistics are comparable since they are ratios (the effects of the weights cancel) and the model terms are unchanged. You can see that the $R^2$ values are somewhat larger for the weighted analysis, which occurs because the effect of the largest residuals has been reduced. Also, the estimated equation has a smaller coefficient for (Carats)$^2$. In other words, the curve has a somewhat smaller upward curvature, which is presumably due to the lesser influence of the very high-priced diamonds.

Another feature of the weighted analysis is that the prediction intervals are much narrower for the smaller diamonds than for the large diamonds. This difference can be seen by a plot comparing the prediction intervals for the unweighted and weighted analyses.

- Select **Confid Curves: Fit** from the pop-up menu beside **Polynomial Fit Degree=2**.

The resulting plots in Figure 3.24 and Figure 3.25 clearly show the differences in the prediction intervals. Although all are possibly too wide to make the estimates very useful for all values of the Carats variable, the intervals based on weighted least squares are at least equivalent in relative magnitudes.

*Figure 3.24* Mean Confidence Intervals for Weighted Regression

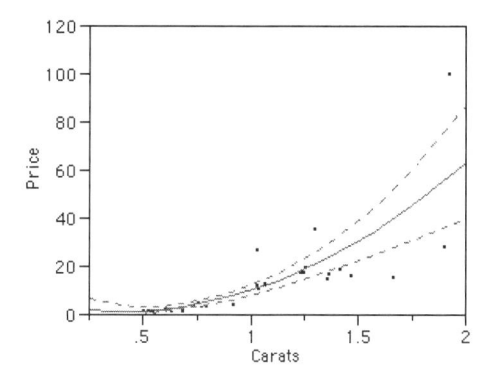

*Figure 3.25* Mean Confidence Intervals for Unweighted Regression

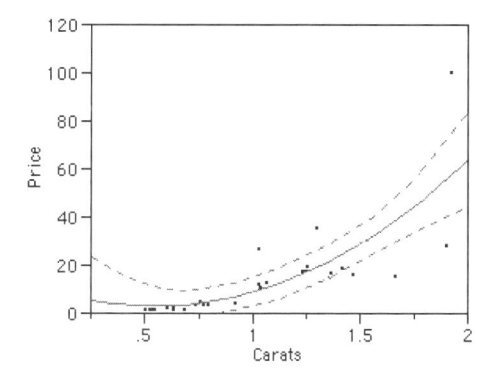

## 3.5 Summary

This chapter is titled "Observations" because it is concerned with aspects of observations that can cause a regression analysis to be of questionable value. Most of the focus has been on problems with the random error, but it has been shown that problems may exist with the independent variables as well.

The problems comprise four major types that may occur singly or in combination:

- outliers
- specification error
- heterogeneous variances
- nonindependent errors.

The most difficult of these is the problem of outliers, a point illustrated by the large number of statistics that have been developed to detect outliers. Unfortunately, none of these is uniformly superior because outliers can exist in so many ways. Finally, if you have found an outlier (or several), there is no guide as to what action to take.

The other difficulties are somewhat easier to diagnose and remedy, although even for these a degree of subjectivity is often needed to provide a reasonable analysis.

This chapter has demonstrated how JMP can be used to detect violations of assumptions about the error term in the regression model and subsequently to employ some remedial methods. Not only can the violations of assumptions take many forms, but the nature of violations are not always distinct. For example, apparent outliers may be the result of a nonnormal distribution of errors. Therefore, it is important not to use these methods blindly by taking a scattershot approach of doing everything. Instead, methods must be chosen carefully, often on the basis of prior information such as, for example, knowledge of distributions that are known to exist with certain types of data, or outliers resulting from sloppiness that occurs with some regularity from some data sources. As usual, the power of even the most sophisticated computer software is no substitute for the application of human intelligence.

# Chapter 4 Collinearity: Detection and Remedial Measures

*4.1 Introduction 105*

*4.2 Detecting Collinearity 107*

    *4.2.1 Variance Inflation Factors 110*

    *4.2.2 Leverage Plots 110*

    *4.2.3 Analysis of Structure: Principal Components, Eigenvalues, and Eigenvectors 111*

*4.3 Model Restructuring 115*

    *4.3.1 Redefining Variables 116*

    *4.3.2 Multivariate Structure: Principal Component Regression 117*

*4.4 Variable Selection 125*

    *4.4.1 Variable Selection 126*

    *4.4.2 All Possible Models 126*

    *4.4.3 Choosing Useful Models 129*

    *4.4.4 Selection Procedures 132*

    *4.4.5 Stepwise Probabilities 133*

    *4.4.6 A Strategy for Models with Many Variables 136*

*4.5 Summary 136*

## 4.1 Introduction

The validity of inferences resulting from a regression analysis assumes the use of a model with a specified set of independent variables. However, in many cases, you do not know specifically what variables should be included in a model. Hence, you may propose an initial model, often containing a large number of independent variables, and use a statistical analysis in hopes of revealing the correct model. This approach has two major problems:

❏ The model and associated hypotheses are generated by the data, thus invalidating significance levels (*p* values). This problem is related to the control of Type I errors in multiple comparisons, and although the problem has been partially solved for that application, it has not been solved for variable selection in regression. Therefore, *p* values provided by computer outputs for models obtained by such methods cannot be taken literally. For this reason, the column titles for *F* ratios and their corresponding *p* values are enclosed in quotation marks (see Figure 4.12 on page 127).

❏ The inclusion of a large number of variables in a regression model often results in *collinearity*, which is defined as a high degree of correlation among several independent variables. This occurs when too many variables have been put into the model and a number of different variables measure similar phenomena.

The existence of collinearity is not a violation of the assumptions underlying the use of regression analysis. In other words, the existence of collinearity does not affect the estimation of the dependent variable. The resulting $\hat{y}$ values are the best linear unbiased estimates of the conditional means of the population. Depending on the purpose of the regression analysis, collinearity may, however, limit the usefulness of the results as follows:

❏ The existence of collinearity tends to inflate the variances of predicted values, that is, predictions of the response variable for sets of *x* values, especially when these values are not in the sample.

❏ The existence of collinearity tends to inflate the variances of the parameter estimates. A partial regression coefficient measures the effect of the corresponding independent variable, holding constant all other variables. A high correlation among the independent variables makes the estimation and interpretation of such a coefficient difficult. In other words, when collinearity exists, partial coefficients are trying to estimate something that does not occur in the data. Therefore, collinearity often results in coefficient estimates that have large variances with consequential lack of statistical significance, or have incorrect signs or magnitude (Myers 1990, Section 3.7). This is an especially troublesome result when it is important to ascertain the structure of the relationship of the response to the various independent variables.

Because the use and interpretation of regression coefficients are very important for many regression analyses, you should ascertain whether collinearity exists. Then, if collinearity is deemed to exist, it is important to ascertain the nature of the collinearity, that is, the nature of the linear relationships among the independent variables. The final step is to combat the effects of collinearity.

"Detecting Collinearity" presents some methods available in JMP for the detection of collinearity. You will see that collinearity is not difficult to detect, but once it is detected, the nature of the collinearity may be more difficult to diagnose.

Alleviating the effects of collinearity is even more difficult, and the methods used depend on the ultimate purpose of the regression analysis. In fact, there is no universally optimal strategy for this task, and, furthermore, results obtained from any strategy are often of questionable validity and usefulness.

The most obvious and therefore most frequently used strategy is to implement a model with fewer independent variables. Since there is often no *a priori* criterion for the selection of variables, an automated, data-driven search procedure is most frequently used. Implementation of such variable selection procedures is often called *model building*. However, since these methods use the data to select the model, they are more appropriately called *data dredging*. This approach has two major drawbacks:

❑ It is not appropriate if you are trying to ascertain the structure of the regression relationship.

❑ The results of the variable selection procedures often do not provide a clear choice of an optimal model.

Procedures for variable selection using JMP are presented in "Variable Selection" on page 125.

When it is important to study the nature of the regression relationship, it may be useful to redefine the variables in the model. Such redefinitions may be simply based on knowledge of the variables or on a multivariate analysis of the independent variables. Variable redefinition procedures are presented in "Redefining Variables" on page 116.

## 4.2 Detecting Collinearity

The example used for detecting and combatting the effects of collinearity is the BOQ data used for outlier detection in Chapter 3, "Observations," omitting the impossible observation 25.

- Open BOQ.JMP.
- Select row 25.
- From the **Rows** menu, select **Exclude/Unexclude**.

Three sets of statistics that may be useful for ascertaining the degree and nature of collinearity are available from JMP. These statistics are

❏ $p$ values and $F$ ratios showing the relative degree of significance of the model and its individual parameters

❏ standard errors of the parameter estimates

❏ the *variance inflation factors*, often referred to as *VIF*

❏ an analysis of the structure of the **X'X** matrix, available through custom scripting. An example script is presented in "Regression Matrices" on page 241.

In addition, JMP provides a useful graphical tool known as a *leverage plot* (Sall 1990), which reveals collinearity at a glance.

JMP provides these statistics when you complete the following steps:

- Select **Analyze** → **Fit Model**.

- Select MANH in the variables list and click the **Y** button.

- Select OCCUP, CHECKIN, HOURS, COMMON, WINGS, CAP, and ROOMS and click the **Add** button.

- Select **Effect Leverage** from the **Emphasis** drop-down list.

- Click **Run Model**.

To reveal the variance inflation factors, which are initially hidden,

- Right-click (Control-click on the Macintosh) in the body of the **Parameter Estimates** table.

- From the menu that appears, select **Columns** → **VIF**.

They are appended to the listing of parameter estimates, as seen in Figure 4.1.

A comparison of the relative degrees of statistical significance of the model with those of the partial regression coefficients reveals collinearity. The overall model is highly significant with an $F$ value of 154.3185 and a $p$ value smaller than 0.0001. The smallest $p$ value for a partial regression coefficient is 0.0002, which is certainly not large but is definitely larger than that for the overall model. This type of result is a natural consequence of collinearity: the overall model may fit the data quite well, but because several independent variables are measuring similar phenomena, it is difficult to determine which of the individual variables contribute significantly to the regression relationship.

***Figure 4.1***
*Regression for BOQ Data, Omitting Observation 25*

**Whole Model**
**Actual by Predicted Plot**

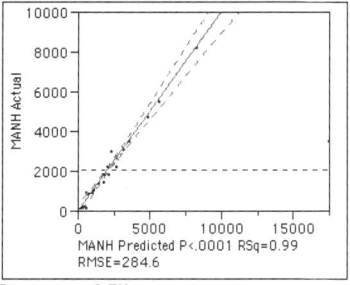

[Plot: MANH Actual vs MANH Predicted, P<.0001 RSq=0.99 RMSE=284.6]

**Summary of Fit**

| | |
|---|---|
| RSquare | 0.985405 |
| RSquare Adj | 0.979019 |
| Root Mean Square Error | 284.6035 |
| Mean of Response | 2050.007 |
| Observations (or Sum Wgts) | 24 |

**Analysis of Variance**

| Source | DF | Sum of Squares | Mean Square | F Ratio |
|---|---|---|---|---|
| Model | 7 | 87497673 | 12499668 | 154.3185 |
| Error | 16 | 1295987 | 80999.171 | Prob > F |
| C. Total | 23 | 88793659 | | <.0001 |

**Parameter Estimates**

| Term | Estimate | Std Error | t Ratio | Prob>|t| | VIF |
|---|---|---|---|---|---|
| Intercept | 171.47336 | 148.8617 | 1.15 | 0.2663 | |
| OCCUP | 21.045622 | 4.289049 | 4.91 | 0.0002 | 43.632217 |
| CHECKIN | 1.4263228 | 0.33071 | 4.31 | 0.0005 | 4.5415396 |
| HOURS | -0.089268 | 1.163532 | -0.08 | 0.9398 | 1.3607642 |
| COMMON | 7.6503311 | 8.438352 | 0.91 | 0.3781 | 4.0608297 |
| WINGS | -5.30231 | 9.452761 | -0.56 | 0.5826 | 3.7999573 |
| CAP | -4.074748 | 3.30195 | -1.23 | 0.2350 | 56.60333 |
| ROOMS | 0.3319106 | 6.813987 | 0.05 | 0.9618 | 178.70159 |

**Effect Tests**

| Source | Nparm | DF | Sum of Squares | F Ratio | Prob > F |
|---|---|---|---|---|---|
| OCCUP | 1 | 1 | 1950212.8 | 24.0769 | 0.0002 |
| CHECKIN | 1 | 1 | 1506682.9 | 18.6012 | 0.0005 |
| HOURS | 1 | 1 | 476.8 | 0.0059 | 0.9398 |
| COMMON | 1 | 1 | 66577.2 | 0.8219 | 0.3781 |
| WINGS | 1 | 1 | 25485.5 | 0.3146 | 0.5826 |
| CAP | 1 | 1 | 123350.5 | 1.5229 | 0.2350 |
| ROOMS | 1 | 1 | 192.2 | 0.0024 | 0.9618 |

**Residual by Predicted Plot**

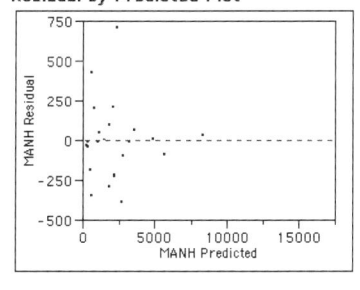

[Plot: MANH Residual vs MANH Predicted]

### 4.2.1 Variance Inflation Factors

The variance inflation factors are useful in determining which variables may be correlated or collinear. For the $i$th independent variable, the variance inflation factor is defined as $1/(1 - R_i^2)$, where $R_i^2$ is the coefficient of determination for the regression of the $i$th independent variable on all other independent variables. It can be shown that the variance of the estimate of the corresponding regression coefficient is larger by that factor than it would be if there were no collinearity. In other words, the VIF statistics show how collinearity has increased the instability of the coefficient estimates.

There are no formal criteria for determining the magnitude of variance inflation factors that cause poorly estimated coefficients. Some authorities (Myers 1990, Chapter 8) state that values exceeding 10 may be cause for concern, but this value is arbitrary. Actually, for models with low coefficients of determination ($R^2$) for the regression, estimates of coefficients that exhibit relatively small variance inflation factors may still be unstable, and vice versa. In Figure 4.1 the regression $R^2$ is a rather high 0.9854. Since $1/(1 - R^2) = 68.5$, any variables associated with VIF values exceeding 68.5 are more closely related to the other independent variables than they are to the dependent variable. The coefficient of **ROOMS** has a VIF value larger than 68.5, and it is certainly not statistically significant. You may conclude, therefore, that collinearity exists that decreases the reliability of the coefficient estimates. The overall regression is so strong, however, that some coefficients may still be meaningful.

### 4.2.2 Leverage Plots

An important feature of JMP is its emphasis on graphical representations. Figure 4.1 differs from the reports of other chapters, in that it shows a graphic with the textual reports for a statistical analysis. This is the preferred method of looking at analyses, so JMP generally gives such plots by default. For general linear hypotheses, both significance and collinearity can be seen through a graphical tool called the *leverage plot*. Leverage plots were introduced by Sall (1990) as an extension of the partial regression residual plots of Belsley, Kuh, and Welsch (1980).

For an effect, the leverage plot displays a horizontal line to represent the model without the effect in it. A sample leverage plot is shown in Figure 4.2. A slanted line represents the full model. Confidence curves, represented as dotted lines in the leverage plot, give a graphical indication of whether the effect is significant. If it is significant, the dotted lines will not include the horizontal line. If the effect is nonsignificant, the dotted lines will contain the horizontal line.

***Figure 4.2***
*Leverage Plot*

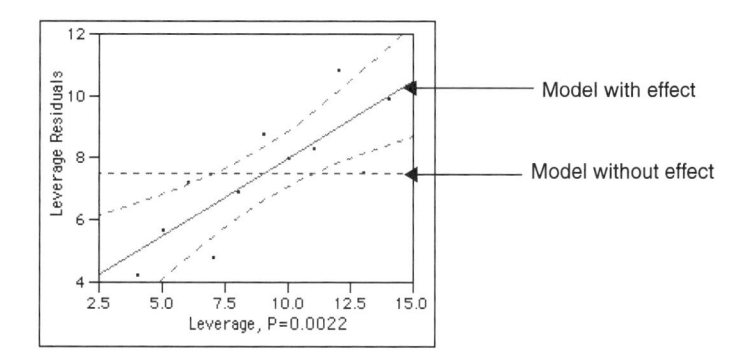

Because of their construction, the values on the *X*-axis turn out to be the predicted values for the model. The *Y*-axis of the leverage plot is the leverage residual of the model. If an effect is involved in collinearity, the plot will appear to shrink horizontally toward the center of the plot. Examples of this effect are shown in Figure 4.3 for two variables involved in the present example. Notice the collapse of the points toward the center of the plot and the flared confidence intervals for the plot on the right.

***Figure 4.3***
*Leverage Plot Reflecting Collinearity*

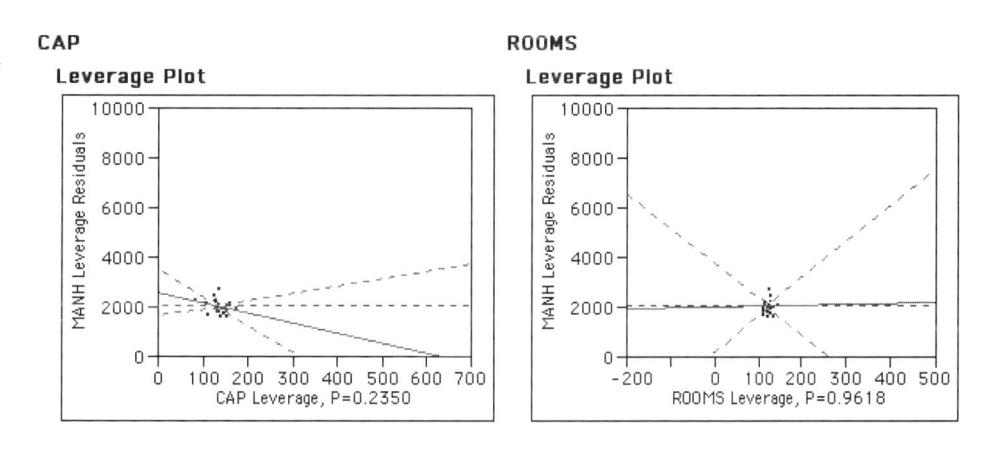

## 4.2.3 Analysis of Structure: Principal Components, Eigenvalues, and Eigenvectors

Both the analysis of the structure of collinearity and attempts to alleviate the effects of collinearity make use of a multivariate statistical technique called *principal components*.

*Multivariate analysis* is the study of variation involving multiple response variables. *Principal component analysis* is a multivariate analysis technique that attempts to describe interrelationships among a set of variables. Starting with a set of observed values on a set of $m$ variables, this method uses linear transformations to create a new set of variables, called the *principal components*, which are defined as

$$Z = X\Gamma$$

where

$Z$ is the matrix of principal component variables

$X$ is the matrix of observed variables

$\Gamma$ is a matrix of coefficients that relate $Z$ to $X$.

The principal component transformation has the following properties:

- The principal component variables, or simply *components*, are jointly uncorrelated.

- The first principal component has the largest variance of any linear function of the original variables (subject to a scale constraint). The second component has the second largest variance, and so on.

Although the principal components exhibit absolutely no collinearity, they are not guaranteed to provide useful interpretations.

Principal components may be obtained by computing the eigenvalues and eigenvectors of the correlation or covariance matrix. In most applications, however, the correlation matrix is used so that the scales of measurement of the original variables do not affect the components.

The eigenvalues are the variances of the components. If the correlation matrix has been used, the variance of each input variable is one. Therefore, the sum of the variances is equal to the number of variables. Because of the scale constraint of the principal component transformation, the sum of variances (eigenvalues) of the components is also equal to the number of variables, but the variances are not equal.

The eigenvectors, which are columns of $\Gamma$, are the coefficients of the linear equations that relate the component variables to the original variables.

A set of eigenvalues of nonzero magnitudes indicates that there is little collinearity, while eigenvalues that are close to zero indicate the presence of collinearity.

In fact, the number of large (usually greater than unity) eigenvalues may be taken as an indication of the true number of variables (sometimes called *factors*) needed to describe the behavior of the full set of variables. In other words, a small number of large eigenvalues indicates that a small number of component variables describes most of the variability of the originally observed variables. Because of the scale constraint, a number of large eigenvalues implies that there will be some small eigenvalues, and such values imply that some component variables have small variances. In fact, zero-valued eigenvalues indicate that exact collinearity (see "Exact Collinearity: Linear Dependency" on page 67) exists among the *x* variables; hence the existence of very small eigenvalues implies severe collinearity. For more complete descriptions of principal components, see Johnson and Wichern (1982) and Morrison (1976).

Principal component variables with very small variances are of interest in identifying sources of collinearity, as shown in this section. Principal component variables with large variances are used in attempts to provide better interpretation of the regression.

The analysis of the structure of relationships among a set of variables is afforded by an analysis of the eigenvalues and eigenvectors of $\mathbf{X'X}$. Such an analysis can be performed in two ways:

❑ by using the raw (not centered) variables, including the variable used to estimate the intercept, and scaling the variables such that the $\mathbf{X'X}$ matrix has ones on the diagonal.

❑ by using scaled and centered variables and excluding the intercept variable. In this case, $\mathbf{X'X}$ is the correlation matrix.

Because the first method is suggested by use of the dummy variable to estimate the intercept, you may be tempted to think of that variable simply as one of the variables that can be involved in collinearity. This is not an appropriate conclusion for many situations. The intercept is an estimate of the response at the origin, that is, where all independent variables are zero. It is chosen for mathematical convenience rather than to provide a useful parameter. In fact, for most applications the intercept represents an extrapolation far beyond the reach of the data. For this reason the inclusion of the intercept in the study of collinearity can be useful only if the intercept has some physical interpretation and is within reach of the actual data space.

Centering the variables places the intercept at the means of all the variables. Therefore, if the variables have been centered, the intercept has no effect on the collinearity of the other variables (Belsley, Kuh, and Welsch 1980). Centering is also consistent with the computation of the variance inflation factors that are based on first centering the variables. Therefore, the analysis presented here is on centered variables.

**114** *Collinearity: Detection and Remedial Measures*

To compute a principal components analysis on this data,

- Select **Analyze** → **Multivariate Methods** → **Multivariate**.
- Highlight all the variables except MANH and click the **Y, Columns** button.
- When the Multivariate report appears, select **Principal Components** → **on Correlations** from the platform pop-up menu.

This provides the eigenvectors and variance proportions associated with the eigenvalues.

Figure 4.4 shows the portion of the output from the principal components analysis.

*Figure 4.4 Principal Components Analysis*

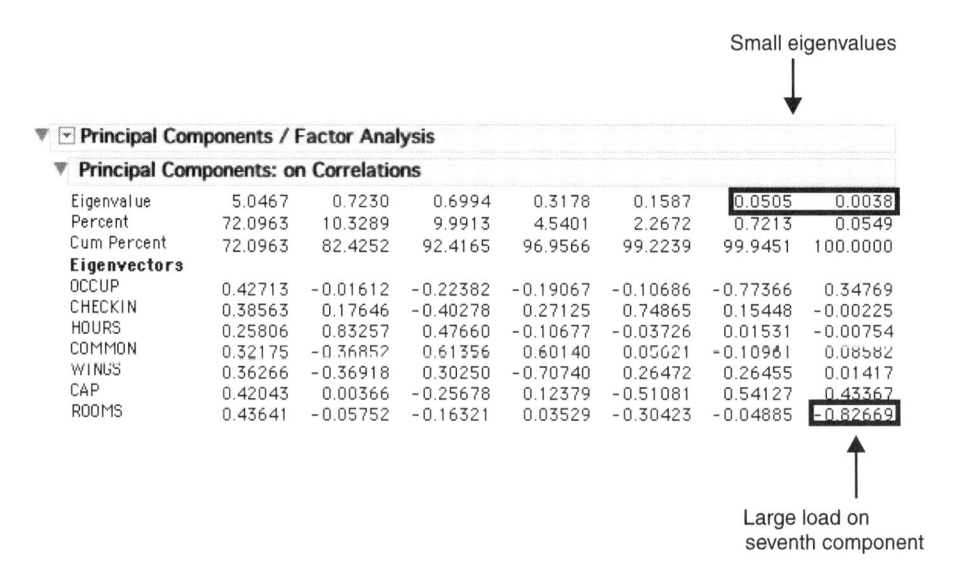

Small eigenvalues ↓

**Principal Components / Factor Analysis**
**Principal Components: on Correlations**

| | | | | | | | |
|---|---|---|---|---|---|---|---|
| Eigenvalue | 5.0467 | 0.7230 | 0.6994 | 0.3178 | 0.1587 | 0.0505 | 0.0038 |
| Percent | 72.0963 | 10.3289 | 9.9913 | 4.5401 | 2.2672 | 0.7213 | 0.0549 |
| Cum Percent | 72.0963 | 82.4252 | 92.4165 | 96.9566 | 99.2239 | 99.9451 | 100.0000 |

**Eigenvectors**

| | | | | | | | |
|---|---|---|---|---|---|---|---|
| OCCUP | 0.42713 | -0.01612 | -0.22382 | -0.19067 | -0.10686 | -0.77366 | 0.34769 |
| CHECKIN | 0.38563 | 0.17646 | -0.40278 | 0.27125 | 0.74865 | 0.15448 | -0.00225 |
| HOURS | 0.25806 | 0.83257 | 0.47660 | -0.10677 | -0.03726 | 0.01531 | -0.00754 |
| COMMON | 0.32175 | -0.36852 | 0.61356 | 0.60140 | 0.05021 | -0.10961 | 0.08582 |
| WINGS | 0.36266 | -0.36918 | 0.30250 | -0.70740 | 0.26472 | 0.26455 | 0.01417 |
| CAP | 0.42043 | 0.00366 | -0.25678 | 0.12379 | -0.51081 | 0.54127 | 0.43367 |
| ROOMS | 0.43641 | -0.05752 | -0.16321 | 0.03529 | -0.30423 | -0.04885 | -0.82669 |

↑ Large load on seventh component

The first row of this output consists of the eigenvalues of the correlation matrix of the set of independent variables. The eigenvalues are arranged from largest to smallest. The severity of collinearity is revealed by the near-zero values of these eigenvalues. Large variability among the eigenvalues indicates a greater degree of collinearity. Two features of these eigenvalues are of interest:

❑ Eigenvalues of zero indicate linear dependencies or exact collinearities. Therefore, very small eigenvalues indicate near-linear dependencies or high degrees of collinearity. There are two eigenvectors that may be considered very small in this set, implying the possibility of two sets of very strong relationships among the variables.

❑ The square root of the ratio of the largest to smallest eigenvalue is called the *condition number*. This value, 36.44, provides a single statistic for indicating the severity of collinearity. Criteria for a condition number to signify serious collinearity are arbitrary, with the value 30 often quoted. Myers (1990, Chapter 7) mentions that the square of the condition number in excess of 1000 indicates serious collinearity. The condition number of 36.44 for this example indicates some collinearity.

The Eigenvectors section of the output may indicate which variables are involved in the near-linear dependencies. For example, looking at the seventh eigenvalue, the value –0.82 in the OCCUP column shows that a large portion of the variability in OCCUP is attributed to the seventh principal component.

The set of principal component variables may be used as independent variables in a regression analysis. Such an analysis is called *principal component regression* (see "Multivariate Structure: Principal Component Regression" on page 117 for a thorough example). Since the components are uncorrelated, there is no collinearity in the regression, and you can easily determine the important coefficients. Then, if the coefficients of the principal components transformations imply meaningful interpretation of the components, the regression may shed light on the underlying regression relationships. Unfortunately, such interpretations are not always obvious.

## 4.3 Model Restructuring

In many cases, the effects of collinearity may be alleviated by redefining the model. For example, in an analysis of economic time series data, variables such as GNP, population, production of steel, and so on, tend to be highly correlated because all are affected by inflation and the total size of the economy. Deflating such variables by a price index and population reduces collinearity. Model redefinition is illustrated with the BOQ data in "Redefining Variables" below.

In situations where a basis for model redefinition is not obvious, it may be useful to implement multivariate techniques to study the structure of collinearity and consequently to use the results of such a study to provide a better understanding of the regression relationships. One such multivariate method is principal components, which generates a set of artificial uncorrelated variables that can then be used in a regression model. Implementing a principal component regression using JMP is presented in "Multivariate Structure: Principal Component Regression" on page 117.

### 4.3.1 Redefining Variables

The various collinearity statistics in the BOQ data demonstrate that many of the variables are related to the size of the establishment. The regression, then, primarily illustrates the relationship that larger establishments require more manpower. It is, however, more interesting to ascertain what other characteristics of Bachelor Officers Quarters require more or less manpower. You may be able to answer this question by redefining the variables in the model to measure per room characteristics; that is, estimate the relationship of the per room man-hour requirement to the per room occupancy rate, and so on.

The data set BOQ Relative contains variables defined as follows:

relocc = occup / rooms

relcheck = checkin / rooms

relcom = common / rooms

relwings = wings / rooms

relcap = cap / rooms

relman = manh / rooms

Figure 4.5 shows the resulting variables along with the HOURS variable, which is not redefined, and also the ROOMS variable.

The redefined variables reveal some features of the data that were not originally apparent. For example, the relCHECK variable shows that establishment 12 has a very high turnover rate while establishments 3 and 7 have low turnover rates. Now perform the regression:

- Select **Analyze → Fit Model**.
- Assign relMAN as the Y variable.
- Assign all other rel variables, as well as ROOMS and HOURS, as effects in the model.
- Click **Run Model**.

The purpose of keeping the ROOMS variable in the model is to ascertain whether there are economies of scale—that is, man-hour requirements per room decrease for larger establishments. Figure 4.6 shows the results of the regression.

You can see from the leverage plots in Figure 4.7 that the collinearity has been decreased somewhat but the regression is not statistically significant. In other words, there is little evidence that factors other than size affect manpower

*Figure 4.5*
*BOQ Relative Data*

| HOURS | ROOMS | relOCCUP | relCHECKIN | relCOMMON | relWINGS | relCAP | relMANH |
|---|---|---|---|---|---|---|---|
| 4.000 | 6.000 | 0.333 | 0.667 | 0.210 | 0.167 | 1.000 | 30.038 |
| 40.000 | 5.000 | 0.600 | 0.316 | 0.250 | 0.200 | 1.000 | 36.522 |
| 42.500 | 25.000 | 0.212 | 0.067 | 0.312 | 0.120 | 1.000 | 7.997 |
| 168.000 | 8.000 | 0.875 | 0.296 | 0.125 | 0.125 | 0.875 | 35.569 |
| 168.000 | 19.000 | 0.868 | 0.434 | 0.059 | 0.105 | 1.000 | 14.073 |
| 40.000 | 13.000 | 1.277 | 1.829 | 0.077 | 0.077 | 1.000 | 12.645 |
| 40.000 | 36.000 | 0.719 | 0.083 | 0.000 | 0.083 | 1.000 | 27.753 |
| 168.000 | 47.000 | 0.679 | 0.853 | 0.117 | 0.128 | 1.000 | 19.826 |
| 40.000 | 77.000 | 0.515 | 0.661 | 0.355 | 0.130 | 1.000 | 12.262 |
| 168.000 | 48.000 | 0.925 | 3.328 | 0.012 | 0.375 | 1.000 | 22.984 |
| 168.000 | 66.000 | 0.827 | 3.138 | 0.118 | 0.091 | 1.000 | 21.028 |
| 168.000 | 37.000 | 1.531 | 10.092 | 0.163 | 0.108 | 0.973 | 40.257 |
| 168.000 | 196.000 | 0.485 | 1.878 | 0.154 | 0.046 | 1.490 | 9.418 |
| 168.000 | 120.000 | 0.806 | 1.722 | 0.149 | 0.117 | 1.000 | 15.764 |
| 168.000 | 210.000 | 0.461 | 3.225 | 0.097 | 0.048 | 1.438 | 8.956 |
| 168.000 | 130.000 | 0.749 | 1.962 | 0.146 | 0.046 | 1.269 | 17.447 |
| 168.000 | 131.000 | 0.781 | 2.205 | 0.160 | 0.107 | 1.000 | 23.180 |
| 168.000 | 115.000 | 0.959 | 3.565 | 0.174 | 0.104 | 1.000 | 22.855 |
| 168.000 | 179.000 | 0.636 | 5.480 | 0.137 | 0.034 | 0.927 | 19.888 |
| 168.000 | 192.000 | 0.700 | 0.759 | 0.135 | 0.062 | 1.000 | 11.603 |
| 168.000 | 202.000 | 0.740 | 1.158 | 0.154 | 0.069 | 0.916 | 15.422 |
| 168.000 | 237.000 | 0.796 | 3.954 | 0.192 | 0.110 | 1.000 | 20.271 |
| 168.000 | 363.000 | 0.757 | 1.915 | 0.128 | 0.160 | 1.000 | 15.262 |
| 168.000 | 453.000 | 0.849 | 3.253 | 0.016 | 0.053 | 1.192 | 18.249 |
| 168.000 | 242.000 | 3.352 | 2.952 | 0.094 | 0.070 | 1.000 | 14.605 |

requirements. It is, however, possible that variable selection may reveal that some of these variables are useful in determining the manpower requirements (see "Variable Selection" on page 125).

### 4.3.2 Multivariate Structure: Principal Component Regression

Principal component regression is illustrated here with the BOQ data. The analysis is composed of two parts:

1. Use the Multivariate platform to perform the principal component analysis.
2. Use the Fit Model platform to perform the regression of the dependent variable on the set of component variables.

To run the principal components analysis,

- Return to the original BOQ data set (with observation 25 still excluded).
- Select **Analyze** → **Multivariate Methods** → **Multivariate**.
- Select all variables except MANH and click the **Y, Columns** button.
- Click **OK**.

**118** *Collinearity: Detection and Remedial Measures*

***Figure 4.6**
Regression
with
Redefined
Variables*

**Whole Model**

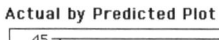

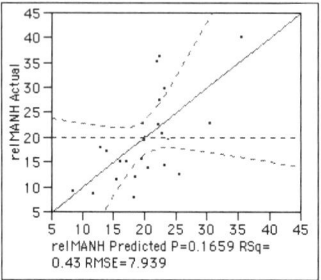

**Actual by Predicted Plot**

relMANH Predicted P=0.1659 RSq=
0.43 RMSE=7.939

**Summary of Fit**

| | |
|---|---|
| RSquare | 0.434556 |
| RSquare Adj | 0.187174 |
| Root Mean Square Error | 7.939016 |
| Mean of Response | 19.9695 |
| Observations (or Sum Wgts) | 24 |

**Analysis of Variance**

| Source | DF | Sum of Squares | Mean Square | F Ratio |
|---|---|---|---|---|
| Model | 7 | 775.0143 | 110.716 | 1.7566 |
| Error | 16 | 1008.4475 | 63.028 | Prob > F |
| C. Total | 23 | 1783.4618 | | 0.1659 |

**Parameter Estimates**

| Term | Estimate | Std Error | t Ratio | Prob>|t| |
|---|---|---|---|---|
| Intercept | 36.881423 | 21.07922 | 1.75 | 0.0993 |
| relOCCUP | 1.6689142 | 10.01957 | 0.17 | 0.8698 |
| relCHECKIN | 1.5805865 | 1.085976 | 1.46 | 0.1649 |
| relCOMMON | -12.94336 | 25.50015 | -0.51 | 0.6187 |
| relWINGS | 20.207212 | 26.2219 | 0.77 | 0.4522 |
| relCAP | -16.02822 | 13.56252 | -1.18 | 0.2546 |
| ROOMS | -0.019429 | 0.01818 | -1.07 | 0.3010 |
| HOURS | -0.021741 | 0.036701 | -0.59 | 0.5619 |

**Effect Tests**

| Source | Nparm | DF | Sum of Squares | F Ratio | Prob > F |
|---|---|---|---|---|---|
| relOCCUP | 1 | 1 | 1.74865 | 0.0277 | 0.8698 |
| relCHECKIN | 1 | 1 | 133.51469 | 2.1183 | 0.1649 |
| relCOMMON | 1 | 1 | 16.23836 | 0.2576 | 0.6187 |
| relWINGS | 1 | 1 | 37.42984 | 0.5939 | 0.4522 |
| relCAP | 1 | 1 | 88.02845 | 1.3967 | 0.2546 |
| ROOMS | 1 | 1 | 71.98982 | 1.1422 | 0.3010 |
| HOURS | 1 | 1 | 22.11883 | 0.3509 | 0.5619 |

**Residual by Predicted Plot**

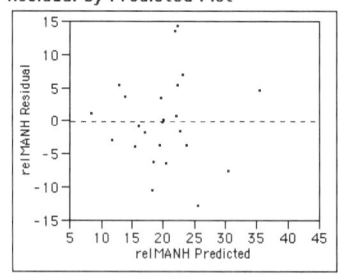

*Figure 4.7* Leverage Plots

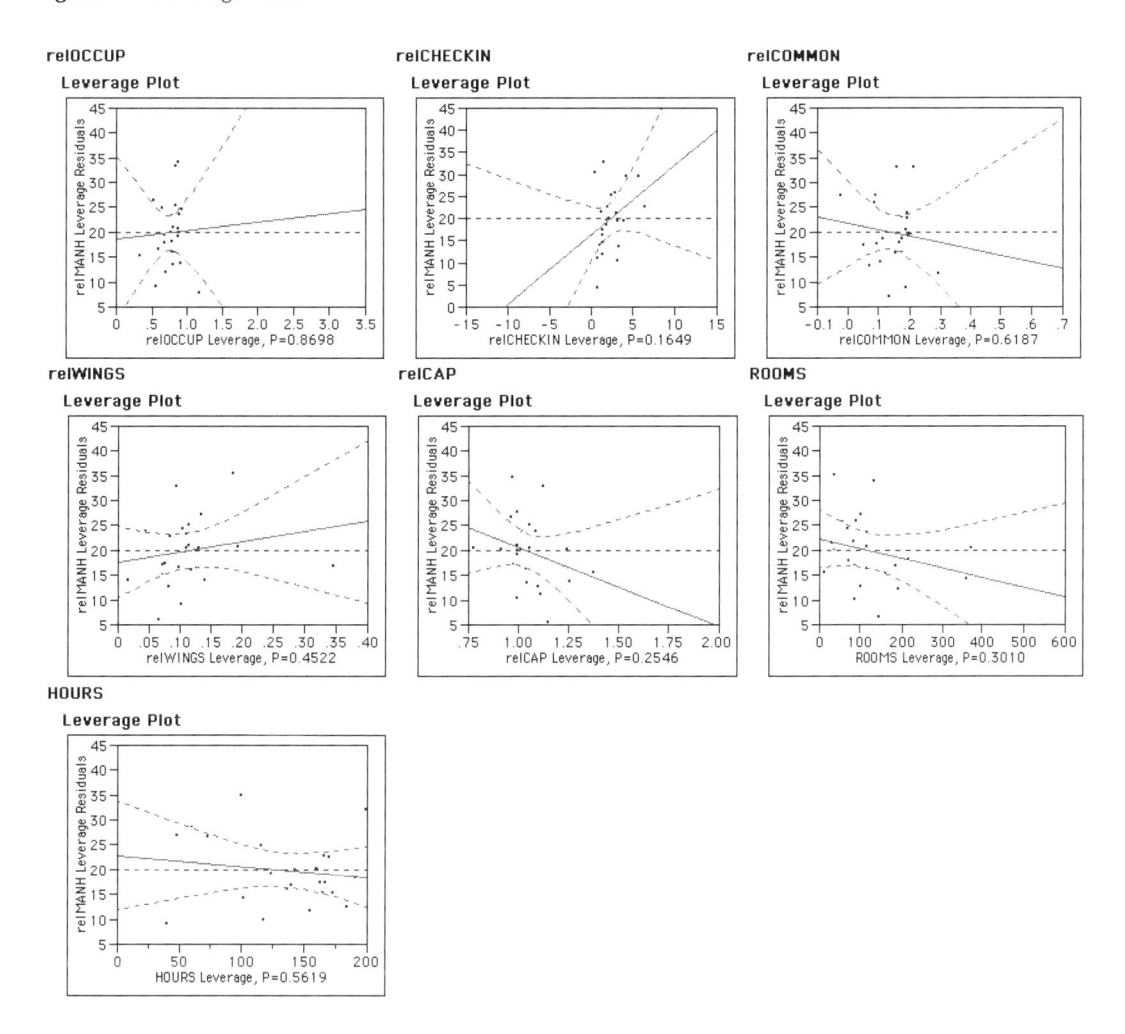

When the multivariate report appears,

- Select **Principal Components → On Correlations** from the platform pop-up menu.

The results of the principal components analysis using the independent variables from the BOQ data appear in Figure 4.8.

**120** Collinearity: Detection and Remedial Measures

*Figure 4.8*
*Multivariate Report*

**Multivariate**

**Correlations**

|        | OCCUP  | CHECKIN | HOURS  | COMMON | WINGS  | CAP    | ROOMS  |
|--------|--------|---------|--------|--------|--------|--------|--------|
| OCCUP  | 1.0000 | 0.8571  | 0.4785 | 0.5688 | 0.7668 | 0.9270 | 0.9708 |
| CHECKIN| 0.8571 | 1.0000  | 0.4607 | 0.4640 | 0.5460 | 0.8452 | 0.8545 |
| HOURS  | 0.4785 | 0.4607  | 1.0000 | 0.3809 | 0.3736 | 0.4634 | 0.4799 |
| COMMON | 0.5688 | 0.4640  | 0.3809 | 1.0000 | 0.6827 | 0.5878 | 0.6579 |
| WINGS  | 0.7668 | 0.5460  | 0.3736 | 0.6827 | 1.0000 | 0.6722 | 0.7581 |
| CAP    | 0.9270 | 0.8452  | 0.4634 | 0.5878 | 0.6722 | 1.0000 | 0.9785 |
| ROOMS  | 0.9708 | 0.8545  | 0.4799 | 0.6579 | 0.7581 | 0.9785 | 1.0000 |

1 rows not used due to missing values.

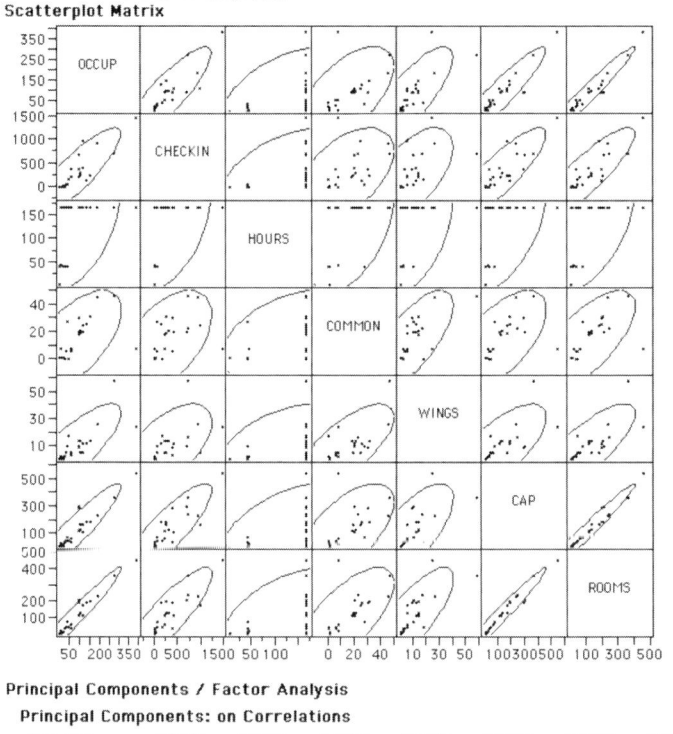

**Scatterplot Matrix**

**Principal Components / Factor Analysis**

**Principal Components: on Correlations**

| Eigenvalue  | 5.0467  | 0.7230   | 0.6994   | 0.3178   | 0.1587   | 0.0505   | 0.0038   |
|-------------|---------|----------|----------|----------|----------|----------|----------|
| Percent     | 72.0963 | 10.3289  | 9.9913   | 4.5401   | 2.2672   | 0.7213   | 0.0549   |
| Cum Percent | 72.0963 | 82.4252  | 92.4165  | 96.9566  | 99.2239  | 99.9451  | 100.0000 |

**Eigenvectors**

| OCCUP   | 0.42713 | -0.01612 | -0.22382 | -0.19067 | -0.10686 | -0.77366 | 0.34769  |
| CHECKIN | 0.38563 | 0.17646  | -0.40278 | 0.27125  | 0.74865  | 0.15448  | -0.00225 |
| HOURS   | 0.25806 | 0.83257  | 0.47660  | -0.10677 | -0.03726 | 0.01531  | -0.00754 |
| COMMON  | 0.32175 | -0.36852 | 0.61356  | 0.60140  | 0.05621  | -0.10961 | 0.08582  |
| WINGS   | 0.36266 | -0.36918 | 0.30250  | -0.70740 | 0.26472  | 0.26455  | 0.01417  |
| CAP     | 0.42043 | 0.00366  | -0.25678 | 0.12379  | -0.51081 | 0.54127  | 0.43367  |
| ROOMS   | 0.43641 | -0.05752 | -0.16321 | 0.03529  | -0.30423 | -0.04885 | -0.82669 |

To save the results of the principal components analysis,

🖱 Select **Save Principal Components** from the pop-up menu on the Principal Components report.

✋ When prompted for how many components to save, enter 7 and click **OK**.

The first portion of the output provides the correlation coefficients and a scatterplot matrix. You can easily see the very high correlations among OCCUP, CAP, and ROOMS, but other correlations are also quite high. To see a report containing all pairwise correlations (Figure 4.9),

✋ Select **Pairwise Correlations** from the platform pop-up menu.

*Figure 4.9*
*Pairwise Correlations*

```
Pairwise Correlations
Variable  by Variable  Correlation  Count  Signif Prob   -.8-.6-.4-.2 0 .2 .4 .6 .8
CHECKIN   OCCUP          0.8571       24    0.0000
HOURS     OCCUP          0.4785       24    0.0180
HOURS     CHECKIN        0.4607       24    0.0235
COMMON    OCCUP          0.5688       24    0.0037
COMMON    CHECKIN        0.4640       24    0.0224
COMMON    HOURS          0.3809       24    0.0663
WINGS     OCCUP          0.7668       24    0.0000
WINGS     CHECKIN        0.5460       24    0.0058
WINGS     HOURS          0.3736       24    0.0722
WINGS     COMMON         0.6827       24    0.0002
CAP       OCCUP          0.9270       24    0.0000
CAP       CHECKIN        0.8452       24    0.0000
CAP       HOURS          0.4634       24    0.0226
CAP       COMMON         0.5878       24    0.0025
CAP       WINGS          0.6722       24    0.0003
ROOMS     OCCUP          0.9708       24    0.0000
ROOMS     CHECKIN        0.8545       24    0.0000
ROOMS     HOURS          0.4799       24    0.0176
ROOMS     COMMON         0.6579       24    0.0005
ROOMS     WINGS          0.7581       24    0.0000
ROOMS     CAP            0.9785       24    0.0000
```

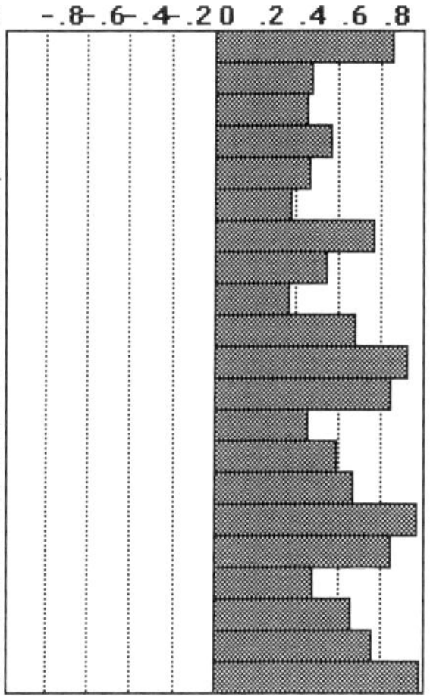

The second portion of Figure 4.8 provides information on the eigenvalues of the correlation matrix. The eigenvalues are located in the first row. Since there are seven variables, there are also seven eigenvalues, arranged from high to low.

The principal components have been computed from the standardized variables, that is, from the correlation matrix. Therefore, the sum of the variances of the original seven variables, as well as the sum of variances of the seven new principal component variables, is seven. This is a measure of the total variation inherent in the entire set of data. As previously noted, the variances of the principal components are given by the individual eigenvalues. The first principal component shows a very large variance (5.05), the second and third have modest variances (0.72 and 0.70), and the remainder have very small variances (less than 0.5). Remember, an eigenvalue of zero implies exact linear dependency.

The proportion of total variation accounted for by each of the components is obtained by dividing each of the eigenvalues by the total variation. These quantities are given in the Percent row. You can see that the first component accounts for 5.04 / 7 = 72% of the total variation, a result that is typical when a single factor, in this case the size of the establishment, is a common factor in the variability among the original variables.

The cumulative proportions printed in the Cum Percent row indicate for each component the proportion of the total variation of the original set of variables explained by all components up to and including that one. For example, 92% of the total variation in the seven variables is explained by only three components. This is another indication that the original set of variables contains redundant information.

The columns of the final portion of the output give the eigenvectors for each of the principal components. These coefficients, which relate the components to the original variables, are scaled so that their sum of squares is unity. This allows for finding which, if any, of the original variables dominate a component.

The coefficients of the first principal component show a positive relationship with all variables, with somewhat larger contributions from OCCUP, CAP, and ROOMS. As expected, this component measures the size of the establishment. The second component is dominated by HOURS. This shows that among these establishments there is a variability in operating hours that is independent of size. The third component is dominated by COMMON and is also somewhat a function of HOURS and, negatively, of CHECKIN. This component indicates variability among the establishments that reflects large common areas and longer hours of operation but a relatively low number of check-ins. Interpretation of components having small eigenvalues, such as components four through seven, is not usually useful, although such components may reveal data anomalies (see Figure 4.11).

Next, you can perform a regression of MANH on the principal components. The principal components are stored in the data table. To perform the regression,

- Select **Analyze → Fit Model**
- Enter MANH as the Y variable.
- Enter all seven principal components as the X variables.
- Click **Run Model**.
- Right-click (Control-click on the Macintosh) on the **Parameter Estimates** table and select **Column → VIF**.

The results appear in Figure 4.10.

The statistics for the overall regression (SS model and SS error) are, by definition, the same as for the regression with the seven original variables (see Figure 4.1). However, the statistics for the individual variables in the model tell a

*Figure 4.10
Principal
Component
Regression
(Minimal
Report)*

**Response MANH**

**Summary of Fit**

| | |
|---|---|
| RSquare | 0.985405 |
| RSquare Adj | 0.979019 |
| Root Mean Square Error | 284.6035 |
| Mean of Response | 2050.007 |
| Observations (or Sum Wgts) | 24 |

**Analysis of Variance**

| Source | DF | Sum of Squares | Mean Square | F Ratio |
|---|---|---|---|---|
| Model | 7 | 87497673 | 12499668 | 154.3185 |
| Error | 16 | 1295987 | 80999.171 | Prob > F |
| C. Total | 23 | 88793659 | | <.0001 |

**Parameter Estimates**

| Term | Estimate | Std Error | t Ratio | Prob>|t| | VIF |
|---|---|---|---|---|---|
| Intercept | 2050.0071 | 58.09445 | 35.29 | <.0001 | |
| Prin1 | 827.09516 | 26.41624 | 31.31 | <.0001 | 1 |
| Prin2 | 40.582716 | 69.79101 | 0.58 | 0.5690 | 1 |
| Prin3 | -470.6726 | 70.96047 | -6.63 | <.0001 | 1 |
| Prin4 | -173.9671 | 105.2672 | -1.65 | 0.1179 | 1 |
| Prin5 | 461.60751 | 148.9635 | 3.10 | 0.0069 | 1 |
| Prin6 | -1733.067 | 264.1041 | -6.56 | <.0001 | 1 |
| Prin7 | 405.07458 | 957.6936 | 0.42 | 0.6779 | 1 |

**Effect Tests**

| Source | Nparm | DF | Sum of Squares | F Ratio | Prob > F |
|---|---|---|---|---|---|
| Prin1 | 1 | 1 | 79405328 | 980.3227 | <.0001 |
| Prin2 | 1 | 1 | 27388 | 0.3381 | 0.5690 |
| Prin3 | 1 | 1 | 3563571 | 43.9952 | <.0001 |
| Prin4 | 1 | 1 | 221222 | 2.7312 | 0.1179 |
| Prin5 | 1 | 1 | 777797 | 9.6025 | 0.0069 |
| Prin6 | 1 | 1 | 3487875 | 43.0606 | <.0001 |
| Prin7 | 1 | 1 | 14491 | 0.1789 | 0.6779 |

different story. Since the components are uncorrelated, the VIFs are all unity. You can also verify that the partial sums of squares add to the model sum of squares. According to the *t* statistics for the parameter estimates, there appear to be four components of importance for estimating man-hour requirements. The most important component is Prin1, followed in importance by Prin3 and Prin6, and to a lesser degree Prin5.

Prin1 is clearly the component associated with size of establishment. In fact, this component accounts for over 90% of the variation explained by the model (Partial SS/Model SS). The second component apparently does nothing—that is, the hours of operation apparently have no effect on manpower requirements. Component three was associated with common areas, hours, and (negatively) check-ins. The negative coefficient indicates lower man-hour requirements for establishments having larger common areas, longer desk hours, and lower turnover.

Because principal components with very small variances are usually not useful, strong relationships of such components with the dependent variable are an

**124** *Collinearity: Detection and Remedial Measures*

apparent contradiction and may very well indicate data anomalies. You can investigate this by plotting the component variables against the dependent variable. In this example, components three and six have small variances and appear important, so they are therefore logical candidates for such plots.

- Select **Graph** → **Overlay Plot**.
- Select Prin3 and Prin6 as Y variables.
- Select MANH as the X variable.
- Click **OK**.
- When the single, overlaid plot appears, select **Overlay** from the platform pop-up menu to separate the plots.

The results appear in Figure 4.11.

***Figure 4.11***
*Plots of Components Three and Six*

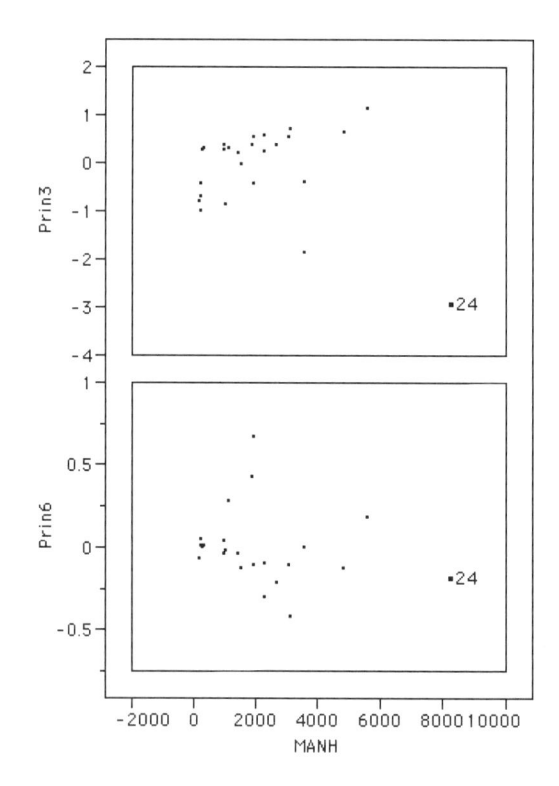

You can see that the relationships of both Prin3 and Prin6 with MANH are dominated by one observation, which can be identified as number 24. Remember that observation 24 was unusual in having very high turnover and small common areas, which have relatively large coefficients for component three. Omitting this observation would most certainly change the results. The relationship of Prin6 to MANH is also affected by observation 24, but the reason for this is not clear. Of course, this is not justification for omitting observation 24.

Principal components that have large eigenvalues can also be used to re-create values of the original variables reflecting only the variation explained by these components.

In summary, principal component regression has helped somewhat to interpret the structure of the regression, although the interpretation is not clear-cut, which is common with this type of analysis. Slightly more interpretable results are obtained by using rotated principal components, which are available in the Multivariate platform. Presentation of such methods is beyond the scope of this book.

## 4.4 Variable Selection

When a number of variables in a regression analysis do not appear to contribute significantly to the predictive power of the model, it is natural to try to find a suitable subset of important or useful variables. The use of regression methodology assumes that you have specified the appropriate model, but in many cases theory or intuitive reasoning does not supply such a model. In such situations, it is customary to use an automated procedure that uses information on the estimated coefficients to select a suitable subset of variables for a final model.

An optimum subset model is one that, for a given number of variables, produces the minimum error sum of squares, or, equivalently, the maximum $R^2$. In a sense, the only way to ensure finding optimum subsets is to examine all possible subsets. This procedure, for $m$ independent variables, requires computing statistics for $m!/[p!(m-p)!]$ regression equations for subsets of size $p$ from an $m$-variable model, or requires computing $2^m$ equations for finding optimum subsets for all subset sizes. Fortunately, optimal search procedures, highly efficient algorithms, and high-speed-computing capabilities make such a procedure feasible for models with a moderate number of variables, because they reduce the number of subsets that actually need to be examined. Such a procedure is implemented by an option in JMP's Stepwise platform, and it is normally recommended for models containing fewer than 25 variables. This method is presented in "All Possible Models" on page 126.

Because these selection methods often produce a bewildering array of results, statistics have been developed to assist in choosing suitable subset models. The use of such statistics is presented in "Choosing Useful Models" on page 129. Popular alternatives to the guaranteed optimum subset selection are the step-type procedures that add or delete variables one at a time until, by some criterion, a reasonable stopping point is reached. These procedures do not guarantee finding optimum subsets, but they work quite well in many cases and are especially useful for models with many variables.

Before continuing, it is necessary to point out that variable selection is not always appropriate, although it is easy to do. In fact, it may produce misleading results. Additional comments on this issue are presented in "Summary" on page 136.

### 4.4.1 Variable Selection

All selection methods in JMP are implemented using the **Stepwise** personality of the Fit Model dialog. To proceed with variable selections using the BOQ data set,

- Select **Analyze** → **Fit Model**.

- Assign MANH as the Y variable.

- Assign OCCUP, CHECKIN, HOURS, COMMON, WINGS, CAP, and ROOMS as X variables.

- Select **Stepwise** from the **Personality** drop-down list.

The Stepwise Control Panel appears (Figure 4.12). This is the control panel that allows for automated variable selection.

### 4.4.2 All Possible Models

Guaranteed optimum subsets are obtained by using the All Possible Models command. You can use this method as follows:

- Select **All Possible Models** from the platform pop-up menu.

The output from the All Possible Models option (Figure 4.13) provides, for each subset size, the variables included in the models, listed in order of decreasing $R^2$, along with the RSquare and sqrt(MS) statistics. Sqrt(MS) is the square root of the mean square of the regression. In addition, Mallows' $C_p$ can be requested.

- Right-click (Control-click on the Macintosh) in the **All Possible Models** table.

- Select **Columns** → **Cp**.

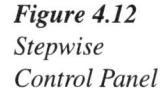

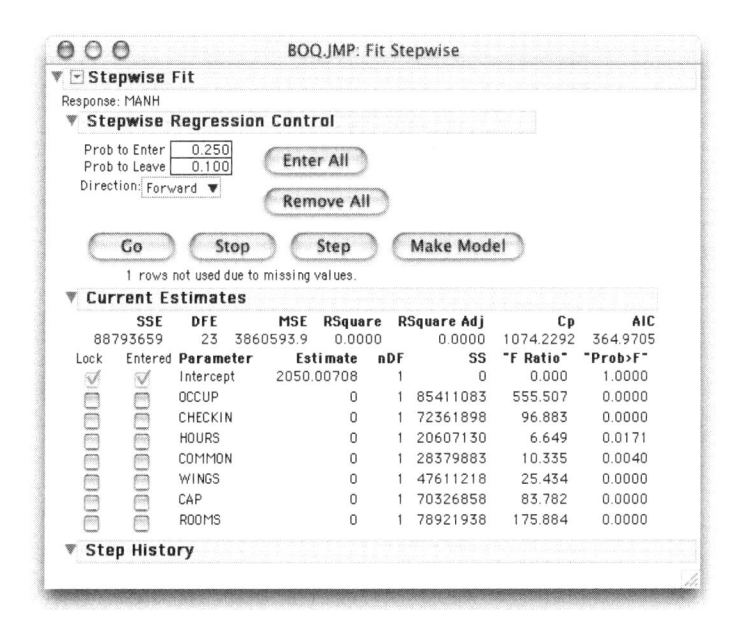

**Figure 4.12**
*Stepwise Control Panel*

A portion of the results appear in Figure 4.13.

The best models for each subset size are highlighted in this report. You can see that $R^2$ remains virtually unchanged down to subsets of size three, indicating that the three-variable model including OCCUP, CHECKIN, and CAP may be most useful. Additional considerations in this selection are presented in "Choosing Useful Models" on page 129.

In addition to the text reports, a plot of the sqrt(MS) versus the number of parameters in the model (Figure 4.14) appears at the bottom of the report.

A similar plot can be made for the Mallows' $C_p$ information.

- Right-click (Control-click on the Macintosh) in the All Possible Models report and select **Make into Data Table**.

This data table contains a lot of information. In fact, it is difficult to see the pattern of the $C_p$ statistic with all the points included on the plot. To simplify the plot, only consider the best four models for each subset.

- Hold down the Control key (on Windows) or the ⌘ key (on Macintosh) and select the first four rows for each subset size.

Note that there is only one point for subset size 7, so a total of 25 rows should be selected.

**Figure 4.13**
*Regression for BOQ Data Using All Possible Regressions*

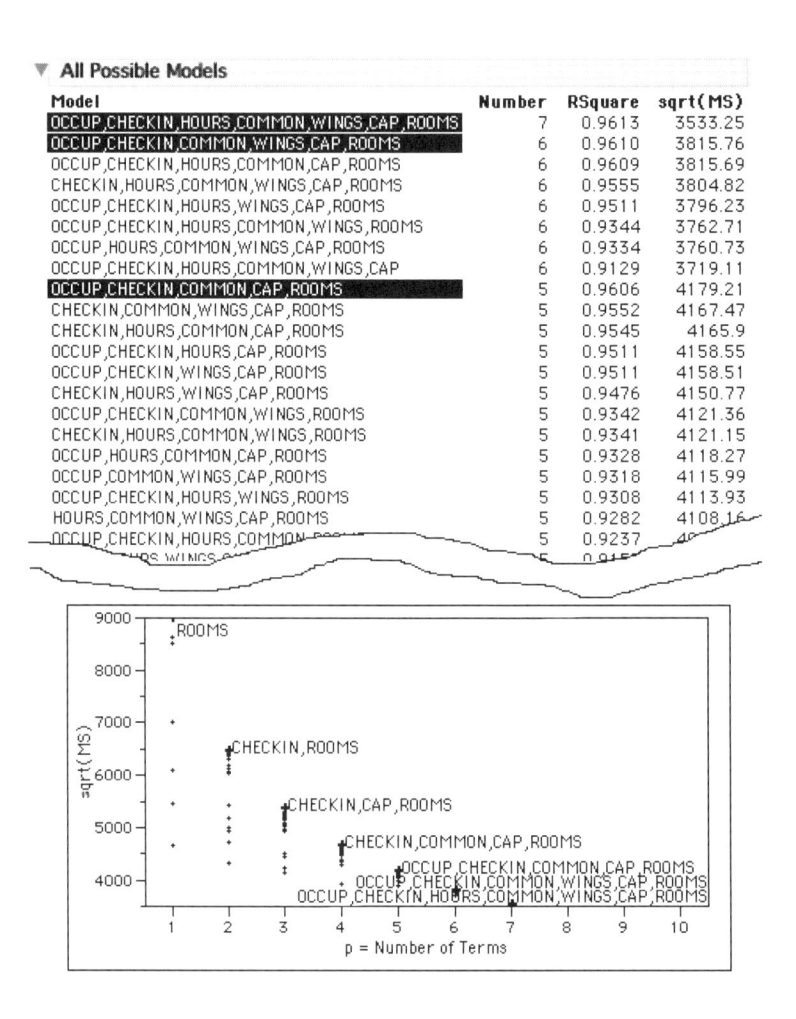

**All Possible Models**

| Model | Number | RSquare | sqrt(MS) |
|---|---|---|---|
| OCCUP,CHECKIN,HOURS,COMMON,WINGS,CAP,ROOMS | 7 | 0.9613 | 3533.25 |
| OCCUP,CHECKIN,COMMON,WINGS,CAP,ROOMS | 6 | 0.9610 | 3815.76 |
| OCCUP,CHECKIN,HOURS,COMMON,CAP,ROOMS | 6 | 0.9609 | 3815.69 |
| CHECKIN,HOURS,COMMON,WINGS,CAP,ROOMS | 6 | 0.9555 | 3804.82 |
| OCCUP,CHECKIN,HOURS,WINGS,CAP,ROOMS | 6 | 0.9511 | 3796.23 |
| OCCUP,CHECKIN,HOURS,COMMON,WINGS,ROOMS | 6 | 0.9344 | 3762.71 |
| OCCUP,HOURS,COMMON,WINGS,CAP,ROOMS | 6 | 0.9334 | 3760.73 |
| OCCUP,CHECKIN,HOURS,COMMON,WINGS,CAP | 6 | 0.9129 | 3719.11 |
| OCCUP,CHECKIN,COMMON,CAP,ROOMS | 5 | 0.9606 | 4179.21 |
| CHECKIN,COMMON,WINGS,CAP,ROOMS | 5 | 0.9552 | 4167.47 |
| CHECKIN,HOURS,COMMON,CAP,ROOMS | 5 | 0.9545 | 4165.9 |
| OCCUP,CHECKIN,HOURS,CAP,ROOMS | 5 | 0.9511 | 4158.55 |
| OCCUP,CHECKIN,WINGS,CAP,ROOMS | 5 | 0.9511 | 4158.51 |
| CHECKIN,HOURS,WINGS,CAP,ROOMS | 5 | 0.9476 | 4150.77 |
| OCCUP,CHECKIN,COMMON,WINGS,ROOMS | 5 | 0.9342 | 4121.36 |
| CHECKIN,HOURS,COMMON,WINGS,ROOMS | 5 | 0.9341 | 4121.15 |
| OCCUP,HOURS,COMMON,CAP,ROOMS | 5 | 0.9328 | 4118.27 |
| OCCUP,COMMON,WINGS,CAP,ROOMS | 5 | 0.9318 | 4115.99 |
| OCCUP,CHECKIN,HOURS,WINGS,ROOMS | 5 | 0.9308 | 4113.93 |
| HOURS,COMMON,WINGS,CAP,ROOMS | 5 | 0.9282 | 4108.16 |
| OCCUP,CHECKIN,HOURS,COMMON | 5 | 0.9237 | |

- Select **Tables → Subset** and click **OK** in the dialog that appears.

This produces a data table containing only the 25 selected observations.

- Right-click (Control-click on the Macintosh) on the word Model in the columns pane on the left side of the data table.

- Pick **Label/Unlabel** from the menu that appears.

- Select **Graph → Overlay Plot**.

- Assign Cp to Y and Number to X.

**Figure 4.14**
*All Possible Models Plot*

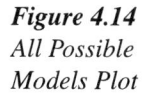

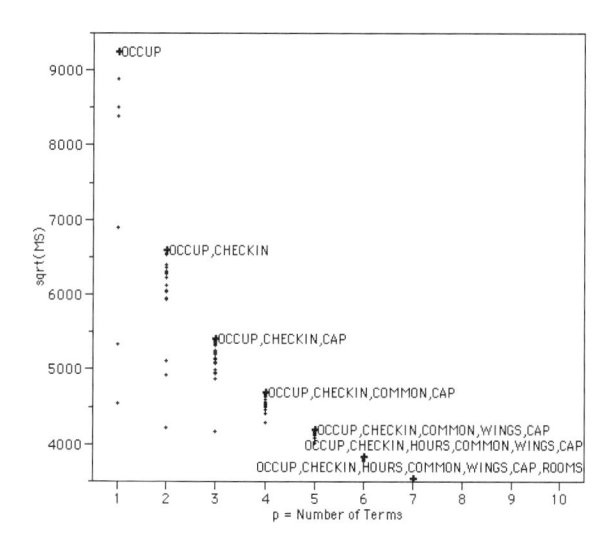

[Scatter plot: x-axis "p = Number of Terms" from 1 to 10; y-axis "sqrt(MS)" from 4000 to 9000. Labeled points: OCCUP; OCCUP,CHECKIN; OCCUP,CHECKIN,CAP; OCCUP,CHECKIN,COMMON,CAP; OCCUP,CHECKIN,COMMON,WINGS,CAP; OCCUP,CHECKIN,HOURS,COMMON,WINGS,CAP; OCCUP,CHECKIN,HOURS,COMMON,WINGS,CAP,ROOMS.]

Now, add a reference line showing ($p + 1$), where $p$ is the number of variables in the model. To add this line, we must add a short graphics script to the plot. The script uses the YFunction JSL command as follows.

- Right-click in the body of the plot and select **Add Graphics Script** from the menu that appears.

- Type YFunction(x+1,x) in the edit box that appears.

This tells JMP to plot the function $y = x + 1$ on the plot. The second argument (a single x) specifies the name of the independent variable in the plot. So, for example, an equivalent JSL expression would be YFunction(var + 1, var) or YFunction(XYZ + 1, XYZ).

- Click **OK**.

The finished plot appears in Figure 4.15.

Let the mouse pointer rest over any point in the plot, and that point is labeled with its corresponding model. Further discussion of Mallows' $C_p$ and a discussion of its plot are contained in the next section.

## 4.4.3 Choosing Useful Models

An examination of the $R^2$ values in Figure 4.13 does not reveal any obvious choices for selecting a most useful subset model. A number of other statistics

**Figure 4.15**
*Mallows' $C_p$ Plot*

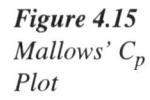

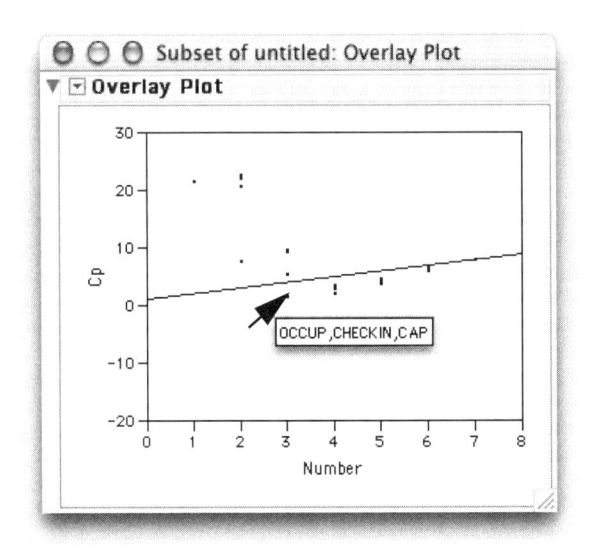

have been developed to aid in making these choices and are available as additional options with the All Possible Models command. Among these, the most frequently used is the $C_p$ statistic, proposed by Mallows (1973).

In the original presentation of the $C_p$ statistic, the intercept coefficient is also considered as a candidate for selection, so that in that presentation the number of variables in the model is one more than what is defined here and results in the +1 elements in the equations. As implied in the collinearity discussion, allowing the deletion of the intercept is not normally useful.

This statistic is a measure of total squared error for a subset model containing $p$ independent variables. The total squared error is a measure of the error variance plus the bias introduced by not including important variables in a model. It may, therefore, indicate when variable selection is deleting too many variables. The $C_p$ statistic is computed as follows:

$$C_p = \frac{SSE(p)}{MSE} - (N - 2p) + 1$$

where

*MSE* is the error mean square for the full model (or some other estimate of pure error)

*SSE(p)* is the error sum of squares for the subset model containing $p$ independent variables (*not* including the intercept)

*N* is total sample size.

For any given number of selected variables, larger $C_p$ values indicate equations with larger error mean squares. For any subset model $C_p > (p+1)$, there is evidence of bias due to an incompletely specified model. On the other hand, if there are values of $C_p < (p+1)$, the full model is said to be *overspecified*, meaning that it contains too many variables.

Mallows recommends that $C_p$ be plotted against $p$, and further recommends selecting that subset size where the minimum $C_p$ first approaches $(p+1)$, starting from the full model. The magnitudes of differences in the $C_p$ statistic between the optimum and near-optimum models for each subset size are also of interest.

The pattern of $C_p$ values shown in Figure 4.15 is quite typical for situations where collinearity is serious. Starting with $p = 7$, they initially become smaller than $(p+1)$, as fewer variables are included, but eventually start to increase. In this plot, there is a definite corner at Number=3, where the $C_p$ values increase rapidly with smaller subset sizes. Hence, a model with three variables appears to be a good choice.

A second criterion is the difference in $C_p$ between the optimum and second optimum subset for each subset size. In the above models with four or more variables, these differences are very small, which implies that the collinearity allows interchange of variables without affecting the fit of the model. However, the difference is larger with three variables, implying that the degree of collinearity has decreased. You can now estimate the best three-variable model using the information from Figure 4.15.

- Select **Analyze → Fit Model.**
- Assign MANH to the Y variable and OCCUP, CHECKIN, CAP as effects in the model.
- Click **Run Model**.

**Note**  Since this model has been specified by the data, the *p* values cannot be used literally but may be useful for determining the relative importance of the variables.

It does appear that more turnover (CHECKIN) requires additional manpower. The negative coefficient for CAP may reflect fewer man-hours for a larger proportion of vacant rooms.

**Response MANH**

**Summary of Fit**

| | |
|---|---|
| RSquare | 0.983853 |
| RSquare Adj | 0.981431 |
| Root Mean Square Error | 267.7415 |
| Mean of Response | 2050.007 |
| Observations (or Sum Wgts) | 24 |

**Analysis of Variance**

| Source | DF | Sum of Squares | Mean Square | F Ratio |
|---|---|---|---|---|
| Model | 3 | 87359949 | 29119983 | 406.2186 |
| Error | 20 | 1433710 | 71685.504 | Prob > F |
| C. Total | 23 | 88793659 | | <.0001 |

**Parameter Estimates**

| Term | Estimate | Std Error | t Ratio | Prob>|t| |
|---|---|---|---|---|
| Intercept | 207.86486 | 78.28539 | 2.66 | 0.0152 |
| OCCUP | 20.671626 | 1.751235 | 11.80 | <.0001 |
| CHECKIN | 1.4362433 | 0.293658 | 4.89 | <.0001 |
| CAP | -3.453968 | 1.141095 | -3.03 | 0.0067 |

**Effect Tests**

| Source | Nparm | DF | Sum of Squares | F Ratio | Prob > F |
|---|---|---|---|---|---|
| OCCUP | 1 | 1 | 9988307.0 | 139.3351 | <.0001 |
| CHECKIN | 1 | 1 | 1714758.1 | 23.9206 | <.0001 |
| CAP | 1 | 1 | 656786.8 | 9.1621 | 0.0067 |

▶ **Effect Details**

## 4.4.4 Selection Procedures

Several step-type selection procedures are available as alternatives to the All Possible Models. Starting with some given model, these procedures can

❑ add a variable to the model

❑ delete a variable from the model

❑ exchange a variable in the model for one that is not in the model.

Three different step-type selection procedures are available as options in the Stepwise Regression Control Panel. All are available through the Direction drop-down list. Additional options for these methods are detailed after the descriptions. The selection methods are as follows.

### Forward Selection

Foward selection begins by finding the variable that produces the optimum one-variable model. In the second step, the procedure finds the variable that, when added to the already chosen variable, results in the largest reduction in the residual sum of squares (largest increase in $R^2$). The third step finds the variable that, when added to the two already chosen, gives the minimum residual sum of squares (maximum $R^2$). The process continues until no variable considered for addition to the model provides a reduction in sum of squares considered statistically significant at a level specified by the user (see "Stepwise Probabilities" later in this section). An important feature of this method is that once a variable has been selected, it stays in the model.

### Backward Elimination

Backward elimination begins by computing the regression with all independent variables entered in the control panel. The statistics for the partial coefficients are examined to find the variable that contributes least to the fit of the model, that is, the coefficient with the largest $p$ value (smallest partial $F$ value). That variable is deleted from the model and the resulting equation is examined for the variable now contributing the least, which is then deleted, and so on. The procedure stops when all coefficients remaining in the model are statistically significant at a level specified by the user (see "Stepwise Probabilities" below). With this method, once a variable has been deleted, it is deleted permanently.

### Mixed Selection

Mixed selection begins like forward selection, but after a variable has been added to the model, the resulting equation is examined to see if any coefficient has a sufficiently large $p$ value (see "Stepwise Probabilities" below) to suggest that a variable should be dropped. This procedure continues until no additions or deletions are indicated according to significance levels chosen by the user.

## 4.4.5 Stepwise Probabilities

For all three methods, you may specify desired significance levels for stopping the addition or elimination of variables by entering the levels beside **Prob to Enter** and **Prob to Leave** in the Stepwise Control Panel.

The smallest permissible value for **Prob to Leave** is 0.0001, which almost always ensures that the final equation obtained by backward elimination contains only one variable, while the maximum **Prob to Enter** of 0.99 usually includes all variables when forward selection has stopped. It is again important to note that, since variable selection is an exploratory rather than confirmatory analysis, the **Prob to Leave** and **Prob to Enter** values do not have the usual connotation as probabilities of erroneously rejecting the null hypothesis of the nonexistence of the coefficients in any selected model.

Because the outputs from the step-type selection procedures are quite lengthy, they are illustrated here only with the Forward direction using the redefined variables of the BOQ data. Since the overall seven-variable model has a rather high $p$ value, the default **Prob to Enter** of 0.10 most likely selects only a few variables.

- Using the BOQ Relative data set, select **Analyze → Fit Model**.

- Enter relMANH as the Y variable and the other rel variables as effects.

**134** *Collinearity: Detection and Remedial Measures*

- From the Stepwise Control Panel, enter 0.10 as the **Prob to Enter** and select **Forward** as the **Direction**.
- Select **Step** to enter the first variable into the model.
- Select **Step** again to enter another variable in the model.

The Step button can be used repeatedly to watch the model being built.

- Select **Go** to proceed fully through the model selection, and see the results in Figure 4.16.

*Figure 4.16 Forward Selection for Redefined Variables*

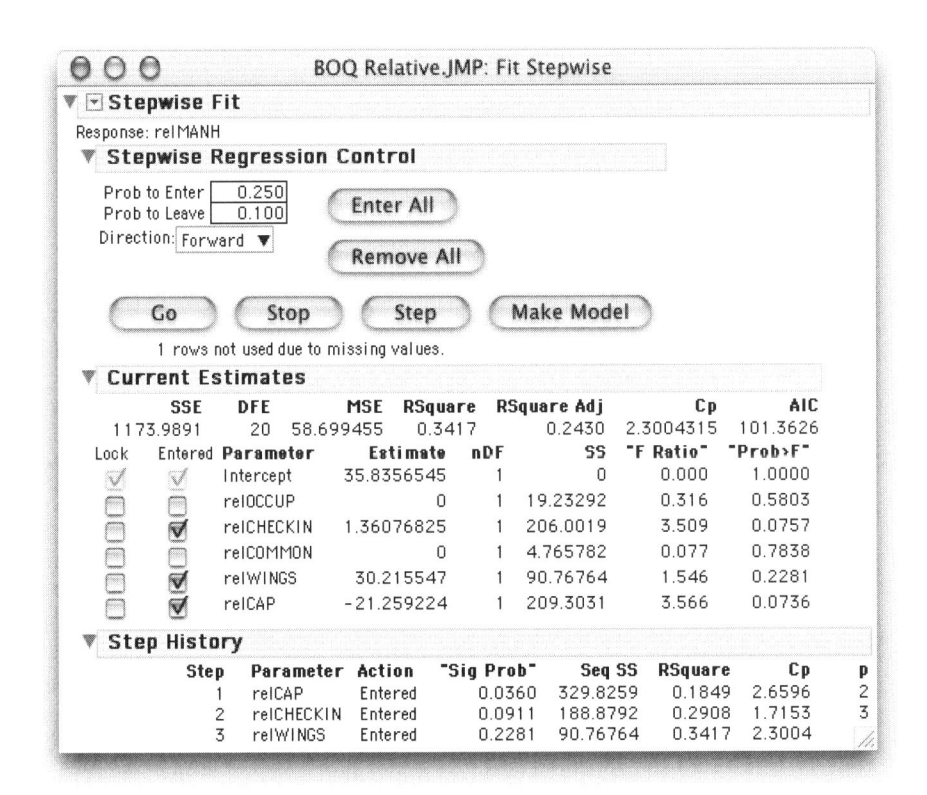

```
                    BOQ Relative.JMP: Fit Stepwise
▼ Stepwise Fit
Response: relMANH
  ▼ Stepwise Regression Control
    Prob to Enter  0.250
    Prob to Leave  0.100      Enter All
    Direction: Forward
                              Remove All

         Go        Stop        Step       Make Model
    1 rows not used due to missing values.
  ▼ Current Estimates
         SSE      DFE        MSE     RSquare   RSquare Adj      Cp        AIC
      1173.9891   20      58.699455  0.3417       0.2430    2.3004315  101.3626
    Lock  Entered Parameter    Estimate   nDF      SS     "F Ratio"   "Prob>F"
      ✓     ✓     Intercept   35.8356545   1        0       0.000      1.0000
      ☐     ☐     relOCCUP            0    1     19.23292   0.316      0.5803
      ☐     ✓     relCHECKIN   1.36076825  1    206.0019    3.509      0.0757
      ☐     ☐     relCOMMON           0    1      4.765782  0.077      0.7838
      ☐     ✓     relWINGS     30.215547   1     90.76764   1.546      0.2281
      ☐     ✓     relCAP      -21.259224   1    209.3031    3.566      0.0736
  ▼ Step History
         Step  Parameter   Action    "Sig Prob"   Seq SS    RSquare    Cp      p
          1    relCAP      Entered     0.0360    329.8259   0.1849   2.6596    2
          2    relCHECKIN  Entered     0.0911    188.8792   0.2908   1.7153    3
          3    relWINGS    Entered     0.2281     90.76764  0.3417   2.3004
```

For each step, the Step History describes the action taken. In this case, Step 1 selects relCAP, and an abbreviated output summarizes the resulting model. In the same fashion, Step 2 adds relCHECKIN and Step 3 adds relWINGS. At the end of the selection is a summary of the selection process.

Remember that the *F* and *p* values cannot be taken literally, which is why they are presented in quotation marks. However, you can use them as a measure of relative importance. In the three-variable model, CHECKIN appears to have some importance and the other variables have *p* values sufficiently small to indicate that they should not be ignored. Also, the signs of the coefficients do make sense, in that manpower requirements increase with greater turnover but decrease with overall size (economy of scale) and fewer unused rooms.

Once the final model has been selected,

- Click the **Make Model** button to open a Fit Model dialog with the variables preselected in their appropriate roles.
- Click **Run Model** in the Fit Model dialog to run the model.

Output for the model fit appears in Figure 4.17.

It is worth repeating that the step-type procedures do not necessarily produce optimum selections. Temper the results with any knowledge of the underlying process.

*Figure 4.17 Output after* **Make Model** *Command*

**Response relMANH**

**Summary of Fit**

| | |
|---|---|
| RSquare | 0.341736 |
| RSquare Adj | 0.242996 |
| Root Mean Square Error | 7.661557 |
| Mean of Response | 19.9695 |
| Observations (or Sum Wgts) | 24 |

**Analysis of Variance**

| Source | DF | Sum of Squares | Mean Square | F Ratio |
|---|---|---|---|---|
| Model | 3 | 609.4727 | 203.158 | 3.4610 |
| Error | 20 | 1173.9891 | 58.699 | Prob > F |
| C. Total | 23 | 1783.4618 | | 0.0357 |

**Parameter Estimates**

| Term | Estimate | Std Error | t Ratio | Prob>|t| |
|---|---|---|---|---|
| Intercept | 35.835655 | 13.1068 | 2.73 | 0.0128 |
| relCHECKIN | 1.3607683 | 0.726383 | 1.87 | 0.0757 |
| relWINGS | 30.215547 | 24.29864 | 1.24 | 0.2281 |
| relCAP | -21.25922 | 11.2584 | -1.89 | 0.0736 |

**Effect Tests**

| Source | Nparm | DF | Sum of Squares | F Ratio | Prob > F |
|---|---|---|---|---|---|
| relCHECKIN | 1 | 1 | 206.00187 | 3.5094 | 0.0757 |
| relWINGS | 1 | 1 | 90.76764 | 1.5463 | 0.2281 |
| relCAP | 1 | 1 | 209.30306 | 3.5657 | 0.0736 |

### 4.4.6 A Strategy for Models with Many Variables

Because All Possible Models allows you to investigate all models, it not only provides the optimum models for all subset sizes, but it also provides information on other subsets that, although not strictly optimal, may be very useful. However, the All Possible Models method simply cannot be used for problems with a large number of variables. In such cases, step-type procedures provide an alternative. An especially attractive alternative is to use both the Forward and Backward methods with the Prob to Enter and Prob to Leave parameters set to provide the entire range (usually Prob to Enter = 0.99 and Prob to Leave = 0.0001). The closeness of agreement of the two methods provides some clues to true optimality: if they are identical it is quite likely that optimality has been achieved.

In addition, these methods may indicate approximately how many variables are needed. Then, for example, if only a few are needed, you may be able to implement the All Possible Models method for that limited number of variables.

## 4.5 Summary

This chapter has presented several methods of detecting collinearity and two types of remedial methods of combatting the effects of collinearity. It can be argued that the two types have different purposes:

- ❏ Model redefinition, including complete principal components regression, is used to investigate the structure of the relationships.

- ❏ Variable selection is used to find the smallest (most economical) set of variables needed for estimating the dependent variable.

These different objectives are, of course, not mutually exclusive, and most regression analyses involve both of them to some degree. It is, however, useful to keep both objectives in mind when planning a strategy for analysis.

However, because it is the easiest to use, variable selection is the most frequently used method. This is unfortunate, not only because it may be the incorrect strategy, but also because there are some side effects from using variable selection.

The least-squares properties of providing unbiased estimates of the regression coefficients and error variance assume that the true model has been specified. However, models resulting from variable selection may not be the true model; hence, the resulting estimates may not have these favorable properties. In fact, if the selection process deletes variables that are in the true model, it is clear that all estimates are biased. On the other hand, if variables not in the true model have not been deleted, the purpose of variable selection has not been accomplished.

The other negative aspect of variable selection has already been noted—that is, $p$ values obtained with selected models may not be taken literally. There is, in fact, no theory that specifies what the true $p$ values can be, except that they are probably quite a bit larger than those printed by the output.

If variable selection is used, it is important to stress that, if possible, the use of prior information to choose a set of suitable variables is preferable to automated variable selection. In other words, the brute force of the computer is no substitute for knowledge about the data and existing relationships. For example, the relative cost of measuring the different independent variables should have a bearing on which variables to keep in a model that you use to predict values of the dependent variable. Another case in point is the polynomial model where a natural ordering of parameters exists, which suggests a predetermined order of variable selection. (See Chapter 5, "Polynomial and Smoothing Models.")

An interesting demonstration of how poorly automatic variable selection works is to randomly split a data set into two parts and perform these methods on each part. The differences in the results are often quite striking and informative. For this reason, results of all analyses, and especially those resulting from variable selections, should be interpreted with caution.

# Chapter 5 Polynomial and Smoothing Models

*5.1 Introduction 139*

*5.2 Polynomial Models with One Independent Variable 140*
    *5.2.1 Polynomial Centering 141*
    *5.2.2 Analysis Using Fit Y by X 145*
    *5.2.3 Analysis Using Fit Model 148*

*5.3 Polynomial Models with Several Variables 151*

*5.4 Response Surface Plots 156*

*5.5 A Three-Factor Response Surface Experiment 158*

*5.6 Smoothing Data 167*
    *5.6.1 The Moving Average 167*
    *5.6.2 The Time Series Platform 169*
    *5.6.3 Smoothing Splines 172*

*5.7 Summary 173*

## 5.1 Introduction

In the regression models presented in earlier chapters, all relationships among variables have been described by straight lines. In this chapter, linear regression methods are used to estimate parameters of models that cannot be described by straight lines.

One popular method used for this purpose is the *polynomial* model, in which the dependent variable is related to functions of the powers of one or more independent variables.

Another popular model is called *curve fitting*, where the purpose of the statistical analysis is to define a relatively smooth curve or surface that describes the behavior of the response variable without any reference to a meaningful model. A smooth curve does not necessarily have to be represented by a regression model with parameters. A frequently used curve-fitting procedure that does not emphasize parameters is the cubic spline.

Further, data can be smoothed to clarify underlying patterns that may be obscured with the variability of the data. Several smoothing techniques are shown in this chapter.

Methods that attempt to fit models with meaningful parameters are discussed in Chapter 6, "Special Applications of Linear Models," and in Chapter 7, "Nonlinear Models."

## 5.2 Polynomial Models with One Independent Variable

A one-variable polynomial model is defined as follows:

$$y = \beta_0 + \beta_1 x + \beta_2 x^2 + \ldots + \beta_m x^m + \varepsilon$$

where $y$ represents the dependent variable and $x$ the independent variable. The highest exponent, or power, of $x$ used in the model is known as the *degree* of the model, and it is customary for a model of degree $m$ to include all terms with lower powers of the independent variable.

Although the polynomial model describes a curvilinear response, it is still a linear regression model because it is linear in its parameters. In other words, you can use the values of the required powers of the independent variable as the set of independent variables in a multiple linear regression analysis for a polynomial model. Consequently, all statistics and estimates produced by the implementation of that model have the same connotation as in any linear regression analysis, although the practical implications of some of the results may differ.

Polynomial models are primarily used as a means to fit a relatively smooth curve to a set of data. In this situation, the polynomial model itself is of little practical use, and therefore the degree of polynomial required to fit a set of data is not usually known *a priori*. Therefore, it is customary to build an appropriate polynomial model by sequentially fitting equations with higher-order terms until a satisfactory degree of fit has been accomplished. In other words, you start by fitting a simple linear regression of $y$ on $x$. Then you specify a model with linear and quadratic terms, to ascertain if adding the quadratic term improves the fit by significantly reducing the residual mean square. You can then continue by adding and testing the contribution of a cubic term, then a fourth-power term, and so on, until no additional terms are needed.

A polynomial regression model is illustrated here using data collected to determine how growth patterns of fish are related to temperature. A curve describing how an organism grows with time is called a *growth curve*. It usually shows rapid initial growth, which gradually becomes slower and may eventually cease. Mathematical biologists have developed many sophisticated models to fit growth curves (see "Fitting a Growth Curve with the Nonlinear Platform" on page 229). However, a polynomial model often provides a convenient and easy approximation to such curves.

Fingerlings of a particular species of fish were put into four tanks, which were kept at temperatures of 25, 27, 29, and 31 degrees Celsius, respectively. After 14 days, and weekly thereafter, one fish was randomly selected from each tank and its length was measured. The data from this experiment are given in Table 5.1 and stored in the Fish.jmp data file.

The data set Fish.jmp consists of 84 observations containing the variables Age, Temperature, and Length. The data for the fish kept at 29 degrees are used to approximate the growth curve with a fourth-degree polynomial in Age for the dependent variable Length. (The entire data set is used later.)

The polynomial regression is estimated using Fit Model, with Length as the dependent variable and Age (and perhaps its powers) as the independent variable.

First, select the data for fish kept at 29 degrees.

- Select **Rows** → **Row Selection** → **Select Where**.
- Select Temperature from the variables list.
- Make sure **equals** is selected as the condition.
- Type 29 in the box to the right of the condition, as shown in Figure 5.1.
- Click **OK**.

Now, make a new table consisting of this subset of data.

- Select **Tables** → **Subset**
- Click **OK**.

The data set Subset of Fish appears (Figure 5.2).

### 5.2.1 Polynomial Centering

When a model contains polynomial or interaction terms, they are automatically centered by JMP. Without centering, spurious correlation is introduced between the higher-order terms and the main effects. Centering improves the interpretability of the parameters, the meaningfulness of the tests, and the accuracy of the numerics.

To see this, examine the scatterplot matrix in Figure 5.3. It shows the correlations among the variables Age, Weight, and Age*Weight from the Fish29.jmp data table.

*Table 5.1* Fish Data

| Age | Temp 25 | Temp 27 | Temp 29 | Temp 31 |
|---|---|---|---|---|
| 14 | 620 | 625 | 590 | 590 |
| 21 | 910 | 820 | 910 | 910 |
| 28 | 1315 | 1215 | 1305 | 1205 |
| 35 | 1635 | 1515 | 1730 | 1605 |
| 42 | 2120 | 2110 | 2140 | 1915 |
| 49 | 2300 | 2320 | 2725 | 2035 |
| 56 | 2600 | 2805 | 2890 | 2140 |
| 63 | 2925 | 2940 | 3685 | 2520 |
| 70 | 3110 | 3255 | 3920 | 2710 |
| 77 | 3315 | 3620 | 4325 | 2870 |
| 84 | 3535 | 4015 | 4410 | 3020 |
| 91 | 3710 | 4235 | 4485 | 3025 |
| 98 | 3935 | 4315 | 4515 | 3030 |
| 105 | 4145 | 4435 | 4480 | 3025 |
| 112 | 4465 | 4495 | 4520 | 3040 |
| 119 | 4510 | 4475 | 4545 | 3177 |
| 126 | 4530 | 4535 | 4525 | 3180 |
| 133 | 4545 | 4520 | 4560 | 3180 |
| 140 | 4570 | 4600 | 4565 | 3257 |
| 147 | 4605 | 4600 | 4626 | 3166 |
| 154 | 4600 | 4600 | 4566 | 3214 |

Note the strong correlation between Age and Age*Length. It appears to be quite strongly positive. After each variable is standardized, a scatterplot matrix of the same relationships looks quite different (Figure 5.4).

Centered values show the true correlation relationship (weakly negative). For this reason, JMP centers interaction terms by default. It can be removed using either of the following methods.

*Polynomial Models with One Independent Variable* **143**

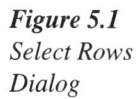

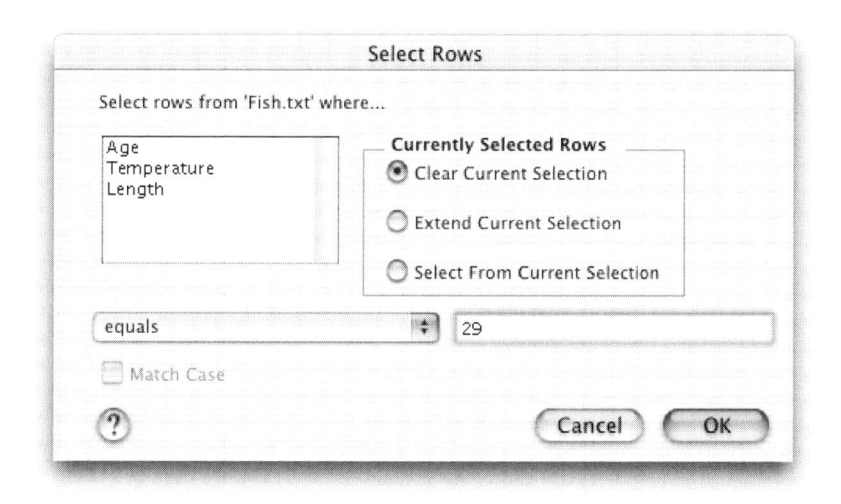

**Figure 5.1**
*Select Rows Dialog*

**Figure 5.2**
*Subset of Fish Data Set*

| Age | Temperature | Length |
|---|---|---|
| 14 | 29 | 590 |
| 21 | 29 | 910 |
| 28 | 29 | 1305 |
| 35 | 29 | 1730 |
| 42 | 29 | 2140 |
| 49 | 29 | 2725 |
| 56 | 29 | 2890 |
| 63 | 29 | 3685 |
| 70 | 29 | 3920 |
| 77 | 29 | 4325 |
| 84 | 29 | 4410 |
| 91 | 29 | 4485 |
| 98 | 29 | 4515 |
| 105 | 29 | 4480 |
| 112 | 29 | 4520 |
| 119 | 29 | 4545 |
| 126 | 29 | 4525 |
| 133 | 29 | 4560 |
| 140 | 29 | 4565 |
| 147 | 29 | 4626 |
| 154 | 29 | 4566 |

❏ In Fit Y by X, select **Fit Special** from the platform pop-up menu after the scatterplot appears. Uncheck the **Centered Polynomial** checkbox in the dialog that appears.

❏ In Fit Model, uncheck the **Center Polynomials** menu selection from the pop-up menu in the Fit Model launch dialog.

Note the essential difference between the two platforms. In Fit Y by X, centering is altered after the report is produced. In Fit Model, it is altered in the launch dialog.

**144** *Polynomial and Smoothing Models*

*Figure 5.3*
*Uncentered* Age *and* Weight *Data*

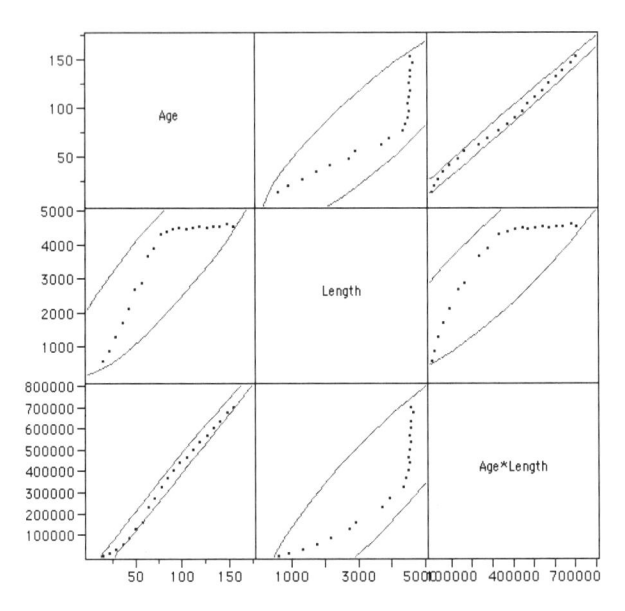

*Figure 5.4*
*Centered* Age *and* Weight *Data*

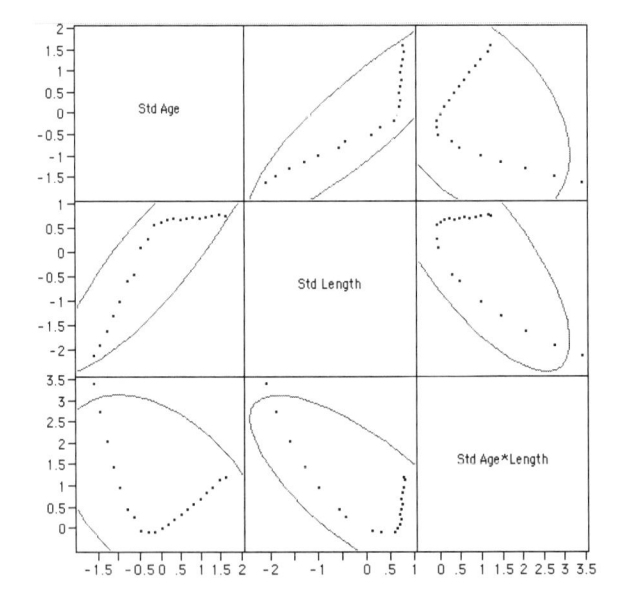

## 5.2.2 Analysis Using Fit Y by X

With only one independent variable, Fit Y by X is an obvious option for analysis of the Fish29 data. It provides a quick and interactive method of trying several models to see which one fits the best. However, it does not contain all the traditional diagnostic statistics that are contained in the Fit Model platform, and it is not an option when more than one factor is in the model. Therefore, a similar analysis to this is presented in the section "Analysis Using Fit Model" on page 148.

First,

- Select **Analyze → Fit Y by X**.
- Select Length in the variable list and click the **Y, Response** button.
- Select Age and click the **X, Factor** button.
- Click **OK**.

A scatterplot of Length by Age appears, as in Figure 5.5.

*Figure 5.5*
*Scatterplot of*
Length *by* Age

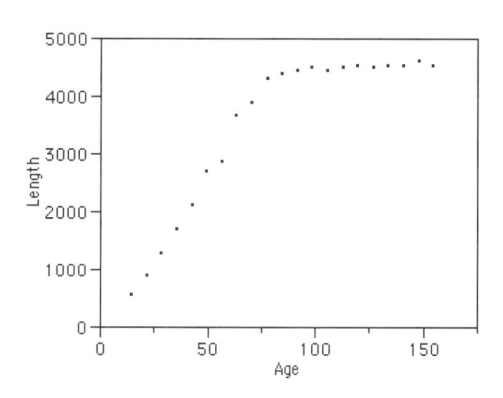

There is an obvious curvature to the data, so a polynomial model is justified. You should try several degrees of polyomials to examine their fits.

- Select **Fit Line** from the platform pop-up menu located in the top-left corner of the report.
- Select **Fit Polynomial → 2, quadratic** from the platform pop-up menu.
- Repeat this process for third- and fourth-degree polynomials.

## 146 *Polynomial and Smoothing Models*

The graphical portion of the output is shown in Figure 5.6.

**Figure 5.6**
*Several Fits*

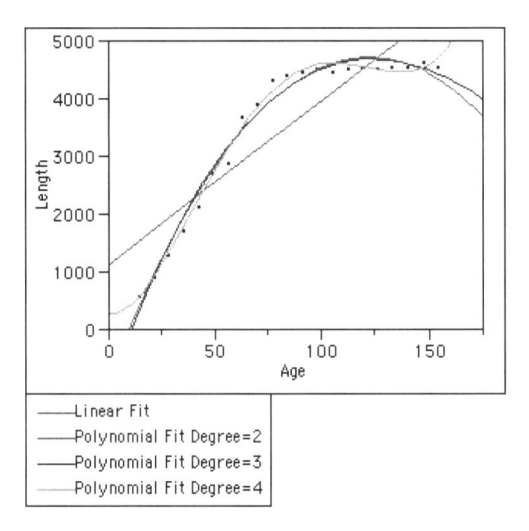

Examine the text reports below the fits. The linear and polynomial models show all their terms as significant. The cubic model shows that its cubic term is not significant ($p = 0.3507$).

The output from the fourth-degree polynomial is shown in Figure 5.7.

The *F* ratio shows that the overall model is significant ($p < 0.001$). The $R^2$ shows a good match between the fit and the model. Also, the *p* value of the fourth-degree term (found in the Parameter Estimates portion of the report) is significant at $p < 0.0001$.

Note that all terms above the first degree are centered. Although it is possible to get an uncentered model (using Fit Special), the centered model makes all the *p* values interpretable.

It may be useful to remove the lower-order fits to compare the cubic and quartic curves.

- From the pop-up menu beside **Linear Fit** and **Polynomial Fit Degree=2**, select **Remove Fit**.

This plot (Figure 5.8) clearly shows the limited improvement due to the cubic and fourth-degree terms. In fact, the fourth-order polynomial curve shows a peculiar hook at the upper end that is not typical of growth curves. Of course, the quadratic curve shows negative growth in this region, so it is also unsatisfactory. In

**Figure 5.7**
*Fourth-Degree Polynomial Output*

**Polynomial Fit Degree=4**

Length = 2161.5789 + 26.129248 Age − 0.6766749 (Age−84)^2 + 0.000686 (Age−84)^3 + 0.0000663 (Age−84)^4

**Summary of Fit**

| | |
|---|---|
| RSquare | 0.994508 |
| RSquare Adj | 0.993135 |
| Root Mean Square Error | 114.9017 |
| Mean of Response | 3524.619 |
| Observations (or Sum Wgts) | 21 |

**Analysis of Variance**

| Source | DF | Sum of Squares | Mean Square | F Ratio |
|---|---|---|---|---|
| Model | 4 | 38250790 | 9562698 | 724.3145 |
| Error | 16 | 211239 | 13202 | Prob > F |
| C. Total | 20 | 38462029 | | <.0001 |

**Parameter Estimates**

| Term | Estimate | Std Error | t Ratio | Prob>\|t\| |
|---|---|---|---|---|
| Intercept | 2161.5789 | 133.8503 | 16.15 | <.0001 |
| Age | 26.129248 | 1.490789 | 17.53 | <.0001 |
| (Age−84)^2 | −0.676675 | 0.055759 | −12.14 | <.0001 |
| (Age−84)^3 | 0.000686 | 0.000424 | 1.62 | 0.1255 |
| (Age−84)^4 | 0.0000663 | 0.000012 | 5.68 | <.0001 |

**Figure 5.8**
*Cubic and Quartic Graphs*

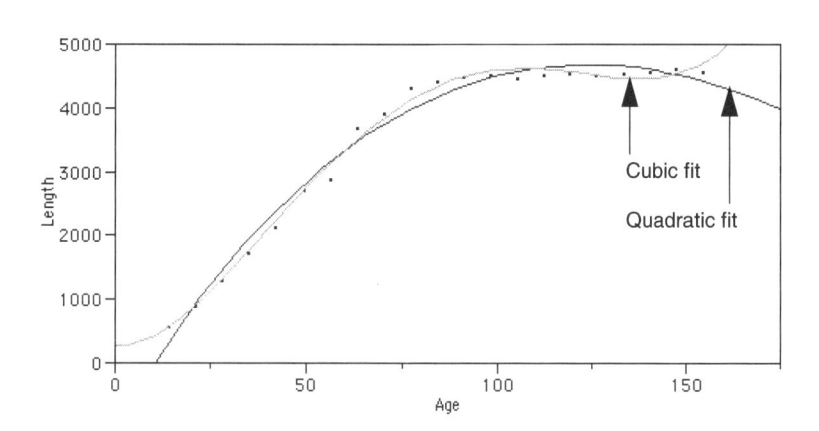

other words, the polynomial model may be unsatisfactory for this data set. Alternate models for use with this data set are presented in "Estimating the Exponential Decay Model" on page 216.

Another method of checking the appropriateness of a model is to plot the residual values. The plot of residual values from the quartic polynomial is obtained by the following:

🖰 From the pop-up menu beside **Polynomial Fit Degree=4**, select **Plot Residuals**.

The resulting plot, which appears in Figure 5.9, shows a systematic pattern that is typical of residual plots when the specified degree of polynomial is inadequate. In this case, the W-shaped pattern is due to the fourth-degree term, which was statistically significant.

*Figure 5.9 Plot of Residuals from Quadratic Model*

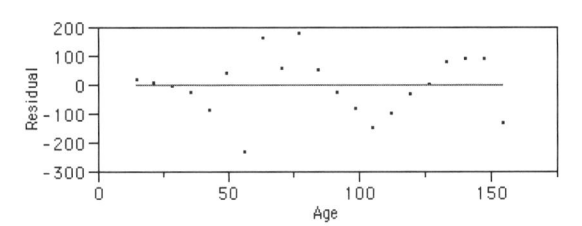

### 5.2.3 Analysis Using Fit Model

A similar analysis can be accomplished with the Fit Model platform. Although it is less interactive graphically, it allows for deeper investigation of the model than Fit Y by X and has several features that Fit Y by X does not.

Again using the subset of the original data,

- Select **Analyze → Fit Model**.
- Select Length from the list of variables and click the **Y** button.
- Select Age from the variables list.
- In the **Degree** box, enter 4.
- From the **Macros** drop-down list, select **Polynomial to Degree**.

The model now has the dependent variable Length as a model of Age, Age*Age, Age*Age*Age, and Age*Age*Age*Age (Figure 5.10).

- Click **Run Model**.
- When the model appears, Select **Estimates → Sequential Tests**.

Partial output is shown in Figure 5.11.

Numbers have been added to Figure 5.11 for the following points.

1. The test for the entire model is statistically significant since the $p$ value for the test for Model is less than 0.0001. The large value for the coefficient of determination (Rsquare) is 0.9945, showing that the model accounts for a

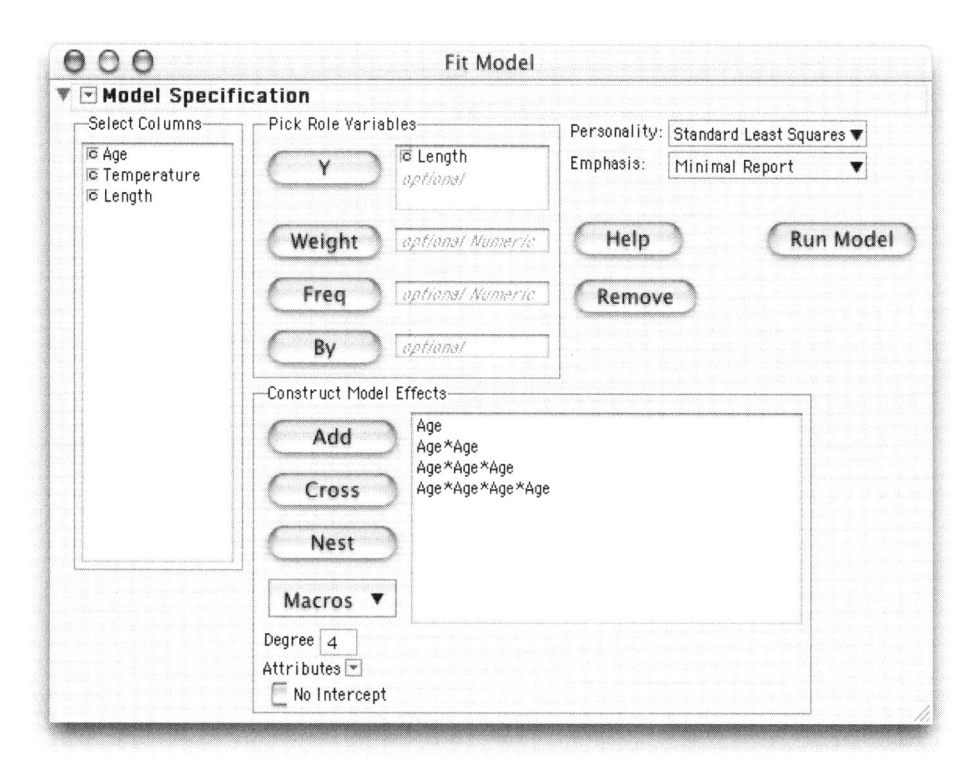

*Figure 5.10* Fit Model Dialog for the Fish Example

large portion of the variation in fish lengths. The residual standard deviation (Root Mean Square Error) is 114.9, indicating how well the fourth-degree polynomial curve fits the data.

2. The Sequential sums of squares are used to determine what order of polynomial model is really needed. The Sequential (Type 1) Tests give the contribution to the model SS for each independent variable as it is added to the model in the order listed in the Fit Model dialog (see "Sequential and Partial: Two Types of Sums of Squares" on page 41). Since there is only one degree of freedom, dividing these sequential sums of squares by the residual mean square provides $F$ statistics that are used to test whether these additional contributions to the regression sum of squares justify addition of the corresponding terms to the model.

In this example, the sequential sum of squares for the linear regression on Age is 30305600; dividing by the residual mean square of 13202 gives an $F$ ratio of 2295.46, which clearly establishes that adding the Age term makes a

**Figure 5.11**
*Partial Output from Fit Model*

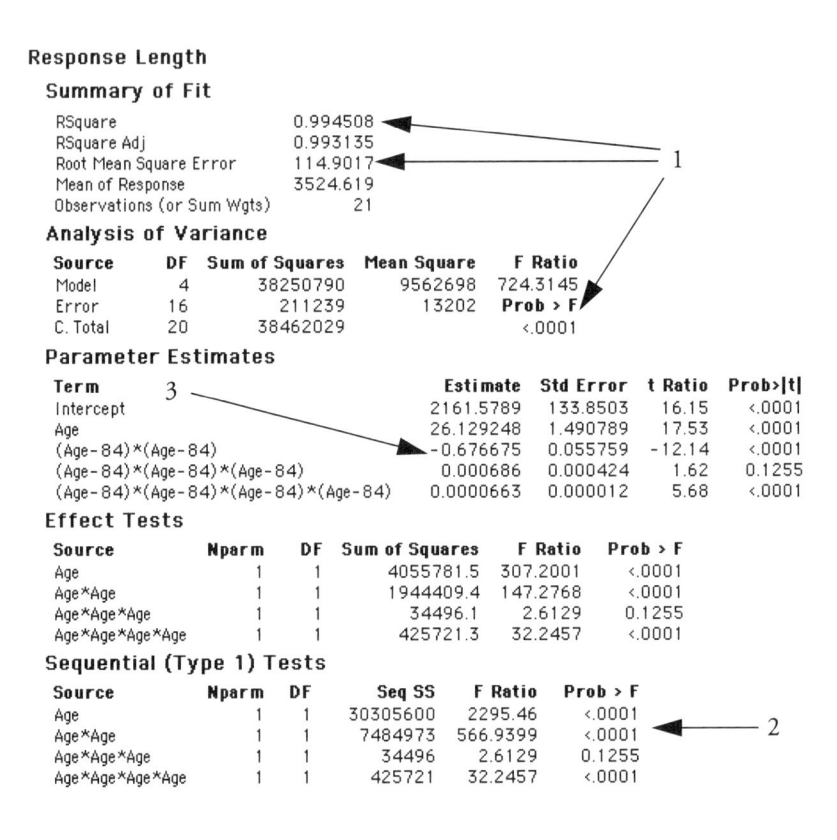

**Response Length**

**Summary of Fit**

| | |
|---|---|
| RSquare | 0.994508 |
| RSquare Adj | 0.993135 |
| Root Mean Square Error | 114.9017 |
| Mean of Response | 3524.619 |
| Observations (or Sum Wgts) | 21 |

⟵ 1

**Analysis of Variance**

| Source | DF | Sum of Squares | Mean Square | F Ratio |
|---|---|---|---|---|
| Model | 4 | 38250790 | 9562698 | 724.3145 |
| Error | 16 | 211239 | 13202 | Prob > F |
| C. Total | 20 | 38462029 | | <.0001 |

**Parameter Estimates**

| Term  3 | Estimate | Std Error | t Ratio | Prob>\|t\| |
|---|---|---|---|---|
| Intercept | 2161.5789 | 133.8503 | 16.15 | <.0001 |
| Age | 26.129248 | 1.490789 | 17.53 | <.0001 |
| (Age-84)*(Age-84) | -0.676675 | 0.055759 | -12.14 | <.0001 |
| (Age-84)*(Age-84)*(Age-84) | 0.000686 | 0.000424 | 1.62 | 0.1255 |
| (Age-84)*(Age-84)*(Age-84)*(Age-84) | 0.0000663 | 0.000012 | 5.68 | <.0001 |

**Effect Tests**

| Source | Nparm | DF | Sum of Squares | F Ratio | Prob > F |
|---|---|---|---|---|---|
| Age | 1 | 1 | 4055781.5 | 307.2001 | <.0001 |
| Age*Age | 1 | 1 | 1944409.4 | 147.2768 | <.0001 |
| Age*Age*Age | 1 | 1 | 34496.1 | 2.6129 | 0.1255 |
| Age*Age*Age*Age | 1 | 1 | 425721.3 | 32.2457 | <.0001 |

**Sequential (Type 1) Tests**

| Source | Nparm | DF | Seq SS | F Ratio | Prob > F |
|---|---|---|---|---|---|
| Age | 1 | 1 | 30305600 | 2295.46 | <.0001 |
| Age*Age | 1 | 1 | 7484973 | 566.9399 | <.0001 | ⟵ 2
| Age*Age*Age | 1 | 1 | 34496 | 2.6129 | 0.1255 |
| Age*Age*Age*Age | 1 | 1 | 425721 | 32.2457 | <.0001 |

better model than one without the **Age** term. The additional contribution of the quadratic term, designated **Age*Age**, is 7484973, and the $F$ ratio is 566.9. Therefore, the addition of this term can be justified. The $F$ ratio for adding the cubic term is 2.61. This is not statistically significant, so the inclusion of this term cannot be justified. Nevertheless, you can continue to check for additional terms. The $F$ ratio for adding the fourth-degree term is 32.25, which is significant, providing evidence that this term should be included. You could, of course, continue if you had specified a higher-order polynomial in the Fit Model statement. However, polynomials beyond the fourth degree are not often used.

3. In this example, the estimated equation, obtained from the portion of the output labeled **Parameter Estimate**, is

$$\text{Length} = 2161.6 + 26.12(\text{Age}) - 0.67(\text{Age} - 84)^2 + 0.000686(\text{Age} - 84)^3 + 0.00007(\text{Age} - 84)^4$$

As noted, the polynomial model is only used to approximate a curve. Therefore, the individual polynomial terms have no practical interpretation and the remainder of the statistics for the coefficients are of little interest.

A residual plot (Figure 5.12) is obtained as follows:

- Select **Row Diagnostics** → **Plot Residual by Row**.
- Select **Row Diagnostics** → **Plot Residual by Predicted**.

Their interpretation is the same as that in the Fit Y by X analysis.

*Figure 5.12*
*Fit Model*
*Residual Plot*

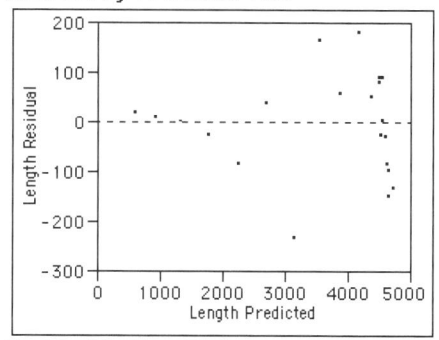

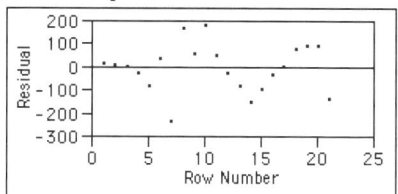

## 5.3 Polynomial Models with Several Variables

Polynomial models with several variables contain terms involving powers of the various variables, and can include cross-products among these variables. The cross-product terms measure interactions among the effects of the variables. For example, consider the two-variable model:

$$y = \beta_0 + \beta_1 x_1 + \beta_2 x_2 + \beta_{12} x_1 x_2$$

The coefficient $\beta_{12}$ indicates how the linear effect of $x_1$ is affected by $x_2$, or vice versa. This is apparent in the following rearrangement of terms:

$$y = \beta_0 + (\beta_1 + \beta_{12}x_2)x_1 + \beta_2 x_2$$

The coefficient $\beta_{12}$ specifies how the linear effect of $x_1$ changes with $x_2$. This change is linear in $x_2$. This effect is referred to as the *linear-by-linear interaction*. The interaction effect is symmetric since it also shows how the linear coefficient in $x_2$ is affected by $x_1$. Cross-products involving higher-order terms have equivalent connotations, although their interpretation might become more difficult.

One consequence of the greater complexity of models with polynomials in several variables is that the sequential sums of squares are no longer useful in selecting the appropriate degree of model. Likewise, the partial sums of squares (shown by default) are of little use since, as was the case for one-variable models, it is not customary to omit lower-order terms. A similar restriction also applies to cross-product terms. In fact, JMP automatically deletes any interaction terms from the Fit Model dialog when their corresponding main effect is deleted. If a cross-product of two linear terms has been included, you should include the individual linear terms. In such models, the following questions are of primary interest:

❑ Does the entire model help to explain the behavior of the response variable?

❑ Are all factors or variables needed?

❑ Is there a need for quadratic and higher-order terms?

❑ Is there a need for cross-product terms?

❑ Is the model adequate?

Obviously, the statistics supplied by a single run of a regression model cannot answer all of these questions.

Since polynomial models with several variables can easily become extremely cumbersome and consequently difficult to interpret, it is common practice to restrict the degree of polynomial terms to be used for such models. The most frequently used model of this type is called the *quadratic response surface model*, in which the maximum total exponent of any term is two. In other words, this model includes all linear and quadratic terms in the individual variables and all pairwise cross-products of linear terms.

The Fit Model platform is used for building and evaluating such a quadratic response surface model. The implementation of this procedure for estimating the response surface regression is illustrated by estimating the quadratic response surface regression relating the Length of fish to Age and Temperature using the data in Figure 5.2 on page 143.

The procedure is implemented with the following steps.

- Bring the original **Fish** data to the front by clicking on their window or using the **Window** menu.
- Select **Analyze → Fit Model**.
- Select **Length** from the list of variables and click the **Y** button.
- Select both **Age** and **Temperature** from the list of variables. (Shift-click one variable name, then the other, to select them both.)
- Click the **Macros** drop-down list and select **Response Surface** from the menu that appears.

The dialog should appear as in Figure 5.13.

*Figure 5.13* Fit Model for Response Surface

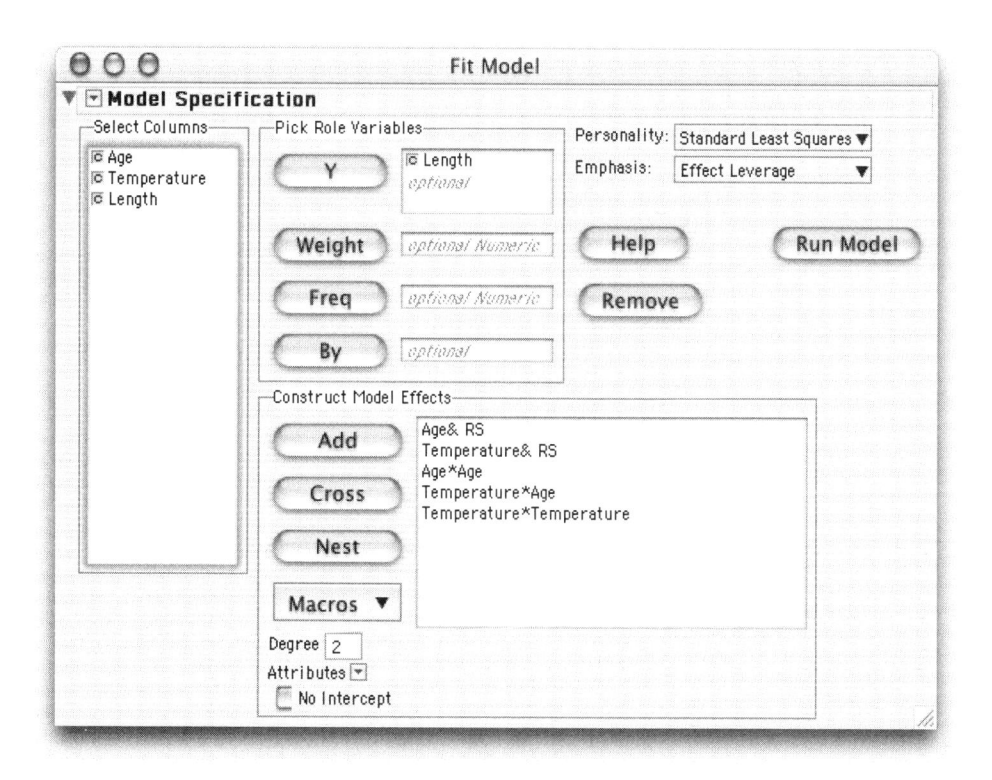

**154** *Polynomial and Smoothing Models*

Note that JMP appends &RS to the names of the main effect variables. This shows that they are response surface effects. Extra output for the response surface is appended to the report that appears when Run Model is clicked.

For this example, the regression model estimated by the procedure is

$$\text{Length} = \beta_0 + \beta_1(\text{Age}) + \beta_2(\text{Temperature}) + \beta_3(\text{Age}-\overline{\text{Age}})^2 + \beta_4(\text{Temperature}-\overline{\text{Age}})(\text{Age}) + \beta_5(\text{Temperature}-\overline{\text{Age}})^2$$

🖱 Click **Run Model**.

The results of implementing Fit Model on the fish data appear in Figure 5.14.

Because the interpretation of results from the search for the optimum response may be affected by the scales of measurement of the factor variables, the scales are centered to have maximum and minimum values of +1 and –1 for the computations required for this procedure. However, all of the statistics in the output are, except where noted, converted to the original scales.

The numbers next to the arrows in Figure 5.14 have been added to key the descriptions that follow:

1. The *F* ratio of 385.39 indicates a statistically significant model, which is supported by an $R^2$ of 0.96.

2. Because response surface analysis is sometimes performed to obtain information on optimum estimated response, JMP also supplies information to assist in determining if the estimated response surface exhibits such an optimum. First, the partial derivatives of the estimated response surface equation are calculated and a critical point is found. The factors for the stationary point are given in the Variable column, and the estimated response at this point is denoted as Predicted Value at Solution. For this example, the stationary points are Age = 138.3 and Temperature = 26.5, where the estimated response is 4762.4. JMP checks to see if these values are in the range of data, and prints a message when they are not. Because the stationary point may be a maximum, minimum, or saddle point, a canonical analysis is performed to ascertain which of these it is. In this case, the point is a maximum. The eigenvalues and eigenvectors required for the analysis might yield additional information about the shape of the response surface (Myers 1976).

Additional statistics on the output include some overall descriptive measures, the residual sum of squares, and the mean square.

Parameter estimates from the centered data are shown by default in the Scaled Estimates report (unless Minimal Report is selected as the Emphasis in the Fit Model dialog). If they are not showing, they can be displayed.

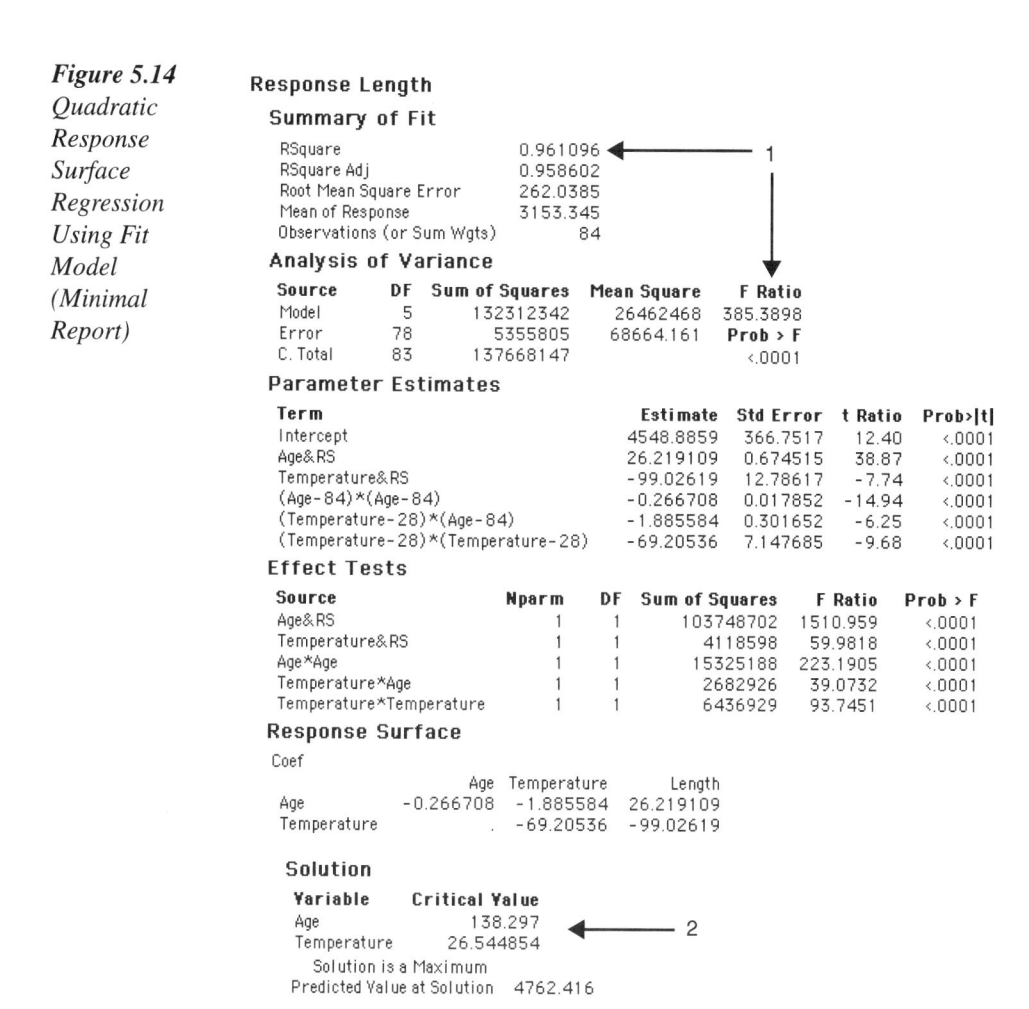

*Figure 5.14*
*Quadratic Response Surface Regression Using Fit Model (Minimal Report)*

**Response Length**

**Summary of Fit**

| | |
|---|---|
| RSquare | 0.961096 |
| RSquare Adj | 0.958602 |
| Root Mean Square Error | 262.0385 |
| Mean of Response | 3153.345 |
| Observations (or Sum Wgts) | 84 |

← 1

**Analysis of Variance**

| Source | DF | Sum of Squares | Mean Square | F Ratio |
|---|---|---|---|---|
| Model | 5 | 132312342 | 26462468 | 385.3898 |
| Error | 78 | 5355805 | 68664.161 | Prob > F |
| C. Total | 83 | 137668147 | | <.0001 |

**Parameter Estimates**

| Term | Estimate | Std Error | t Ratio | Prob>|t| |
|---|---|---|---|---|
| Intercept | 4548.8859 | 366.7517 | 12.40 | <.0001 |
| Age&RS | 26.219109 | 0.674515 | 38.87 | <.0001 |
| Temperature&RS | -99.02619 | 12.78617 | -7.74 | <.0001 |
| (Age-84)*(Age-84) | -0.266708 | 0.017852 | -14.94 | <.0001 |
| (Temperature-28)*(Age-84) | -1.885584 | 0.301652 | -6.25 | <.0001 |
| (Temperature-28)*(Temperature-28) | -69.20536 | 7.147685 | -9.68 | <.0001 |

**Effect Tests**

| Source | Nparm | DF | Sum of Squares | F Ratio | Prob > F |
|---|---|---|---|---|---|
| Age&RS | 1 | 1 | 103748702 | 1510.959 | <.0001 |
| Temperature&RS | 1 | 1 | 4118598 | 59.9818 | <.0001 |
| Age*Age | 1 | 1 | 15325188 | 223.1905 | <.0001 |
| Temperature*Age | 1 | 1 | 2682926 | 39.0732 | <.0001 |
| Temperature*Temperature | 1 | 1 | 6436929 | 93.7451 | <.0001 |

**Response Surface**

Coef

| | Age | Temperature | Length |
|---|---|---|---|
| Age | -0.266708 | -1.885584 | 26.219109 |
| Temperature | . | -69.20536 | -99.02619 |

**Solution**

| Variable | Critical Value | |
|---|---|---|
| Age | 138.297 | ← 2 |
| Temperature | 26.544854 | |

Solution is a Maximum
Predicted Value at Solution  4762.416

🖱 From the platform pop-up menu, select **Effect Screening → Scaled Estimates**.

The results are shown in Figure 5.15. However, as before, the statistics for the lower-order terms are not particularly useful.

*Figure 5.15 Scaled Estimates*

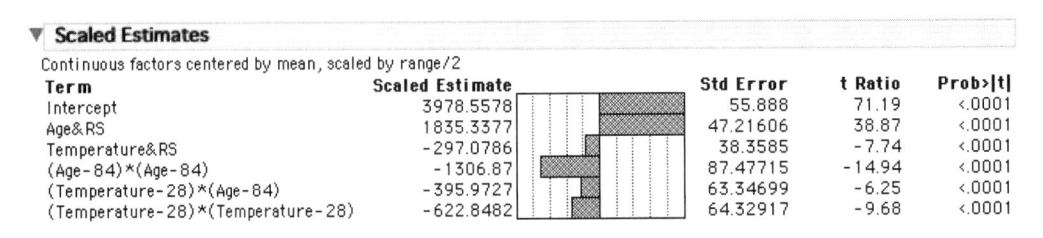

**Scaled Estimates**

Continuous factors centered by mean, scaled by range/2

| Term | Scaled Estimate | Std Error | t Ratio | Prob>|t| |
|---|---|---|---|---|
| Intercept | 3978.5578 | 55.888 | 71.19 | <.0001 |
| Age&RS | 1835.3377 | 47.21606 | 38.87 | <.0001 |
| Temperature&RS | -297.0786 | 38.3585 | -7.74 | <.0001 |
| (Age-84)*(Age-84) | -1306.87 | 87.47715 | -14.94 | <.0001 |
| (Temperature-28)*(Age-84) | -395.9727 | 63.34699 | -6.25 | <.0001 |
| (Temperature-28)*(Temperature-28) | -622.8482 | 64.32917 | -9.68 | <.0001 |

## 5.4 Response Surface Plots

As in the case of a one-variable polynomial regression, graphic representations can be used to show the nature of the estimated curve. For multidimensional polynomial regressions, such plots are called *response surface plots*. A popular plot of this type is a *contour plot*, in which contours of equal response are plotted for a grid of values of the independent variables. Such a plot may be obtained using the Fit Model platform. Also available are three-dimensional mesh plot representations.

As an example of a response surface plot, a plot is made for the estimated quadratic response surface for the fish lengths produced in the previous section. In addition, a residual plot might be useful for investigating specification error or detecting possible outliers.

The residual plot is part of the standard output of the Fit Model platform when Effect Leverage is selected as the Emphasis of the model. If the plot is not showing,

- Select **Row Diagnostics** → **Plot Residual by Predicted**.

The results are shown in Figure 5.16. To add the Contour Profiler, which contains a contour plot and a three-dimensional mesh plot of the surface (Figure 5.17),

- Select **Factor Profiling** → **Contour Profiler**.

The two-dimensional contour is shown on the left with large crosshairs traversing it. The Age and Temperature values at this point have a predicted value, shown below Current Y. These crosshairs can be adjusted by dragging the horizontal and vertical lines that make the crosshairs, or by clicking and dragging the intersection of the crosshairs. The value below Current Y changes to reflect the new positions. Alternatively, the sliders next to Age and Temperature at the top of the plot can be used to maneuver the crosshairs. Finally, values can be directly typed into the boxes listed below Current X at the top of the plot.

**Figure 5.16**
*Residual Plot*

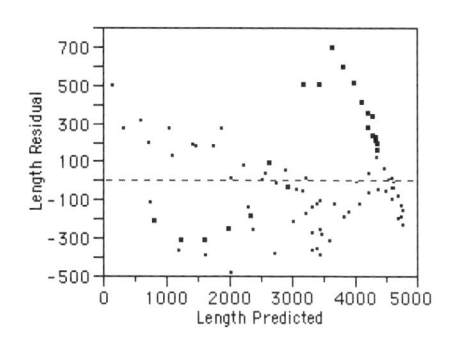

**Figure 5.17**
*Contour Profiler*

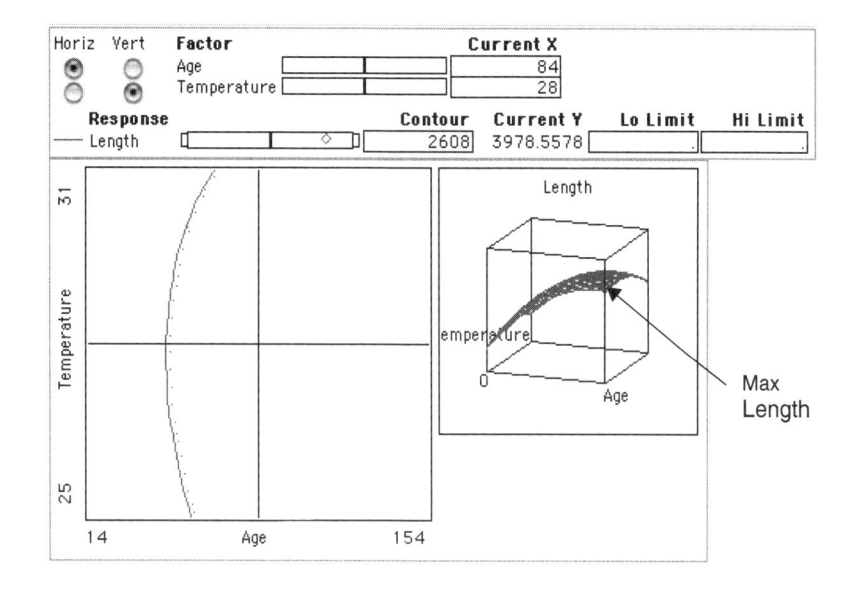

The value of the contour can be adjusted with the slider next to Length listed below Response. The level of the contour is shown below the Contour heading.

To see a grid of values of the contour (rather than the single contour that shows by default),

- Select **Contour Grid** from the platform pop-up menu on the title bar of the Contour Profiler.

- Select Length in the **Specify Response** dialog that appears.

158  *Polynomial and Smoothing Models*

- Another dialog appears that allows specification of the limits and increment of the contours. Accept the default values for now.
- Click **OK** in the **Specify Grid Of Contour Values** dialog.

This addition results in the display in Figure 5.18. Several values of the contour are specified. Dots on one side of the line show increasing values of the response Length.

***Figure 5.18***
*Contour Grid*

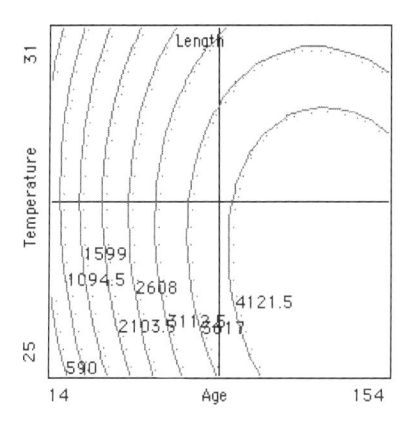

A three-dimensional representation of the response surface is shown at the right of the contour plot.

- Click and drag inside this plot to rotate it and see various views of the surface.

The plot shows the growth of fish with age and temperature. Note, however, that the growth becomes negative with increasing age. The plot also shows that fish grow faster at temperatures of 26 to 28 degrees Celsius.

## 5.5  A Three-Factor Response Surface Experiment

The data for this example come from an experiment concerning a device for automatically shelling peanuts. Dickens and Mason (1962) state that

❑ peanuts flow through stationary sheller bars and rest on the grid, which has perforations just large enough to pass shelled kernels. The grid is reciprocated, and the resulting forces on the peanuts between the moving grid and the stationary bars break open the hulls.

❏ the problem became one of determining the combination of bar grid spacing, length of stroke, and frequency of stroke that would produce the most satisfactory performance.

The performance criteria are

❏ kernel damage

❏ shelling time

❏ unshelled peanuts.

The paper cited above describes three separate experiments; the second one is used for this illustration. The experimental design is a three-factor central composite design consisting of 15 points, with 5 additional observations at the center point (Myers 1976). The data consist of responses resulting from the shelling of 1000 grams of peanuts. The factors of the experiment are the following:

| | |
|---|---|
| Length | length of stroke (inches) |
| Freq | frequency of stroke (strokes per minute) |
| Space | bar grid spacing (inches). |

The response variables are the following:

| | |
|---|---|
| Time | time needed to shell 1000 grams of peanuts (minutes) |
| Unshelled | unshelled peanuts (grams) |
| Damaged | damaged peanuts (percent). |

Figure 5.19 shows the peanut sheller data.

The experimenters want to minimize Time, Unshelled, and Damaged. This criterion can be specified for each data column that is a response variable. The following directions take advantage of a JMP command that allows the specification of more than one variable's attributes at a time. To specify this minimization criterion for the three columns,

🖱 Select the Time, Unshelled, and Damaged columns in the data table.

🖱 Select **Cols → Standardize Attributes**.

🖱 Click the **Column Property** button and select **Response Limits** from the drop-down list.

🖱 In the **Response Limits** dialog that appears, change the **Maximize** setting to **Minimize**.

🖱 Click **OK**.

*Figure 5.19* Peanut.jmp *Data Table*

| Length | Freq | Space | Unshelled | Time | Damaged |
|---|---|---|---|---|---|
| 1 | 175 | 0.86 | 284 | 16 | 3.55 |
| 1.25 | 130 | 0.63 | 149 | 9.25 | 8.23 |
| 1.25 | 130 | 1.09 | 240 | 18 | 3.15 |
| 1.25 | 220 | 0.63 | 155 | 4.75 | 5.26 |
| 1.25 | 220 | 1.09 | 197 | 15.5 | 4.23 |
| 1.75 | 100 | 0.86 | 154 | 13 | 3.54 |
| 1.75 | 175 | 0.48 | 100 | 3.5 | 8.16 |
| 1.75 | 175 | 0.86 | 176 | 7 | 3.27 |
| 1.75 | 175 | 0.86 | 177 | 6.25 | 4.38 |
| 1.75 | 175 | 0.86 | 212 | 6.5 | 3.26 |
| 1.75 | 175 | 0.86 | 200 | 6.5 | 3.57 |
| 1.75 | 175 | 0.86 | 160 | 6.5 | 4.65 |
| 1.75 | 175 | 0.86 | 176 | 6.5 | 4.02 |
| 1.75 | 175 | 1.23 | 195 | 12 | 3.8 |
| 1.75 | 250 | 0.86 | 126 | 5 | 4.05 |
| 2.25 | 130 | 0.63 | 84 | 4 | 9.02 |
| 2.25 | 130 | 1.09 | 145 | 7 | 3 |
| 2.25 | 220 | 0.63 | 97 | 2.25 | 7.41 |
| 2.25 | 220 | 1.09 | 168 | 5.75 | 3.78 |
| 2.5 | 175 | 0.86 | 168 | 3.5 | 3.72 |

Because this experiment has six replications at the center point (observations 8 through 13, where Length=1.75, Freq=175, and Space=0.86), you can obtain an estimate of pure error and consequently perform a test for lack of fit.

Lack of fit is a way of checking how well a regression model fits the data. It tests whether the hypothesized model includes enough terms. If there is a significant lack of fit, the model might need higher-order terms to better explain the data. JMP appends a lack-of-fit report whenever there are replicates in the data. Details of a lack-of-fit test are described below.

For this example, only the variable Unshelled is analyzed. You might want to perform analyses for the other responses and ponder the problem of multiple responses.

- Select **Analyze → Fit Model**.
- Select the Unshelled variable and assign it to the Y role.
- Select Length, Freq, and Space in the variables list.
- Select **Response Surface** from the **Macros** drop-down list.
- Click **Run Model**.

Notice in this report that there is a lack-of-fit report (Figure 5.20). This is because there are replications in the study. JMP computes pure error sum of squares from all observations occurring within identical factor level combinations.

**Figure 5.20**
*Lack-of-Fit Output for* Unshelled

```
Lack Of Fit
Source       DF   Sum of Squares   Mean Square   F Ratio
Lack Of Fit   5       1903.6753       380.735     1.0626
Pure Error    5       1791.5000       358.300     Prob > F
Total Error  10       3695.1753                   0.4742
                                                  Max RSq
                                                  0.9585
```

This sum of squares is subtracted from the residual sum of squares (from the model) to obtain the lack-of-fit sum of squares. This quantity indicates the additional variation that can be explained by adding to the model all additional parameters allowed by the construct of the treatment design. Thus, the ratio of the resulting lack of fit and pure error mean squares provides a test for the possible existence of such additional model terms. In other words, it is a test for the adequacy of the model.

Unshelled's residual sum of squares from the nine-term model is 3695.1753, with 10 degrees of freedom. The pure error is the sum of squares among the six replicated values and has 5 degrees of freedom. The difference, 1903.6753, with 5 degrees of freedom, is the additional sum of squares that could be obtained by adding 5 terms to the model. The $F$ statistic derived from the ratio of the lack of fit to the pure error mean square has a $p$ value of 0.4742. You may conclude that the lack-of-fit test is not significant, so additional Unshelled terms are not needed.

The output for Unshelled appears in Figure 5.21. The output is similar for the other two variables.

The cross-product terms are not significant, indicating that there are no interactions for the Unshelled response. In other words, the responses to any one factor have similar shapes across levels of the other factors. The factor Freq has the smallest effect; in fact, it is not significant at the 0.01 level.

The Response Surface report for Unshelled is shown in Figure 5.22.

The canonical analysis shows that the response surface has a saddle point. This claim means that the response surface has no point at which the response is either maximum or minimum.

Since you are looking for a minimum amount of unshelled peanuts, the existence of a saddle point may be disappointing. Of course, it is possible that the saddle point is not well defined and that a broad range of points may provide a guide for finding optimum operating conditions.

The Contour Profiler may provide insights into the process.

⇨ Select **Factor Profiling** → **Contour Profiler**.

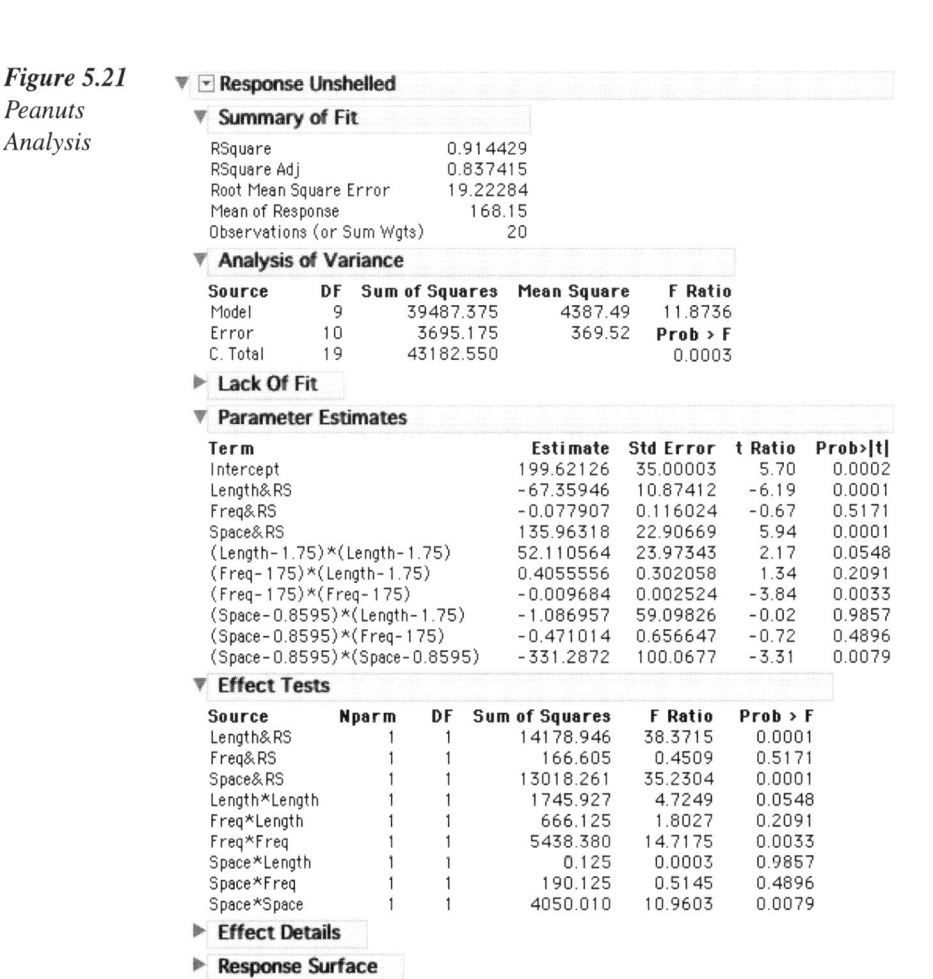

*Figure 5.21*
*Peanuts Analysis*

**Response Unshelled**

**Summary of Fit**

| | |
|---|---|
| RSquare | 0.914429 |
| RSquare Adj | 0.837415 |
| Root Mean Square Error | 19.22284 |
| Mean of Response | 168.15 |
| Observations (or Sum Wgts) | 20 |

**Analysis of Variance**

| Source | DF | Sum of Squares | Mean Square | F Ratio |
|---|---|---|---|---|
| Model | 9 | 39487.375 | 4387.49 | 11.8736 |
| Error | 10 | 3695.175 | 369.52 | Prob > F |
| C. Total | 19 | 43182.550 | | 0.0003 |

▶ **Lack Of Fit**

**Parameter Estimates**

| Term | Estimate | Std Error | t Ratio | Prob>|t| |
|---|---|---|---|---|
| Intercept | 199.62126 | 35.00003 | 5.70 | 0.0002 |
| Length&RS | -67.35946 | 10.87412 | -6.19 | 0.0001 |
| Freq&RS | -0.077907 | 0.116024 | -0.67 | 0.5171 |
| Space&RS | 135.96318 | 22.90669 | 5.94 | 0.0001 |
| (Length-1.75)*(Length-1.75) | 52.110564 | 23.97343 | 2.17 | 0.0548 |
| (Freq-175)*(Length-1.75) | 0.4055556 | 0.302058 | 1.34 | 0.2091 |
| (Freq-175)*(Freq-175) | -0.009684 | 0.002524 | -3.84 | 0.0033 |
| (Space-0.8595)*(Length-1.75) | -1.086957 | 59.09826 | -0.02 | 0.9857 |
| (Space-0.8595)*(Freq-175) | -0.471014 | 0.656647 | -0.72 | 0.4896 |
| (Space-0.8595)*(Space-0.8595) | -331.2872 | 100.0677 | -3.31 | 0.0079 |

**Effect Tests**

| Source | Nparm | DF | Sum of Squares | F Ratio | Prob > F |
|---|---|---|---|---|---|
| Length&RS | 1 | 1 | 14178.946 | 38.3715 | 0.0001 |
| Freq&RS | 1 | 1 | 166.605 | 0.4509 | 0.5171 |
| Space&RS | 1 | 1 | 13018.261 | 35.2304 | 0.0001 |
| Length*Length | 1 | 1 | 1745.927 | 4.7249 | 0.0548 |
| Freq*Length | 1 | 1 | 666.125 | 1.8027 | 0.2091 |
| Freq*Freq | 1 | 1 | 5438.380 | 14.7175 | 0.0033 |
| Space*Length | 1 | 1 | 0.125 | 0.0003 | 0.9857 |
| Space*Freq | 1 | 1 | 190.125 | 0.5145 | 0.4896 |
| Space*Space | 1 | 1 | 4050.010 | 10.9603 | 0.0079 |

▶ **Effect Details**

▶ **Response Surface**

The three-dimensional plot confirms the existence of the saddle point.

In this example, optimum response means lower values of Unshelled. It is not possible to produce a three-factor response surface plot, but you can produce a plot that represents the response curve for two factors for several levels of the third factor. Since there are three different factor combinations for such plots, you must choose which combination is most useful. Often this decision is not easy to make and several possibilities might have to be explored.

It is possible to have all factors and responses appear in a single Contour Profiler.

- Select **Profilers → Contour Profiler** from the drop-down list at the top-level (**Least Squares Fit**) outline node.

*Figure 5.22
Response
Surface
Report*

**Response Surface**

Coef

|        | Length    | Freq      | Space     | Unshelled |
|--------|-----------|-----------|-----------|-----------|
| Length | 52.110564 | 0.4055556 | -1.086957 | -67.35946 |
| Freq   |           | -0.009684 | -0.471014 | -0.077907 |
| Space  |           |           | -331.2872 | 135.96318 |

**Solution**

| Variable | Critical Value |
|----------|----------------|
| Length   | 2.3816281      |
| Freq     | 179.31274      |
| Space    | 1.0606023      |

Solution is a SaddlePoint
Predicted Value at Solution 177.19912

**Canonical Curvature**

Eigenvalues and Eigenvectors

|            |          |          |          |
|------------|----------|----------|----------|
| Eigenvalue | 52.1121  | -0.0103  | -331.288 |
| Length     | 0.99999  | -0.00390 | 0.00142  |
| Freq       | 0.00390  | 0.99999  | 0.00071  |
| Space      | -0.00142 | -0.00070 | 1.00000  |

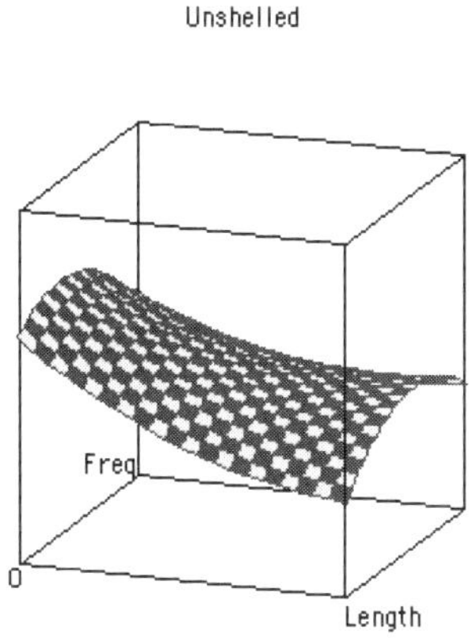

Figure 5.23 appears, showing mesh plots for each of the responses.

To experiment with several levels of the independent variables and see their effect on the responses, use JMP's Prediction Profiler (Figure 5.24). It appears by default in all reports except Minimum Report. If it is not showing,

🖱 Select **Factor Profiling** → **Profiler**.

🖱 When the profiler appears, select **Desirability Functions** from the platform pop-up menu.

*Figure 5.23* Contour Profiler for All Responses

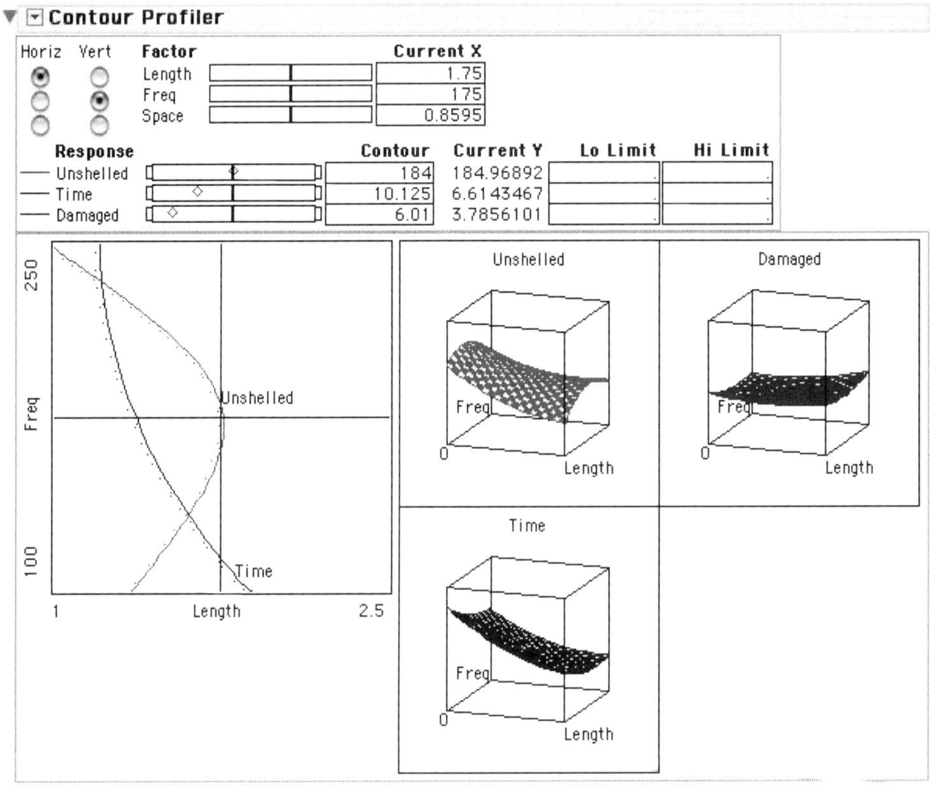

The response variable(s) are listed horizontally; their current levels are in red, above their name. The response variable is plotted on the vertical axis, with its current value printed in red and a horizontal dotted line showing this current value. The desirability profiles that appear to the right side of the plot show, in this case, that each response is to be minimized. These desirability functions would have a different appearance if the value of the response were to be maximized or aimed at a target value. (See the JMP documentation for a complete discussion of desirability profiles.)

Below the response variables, desirability traces appear. There is a desirability trace for each of the factors, with the overall desirability showing on the *Y*-axis. This overall desirability is calculated as the geometric mean of the component desirabilities. Use the desirability traces to get an indication of how to change each factor's values to achieve the desired goal. For example, increasing the value of **Length** increases desirability.

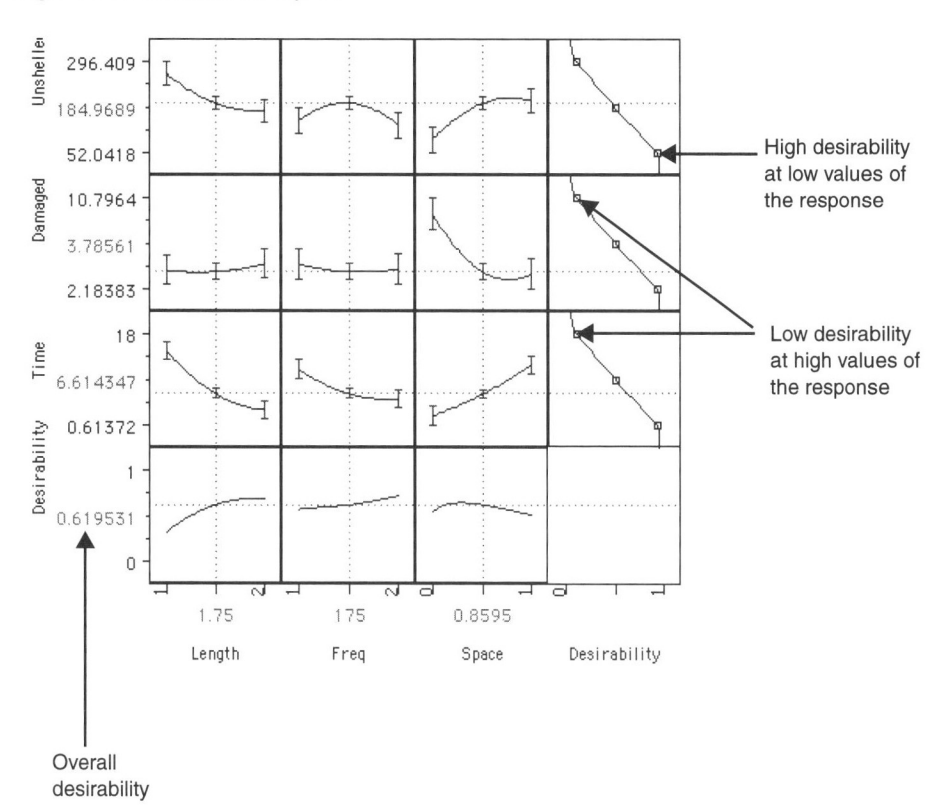

*Figure 5.24* Prediction Profiler

*Figure caption annotations:*
- High desirability at low values of the response
- Low desirability at high values of the response
- Overall desirability

JMP can maximize the desirability functions by selecting Maximize Desirability from the Profiler menu. In this example, JMP must do several series of iterations before it reaches these maximums, so some warnings may appear. The maximized settings appear in Figure 5.25.

To experiment with other values of the factors, drag the horizontal lines to new positions. It appears that increasing Length and decreasing Freq and Space lowers the estimated percent of unshelled peanuts. This hypothesis can be confirmed by experimenting with values in the Contour Profiler, or by requesting a Contour Grid to be added to the contour plot. Grids can be added in contour plots for the individual variables (as in Figure 5.26, which shows the contour for Unshelled) or in the contour plot of all responses.

From these plots you can see that

❑ at low levels, the increase in Freq uniformly increases the percent of unshelled of peanuts by a relatively small amount

**166** *Polynomial and Smoothing Models*

***Figure 5.25***
*Maximized Settings*

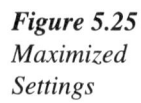

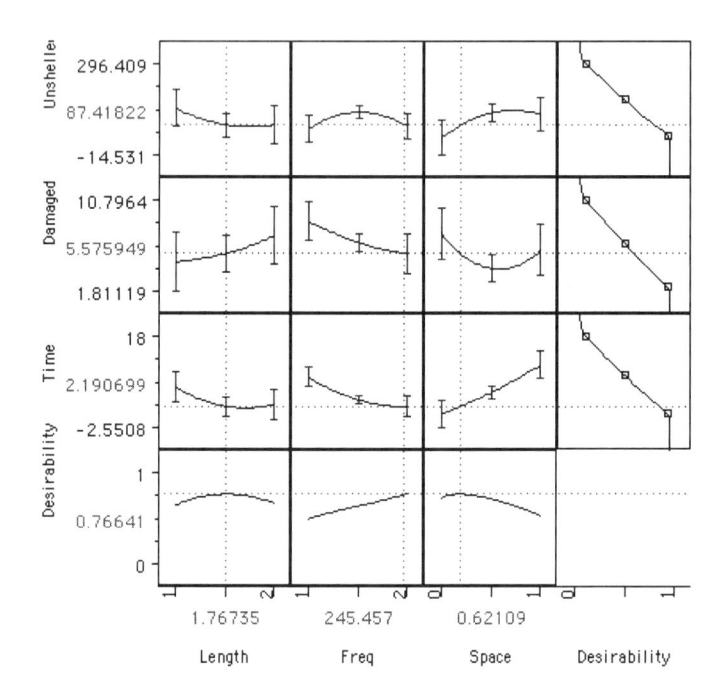

***Figure 5.26***
*Contour Grid for Peanuts Analysis*

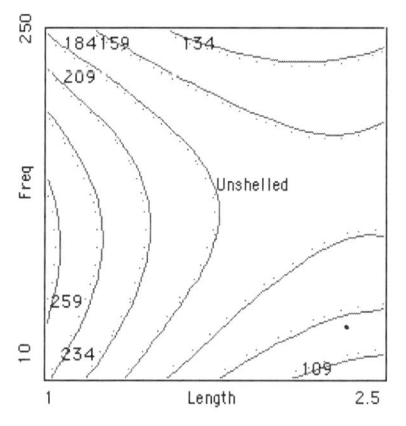

❏ the saddle point is not of interest

❏ the percentage of unshelled peanuts decreases with increasing Length and decreasing Space.

The optimum operating conditions *for unshelled peanuts* should concentrate in regions of higher Freq and Length and lower Space. Optimum conditions that consider all three variables at once should use settings as shown in Figure 5.25.

## 5.6 Smoothing Data

This section provides three methods of smoothing data. These techniques are useful when you are not interested in the form of the underlying model. Both examples are illustrated with data on total exports from the nation of Barbados (export) for the years (year) 1967–1993. The data from the data set Barbexp.jmp are shown in Figure 5.27.

*Figure 5.27*
*Barbados*
*Export Data*

| export | year |
|---|---|
| 53.518 | 1967 |
| 59.649 | 1968 |
| 57.357 | 1969 |
| 62.106 | 1970 |
| 53.182 | 1971 |
| 63.103 | 1972 |
| 83.7 | 1973 |
| 125.555 | 1974 |
| 178.218 | 1975 |
| 137.638 | 1976 |
| 151.055 | 1977 |
| 186.45 | 1978 |
| 232.684 | 1979 |
| 337.291 | 1980 |
| 297.004 | 1981 |
| 372.627 | 1982 |
| 510.165 | 1983 |
| 583.668 | 1984 |
| 496.471 | 1985 |
| 420.614 | 1986 |
| 214.511 | 1987 |
| 248.029 | 1988 |
| 250.35 | 1989 |
| 244.82 | 1990 |
| 241.42 | 1991 |
| 271.384 | 1992 |
| 272.242 | 1993 |

An initial plot of export by year (Figure 5.28) shows some noise in the data. The following techniques smooth the data to eliminate some of this noise.

### 5.6.1 The Moving Average

The moving average approximates or estimates each point of the curve with the mean of a number of adjacent observations. The number of observations to be used is arbitrary: a smaller number gives a better fit, while a larger number gives a smoother curve. For example, values for a five-point centered moving average are obtained as

$$MA_t = (y_{t-2} + y_{t-1} + y_t + y_{t+1} + y_{t+2})/5$$

**Figure 5.28**
*Plot of* export *by* year

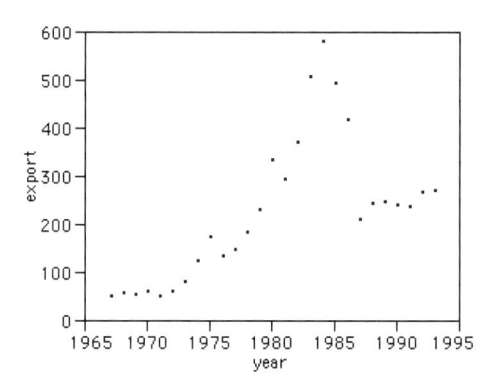

Essentially, this formula looks at a range of two steps ahead and two steps behind each point. To compute moving averages, use the Lag() function in JMP's Formula Editor by completing the following steps.

- Double-click to the right of the last column in the data table to create a new column.
- Name this column Moving Average.
- Right-click (Control-click on the Macintosh) and select **Formula** from the menu that appears.
- From the list of functions, select **Statistical → Mean**.

Since the mean of five columns is to be computed, there need to be five placeholders in the mean function.

- Press the comma (,) key repeatedly to create five placeholders.
- Select the first placeholder, and choose **Row → Lag** from the list of functions.

The lag function takes two arguments: the column it is to take a lagged value of, and the number of periods to lag.

- Select the first argument of the lag() function and click the export column in the columns list.
- Select the second argument in the lag function and enter 2.
- Repeat these steps to fill in the rest of the mean function with lags 1, 0, −1, and −2. Copy and Paste functions are useful in this step.

A lag of 0 indicates the current value, and negative lags look at future values.

The formula should appear as in Figure 5.29.

**Figure 5.29**
*Lag Formula*

$$\text{Mean}\begin{pmatrix} \text{Lag}(export,-2), \\ \text{Lag}(export,-1), \\ \text{Lag}(export,0), \\ \text{Lag}(export,1), \\ \text{Lag}(export,2) \end{pmatrix}$$

- Click **OK** to exit the Formula Editor.

Now, plot the values to see how much the moving average has smoothed the data.

- Select **Graph → Overlay Plot**.
- Assign both export and Moving Average as Y values.
- Assign Year as the X value.

When the plot appears,

- Right-click (Control-click on the Macintosh) on Moving Average in the legend at the bottom of the plot.
- Select **Connect Points** from the menu that appears.
- Repeat the same steps to deselect **Show Points** for the **Moving Average** graph.

The plot should appear as in Figure 5.30.

## 5.6.2 The Time Series Platform

Used for analyzing time series (most of which is beyond the scope of this book), the JMP Time Series platform contains several smoothing methods:

- Simple Exponential Smoothing
- Double (Brown) Exponential Smoothing
- Linear (Holt) Exponential Smoothing
- Damped-Trend Linear Exponential Smoothing
- Seasoned Exponential Smoothing.

**170** *Polynomial and Smoothing Models*

***Figure 5.30**
Moving-
Average Plot*

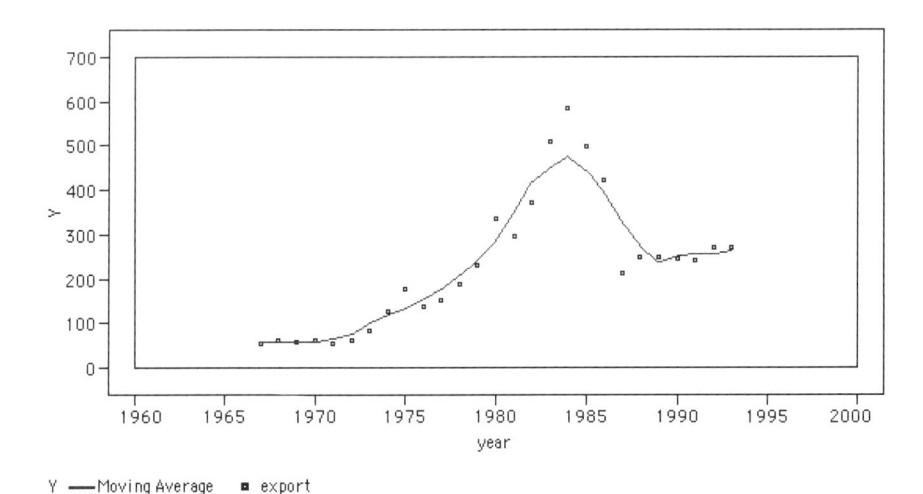

The details of these methods are found in the *JMP Statistics and Graphics Guide*. Simple exponential smoothing is the only one illustrated here.

Simple exponential smoothing fits the model $y_t = \mu_t + a_t$ by smoothing it with the function $L_t = \alpha y_t + (1 - \alpha) L_{t-1}$, where $\alpha$ is the smoothing weight. This is equivalent to fitting the model

$$y_t = \alpha_t + \sum_{j=1}^{\infty} \alpha y_{t-j}$$

This is quite similar to the moving average, except that the value of a row is based on all its lagged values. Each lagged value has a unique weight based on how far in the past it is.

To use this model,

- Select **Analyze → Modeling → Time Series**.
- Specify export as the **Y, Time Series** and Year as the **X, Time ID**.
- Click **OK**.

The Time Series report appears, with a plot of the series and some descriptive statistics and plots.

*Smoothing Data* **171**

- Select **Smoothing Model** → **Simple Exponential Smoothing** from the platform pop-up menu.

- Click **Estimate** on the control panel that appears at the bottom of the report.

A plot of the series and its smoothed values appear, as in Figure 5.31. A vertical line divides known values from forecasts made automatically with the platform.

To save the smoothed values,

- Select **Save Columns** from the platform pop-up menu.

A new data table appears holding the smoothed values, confidence limits, and other values. These values can be cut and pasted into the original data table.

*Figure 5.31*
*Time Series Report*

**Model: Simple Exponential Smoothing**

**Model Summary**

| | |
|---|---|
| DF | 25 |
| Stable | Yes |
| Sum of Squared Errors | 110919.577 |
| Invertible | Yes |
| Variance Estimate | 4436.78306 |
| Standard Deviation | 66.6091815 |
| Akaike's 'A' Information Criterion | 219.320068 |
| Schwarz's Bayesian Criterion | 220.578164 |
| RSquare | 0.79786804 |
| RSquare Adj | 0.79786804 |
| -2LogLikelihood | 217.320068 |

**Parameter Estimates**

| Term | Estimate | Std Error | t Ratio | Prob>|t| |
|---|---|---|---|---|
| Level Smoothing Weight | 1 | 0.1988077 | 5.03 | <.0001 |

**Forecast**

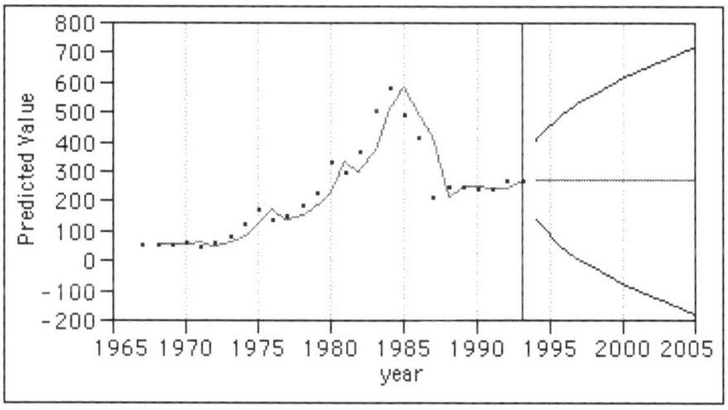

There is far more to the Time Series platform than is shown here (for example, fitting ARIMA and Seasonal ARIMA models). This example is merely to show how the platform can be used as a smoothing device.

### 5.6.3 Smoothing Splines

JMP can fit cubic splines to bivariate data using the Fit Y by X platform. The stiffness of the spline is determined by a parameter $\lambda$, with small values representing flexible splines and large values representing stiff splines. The value of $\lambda$ can be changed interactively, and several spline fits can be fit to compare their prediction power.

To request a spline fit for, say, $\lambda = 1000$,

- Select **Analyze** $\to$ **Fit Y by X**.

- Select export as the Y variable and Year as the X variable.

- Click **OK**.

When the report appears,

- Select **Fit Spline** $\to$ **1000** from the platform pop-up menu.

Results appear like the solid curve shown in Figure 5.32.

*Figure 5.32* Fit Spline Results for Several Values of $\lambda$

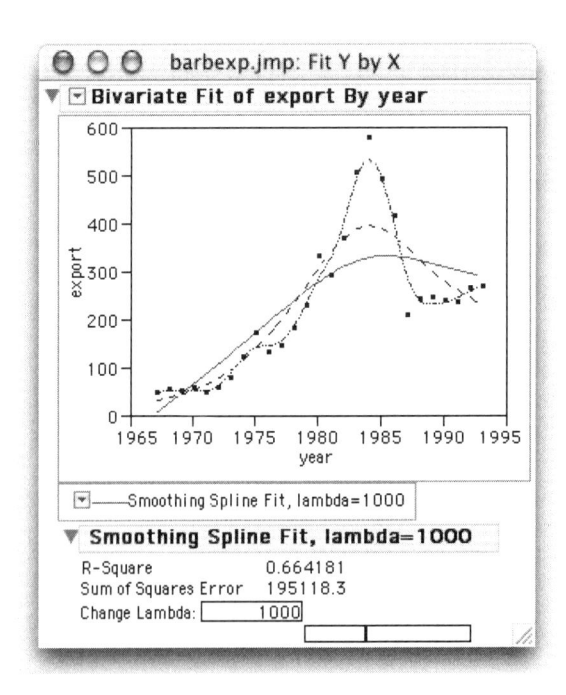

Note the slider that appears below the statistics for the spline fit.

- Click and drag the slider to change the value of $\lambda$ and observe the corresponding change in the curve.

Results that are similar to the moving average are obtained with $\lambda = 10$. There is no hard-and-fast rule that determines what the best spline fit is. You must use your judgment and sense to find a compromise between a smooth-fitting model and the fit to observed values.

To save the predicted values,

- Select **Save Predicteds** from the pop-up menu beside **Smoothing Spline Fit** below the bivariate plot.

## 5.7 Summary

Polynomial models provide reasonable approximations to response models that cannot be described by straight lines. In JMP, they can be analyzed with the Fit Y by X and Fit Model.

An important limitation of polynomial models is that they only provide approximations to a curve, and the model coefficients usually have no practical interpretation. Therefore, if you want a regression where the coefficients have practical interpretation, you might need to look for other types of models. Some of these are explored in Chapter 6, "Special Applications of Linear Models," and in Chapter 7, "Nonlinear Models."

Chapter **6**

# Special Applications of Linear Models

*6.1 Introduction  175*

*6.2 Errors in Both Variables  176*

*6.3 Multiplicative Models  181*

*6.4 Spline Models  191*

*6.5 Indicator Variables  195*

*6.6 Binary Response Variable: Logistic Regression  203*

*6.7 Summary  214*

## 6.1 Introduction

In Chapter 5, "Polynomial and Smoothing Models," you are introduced to the use of polynomial models to analyze relationships that cannot be described by straight lines. Although these polynomial models are very useful, they cannot provide adequate descriptions for all types of relationships. For example, in the data on fish growth, the polynomial model provided a statistically significant fit, but the plot of the resulting curve, even for the fourth-order polynomial, showed some features that did not fit the desired characteristics for such a curve. A number of other regression methods are available for such cases.

Methods presented in this chapter may be analyzed with JMP by adaptations and options of the standard linear regression procedures available in the Fit Model. In "Estimating the Exponential Decay Model" on page 216 you are introduced to the estimation of models that cannot be analyzed in this manner.

Models presented in this chapter include

❑ orthogonal regression, for cases when there is measurement error in both the independent and dependent variables

- log-linear models, where logarithms in a linear regression model provide for estimating a multiplicative model
- spline functions, which allow different functions, usually polynomial models, to be fitted for different regions of the data
- indicator variables, which provide for the estimation of the effect of binary categorical predictors
- logistic regression, which allows for a binary response variable.

## 6.2 Errors in Both Variables

When computing the standard least-squares regression line

$$y = \beta_0 + \beta_1 x + \varepsilon$$

it is assumed that the $y$ variable is subject to error (represented by $\varepsilon$ in the model) but the $x$ variable is not. However, this is not always the case. Frequently, exact values of the independent variables are impossible. Draper and Smith (1998) cite the example of an ornithologist who wanted to measure the distance that a species of bird perched from rural highways. The birds sometimes flew away before the researcher could get an exact position of their perch, so some error in the independent variable was inevitable.

If least-squares regression is performed in cases where both variables are subject to error, there is bias in the slope estimate. The key quantity in determining this bias is the ratio of measurement ($x$) error to the response ($y$) error, written as

$$\lambda = \frac{s_x}{s_y}$$

and the technique of *orthogonal regression* is employed. When the error in $x$ is zero, the value of $\lambda$ is zero and orthogonal regression agrees with least-squares estimates. Similarly, cases where the error in $x$ is small when compared with $y$ yield estimates close to that of ordinary regression.

If the errors in $x$ are large, essentially overpowering the error in $y$, orthogonal regression estimates the slope as if $x$ were regressed on $y$ rather than $y$ on $x$.

This brings up an interesting question. Is a regression of $y$ on $x$ simply the inverse of a regression of $x$ on $y$? An example clarifies the situation. Consider the data in Galton.jmp, the data used by the scientist who gave regression its name. Frances Galton was interested in the relationship between the height of parents and the height of their children. When the child's height is considered the dependent variable and parent's height the independent variable, a regression analysis yields the results in Figure 6.1.

**Figure 6.1**
*Regression of Child's Height on Parent's Height*

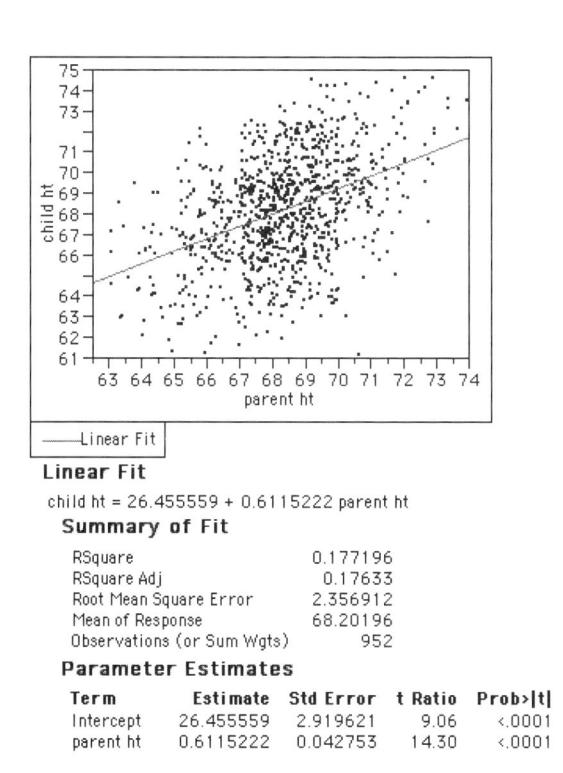

**Linear Fit**
child ht = 26.455559 + 0.6115222 parent ht

**Summary of Fit**

| | |
|---|---|
| RSquare | 0.177196 |
| RSquare Adj | 0.17633 |
| Root Mean Square Error | 2.356912 |
| Mean of Response | 68.20196 |
| Observations (or Sum Wgts) | 952 |

**Parameter Estimates**

| Term | Estimate | Std Error | t Ratio | Prob>|t| |
|---|---|---|---|---|
| Intercept | 26.455559 | 2.919621 | 9.06 | <.0001 |
| parent ht | 0.6115222 | 0.042753 | 14.30 | <.0001 |

Galton's hypothesis was that the slope of this equation should be 1. With a slope of 1, the predicted height of the child is the same as the height of the parent. A slope of less than one—which happened here—indicates that the children tended to have more moderate heights than their parents. In other words, children's heights regressed toward the mean height. Although Galton was examining regression as a biological process, the name regression has become associated with his statistical technique.

Since the slope is less than one when parent's height is *x* and children's height is *y*, it is logical that when those roles are reversed, the slope should be greater than 1. Computing the regression yields the surprising result shown in Figure 6.2.

Not only is the slope not greater than one, but it is less than the slope of the original regression! This demonstrates that one cannot simply reciprocate the slope of

**Figure 6.2**
*Regression of Parent's Height on Child's Height*

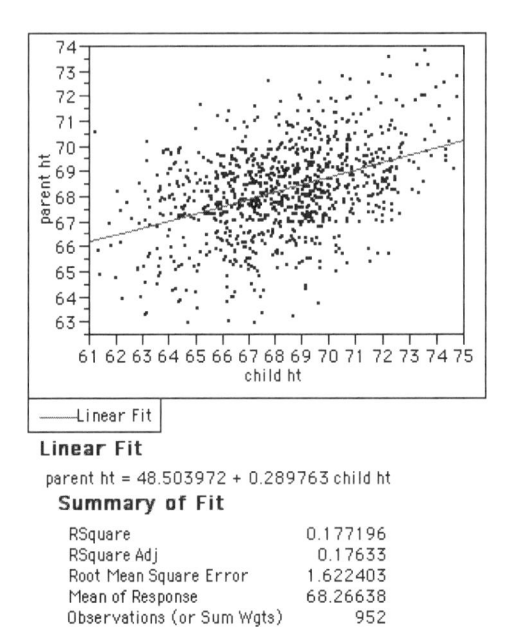

Linear Fit
parent ht = 48.503972 + 0.289763 child ht

**Summary of Fit**

| | |
|---|---|
| RSquare | 0.177196 |
| RSquare Adj | 0.17633 |
| Root Mean Square Error | 1.622403 |
| Mean of Response | 68.26638 |
| Observations (or Sum Wgts) | 952 |

**Parameter Estimates**

| Term | Estimate | Std Error | t Ratio | Prob>|t| |
|---|---|---|---|---|
| Intercept | 48.503972 | 1.382652 | 35.08 | <.0001 |
| child ht | 0.289763 | 0.020258 | 14.30 | <.0001 |

$y$ on $x$ to get the slope of $x$ on $y$. In regression, the errors are minimized along one variable only. Switching the roles is posing a completely different problem.

Geometrically, this can be seen through examining least-squares lines in conjunction with a density ellipse. In Figure 6.3, note that the least-squares regression line intersects the ellipse at the points where the ellipse has vertical tangents. These tangent points, however, are not points along the major axis of the ellipse.

When the roles of $x$ and $y$ are switched, the regression line intersects the ellipse at the points of horizontal tangents. So, connecting the points at the vertical tangents represents the case where $\lambda = 0$. Connecting the points at the horizontal tangents represents the case where $\lambda = \infty$. Orthogonal regressions with variance ratios between 0 and $\infty$ correspond to regression lines between these two extremes.

A (naive, yet) interesting case is where $\lambda$ is estimated from the data. This is, geometrically, the major axis of the ellipse, the direction that accounts for the greatest variation in a single regression. This case is called the *first principal component*.

**Figure 6.3**
*Regression with Density Ellipse*

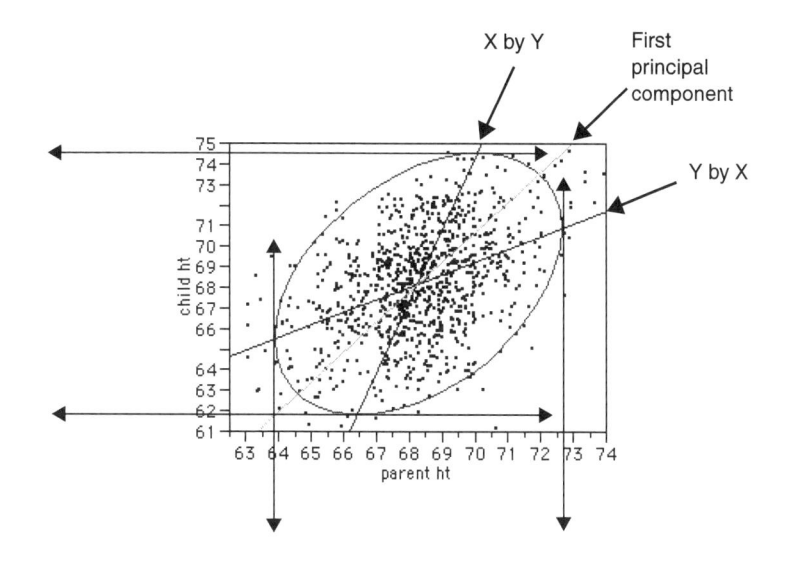

To compute an orthogonal regression in JMP,

❑ Select **Analyze → Fit Y by X** and designate the two variables to be analyzed.

❑ When the analysis appears, select **Fit Orthogonal** from the platform pop-up menu.

There are four choices on this menu for fitting orthogonal regressions.

❑ Univariate Variances, Prin Comp estimates the variances from the $x$ and $y$ columns and constructs $\lambda$ from these estimates.

❑ Equal Variances specifies $\lambda = 1$ and corresponds to the first principal component.

❑ Fit X to Y uses a very large variance ratio, corresponding to the horizontal-tangent case above.

❑ Specified Variance Ratio allows you to enter a variance ratio yourself. This ratio should come from your knowledge of the process under consideration. Note that the variances are not those merely estimated from the data. Rather, they are estimates gained from estimating the variance of $y$ at a fixed value of $x$, and from $x$ estimated at a fixed value of $y$. In other words, replicates are needed for estimation of the variance.

As an example, use the Galton data set.

🖑 Select **Analyze → Fit Y by X**.

🖰  Assign child ht to Y and parent ht to X.

🖰  Click **OK**.

When the analysis appears,

🖰  Select **Density Ellipse → 0.95** from the platform pop-up menu.

This draws the ellipse on the plot. To produce the regression line, the vertical-tangent case above,

🖰  Select **Fit Line**.

To obtain the horizontal-tangent case and the case where the variances are equal,

🖰  Select **Fit Orthogonal → Fit X to Y**.

🖰  Select **Fit Orthogonal → Equal Variances**.

To use the actual data to estimate the appropriate variances and see the first principal component,

🖰  Select **Fit Orthogonal → Univariate Variances, Prin Comp**.

Finally, estimate the regression for values of $\lambda = 2$ and $\lambda = 10$.

🖰  Select **Fit Orthogonal → Specified Variance Ratio** and enter 2 in the dialog that appears. Repeat for $\lambda = 10$.

Notice that all of the Fit Orthogonal lines are between the extreme cases of $\lambda = 0$ and $\lambda = \infty$ (Figure 6.4).

*Figure 6.4*
*Several Fit Orthogonals*

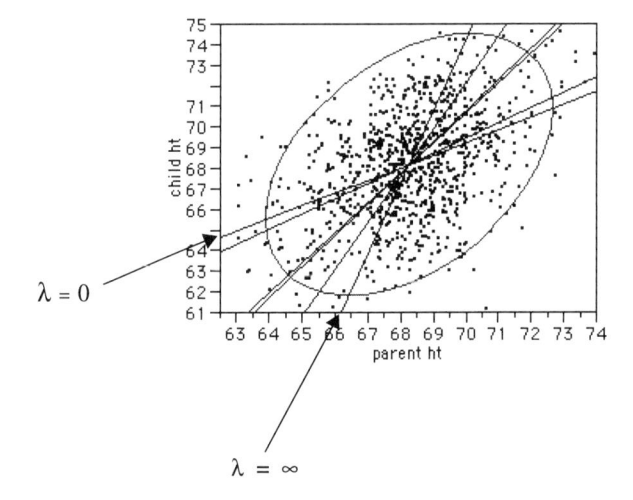

The output from Fit Orthogonal includes confidence limits on the estimates of the slope of the line (Figure 6.5). By default, these limits are calculated for α = 0.05. However, this value can be changed in the edit box that is part of the report, as shown in Figure 6.5.

*Figure 6.5*
*Orthogonal Regression Output*

```
▼ Orthogonal Regression
Variable      Mean     Std Dev   Variance Ratio   Correlation
parent ht   68.26638   1.787649      2.110422        0.4209
child ht    68.20196   2.59697
    Intercept    Slope    LowerCL    UpperCL    Alpha
     -30.9706   1.452729  1.265378   1.667819   0.05000
```

Confidence limit edit box

Unlike ordinary regression, orthogonal regression allows predictions of both $x$ and $y$ values. When you select **Save Predicteds** from the menu beside the fit name, two columns are created in the data table, containing these predicted values.

An inevitable question is which method to use. We offer the following advice.

❏ Using the univariate variances is naive and often is not appropriate.

❏ Assuming equal variances is often reasonable, especially if the measurements are on the same scale and gathered in the same way.

❏ Best of all is when you specify the variances of each variable based on variance estimates. Replicating data points in an experiment provides these estimates.

## 6.3 Multiplicative Models

A linear regression model using the logarithms of the variables is equivalent to estimating a multiplicative model. The following linear model uses logarithms:

$$\log y = \beta_0 + \beta_1(\log x_1) + \beta_2(\log x_2) + \ldots + \beta_m(\log x_m) + \varepsilon$$

It is equivalent to the model

$$y = (e^{\beta_0})(x_1^{\beta_1})(x_2^{\beta_2}) \ldots (x_m^{\beta_m})(e^{\varepsilon})$$

In this multiplicative model the coefficients, called *elasticities,* measure the *percent* change in the dependent variable associated with a *one percent* change in the corresponding independent variable, holding constant all other variables. The intercept is a *scaling factor.* The error component in this model is also multiplicative and exhibits variation that is proportional to the magnitude of the dependent variable (Freund and Wilson 1998, Section 8.2).

The multiplicative model is illustrated with an example in which the weight of lumber is to be estimated from external measurements of the trees. The data set Pines.jmp contains information on a sample of individual pine trees. The dependent variable Weight represents the weight of lumber from a tree. The four independent variables are

Height              the height of the tree

Diameter          the diameter of the tree at breast height (about four feet)

Age                 the age of the tree

Specific Gravity  a measure of the specific gravity of the tree.

Obviously, the first two variables are relatively easy to measure; hence, a model for predicting tree weights using these variables could provide a low-cost estimate of timber yield. The other two variables are included to see if their addition to the model provides for better prediction. Table 6.1 shows the data for estimating tree weights.

The Distribution platform shows histograms of the data shown in Figure 6.6.

*Figure 6.6* Distribution of Pines Data

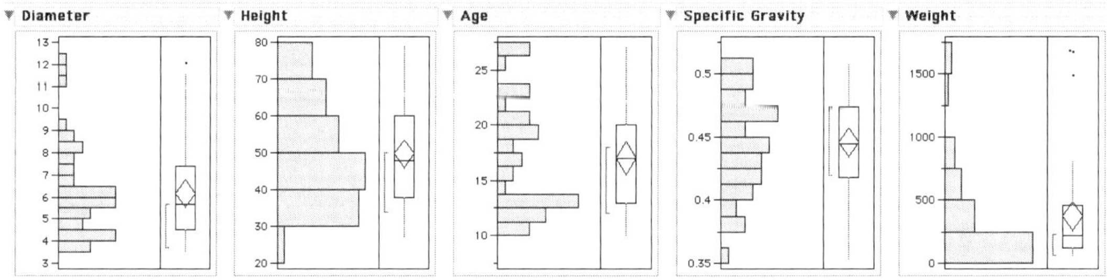

As an initial step, use a linear regression model and examine a residual plot.

- Select **Analyze → Fit Model**.
- Select Weight from the list of variables.
- Click the **Y** button.
- Select Diameter, Height, Age, and Specific Gravity from the list of variables.
- Click the **Add** button.
- Click **Run Model**.

*Table 6.1    Pines Data*

| Diameter | Height | Age | Specific Gravity | Weight |
|---|---|---|---|---|
| 5.7 | 34 | 10 | 0.409 | 174 |
| 8.1 | 68 | 17 | 0.501 | 745 |
| 8.3 | 70 | 17 | 0.445 | 814 |
| 7 | 54 | 17 | 0.442 | 408 |
| 6.2 | 37 | 12 | 0.353 | 226 |
| 11.4 | 79 | 27 | 0.429 | 1675 |
| 11.6 | 70 | 26 | 0.497 | 1491 |
| 4.5 | 37 | 12 | 0.38 | 121 |
| 3.5 | 32 | 15 | 0.42 | 58 |
| 6.2 | 45 | 15 | 0.449 | 278 |
| 5.7 | 48 | 20 | 0.471 | 220 |
| 6 | 57 | 20 | 0.447 | 342 |
| 5.6 | 40 | 20 | 0.439 | 209 |
| 4 | 44 | 27 | 0.394 | 84 |
| 6.7 | 52 | 21 | 0.422 | 313 |
| 4 | 38 | 27 | 0.496 | 60 |
| 12.1 | 74 | 27 | 0.476 | 1692 |
| 4.5 | 37 | 12 | 0.382 | 74 |
| 8.6 | 60 | 23 | 0.502 | 515 |
| 9.3 | 63 | 18 | 0.458 | 766 |
| 6.5 | 57 | 18 | 0.474 | 345 |
| 5.6 | 46 | 12 | 0.413 | 210 |
| 4.3 | 41 | 12 | 0.382 | 100 |
| 4.5 | 42 | 12 | 0.457 | 122 |
| 7.7 | 64 | 19 | 0.478 | 539 |
| 8.8 | 70 | 22 | 0.496 | 815 |
| 5 | 53 | 23 | 0.485 | 194 |

**Table 6.1** Pines Data (Continued)

| Diameter | Height | Age | Specific Gravity | Weight |
|---|---|---|---|---|
| 5.4 | 61 | 23 | 0.488 | 280 |
| 6 | 56 | 23 | 0.435 | 296 |
| 7.4 | 52 | 14 | 0.474 | 462 |
| 5.6 | 48 | 19 | 0.441 | 200 |
| 5.5 | 50 | 19 | 0.506 | 229 |
| 4.3 | 50 | 19 | 0.41 | 125 |
| 4.2 | 31 | 10 | 0.412 | 84 |
| 3.7 | 27 | 10 | 0.418 | 70 |
| 6.1 | 39 | 10 | 0.47 | 224 |
| 3.9 | 35 | 19 | 0.426 | 99 |
| 5.2 | 48 | 13 | 0.436 | 200 |
| 5.6 | 47 | 13 | 0.472 | 214 |
| 7.8 | 69 | 13 | 0.47 | 712 |
| 6.1 | 49 | 13 | 0.464 | 297 |
| 6.1 | 44 | 13 | 0.45 | 238 |
| 4 | 34 | 13 | 0.424 | 89 |
| 4 | 38 | 13 | 0.407 | 76 |
| 8 | 61 | 13 | 0.508 | 614 |
| 5.2 | 47 | 13 | 0.432 | 194 |
| 3.7 | 33 | 13 | 0.389 | 66 |

A portion of the output is shown in Figure 6.7.

The model does fit rather well, and the coefficients have the expected signs. Surprisingly, however, the Height coefficient is not statistically significant. Furthermore, the significance of both the Age and Specific Gravity coefficients ($p < 0.05$) indicates that the model using only the two-dimensional measurements is inadequate. Finally, the residual plot (see Figure 6.8) shows a pattern that suggests a poorly specified model.

*Figure 6.7* Fit Model Output for the Linear Model

**Response Weight**
**Whole Model**
**Actual by Predicted Plot**

**Diameter Leverage Plot**

**Height Leverage Plot**

**Age Leverage Plot**

**Specific Gravity Leverage Plot**

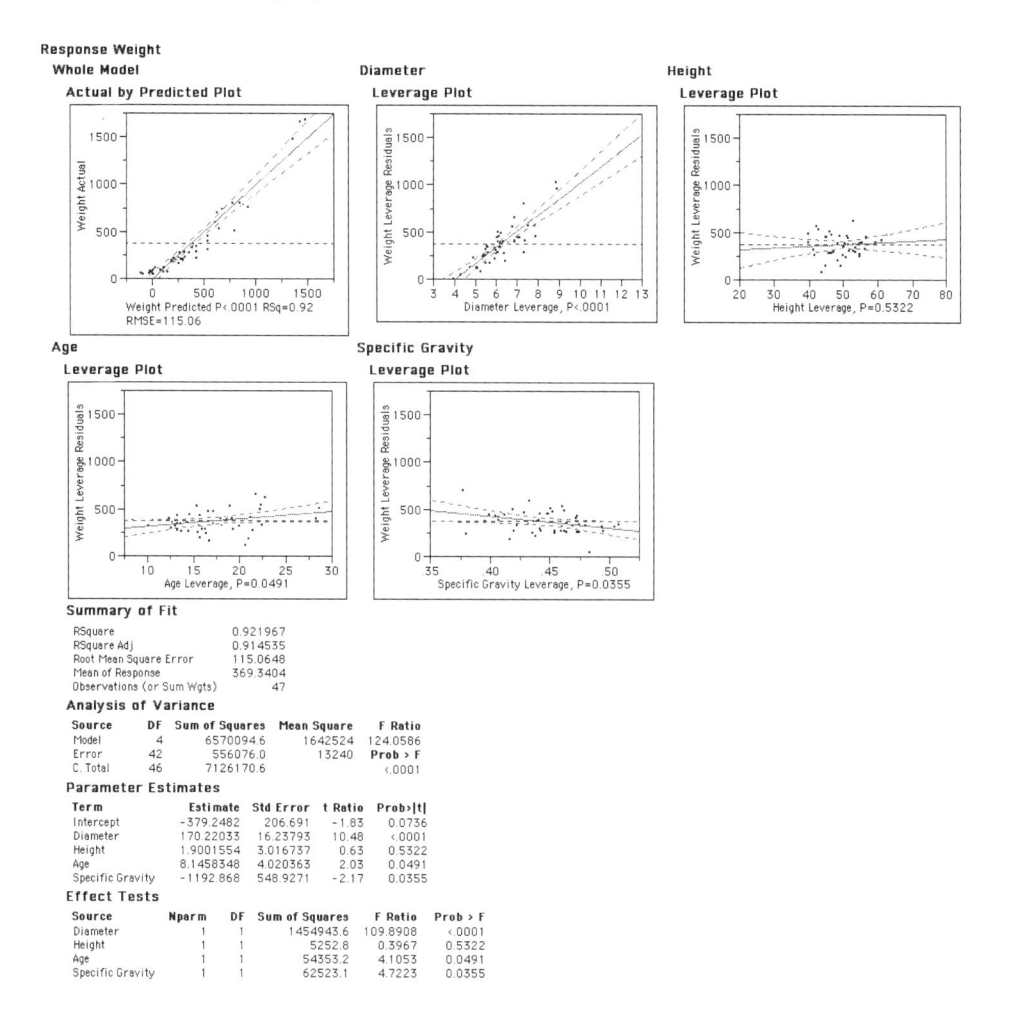

**Summary of Fit**

| | |
|---|---|
| RSquare | 0.921967 |
| RSquare Adj | 0.914535 |
| Root Mean Square Error | 115.0648 |
| Mean of Response | 369.3404 |
| Observations (or Sum Wgts) | 47 |

**Analysis of Variance**

| Source | DF | Sum of Squares | Mean Square | F Ratio |
|---|---|---|---|---|
| Model | 4 | 6570094.6 | 1642524 | 124.0586 |
| Error | 42 | 556076.0 | 13240 | Prob > F |
| C. Total | 46 | 7126170.6 | | <.0001 |

**Parameter Estimates**

| Term | Estimate | Std Error | t Ratio | Prob>|t| |
|---|---|---|---|---|
| Intercept | -379.2482 | 206.691 | -1.83 | 0.0736 |
| Diameter | 170.22033 | 16.23793 | 10.48 | <.0001 |
| Height | 1.9001554 | 3.016737 | 0.63 | 0.5322 |
| Age | 8.1458348 | 4.020363 | 2.03 | 0.0491 |
| Specific Gravity | -1192.868 | 548.9271 | -2.17 | 0.0355 |

**Effect Tests**

| Source | Nparm | DF | Sum of Squares | F Ratio | Prob > F |
|---|---|---|---|---|---|
| Diameter | 1 | 1 | 1454943.6 | 109.8908 | <.0001 |
| Height | 1 | 1 | 5252.8 | 0.3967 | 0.5322 |
| Age | 1 | 1 | 54353.2 | 4.1053 | 0.0491 |
| Specific Gravity | 1 | 1 | 62523.1 | 4.7223 | 0.0355 |

The pattern indicates the need for a curvilinear form, such as a quadratic response function, as well as the possibility of heterogeneous variances. In this case, however, a multiplicative model is more suitable. The amount of lumber in a tree is a function of the volume of the trunk, which is in the shape of a cylinder. The volume of a cylinder is $\pi r^2 h$, where $r$ is the radius and $h$ the height of the cylinder. Thus, a multiplicative model for volume or weight using radius (or diameter) and height is appropriate. Furthermore, it is also reasonable to expect that age and specific gravity have a relative, or multiplicative, effect. A multiplicative model of the form

**Figure 6.8**
*Residual Plot, Linear Model*

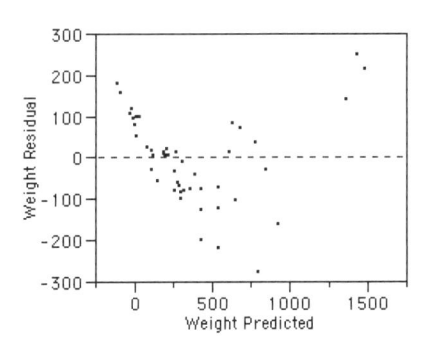

$$y = e^{\beta_0} x_1^{\beta_1} x_2^{\beta_2} \dots x_m^{\beta_m} e^{\varepsilon}$$

is converted to a linear model by taking logarithms of both sides:

$$\log y = \beta_0 + \beta_1 \log x_1 + \beta_2 \log x_2 + \dots + \beta_m \log x_m + \varepsilon$$

Because this is now a linear regression model using the logarithms of the values of the variables, it can be estimated by any procedure that can perform linear regressions. The new columns are created using JMP's Formula Editor.

First, create columns to hold the log values.

- Select **Cols → Add Multiple Columns**.
- Request 5 new columns.
- Click **OK**.

Once the columns are created,

- Click once on the first column heading to select it.
- Type the new name of the column, logDiameter, and press Return.
- Right-click (Control-click on the Macintosh) on the logDiameter column heading and select **Formula** from the menu that appears.

When the Formula Editor appears,

- Select **Transcendental → Log** from the list of functions.
- Select Diameter from the list of data table columns.

The formula should now say log(Diameter).

- Click **OK**.

- 🖱 Repeat these steps to create the columns logHeight, logSpecific Gravity, logAge, and logWeight.

The data table is included as Pines log.jmp.

The new variables, logDiameter through logWeight, are now available for use in the multiplicative model. You can now use these variables with Fit Model and examine the residual plot.

- 🖱 Select **Analyze** → **Fit Model**.
- 🖱 Assign logWeight as the Y variable.
- 🖱 Assign the other four log variables as effects by selecting them and clicking the **Add** button.
- 🖱 Click **Run Model**.

Figure 6.9 shows some of the output.

Note that both $R^2$ and $F$ statistics indicate that the overall fit of this model is quite good. Furthermore, both the logDiameter and logHeight coefficients are highly significant, while neither of the other variables contributes significantly. Finally, the coefficients for logDiameter and logHeight are quite close to 2 and unity, respectively, which are the values you would expect with a model based on the cylindrical shape of the tree trunk. You can, in fact, test the hypotheses that these values are correct as follows:

- 🖱 Select **Estimates** → **Custom Test**.
- 🖱 For the first test, enter a 1 beside logDiameter and a 2 beside =.
- 🖱 Click **OK**.

The dialog and output are shown in Figure 6.10.

For the second test,

- 🖱 Again select **Estimates** → **Custom Test**.
- 🖱 Enter a 1 beside logHeight and a 1 beside =.
- 🖱 Click **OK**.

The dialog and output are shown in Figure 6.11.

The residuals from this model (see Figure 6.12) appear to show virtually no patterns suggesting specification errors. There are some suspiciously large residuals for some of the smaller values of the predicted values that may require further scrutiny. Of course, these residuals show relative errors and therefore do not nec-

**188** *Special Applications of Linear Models*

*Figure 6.9 Partial Output for Multiplicative Model*

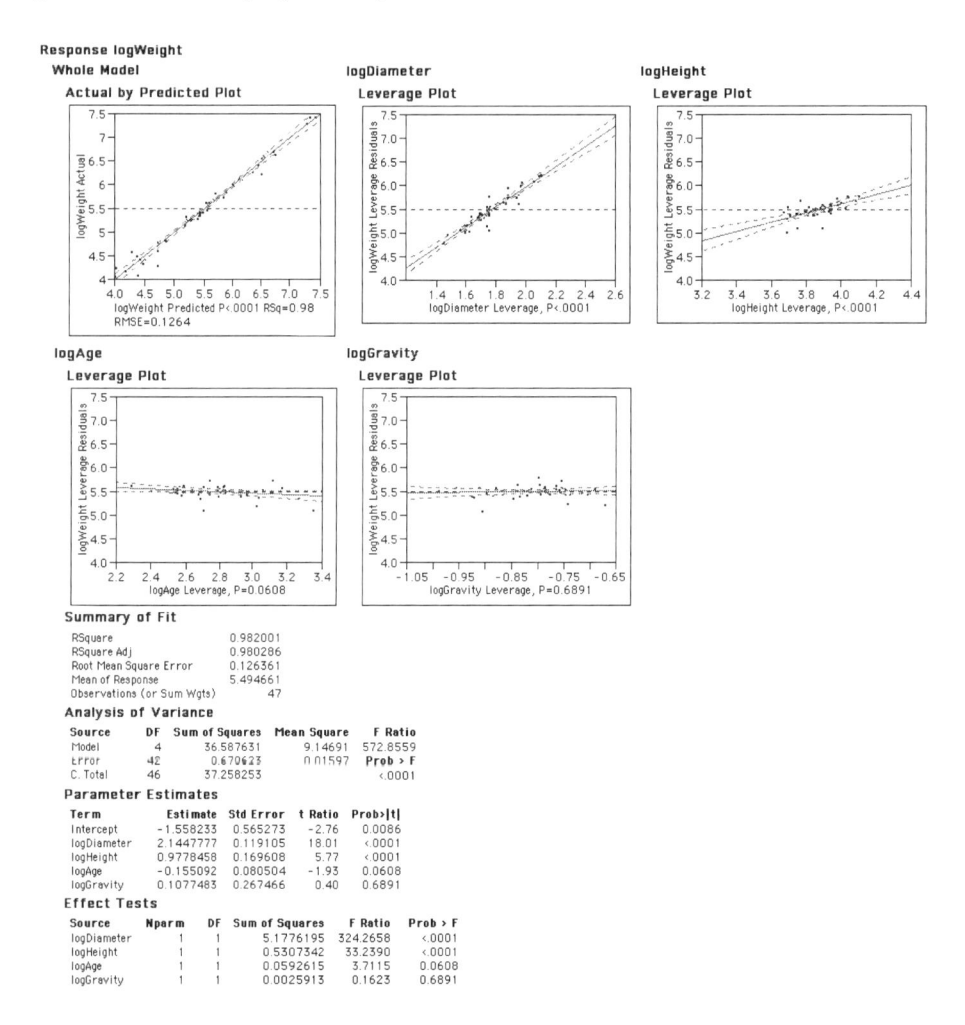

```
Response logWeight
Whole Model                              logDiameter                    logHeight
Actual by Predicted Plot                 Leverage Plot                  Leverage Plot
```

**Summary of Fit**

| | |
|---|---|
| RSquare | 0.982001 |
| RSquare Adj | 0.980286 |
| Root Mean Square Error | 0.126361 |
| Mean of Response | 5.494661 |
| Observations (or Sum Wgts) | 47 |

**Analysis of Variance**

| Source | DF | Sum of Squares | Mean Square | F Ratio |
|---|---|---|---|---|
| Model | 4 | 36.587631 | 9.14691 | 572.8559 |
| Error | 42 | 0.670623 | 0.01597 | Prob > F |
| C. Total | 46 | 37.258253 | | <.0001 |

**Parameter Estimates**

| Term | Estimate | Std Error | t Ratio | Prob>|t| |
|---|---|---|---|---|
| Intercept | -1.558233 | 0.565273 | -2.76 | 0.0086 |
| logDiameter | 2.1447777 | 0.119105 | 18.01 | <.0001 |
| logHeight | 0.9778458 | 0.169608 | 5.77 | <.0001 |
| logAge | -0.155092 | 0.080504 | -1.93 | 0.0608 |
| logGravity | 0.1077483 | 0.267466 | 0.40 | 0.6891 |

**Effect Tests**

| Source | Nparm | DF | Sum of Squares | F Ratio | Prob > F |
|---|---|---|---|---|---|
| logDiameter | 1 | 1 | 5.1776195 | 324.2658 | <.0001 |
| logHeight | 1 | 1 | 0.5307342 | 33.2390 | <.0001 |
| logAge | 1 | 1 | 0.0592615 | 3.7115 | 0.0608 |
| logGravity | 1 | 1 | 0.0025913 | 0.1623 | 0.6891 |

essarily correspond to large absolute residuals. You can use additional procedures for examining residuals as presented in Chapter 3, "Observations."

It may be of interest to see how well the multiplicative model estimates actual weights rather than logarithms of weights. You can do this by taking antilogs of the predicted values from the multiplicative model.

⟡ Select **Save Columns** → **Predicted Values** from the main report's platform pop-up menu.

**Figure 6.10**
*Test* logDiameter =
2 *Dialog and Output*

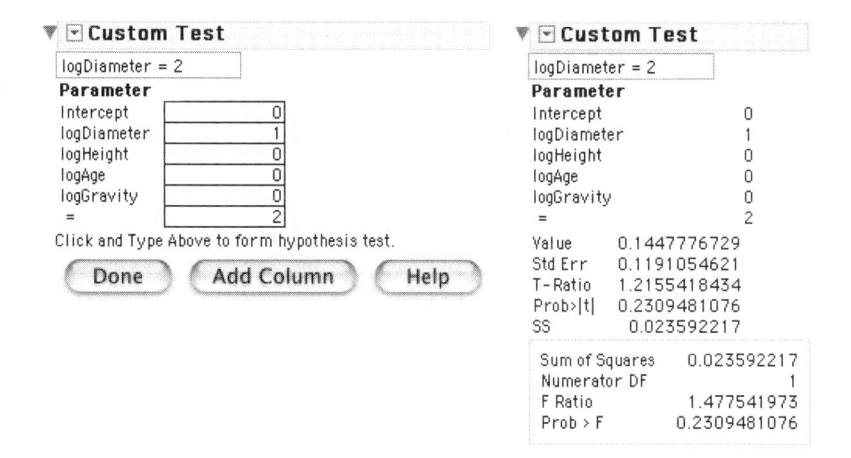

```
▼ ☐ Custom Test
logDiameter = 2
Parameter
Intercept      0
logDiameter    1
logHeight      0
logAge         0
logGravity     0
=              2
Click and Type Above to form hypothesis test.
   Done    Add Column    Help
```

```
▼ ☐ Custom Test
logDiameter = 2
Parameter
Intercept      0
logDiameter    1
logHeight      0
logAge         0
logGravity     0
=              2
Value     0.1447776729
Std Err   0.1191054621
T-Ratio   1.2155418434
Prob>|t|  0.2309481076
SS        0.023592217

Sum of Squares   0.023592217
Numerator DF               1
F Ratio           1.477541973
Prob > F         0.2309481076
```

**Figure 6.11**
*Test* logHeight
= 1 *Dialog and Output*

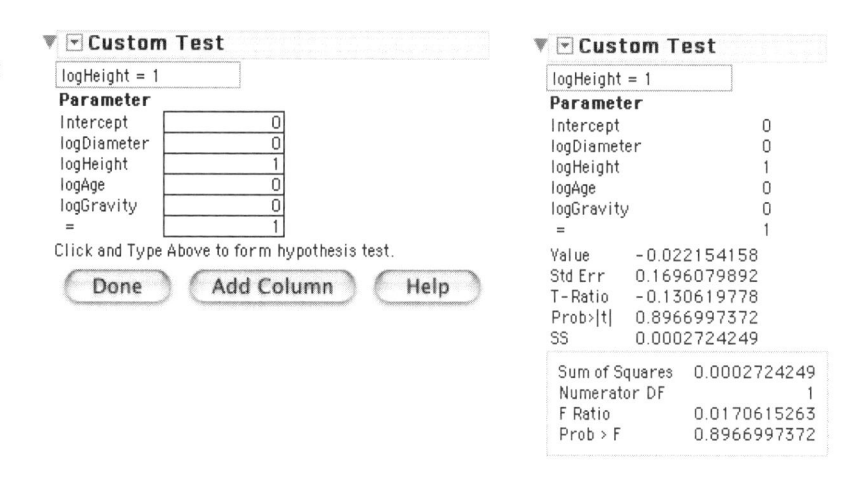

```
▼ ☐ Custom Test
logHeight = 1
Parameter
Intercept      0
logDiameter    0
logHeight      1
logAge         0
logGravity     0
=              1
Click and Type Above to form hypothesis test.
   Done    Add Column    Help
```

```
▼ ☐ Custom Test
logHeight = 1
Parameter
Intercept      0
logDiameter    0
logHeight      1
logAge         0
logGravity     0
=              1
Value    -0.022154158
Std Err   0.1696079892
T-Ratio  -0.130619778
Prob>|t|  0.8966997372
SS        0.0002724249

Sum of Squares   0.0002724249
Numerator DF                1
F Ratio           0.0170615263
Prob > F         0.8966997372
```

This command saves the predicted values into the data table. Now, make a new column to hold the antilogs.

- ✎ Double-click to the right of the last column in the data table to create a new column.

- ✎ Name the column Predicted Antilog Weight.

- ✎ With the column selected, right-click (Control-click on the Macintosh) on the column and select **Formula** from the menu that appears.

When the Formula Editor appears,

**Figure 6.12**
*Estimating Tree Weights: Residual Plot, Log Model*

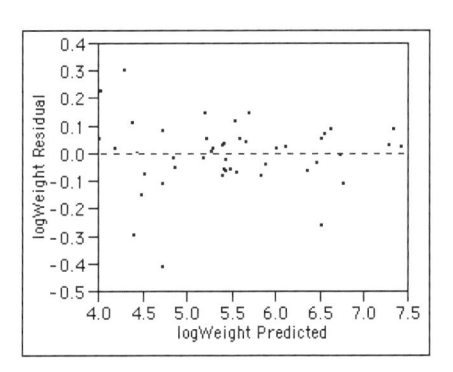

- Select **Transcendental → Exp** from the list of functions.
- Select Predicted logWeight from the list of data table columns.

The formula should now read Exp(Predicted logWeight).

- Click **OK**.

Now, compute the residuals from these new predictions.

- Add another column to the data table.
- Name the column Residuals antilog Weight.
- Bring up the Formula Editor.
- Enter the formula Weight – Predicted Antilog Weight.
- Click **OK**.

Finally, analyze these residuals to see them plotted and to get some summary statistics.

- Select **Analyze → Fit Y by X**.
- Assign Residuals Antilog Weight to the Y role.
- Assign Predicted Antilog Weight to the X role.
- Click **OK**.

When the scatterplot appears,

- Select **Fit Mean** from the platform pop-up menu.

The Fit Mean report is closed by default.

⇐ Click on the disclosure icon next to the **Fit Mean** outline bar to open the Fit Mean report.

The analysis should now appear as in Figure 6.13.

*Figure 6.13*
*Residual Plot of the Exponentiated Log Residuals*

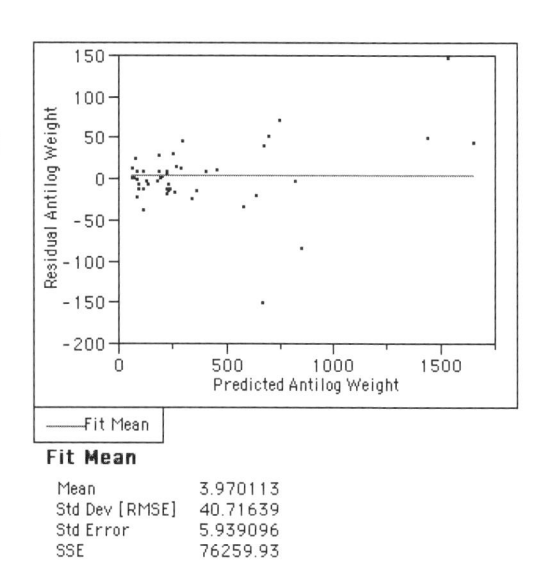

```
Fit Mean
Mean         3.970113
Std Dev [RMSE] 40.71639
Std Error    5.939096
SSE          76259.93
```

The mean residual is 3.97, and the error sum of squares (SSE) is 76,259. You can see that the sum of residuals is not zero, which illustrates the well-known fact that estimated or predicted values obtained in this manner are biased. However, the error sum of squares is smaller than that obtained by the linear model.

These residuals do not have the obvious specification error pattern exhibited by the residuals of the linear model. They do, however, show the typical pattern of multiplicative errors, where larger residuals are associated with larger values of the response variable.

## 6.4 Spline Models

In a review paper on spline models, Smith (1979) gives the following definition:

> Splines are generally defined to be piecewise polynomials of degree $n$ whose function values and first $(n-1)$ derivatives agree at points where they join. The abscissas of these joint points are called knots. Polynomials

may be considered a special case of splines with no knots, and piecewise (sometimes also called grafted or segmented) polynomials with fewer than the maximum number of continuity restrictions may also be considered splines. The number and degrees of polynomial pieces and the number and position of knots may vary in different situations.

First consider splines with known knots, that is, splines for which the values of the independent variable are known for the joint points. Fitting spline models with known knots is much easier than fitting them with unknown knots, because with known knots you can use linear regression methods. Estimation of spline models with unknown knots requires the use of nonlinear methods.

You can fit a spline of two straight lines with known knots to the fish growth at 29 degrees, as shown in Table 5.1 on page 142 and the Fish29.jmp data table.

Judging from the plot in Figure 5.5, the rate of increase is roughly constant until about Age = 80, at which point growth appears to stop abruptly. A linear spline with knot at Age = 80 would appear to be suitable for these data.

In order to perform a regression analysis, you need to write a linear regression equation to represent the spline model. Define a variable, AgePLUS, as the maximum of Age − 80 and zero:

- Double-click to the right of the last column in the data table to add a new column.

- Name the new column **AgePLUS**.

- Right-click (Control-click on the Macintosh) on the new column and select Formula from the menu that appears.

When the Formula Editor appears,

- Select **Statistical** → **Maximum** from the function list.

The Maximum() function returns the maximum of the two values specified as arguments. Since you are selecting the maximum of two quantities, the Maximum() function needs two arguments.

To add a placeholder for the second argument,

- Press the comma (,) key.

- Click the first argument to highlight it.

- Select Age from the data table columns list.

- Click the subtract (−) key and enter 80.

- Click the second argument in the Maximum() function and enter 0.

## Spline Models

The formula should say Maximum (Age–80,0).

- Click **OK**.

The spline model is represented with the regression equation

$$\text{Length} = \beta_0 + \beta_1(\text{Age}) + \beta_2(\text{AgePLUS}) + \varepsilon$$

which defines the relationship

$$\text{Length} = \beta_0 + \beta_1(\text{Age}) + \varepsilon$$

for Age < 80, and

$$\text{Length} = \beta_0 + \beta_1(\text{Age}) + \beta_2(\text{Age} - 80) + \varepsilon$$

or equivalently,

$$\text{Length} = (\beta_0 - 80*\beta_2) + (\beta_1 + \beta_2)(\text{Age}) + \varepsilon$$

for Age > 80. Notice that both expressions give the same estimated **Length** when Age = 80. In other words, the two line segments are joined at Age = 80. To perform this regression,

- Select **Analyze → Fit Model**.
- Assign Length to the Y role.
- Assign Age and AgePLUS as effects.
- Click **Run Model**.

Results appear in Figure 6.14. The plot of actual values against predicted values shows a good fit of the model to the data.

The fitted equation is

$$\text{Length} = -327.62 + 60.18(\text{Age}) - 58.86\,(\text{AgePLUS})$$

Therefore the fitted spline model for Age < 80 is

$$\text{Length} = -327.62 + 60.1(\text{Age})$$

and

$$\text{Length} = (-327.62 + 58.86*80) + (60.18 - 58.85)(\text{Age})$$
$$= 4376.38 + 1.32(\text{Age})$$

for Age > 80. Notice the small slope of 1.32 for Age > 80.

*Figure 6.14* Linear Spline Regression

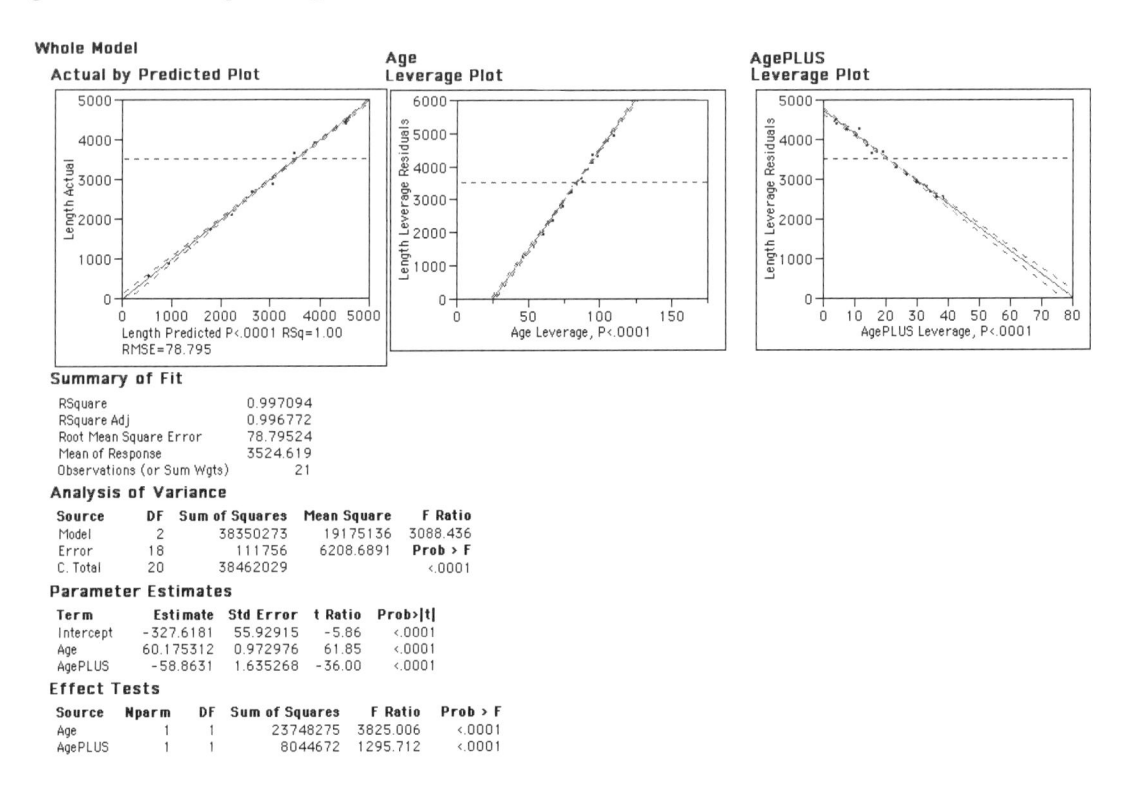

```
Whole Model
Actual by Predicted Plot

Summary of Fit
RSquare                         0.997094
RSquare Adj                     0.996772
Root Mean Square Error          78.79524
Mean of Response                3524.619
Observations (or Sum Wgts)            21

Analysis of Variance
Source    DF   Sum of Squares   Mean Square   F Ratio
Model      2         38350273      19175136  3088.436
Error     18           111756     6208.6891   Prob > F
C. Total  20         38462029                   <.0001

Parameter Estimates
Term        Estimate    Std Error   t Ratio   Prob>|t|
Intercept   -327.6181   55.92915     -5.86     <.0001
Age         60.175312   0.972976     61.85     <.0001
AgePLUS     -58.8631    1.635268    -36.00     <.0001

Effect Tests
Source     Nparm   DF   Sum of Squares   F Ratio   Prob > F
Age            1    1         23748275  3825.006    <.0001
AgePLUS        1    1          8044672  1295.712    <.0001
```

A plot of the actual values against the predicted values gives a good picture of the model. To see a plot of the fit to the actual data,

- Select **Save Columns** → **Predicted Values** from the platform pop-up menu.

This creates a new data table column, Predicted Length.

- Select **Graph** → **Overlay Plot**.
- Assign Length and Predicted Length as Y.
- Assign Age as X.
- Click **OK**.

When the Overlay Plot appears,

- Right-click (Control-click on the Macintosh) on **Predicted Length** in the legend at the bottom of the plot.
- Select **Connect Points** from the menu that appears.
- Repeat the same step to uncheck **Show Points**.

The results should look like Figure 6.15.

*Figure 6.15*
*Overlay Plot of Spline Fit*

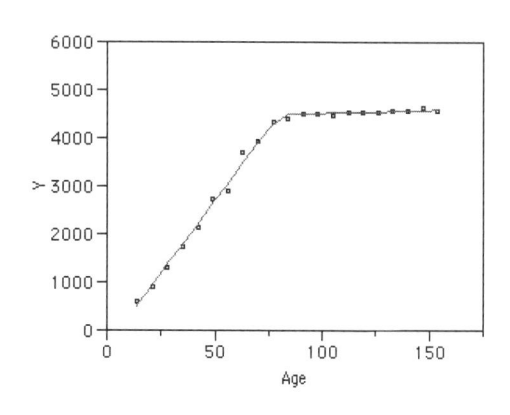

Although a formal test is not available, you can compare the fit of the linear spline to the fit of the fourth-degree polynomial used in Chapter 5. In Figure 6.14, you see Mean Square (Error) = 6208 for the linear spline, while in Figure 5.11 you see Mean Square (Error) = 13,202 for the fourth-degree polynomial, thus indicating a better fit for the spline function.

## 6.5 Indicator Variables

The independent variables in a regression model are usually quantitative; that is, they have a defined scale of measurement. Occasionally, you may need to include qualitative or categorical variables in such a model. This is accomplished by the use of indicator variables. Note that JMP automatically codes nominal and ordinal variables for analyses, but this section is included to give you an appreciation of the process.

The example in Chapter 2 concerned a model for determining operating costs of airlines, stored in the data table air.jmp. It has been argued that long-haul airlines have lower operating costs than short-haul airlines. Recall the variable Type shown in Figure 2.1. This variable is an *indicator* (sometimes called *dummy*) variable that classifies airlines into two groups or classes. Type = 0 defines the short-haul lines with average stage lengths of less than 1200 miles and Type = 1 defines the long-haul lines that have average stage lengths of 1200 miles or longer. Fit a regression with the following steps:

- Select **Analyze → Fit Model**.
- Assign Cost as the Y variable.
- Add Use, Seats, Load, and Type as effects.
- Click **Run Model**.

When Type = 0, Intercept is the intercept for the model describing the short-haul lines. When Type = 1, that is, for the long-haul lines, the intercept is the sum of the Intercept and Type coefficients. The other coefficients are the same for both classes; hence, the Type coefficient simply estimates the difference in levels of operating costs between the two types of airlines regardless of the values of the other variables. In other words, you have estimated a model describing two parallel planes. The results appear in Figure 6.16.

The positive coefficient for Type indicates higher costs for the long-haul lines. However, it is not statistically significant; hence, there is insufficient evidence of a difference in operating costs between the two types of airlines. The other coefficients are interpreted as before and have, in fact, quite similar values to those of the original model. This is to be expected with the insignificant Type coefficient.

The inclusion of the indicator variable only estimates a difference in the average operating cost, but it does not address the possibility that the relationships of cost to the various operating factors differ between types. Such a difference can be estimated by adding to the model variables that are products of the indicator and continuous variables.

A simple example illustrates this principle. Assume the following model:

$$y = \beta_0 + \beta_1 x_1 + \beta_2 x_2 + \beta_3 x_1 x_2$$

where $x_1$ is a continuous variable, and $x_2$ is an indicator variable with values 0 and 1 identifying two classes.

Then, for the first class ($x_2 = 0$), the model equation is

*Figure 6.16 Using an Indicator Variable for an Intercept Shift*

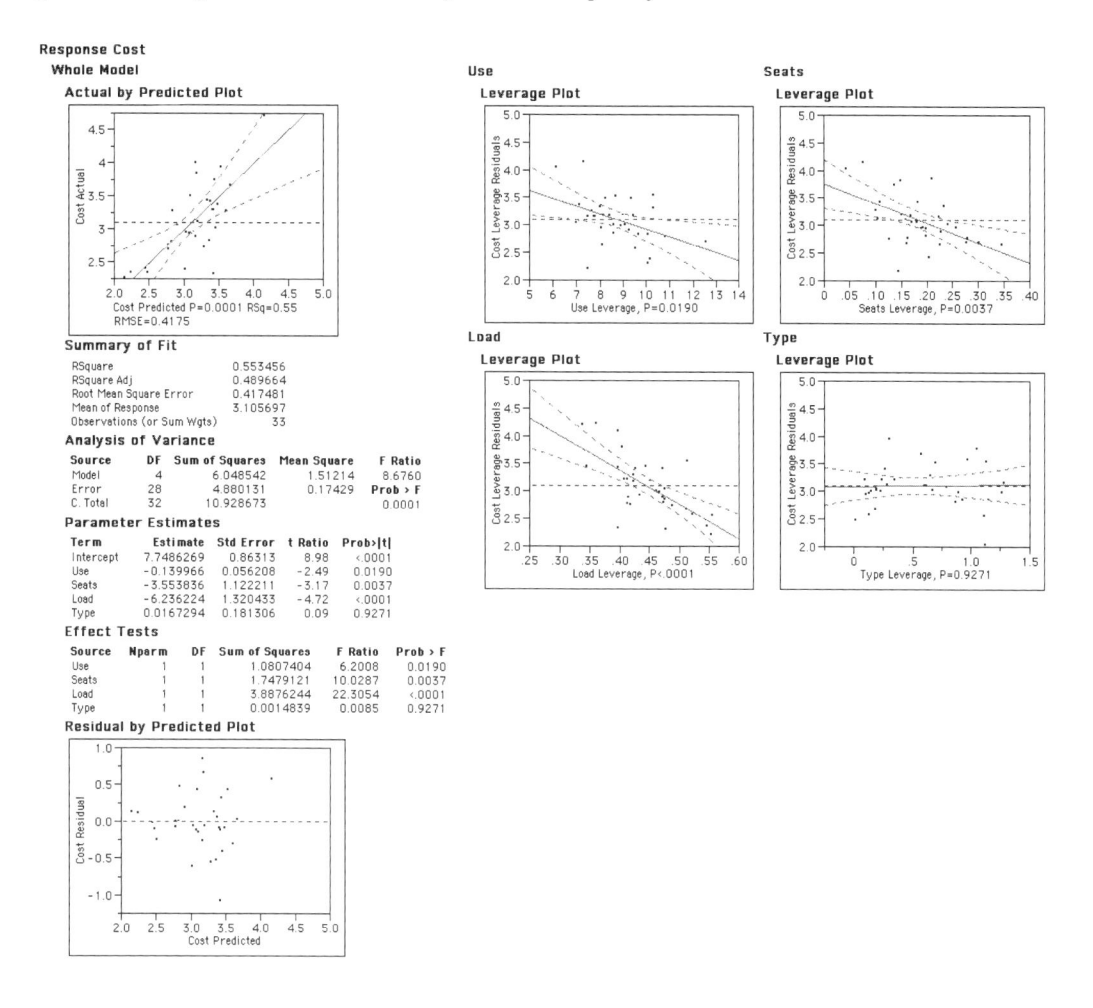

$$y = \beta_0 + \beta_1 x$$

For the other class ($x_2 = 1$), the model equation is

$$y = (\beta_0 + \beta_2) + (\beta_1 + \beta_3)x_1$$

In other words, the slope of the regression of $y$ on $x_1$ is $\beta_1$ for the first class and $\beta_1 + \beta_3$ for the second class. Thus $\beta_3$ is the difference in the regression coefficient between the two classes. The coefficient $\beta_3$ is sometimes referred to as a *slope shift* coefficient, as it allows the slope of the regression line to shift from one class to the next.

You can use this principle to estimate different regression coefficients for the two types of airlines for the three cost factors. You need to add three additional variables to the Fit Model dialog—Use*Type, Seats*Type, and Load*Type. To add these cross-products,

- Use the **Window** menu to bring the Fit Model dialog to the front.
- Select Type in the variables list and select Use in the effects list.
- Click the **Cross** button.
- Select Type in the variables list and select Seats in the effects list.
- Click the **Cross** button.
- Select Type in the variables list and select Load in the effects list.
- Click the **Cross** button.

In this case, we will turn off centering of polynomials. Centering subtracts the mean of each effect from the effect values. This prevents a collinearity problem (discussed later) and allows for meaningful interpretation of the $p$ values for main effects involved in the interaction. However, when the interactions are centered, the equations above become a bit more complicated, partially obscuring the elegance of the indicator variable.

- In the pop-up menu located in the Fit Model dialog, select **Center Polynomials** to turn off centering.

The Fit Model dialog should appear as in Figure 6.17.

- Click **Run Model**.

Two features of the model are of interest:

❑ The Type variable must be included. Leaving this variable out is equivalent to imposing the arbitrary requirement that the intercept is the same for models describing both types of airlines.

❑ The variance inflation factors are not necessary for the analysis, but they do show an important feature of the results of this type of model.

To show the VIFs,

- Right-click (Control-click on the Macintosh) in the body of the **Parameter Estimates** table.
- Select **Columns** → **VIF** from the menu that appears.

Partial results appear in Figure 6.18.

*Figure 6.17* Fit Model Dialog with Crossed Terms

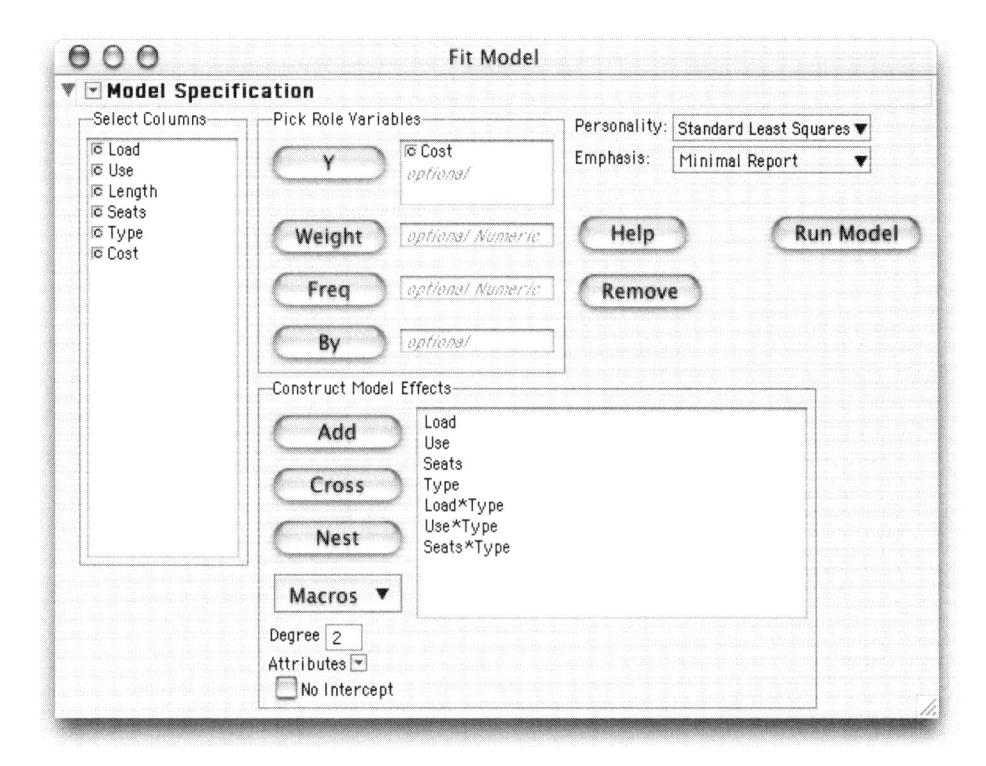

The overall model statistics show that the residual mean square has decreased from 0.174 to 0.103 and the $R^2$ value has increased from 0.5535 to 0.7648. In other words, allowing different coefficients for the two types of airlines has clearly improved the fit of the model. It is now appropriate to test the null hypothesis that the three product coefficients are zero; that is, the effects of all three factors are the same for both types.

- Select **Estimates → Custom Test** from the platform pop-up menu.
- Select **Add Columns** twice to add two columns to the test.
- Enter a 1 in the text box beside each of the interaction terms, one per column, as shown in Figure 6.19.
- Click **Done**.

The results appear in Figure 6.20.

**200**  *Special Applications of Linear Models*

*Figure 6.18*
*Using an Indicator Variable for Slope Shift*

**Response Cost**

**Summary of Fit**

| | |
|---|---|
| RSquare | 0.764772 |
| RSquare Adj | 0.698908 |
| Root Mean Square Error | 0.32067 |
| Mean of Response | 3.105697 |
| Observations (or Sum Wgts) | 33 |

**Analysis of Variance**

| Source | DF | Sum of Squares | Mean Square | F Ratio |
|---|---|---|---|---|
| Model | 7 | 8.357938 | 1.19399 | 11.6114 |
| Error | 25 | 2.570735 | 0.10283 | Prob > F |
| C. Total | 32 | 10.928673 | | <.0001 |

**Parameter Estimates**

| Term | Estimate | Std Error | t Ratio | Prob>\|t\| | VIF |
|---|---|---|---|---|---|
| Intercept | 10.644365 | 1.504313 | 7.08 | <.0001 | |
| Load | -6.964992 | 2.09709 | -3.32 | 0.0028 | 6.1309123 |
| Use | -0.415894 | 0.075479 | -5.51 | <.0001 | 3.7225031 |
| Seats | -6.054836 | 4.324444 | -1.40 | 0.1738 | 46.825437 |
| Type | -4.075799 | 1.723798 | -2.36 | 0.0261 | 232.92861 |
| Load*Type | 0.6118833 | 2.411878 | 0.25 | 0.8018 | 95.463348 |
| Use*Type | 0.4175126 | 0.092134 | 4.53 | 0.0001 | 59.185606 |
| Seats*Type | 2.272941 | 4.417249 | 0.51 | 0.6114 | 110.0634 |

**Effect Tests**

| Source | Nparm | DF | Sum of Squares | F Ratio | Prob > F |
|---|---|---|---|---|---|
| Load | 1 | 1 | 1.1342909 | 11.0308 | 0.0028 |
| Use | 1 | 1 | 3.1219953 | 30.3609 | <.0001 |
| Seats | 1 | 1 | 0.2015866 | 1.9604 | 0.1738 |
| Type | 1 | 1 | 0.5748709 | 5.5905 | 0.0261 |
| Load*Type | 1 | 1 | 0.0066183 | 0.0644 | 0.8018 |
| Use*Type | 1 | 1 | 2.1116427 | 20.5354 | 0.0001 |
| Seats*Type | 1 | 1 | 0.0272264 | 0.2648 | 0.6114 |

*Figure 6.19*
*Custom Test Launch*

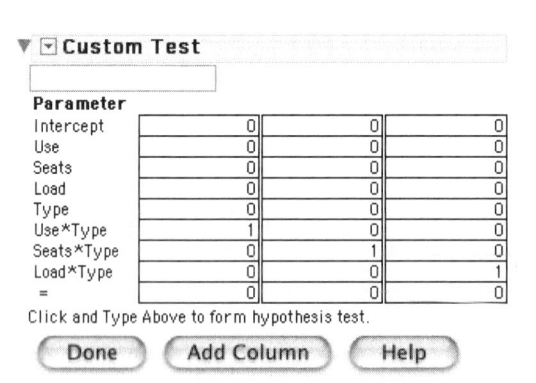

**▼ Custom Test**

**Parameter**

| | | | |
|---|---|---|---|
| Intercept | 0 | 0 | 0 |
| Use | 0 | 0 | 0 |
| Seats | 0 | 0 | 0 |
| Load | 0 | 0 | 0 |
| Type | 0 | 0 | 0 |
| Use*Type | 1 | 0 | 0 |
| Seats*Type | 0 | 1 | 0 |
| Load*Type | 0 | 0 | 1 |
| = | 0 | 0 | 0 |

Click and Type Above to form hypothesis test.

( Done )  ( Add Column )  ( Help )

*Figure 6.20
Custom Test
Results*

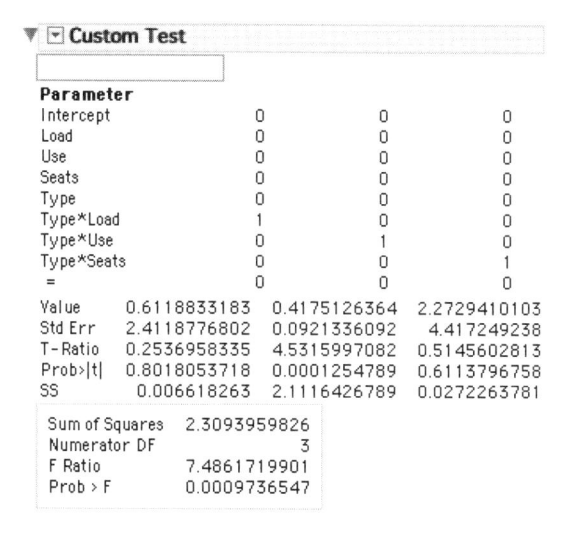

```
Custom Test

Parameter
Intercept              0              0              0
Load                   0              0              0
Use                    0              0              0
Seats                  0              0              0
Type                   0              0              0
Type*Load              1              0              0
Type*Use               0              1              0
Type*Seats             0              0              1
=                      0              0              0
Value      0.6118833183   0.4175126364   2.2729410103
Std Err    2.4118776802   0.0921336092   4.417249238
T-Ratio    0.2536958335   4.5315997082   0.5145602813
Prob>|t|   0.8018053718   0.0001254789   0.6113796758
SS         0.006618263    2.1116426789   0.0272263781

Sum of Squares   2.3093959826
Numerator DF                3
F Ratio          7.4861719901
Prob > F         0.0009736547
```

The test for the three additional coefficients given at the bottom of the output ($p = 0.00098$) indicates that the slope shifts as a whole significantly improve the fit of the model.

The statistics for the coefficients for the product variables show that among these only Use*Type is statistically significant ($p < 0.05$). In other words, the coefficient for the utilization factor is the only one that can be shown to differ between the types.

In checking the statistics for the other coefficients, note that neither Seats nor its change or shift coefficient (Seats*Type) is statistically significant ($p = 0.1738$ and 0.6114, respectively). This appears to contradict the results for the previous models, where the coefficient for Seats does indeed appear to be needed in the model. This apparent contradiction arises from the fact that in this type of model, just as in polynomial models (see Chapter 5), it is not legitimate to test for lower-order terms in the presence of higher-order terms without first centering the variables. In other words, if Use*Type is in the model, and the model is not centered, the test for Use is not meaningful. This high degree of collinearity often found in models of this type is the reason that the **Center Polynomials** option is on by default. In this example, the collinearity is made worse by a large difference in the sizes of planes (Seats) used by the two types of airlines. Note that the variance inflation factors involving Seats and Seats*Type are rather large (see Chapter 4).

For this reason, it is useful to re-estimate the model omitting the two insignificant slope shift terms, Seats*Type and Load*Type.

- Bring the Fit Model dialog to the front.
- Highlight one of the terms in the effects list that is to be removed.
- Click the **Remove** button.
- Repeat for the other term.
- Click **Run Model**.

Note that again the Type variable is kept in the model since it is a lower-order term in the model that still includes one product term.

The results appear in Figure 6.21.

*Figure 6.21 Final Equation for Slope Shift*

**Response Cost**

**Summary of Fit**

| | |
|---|---|
| RSquare | 0.762276 |
| RSquare Adj | 0.718254 |
| Root Mean Square Error | 0.310197 |
| Mean of Response | 3.105697 |
| Observations (or Sum Wgts) | 33 |

**Analysis of Variance**

| Source | DF | Sum of Squares | Mean Square | F Ratio |
|---|---|---|---|---|
| Model | 5 | 8.330670 | 1.66613 | 17.3155 |
| Error | 27 | 2.598002 | 0.09622 | Prob > F |
| C. Total | 32 | 10.928673 | | <.0001 |

**Parameter Estimates**

| Term | Estimate | Std Error | t Ratio | Prob>\|t\| |
|---|---|---|---|---|
| Intercept | 10.141423 | 0.807899 | 12.55 | <.0001 |
| Use | -0.420572 | 0.071163 | -5.91 | <.0001 |
| Seats | -3.872952 | 0.836397 | -4.63 | <.0001 |
| Load | -6.409458 | 0.981754 | -6.53 | <.0001 |
| Type | -3.533493 | 0.741336 | -4.77 | <.0001 |
| Use*Type | 0.4228094 | 0.086819 | 4.87 | <.0001 |

**Effect Tests**

| Source | Nparm | DF | Sum of Squares | F Ratio | Prob > F |
|---|---|---|---|---|---|
| Use | 1 | 1 | 3.3608581 | 34.9281 | <.0001 |
| Seats | 1 | 1 | 2.0631711 | 21.4417 | <.0001 |
| Load | 1 | 1 | 4.1012185 | 42.6223 | <.0001 |
| Type | 1 | 1 | 2.1860207 | 22.7184 | <.0001 |
| Use*Type | 1 | 1 | 2.2821288 | 23.7173 | <.0001 |

At this point, you can construct a test to ascertain the significance of the Use effect for Type=1 airlines. In other words, test the contrast of Use + Use*Type = 0.

- Select **Estimates** → **Custom Test**.
- Enter a 1 in the editable column beside Use and Use*Type.
- Click **Done**.

The results are shown in Figure 6.22.

*Figure 6.22*
*Custom Test Results*

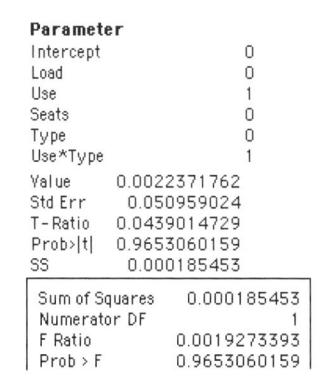

| Parameter | |
|---|---|
| Intercept | 0 |
| Load | 0 |
| Use | 1 |
| Seats | 0 |
| Type | 0 |
| Use*Type | 1 |
| Value | 0.0022371762 |
| Std Err | 0.050959024 |
| T-Ratio | 0.0439014729 |
| Prob>\|t\| | 0.9653060159 |
| SS | 0.000185453 |

| | |
|---|---|
| Sum of Squares | 0.000185453 |
| Numerator DF | 1 |
| F Ratio | 0.0019273393 |
| Prob > F | 0.9653060159 |

The deletion of the two product variables has virtually no effect on the fit of the model and all coefficients are highly significant.

This equation estimates that for the short-haul airlines a one-unit (percent) change in utilization decreases cost by 0.42 cents. On the other hand, for the long-haul lines the corresponding effect is the sum of the coefficients for Use and Use*Type; this estimate is –0.420572 + 0.422809 = 0.002237, or almost zero. The results of the custom test ($p = 0.96$) show that use is not a cost factor for these airlines.

The use of dummy variables is readily extended to more than one categorical variable and also to situations where such variables have more than two categories. In many cases, this type of analysis produces singular normal equations that must be solved by special coding of the categorical levels. JMP's Fit Model facility handles categorical variables automatically and codes the variables so that the estimates can be obtained.

## 6.6 Binary Response Variable: Logistic Regression

In many regression applications the response variable has only two outcomes: an event either did or did not occur. Such a variable is often referred to as a *binary* or *Bernoulli* variable, as its behavior is related to the Bernoulli distribution. A regression model with this type of response can be interpreted as a model that estimates the effect of the independent variables on the probability of the event occurring.

Binary response data typically appear in one of two ways:

1. When observations represent individual subjects, the response is represented by a dummy or indicator variable having any two values. The most commonly used values are zero if the event does not occur and unity if it does.
2. When observations summarize the occurrence of events for each set of unique combinations of the independent variables, the response variable $x/n$ where $x$ is the number of occurrences and $n$ the number of observations in the set.

Regression with a binary response is illustrated with data from a study of carriers of muscular dystrophy (Dystro.jmp). Two groups of women, one consisting of known carriers of the disease and the other a control group, were examined for four types of protein in their blood. It is known that proteins may be used as a screening tool to identify carriers. The variables in the resulting data set are as follows:

CARRIER    coded 0 for control and 1 for carriers

P1    measurement of protein type 1, a type traditionally used for screening

P2    measurement of protein type 2

P3    measurement of protein type 3

P4    measurement of protein type 4.

The objective is to determine the effectiveness of these proteins in identifying carriers of the disease, with special reference to how screening is improved by using measurements of the other proteins. The data are shown in Table 6.2.

Because P1 has been the standard, it will be used to illustrate binomial regression with a single independent variable. Because this looks like a regression problem, you might first try a linear regression model. Since there are only two variables involved in the regression, either Fit Model or Fit Y by X can be used. This example uses Fit Y by X.

- Select **Analyze → Fit Y by X**.
- Assign Carrier to the Y role and P1 to the X role.
- Click **OK**.
- When the report appears, select **Fit Line** from the platform pop-up menu.
- Select **Confid Curves Indiv** from the pop-up menu for **Linear Fit**.
- Double-click the *Y*-axis to bring up the axis specification dialog.
- Enter a **Minimum** of −1 and a **Maximum** of 3.
- Click **OK**.

*Table 6.2* Muscular Dystrophy Data

| id | CARRIER | AGE | P1 | P2 | P3 | P4 |
|---|---|---|---|---|---|---|
| 1 | 1 | 30 | 167 | 89 | 25.6 | 364 |
| 2 | 1 | 41 | 104 | 81 | 26.8 | 245 |
| 3 | 1 | 22 | 30 | 108 | 8.8 | 284 |
| 4 | 1 | 22 | 44 | 104 | 17.4 | 172 |
| 5 | 1 | 20 | 65 | 87 | 23.8 | 198 |
| 6 | 1 | 42 | 440 | 107 | 20.2 | 239 |
| 7 | 1 | 59 | 58 | 88.2 | 11 | 259 |
| 8 | 1 | 35 | 129 | 93.1 | 18.3 | 188 |
| 9 | 1 | 36 | 104 | 87.5 | 16.7 | 256 |
| 10 | 1 | 35 | 122 | 88.5 | 21.6 | 263 |
| 11 | 1 | 29 | 265 | 83.5 | 16.1 | 136 |
| 12 | 1 | 27 | 285 | 79.5 | 36.4 | 245 |
| 13 | 1 | 27 | 25 | 91 | 49.1 | 209 |
| 14 | 1 | 28 | 124 | 92 | 32.2 | 298 |
| 15 | 1 | 29 | 53 | 76 | 14 | 174 |
| 16 | 1 | 30 | 46 | 71 | 16.9 | 197 |
| 17 | 1 | 30 | 40 | 85.5 | 12.7 | 201 |
| 18 | 1 | 30 | 41 | 90 | 9.7 | 342 |
| 19 | 1 | 31 | 657 | 104 | 110 | 358 |
| 20 | 1 | 32 | 465 | 86.5 | 63.7 | 412 |
| 21 | 1 | 32 | 485 | 83.5 | 73 | 382 |
| 22 | 1 | 37 | 168 | 82.5 | 23.3 | 261 |
| 23 | 1 | 38 | 286 | 109.5 | 31.9 | 260 |
| 24 | 1 | 39 | 388 | 91 | 41.6 | 204 |
| 25 | 1 | 39 | 148 | 105.2 | 18.8 | 221 |
| 26 | 1 | 34 | 73 | 105.5 | 17 | 285 |
| 27 | 1 | 35 | 36 | 92.8 | 22 | 308 |
| 28 | 1 | 58 | 19 | 100.5 | 10.9 | 196 |
| 29 | 1 | 58 | 34 | 98.5 | 19.9 | 299 |
| 30 | 1 | 38 | 113 | 97 | 18.8 | 216 |
| 31 | 1 | 30 | 57 | 105 | 12.9 | 155 |
| 32 | 1 | 42 | 78 | 118 | 15.5 | 212 |
| 33 | 0 | 22 | 52 | 83.5 | 10.9 | 176 |
| 34 | 0 | 32 | 20 | 77 | 11 | 200 |
| 35 | 0 | 36 | 29 | 86.5 | 13.2 | 171 |

*Table 6.2* Muscular Dystrophy Data (Continued)

| id | CARRIER | AGE | P1 | P2 | P3 | P4 |
|---|---|---|---|---|---|---|
| 36 | 0 | 22 | 30 | 104 | 22.6 | 230 |
| 37 | 0 | 23 | 40 | 83 | 15.2 | 205 |
| 38 | 0 | 30 | 24 | 78.8 | 9.6 | 151 |
| 39 | 0 | 27 | 15 | 87 | 13.5 | 232 |
| 40 | 0 | 30 | 22 | 91 | 17.5 | 198 |
| 41 | 0 | 25 | 42 | 65.5 | 13.3 | 216 |
| 42 | 0 | 26 | 130 | 80.3 | 17.1 | 211 |
| 43 | 0 | 26 | 48 | 85.2 | 22.7 | 160 |
| 44 | 0 | 27 | 31 | 86.5 | 6.9 | 162 |
| 45 | 0 | 26 | 47 | 53 | 14.6 | 131 |
| 46 | 0 | 27 | 36 | 56 | 18.2 | 105 |
| 47 | 0 | 27 | 24 | 57.5 | 5.6 | 130 |
| 48 | 0 | 31 | 34 | 92.7 | 7.9 | 140 |
| 49 | 0 | 31 | 38 | 96 | 12.6 | 158 |
| 50 | 0 | 35 | 40 | 104.6 | 16.1 | 209 |
| 51 | 0 | 28 | 59 | 88 | 9.9 | 128 |
| 52 | 0 | 28 | 75 | 81 | 10.1 | 177 |
| 53 | 0 | 28 | 72 | 66.3 | 16.4 | 156 |
| 54 | 0 | 27 | 42 | 77 | 15.3 | 163 |
| 55 | 0 | 27 | 30 | 80.2 | 8.1 | 100 |
| 56 | 0 | 28 | 24 | 87 | 3.5 | 132 |
| 57 | 0 | 24 | 26 | 84.5 | 20.7 | 145 |
| 58 | 0 | 23 | 65 | 75 | 19.9 | 187 |
| 59 | 0 | 27 | 34 | 86.3 | 11.8 | 120 |
| 60 | 0 | 25 | 37 | 73.3 | 13 | 254 |
| 61 | 0 | 34 | 73 | 57.4 | 7.4 | 107 |
| 62 | 0 | 34 | 87 | 76.3 | 6 | 87 |
| 63 | 0 | 25 | 35 | 71 | 8.8 | 186 |
| 64 | 0 | 20 | 31 | 61.5 | 9.9 | 172 |
| 65 | 0 | 20 | 62 | 81 | 10.2 | 181 |
| 66 | 0 | 31 | 48 | 79 | 16.8 | 182 |
| 67 | 0 | 31 | 40 | 82.5 | 6.4 | 151 |
| 68 | 0 | 26 | 55 | 85.5 | 10.9 | 216 |
| 69 | 0 | 26 | 32 | 73.8 | 8.6 | 147 |
| 70 | 0 | 21 | 26 | 79.3 | 16.4 | 123 |

This provides the results shown in Figure 6.23.

**Figure 6.23** *Linear Regression with a Binary Response*

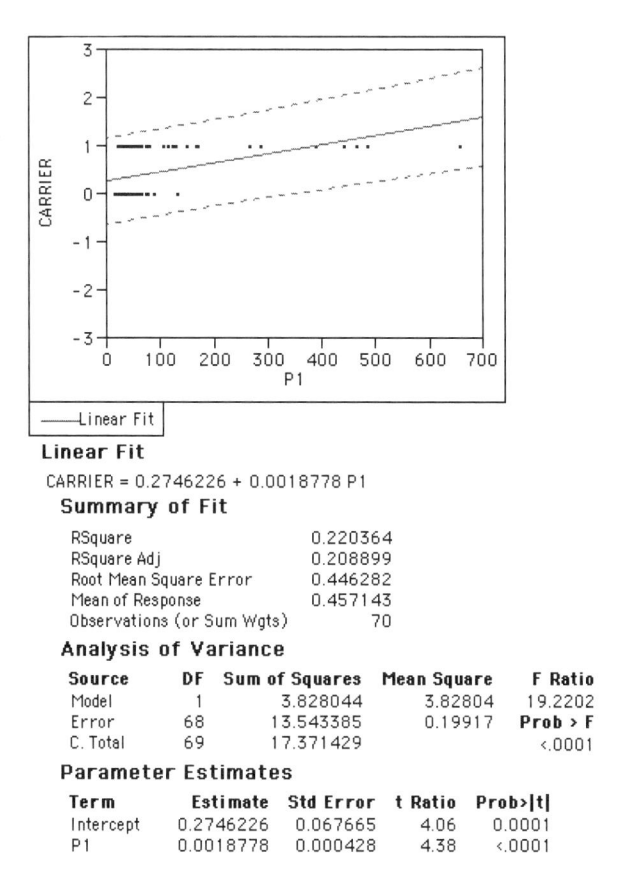

**Linear Fit**

CARRIER = 0.2746226 + 0.0018778 P1

**Summary of Fit**

| | |
|---|---|
| RSquare | 0.220364 |
| RSquare Adj | 0.208899 |
| Root Mean Square Error | 0.446282 |
| Mean of Response | 0.457143 |
| Observations (or Sum Wgts) | 70 |

**Analysis of Variance**

| Source | DF | Sum of Squares | Mean Square | F Ratio |
|---|---|---|---|---|
| Model | 1 | 3.828044 | 3.82804 | 19.2202 |
| Error | 68 | 13.543385 | 0.19917 | Prob > F |
| C. Total | 69 | 17.371429 | | <.0001 |

**Parameter Estimates**

| Term | Estimate | Std Error | t Ratio | Prob>|t| |
|---|---|---|---|---|
| Intercept | 0.2746226 | 0.067665 | 4.06 | 0.0001 |
| P1 | 0.0018778 | 0.000428 | 4.38 | <.0001 |

The regression is certainly significant, and the estimated coefficients suggest that the probability of detecting a carrier increases with measurements of P1.

The plot immediately reveals a problem: the response variable is defined to be zero or one, yet many estimated values and a large portion of the 95% prediction intervals are beyond this range.

Another difficulty with this model is that the variance of the binomial response variable is known to be a function of $p(1-p)$, where $p$ is the probability of the event. This obviously violates the equal variance assumption required by the least-squares estimation process. Thus this particular approach to the regression with a binary response appears to have limited usefulness.

The use of weighted regression may alleviate the unequal variance violation, and the use of the arcsine transformations may provide somewhat better estimates. However, a more useful approach is afforded by the *logistic* regression model. For a single independent variable the model is defined as

$$\log \frac{p}{1-p} = \beta_0 + \beta_1 x + \varepsilon$$

where $p$ is the probability of a response. The resulting response curve asymptotically approaches zero at one end and unity at the other (depending on the sign of $\beta_1$) and thus does not exhibit the difficulty found with the linear response function.

Note that although the regression model is linear on the right side, the left side is a nonlinear function of the response variable $p$. This function is known as the *logit link* function. Because it is not linear, the usual least-squares methods cannot be used to estimate the parameters. Instead, a method known as *maximum likelihood* is used to obtain these estimates.

Given a model specified by a set of parameters and the distribution of the random error, it is possible to obtain a function that describes the likelihood of a sample arising from that model. This expression is used to find those values of the parameters that maximize the likelihood. These estimates are called *maximum likelihood estimates*. Also, since the model includes the specification of the error variance, the equal variance assumption is not required.

For linear regression models with normally distributed errors, the maximum likelihood principle produces a set of linear equations whose solution is the familiar least-squares estimates. However, for the logistic regression model, the equations that must be solved to obtain estimates of the parameters are not linear; hence they must be obtained by numerical methods. This means that there are no formulas for the partitioning of sums of squares and variances of estimates and subsequent test statistics and confidence intervals. However, –2*(logarithm of the likelihood) provides a sample statistic that is related to the $\chi^2$ distribution, which can be used for hypothesis testing. Note that because of the minus sign, smaller values signify higher likelihood, implying a better-fitting model. To maximize the likelihood, we minimize –2*logLikelihood.

The sampling distributions of the parameter estimates are obtained by the use of asymptotic theory, which means that, strictly speaking, they are valid only for infinite sample sizes. However, studies show that they usually do quite well for moderate sample sizes, although this result is not guaranteed.

In JMP, logistic regression is performed exactly as standard least-squares regression is performed. JMP knows which regression to launch based on the modeling type of the variables entered into launch dialogs. If you enter a continuous $Y$ and a continuous $X$, JMP produces standard least-squares output. If you enter a categorical (i.e., nominal or ordinal) *Y* and a continuous *X*, JMP produces logistic regression output.

To change the modeling type of a variable,

- Click on its name in the Columns panel to the left of the data table.
- Select the desired modeling type of the variable from the menu that appears.

In this case, change CARRIER from Continuous to Nominal. The columns panel should appear like the one in Figure 6.24.

*Figure 6.24*
CARRIER *as a Nominal Variable*

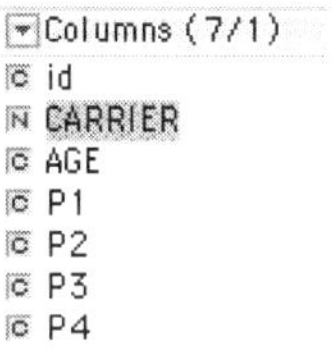

```
Columns (7/1)
 c  id
 N  CARRIER
 c  AGE
 c  P1
 c  P2
 c  P3
 c  P4
```

To perform a logistic regression to estimate the probability of being a carrier as related to P1,

- Select **Analyze → Fit Y by X**.
- Click **Recall** to select CARRIER as the Y variable and P1 as the X variable.
- Click **OK**.

The results are in Figure 6.25. The *X*-axis shows the level of P1 and the *Y*-axis shows the probability that CARRIER = 0 for each value of P1.

The bold numbers have been added to key the descriptions that follow. In this example CARRIER = 0 is the event whose probability you are modeling.

1. The convergence status indicates that the numerical solution method did converge. If this message is different, the results of the analysis may be of questionable value.
2. The test of the global hypothesis is simply the test for the model, that is, the test that all coefficients are zero. In this case it is the test $\beta_1 = 0$. The -Log Likelihood test is the difference in (–2Log L) between the intercept-only model and the full model. The resulting model Chi Square test, computed in this case as 2*13.706, provides a *p* value of <0.0001 for that test. Fit Model output is shown in Figure 6.26.
3. This section provides the estimated parameters and associated tests. The parameters themselves are used for estimating probabilities using the formula

***Figure 6.25***
*Logistic Regression Output*

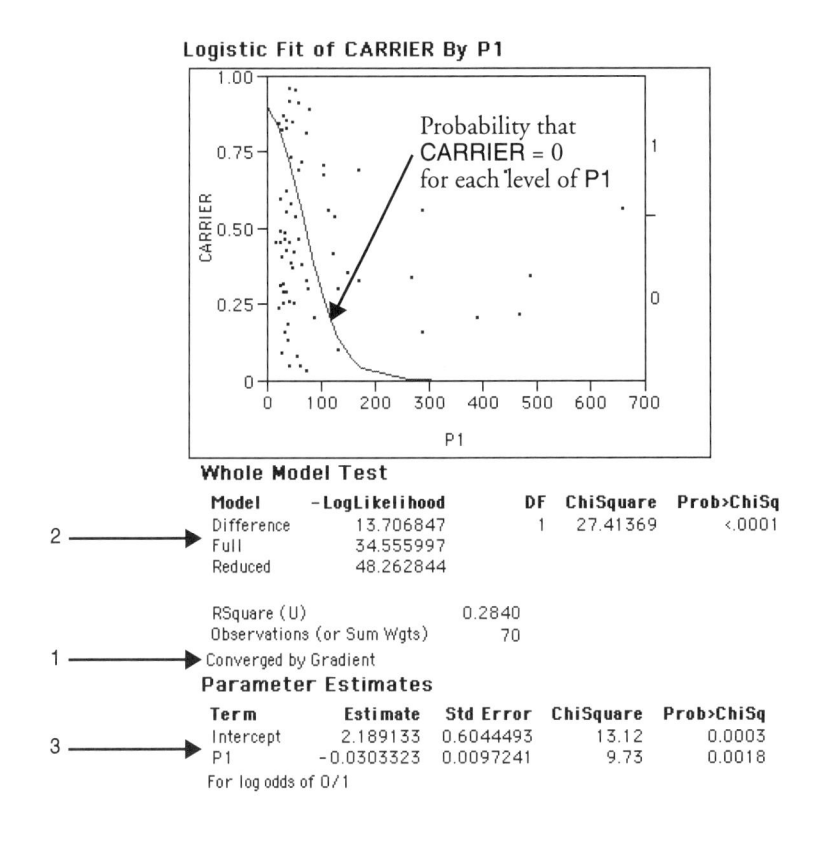

**Logistic Fit of CARRIER By P1**

Probability that CARRIER = 0 for each level of P1

**Whole Model Test**

| Model | −LogLikelihood | DF | ChiSquare | Prob>ChiSq |
|---|---|---|---|---|
| Difference | 13.706847 | 1 | 27.41369 | <.0001 |
| Full | 34.555997 | | | |
| Reduced | 48.262844 | | | |

RSquare (U)  0.2840
Observations (or Sum Wgts)  70
Converged by Gradient

**Parameter Estimates**

| Term | Estimate | Std Error | ChiSquare | Prob>ChiSq |
|---|---|---|---|---|
| Intercept | 2.189133 | 0.6044493 | 13.12 | 0.0003 |
| P1 | −0.0303323 | 0.0097241 | 9.73 | 0.0018 |

For log odds of 0/1

$$\hat{p} = \frac{1}{1 + e^{-\hat{y}}}$$

where $\hat{y}$ is the responses obtained from the estimated parameters.

Some statistics that are not available in Fit Y by X are available in Fit Model.

- Select **Analyze → Fit Model**.
- Assign CARRIER as Y.
- Add P1 as an effect in the model.
- Click **Run Model**.
- From the platform pop-up menu, select **Confidence Intervals**.
- Accept the default 0.05 as the $\alpha$ level.

*Figure 6.26* Logistic Fit Model Output

```
Nominal Logistic Fit for CARRIER
  Whole Model Test
  Model       -LogLikelihood    DF   ChiSquare   Prob>ChiSq
  Difference    13.706847        1    27.41369    <.0001
  Full          34.555997
  Reduced       48.262844

  RSquare (U)                   0.2840
  Observations (or Sum Wgts)       70
  Converged by Gradient
  Lack Of Fit
  Source      DF   -LogLikelihood   ChiSquare
  Lack Of Fit  51      24.328688      48.65738
  Saturated    52      10.227309    Prob>ChiSq
  Fitted        1      34.555997       0.5672
  Parameter Estimates
  Term        Estimate    Std Error   ChiSquare  Prob>ChiSq   Lower 95%    Upper 95%    Odds Ratio   Odds Lower   Odds Upper
  Intercept    2.189133   0.6044493     13.12      0.0003     1.10505588   3.49433015
  P1          -0.0303323  0.0097241      9.73      0.0018    -0.0523608   -0.0139984    3.49e-9      2.52e-15     0.00012503
  For log odds of 0/1
  Effect Wald Tests
  Source   Nparm   DF   Wald ChiSquare   Prob>ChiSq
  P1         1      1      9.7299578       0.0018
```

This adds confidence intervals to the Parameter Estimates table. JMP requires that Confidence Intervals be selected before Odds Ratio.

- From the platform pop-up menu, select **Odds Ratio**.

The odds ratio is calculated as

$$e^{b(\max(P1) - \min(P1))}$$

where $b$ is the parameter estimate for P1. This ratio measures how the fitted probability is multiplied as the regressor changes from its minimum to its maximum. In this example, the estimated odds ratio is $3.49(10^{-9})$.

The Fit Model platform allows you to save the probability formula to the data table.

- From the platform pop-up menu, select **Save Probability Formula**.

This adds several columns to the data table, including the probability that each row is 1, the probability it is 0, and the most likely CARRIER value.

To plot the estimated probabilities, use the following commands.

- Select **Graph → Overlay Plot**.

- Assign Prob[1] and Prob[0] to the Y axis.

- Assign P1 to the X axis.

- Click **OK**.
- Select **Y Options** → **Connect Points** from the platform pop-up menu.

These steps result in the output of Figure 6.27.

*Figure 6.27*
*Predicted Probability Plots*

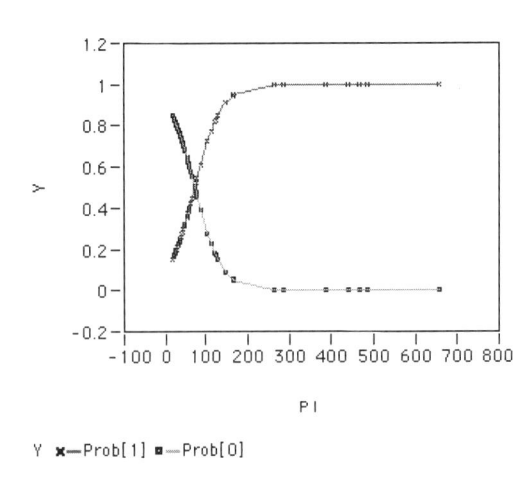

In addition to being able to perform a logistic regression model with several variables, JMP can also perform variable selection procedures. These include the Forward, Backward, and Mixed procedures. The following example uses the Forward procedure.

To perform a stepwise regression, set up the Fit Model dialog exactly as before, and

- Change the **Personality** from **Nominal Logistic** to **Stepwise**.
- Add P2, P3, and P4 as effects in the model.
- Click **Run Model**.

This change presents the familiar stepwise control panel as in Figure 6.28. Proceed exactly as in the least-squares case.

The choice of the most appropriate model is somewhat subjective, much as it was for the results of the continuous selection. The step-type selection procedures do provide $p$ values, but these are, of course, of limited use.

- Change the **Prob to Enter** to 0.05.

*Figure 6.28* Variable Selection

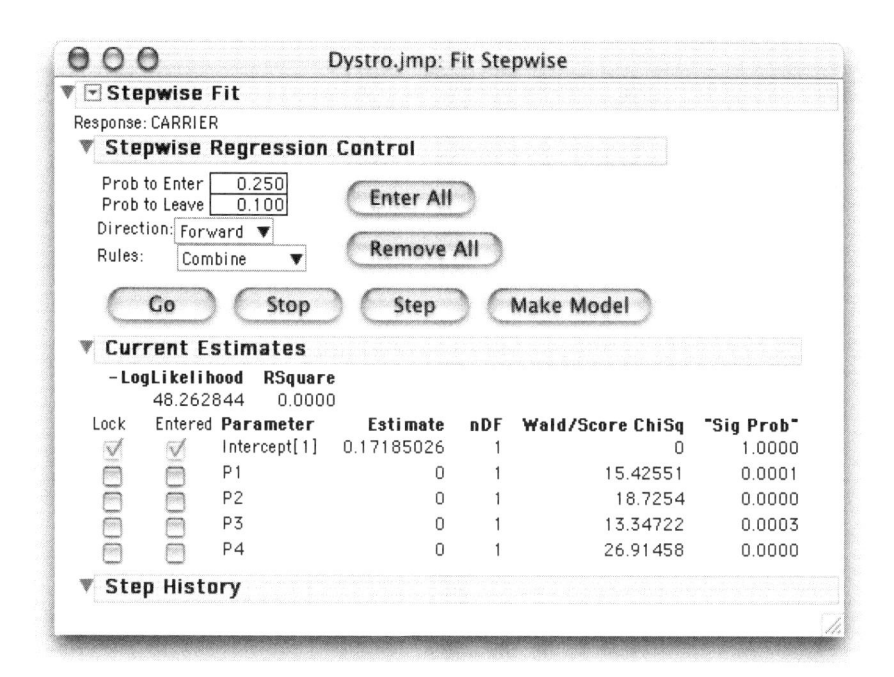

⁻ᵇ  Click **Go**.

The procedure finds a three-variable model, using P1, P2, and P4. To examine the results of this selection,

⁻ᵇ  Click **Make Model**.

When the Fit Model dialog appears,

⁻ᵇ  Click **Run Model**.

The results are shown in Figure 6.29.

The three-variable model does provide a better fit than that obtained from the standard protein P1, especially as indicated by the increase in the $R^2(U)$ statistic.

*Figure 6.29*
*Three-Variable Model*

**Nominal Logistic Fit for CARRIER**

**Whole Model Test**

| Model | -LogLikelihood | DF | ChiSquare | Prob>ChiSq |
|---|---|---|---|---|
| Difference | 28.133099 | 3 | 56.2662 | <.0001 |
| Full | 20.129745 | | | |
| Reduced | 48.262844 | | | |

RSquare (U)  0.5829
Observations (or Sum Wgts)  70
Converged by Gradient

**Lack Of Fit**

| Source | DF | -LogLikelihood | ChiSquare |
|---|---|---|---|
| Lack Of Fit | 66 | 20.129745 | 40.25949 |
| Saturated | 69 | 0.000000 | Prob>ChiSq |
| Fitted | 3 | 20.129745 | 0.9948 |

**Parameter Estimates**

| Term | Estimate | Std Error | ChiSquare | Prob>ChiSq |
|---|---|---|---|---|
| Intercept | 15.653455 | 4.1487674 | 14.24 | 0.0002 |
| P1 | -0.0275736 | 0.0122785 | 5.04 | 0.0247 |
| P2 | -0.0955832 | 0.0398694 | 5.75 | 0.0165 |
| P4 | -0.0268735 | 0.0102669 | 6.85 | 0.0089 |

For log odds of 0/1

**Effect Wald Tests**

| Source | Nparm | DF | Wald ChiSquare | Prob>ChiSq |
|---|---|---|---|---|
| P1 | 1 | 1 | 5.04309761 | 0.0247 |
| P2 | 1 | 1 | 5.74757683 | 0.0165 |
| P4 | 1 | 1 | 6.85126817 | 0.0089 |

## 6.7 Summary

The purpose of this chapter has been to show how linear regression models can be adapted to many situations. JMP can be used to fit a wide variety of models that do not look linear. Using the logarithmic transformation on the dependent variable stabilizes the error variance, and then using the logarithms of the independent variables provides a model whose coefficients are very useful in many applications. The use of specially coded variables allows the fitting of segmented regression or spline models that describe relationships where changes occur too abruptly to be fitted by polynomial models. Finally, indicator variables provide models that describe different relationships for different portions of the data.

Another class of models regresses a linear function of the independent variables on functions of the response variable. An important application of this type of model is the logistic model, which is appropriate for modeling binomial and ordinal responses. Such models are fitted by both Fit Y by X and Fit Model.

# Chapter 7  Nonlinear Models

*7.1 Introduction   215*

*7.2 Estimating the Exponential Decay Model   216*

　*7.2.1 Seeing the Sum of Squares Surface   223*

　*7.2.2 Estimates and Standard Errors   224*

*7.3 Fitting a Growth Curve with the Nonlinear Platform   229*

*7.4 Summary   236*

## 7.1 Introduction

The expression *linear model* refers to a model that is linear in its parameters or that can be made linear by transformation (such as the use of logarithms to estimate a multiplicative model) or redefinition of variables (see the BOQ data in Chapter 4). It is apparent that such linear models need not be linear in terms of the variables. However, many relationships exist that cannot be described by linear models or adaptations of linear models. For example, the model

$$y = \beta e^{\gamma t} + \varepsilon$$

is not linear in its parameters. Specifically, the term $\beta e^{\gamma t}$ is not a linear function of $\gamma$. This particular nonlinear model, called the *exponential growth* (or *decay*) *model*, is used to represent increase (growth) or decrease (decay) over time ($t$) of many types of responses such as population size or radiation counts.

One major advantage of many nonlinear models over, say, polynomial models, is that the parameters represent meaningful physical quantities of the process described by the model. In the above model, the parameter $\beta$ is the initial value of the response (when $t = 0$) and the parameter $\gamma$ is the rate of exponential growth (or decay). A positive value of $\gamma$ indicates growth while a negative value indicates decay.

In addition, the shape of nonlinear models frequently better approximates the data over a wider domain than polynomial models.

When a model is nonlinear in the parameters, the entire process of estimation and statistical inference is radically altered. This departure happens mainly because the normal equations that are solved to obtain least-squares parameter estimates are themselves nonlinear. Solutions of systems of nonlinear equations are not usually available in closed form (mathematical jargon for not being in the form of an equation), but must be obtained by numerical methods. For this reason, closed-form expressions for the partitioning of sums of squares, as well as the consequently obtained statistics for making inferences on the parameters, are also unavailable.

For most applications, the solutions to the normal equations are obtained by means of an iterative process. The process starts with some preliminary estimates of the parameters. These estimates are used to calculate a residual sum of squares and give an indication of which modifications of the parameter estimates may result in reducing the residual sum of squares. This process is repeated until it appears that no further modification of parameter estimates results in a reduction of the residual sum of squares.

The JMP platform for analyzing nonlinear models is the Nonlinear platform. Nonlinear is introduced with an example of the simple exponential decay model in "Estimating the Exponential Decay Model" below. Additional examples of the use of Nonlinear Fit include the logistic growth model (see "Fitting a Growth Curve with the Nonlinear Platform" on page 229).

## 7.2 Estimating the Exponential Decay Model

The data set DECAY comes from an experiment to determine the radioactive decay of a substance. The variable COUNT represents the radiation count recorded at various times (TIME). Figure 7.1 shows the data, and the plot of COUNT versus TIME is given in Figure 7.2. The decrease (decay) of COUNT with TIME is clearly evident.

Notice the curvature of the data, indicating a nonlinear fit. A linear fit shows this quite clearly.

- Select **Fit Line** from the platform pop-up menu.

- When the linear fit appears, select **Plot Residuals** from the **Linear Fit** menu.

The result is shown in Figure 7.3. The U-shaped pattern of the residuals shows that a linear model is not appropriate, even if the correlation is quite good (as in this case).

**Figure 7.1**
*Decay Rate Data*

| COUNT | TIME |
|---|---|
| 383 | 0 |
| 373 | 14 |
| 348 | 43 |
| 328 | 61 |
| 324 | 69 |
| 317 | 74 |
| 307 | 86 |
| 302 | 90 |
| 298 | 92 |
| 280 | 117 |
| 268 | 133 |
| 261 | 138 |
| 244 | 165 |
| 200 | 224 |
| 197 | 236 |
| 185 | 253 |
| 180 | 265 |
| 120 | 404 |
| 112.5 | 434 |

**Figure 7.2**
*Plot of Decay Rate Data*

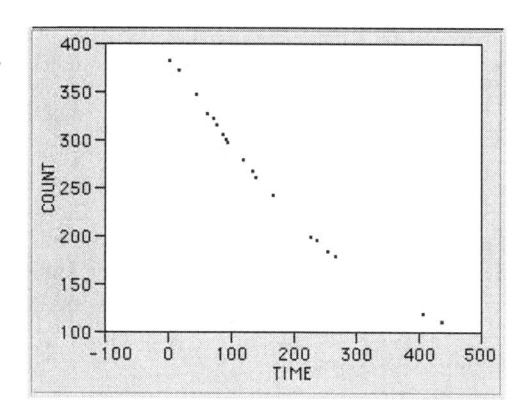

Since the curve is nonlinear, some knowledge of the process should be used to determine a likely form of the model. Radioactive decay is known to follow the familiar exponential function

$$y = be^{cx}$$

so that would be an appropriate next step for the model.

The Nonlinear platform requires that a column in the data table contain the estimation model. The model in this case is

COUNT = b*exp(c*TIME)

**Figure 7.3**
*Linear Fit Results*

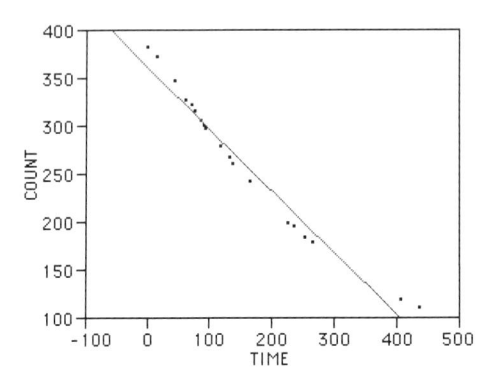

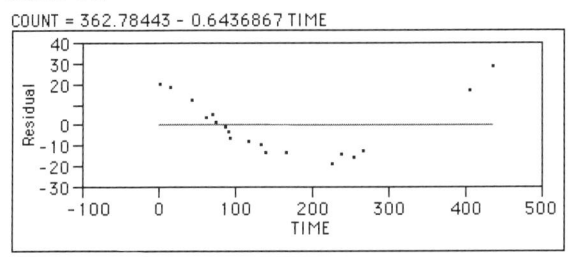

where b and c are parameters to be estimated. Providing good starting values for these parameters is quite important, because poor starting values can increase computing time and may even prevent finding correct estimates of the parameters. Starting values are usually educated guesses, although some preliminary calculations may be used for this purpose.

In this example, b is the expected COUNT at TIME = 0, which should be close to the observed value of 383. The initial value for c is obtained by using the observed COUNT for a specific TIME and solving for c. Choose TIME = 117, where COUNT = 280, and solve

$$280 = 380e^{117c}$$

Taking logarithms makes this a linear equation, which is easily solved to obtain the initial value c = −0.0026.

To construct a column with the model and parameters,

- Double-click to the right of the last column in the data table to add a new column called **Model Formula**.

- Right-click (Control-click on the Macintosh) on the new column and select **Formula** from the menu that appears.

*Estimating the Exponential Decay Model* **219**

The Formula Editor appears, with a list of data table columns in the upper left.

- Click on the drop-down list that currently says **Table Columns** and select **Parameters** from the menu that appears.

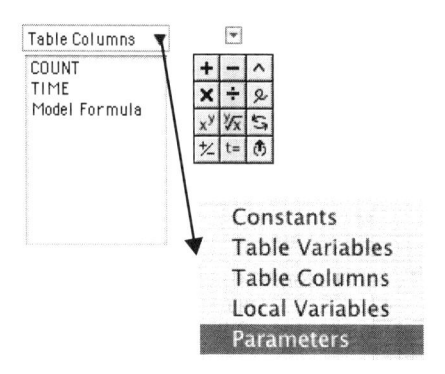

- Double-click on **New Parameter**.

In the dialog that appears,

- Enter b as the name of the parameter. Enter 380 as the initial value of the parameter.

- Repeat these steps to make a parameter named c with an initial value of –0.0026.

Now, construct a formula using these parameters.

- Click b in the parameters list.
- Click the multiplication key in the formula keypad.
- Select **Transcendental** → **Exp** from the functions list.
- Click c in the Parameters list to enter it as the argument for the Exp function.
- Click the multiplication key in the formula keypad.
- Change the **Parameters** list back to **Table Columns**.
- Click TIME in the columns list.
- Click **OK**.

**Figure 7.4**
*Model Formula*

b*Exp(c*TIME)

The formula should appear as in Figure 7.4.

Now, launch the Nonlinear platform.

◦ Select **Analyze** → **Modeling** → **Nonlinear**.

In the dialog that appears,

◦ Select COUNT as the **Y, Response** variable.

◦ Select Model Formula as the **X, Predictor Formula**.

◦ Click **OK**.

◦ From the platform pop-up menu, select **Plot** to see a plot of the data.

The Nonlinear Control Panel appears, as in Figure 7.5.

You can see the differences between running Nonlinear and Fit Model.

❑ In Nonlinear, you must specify the complete model (except for the error) in a data table column, whereas in Fit Model you need to specify only the names of dependent and independent variables.

❑ In Nonlinear, you must specify the names of the parameters in the column formula statement.

❑ The column formula is also used to provide starting values of the parameters that initiate the iterative estimation procedure. In this case, the starting values are specified as b = 380 and c = –0.0026.

To begin the fitting process (called "driving the platform"),

◦ Click **Go** in the Control Panel.

The output appears in Figure 7.6.

The top portion of the output summarizes the iterative solution process. Under Report (near the top of the output) you see the iterative procedure converged.

The Solution portion of the report shows statistics on the fit of the model, estimated parameters, and their standard errors. Confidence limits initially show as missing, but can be computed.

◦ Click the **Confidence Limits** button in the Control Panel.

*Figure 7.5*
*Nonlinear*
*Control Panel*

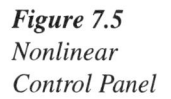

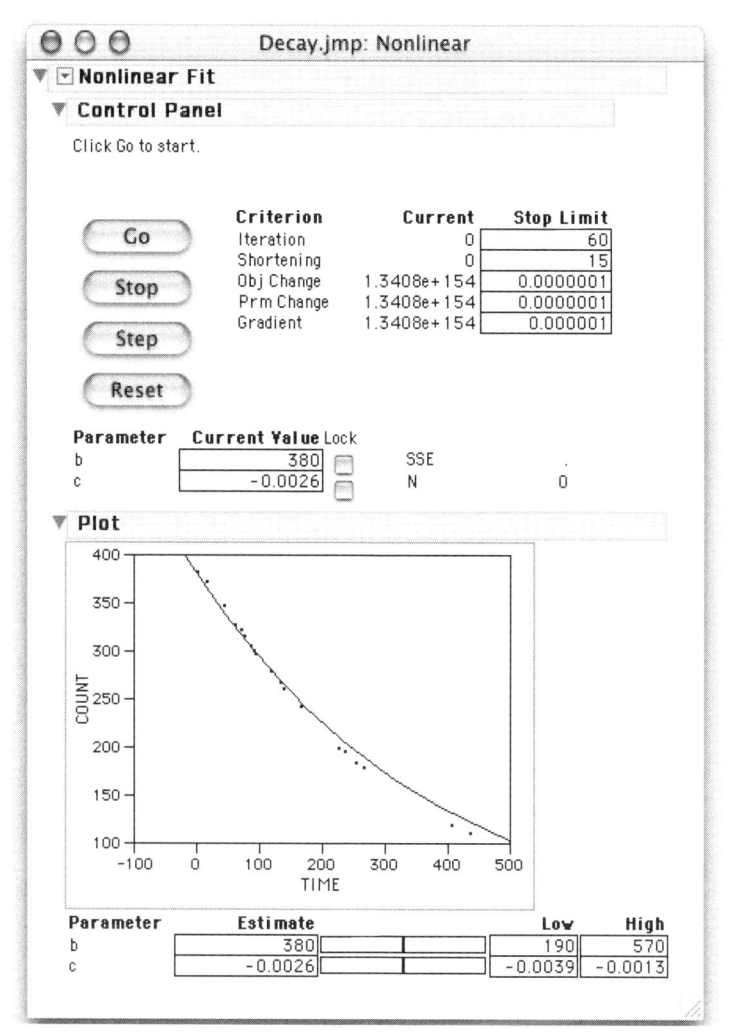

The parameter estimates provide the estimated model

COUNT = 390.34$e^{-0.00289*\text{time}}$

The estimated initial count is 390.34 and the estimated exponential decay rate is –0.00289. This means that the expected count at time $t$ is $e^{0.00289}$ = 0.997 times the count at time $t - 1$. In other words, the estimated rate of decay is (1 – 0.997) = 0.003, or approximately 0.3% per time period.

**Figure 7.6** *Output from Nonlinear Fit for Decay Data*

**Nonlinear Fit**

**Control Panel**

Report
Converged in Objective Function

| Criterion | Current | Stop Limit |
|---|---|---|
| Iteration | 3 | 60 |
| Shortening | 0 | 15 |
| Obj Change | 4.44847e-8 | 0.0000001 |
| Prm Change | 0.0000089552 | 0.0000001 |
| Gradient | 0.0000064048 | 0.000001 |

| Parameter | Current Value | Lock | | |
|---|---|---|---|---|
| b | 390.33778738 | | SSE | 143.06140519 |
| c | -0.002890881 | | N | 19 |

Edit Alpha 0.050
Convergence Criterion 0.00001
Goal SSE for CL

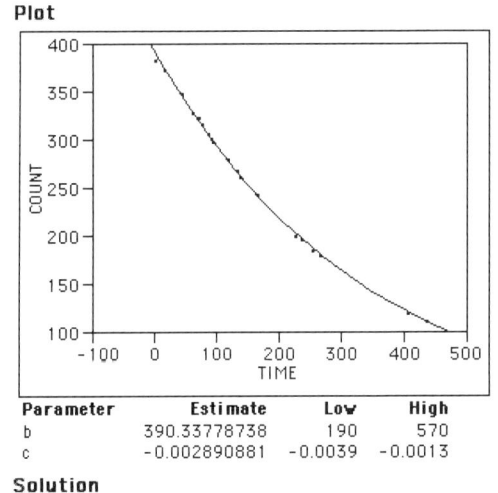

**Plot**

| Parameter | Estimate | Low | High |
|---|---|---|---|
| b | 390.33778738 | 190 | 570 |
| c | -0.002890881 | -0.0039 | -0.0013 |

**Solution**

| SSE | DFE | MSE | RMSE |
|---|---|---|---|
| 143.06140519 | 17 | 8.4153768 | 2.9009269 |

| Parameter | Estimate | ApproxStdErr | Lower CL | Upper CL |
|---|---|---|---|---|
| b | 390.33778738 | 1.45050905 | . | . |
| c | -0.002890881 | 0.00002968 | . | . |

The estimated decay rate coefficient is used to get an estimated half-life, the time at which one half of the radiation has occurred. This is computed as T2 = ln(2)/−0.00289 = 240 time periods.

## 7.2.1 Seeing the Sum of Squares Surface

Nonlinear regression, like linear regression, minimizes the sum of squares of the residuals from the model to the predicted values, although in a more complicated manner. To aid in the visualization of this process, JMP provides a way to see the surface that is used in the minimization process.

- From the Nonlinear pop-up menu, select **SSE Grid**.

This appends a control panel that allows specification of the grid of values over which the plot is made.

For this example,

- Press **Go** to accept the default values.

A new data table appears containing a grid of values for the parameters b and c, as well as the values of SSE for each pair of parameter values. To see a three-dimensional plot of these values,

- Select **Graph → Spinning Plot**.
- Enter all three variables (b, c, and SSE) as **Y, Columns**.
- Click **OK**.

A plot of the SSE surface appears (Figure 7.7).

**Figure 7.7**
*Spinning Plot of SSE*

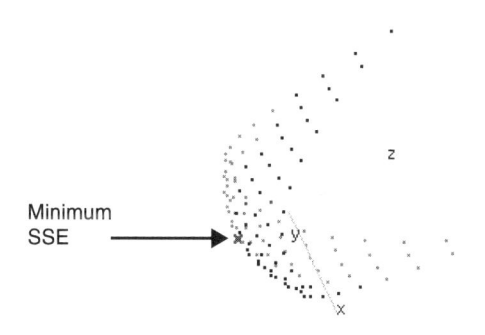

- Select the hand tool from the **Tools** menu (or from the toolbar if it is visible).
- Click and drag it inside the spinning plot to examine the plot from several angles.

Note that the minimum of the SSE values is indicated by a special marker and color.

The standard errors of the estimated coefficients and the confidence intervals are asymptotic. This means that the formulas used for the computations are only approximately correct because they are based on mathematical theory that is valid only for very large sample sizes. The 95% confidence interval in this case indicates that the true exponential decay rate is between –0.00295 and –0.00283.

The **Correlation of Estimates** portion (Figure 7.8) shows the approximate correlations between the estimated coefficients. You can see that there exists a moderately large negative correlation between the estimates of the two coefficients.

*Figure 7.8 Correlation of Estimates*

```
Correlation of Estimates

        b         c
b   1.0000   -0.7603
c  -0.7603    1.0000
```

## 7.2.2 Estimates and Standard Errors

To save the estimates of the model with the current parameters,

- Click the **Save Estimates** button.

This saves the estimates in the Model Formula column that was created to hold the formula.

Confidence limits on the mean or on individuals can be saved from the platform pop-up menu. For this example, save confidence limits on an individual prediction.

- Click **Save Indiv Confid Limits** from the platform pop-up menu.

This appends two columns, LowerI and UpperI, to the data table.

Residuals must be computed using the JMP Formula Editor.

- Double-click to the right of the last column in the data table to create a new column.

- Name the new column Residuals.

- Right-click (Control-click on the Macintosh) on the new column and choose **Formula** from the menu that appears.

When the Formula Editor appears,

## Estimating the Exponential Decay Model

- Select COUNT from the list of columns.
- Click the subtract key (–) on the Formula Editor keypad.
- Select Model Formula from the list of columns.

The formula should now say COUNT – Model Formula.

- Click **OK**.

Now, to generate a plot of the residuals,

- Select **Graph** → **Overlay Plot**.
- Assign Residual to the *y*-axis and TIME to the *x*-axis.
- Click **OK**.

When the plot appears, add a reference line at *y* = 0.

- Double click on the *y*-axis.
- Click the **Add Ref Line** button to add the reference line.

The resulting plot is shown in Figure 7.9. The only outstanding feature is the rather large negative residual for the first observation.

*Figure 7.9*
*Residual Plot*

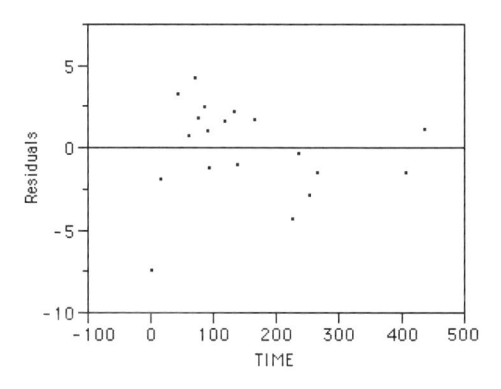

It is always a good idea to examine residuals, and in this case it may indicate whether the residual for the first point is an outlier or not.

- Select **Analyze** → **Distribution**.
- Select Residual as the **Y, Columns** variable.
- Click **OK**.

The resulting output (Figure 7.10) does show that the first point is a mild outlier.

**Figure 7.10** Distribution of Residual

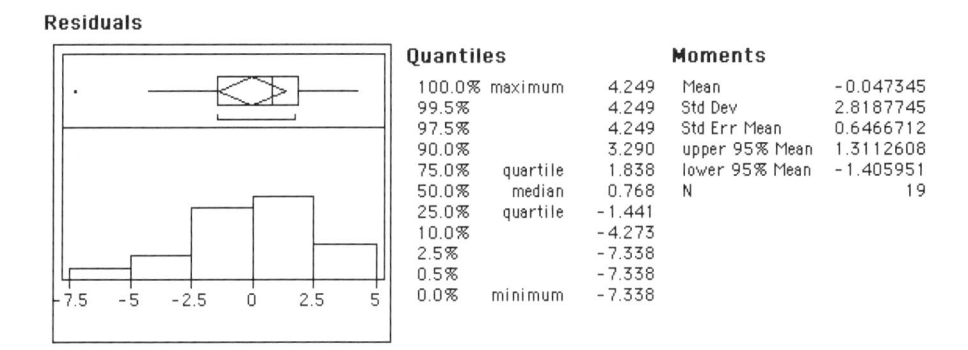

Residuals

| Quantiles | | | Moments | |
|---|---|---|---|---|
| 100.0% | maximum | 4.249 | Mean | -0.047345 |
| 99.5% | | 4.249 | Std Dev | 2.8187745 |
| 97.5% | | 4.249 | Std Err Mean | 0.6466712 |
| 90.0% | | 3.290 | upper 95% Mean | 1.3112608 |
| 75.0% | quartile | 1.838 | lower 95% Mean | -1.405951 |
| 50.0% | median | 0.768 | N | 19 |
| 25.0% | quartile | -1.441 | | |
| 10.0% | | -4.273 | | |
| 2.5% | | -7.338 | | |
| 0.5% | | -7.338 | | |
| 0.0% | minimum | -7.338 | | |

To explain this residual, examine a plot of the predicted values. Since they are saved to the data table, plot the confidence curves for an individual prediction as well.

- Select **Graph** → **Overlay Plot**.
- Designate COUNT, Model Formula, LowerI, and UpperI as Y variables.
- Designate TIME as the X variable.
- Click **OK**.

When the plot appears,

- Right-click (Control-click on the Macintosh) on the LowerI and UpperI columns in the legend at the bottom of the plot to reveal menus that show/hide points, and change colors, line styles, and markers. Several have been changed from their defaults.

The plot appears in Figure 7.11.

The box plot in Figure 7.10 indicates a problem with the observation at TIME=0, which appears to be due to an almost linear decay for the first three time periods, a phenomenon that is supported by the plot of actual and predicted values. The histogram and box plots show a slight left skewness for the distribution of residuals that is not serious enough to cause difficulty.

Although most nonlinear models must be fitted by an iterative procedure such as the one used in the Nonlinear platform, some may be linearized and the linear-

*Figure 7.11* Predicted Values

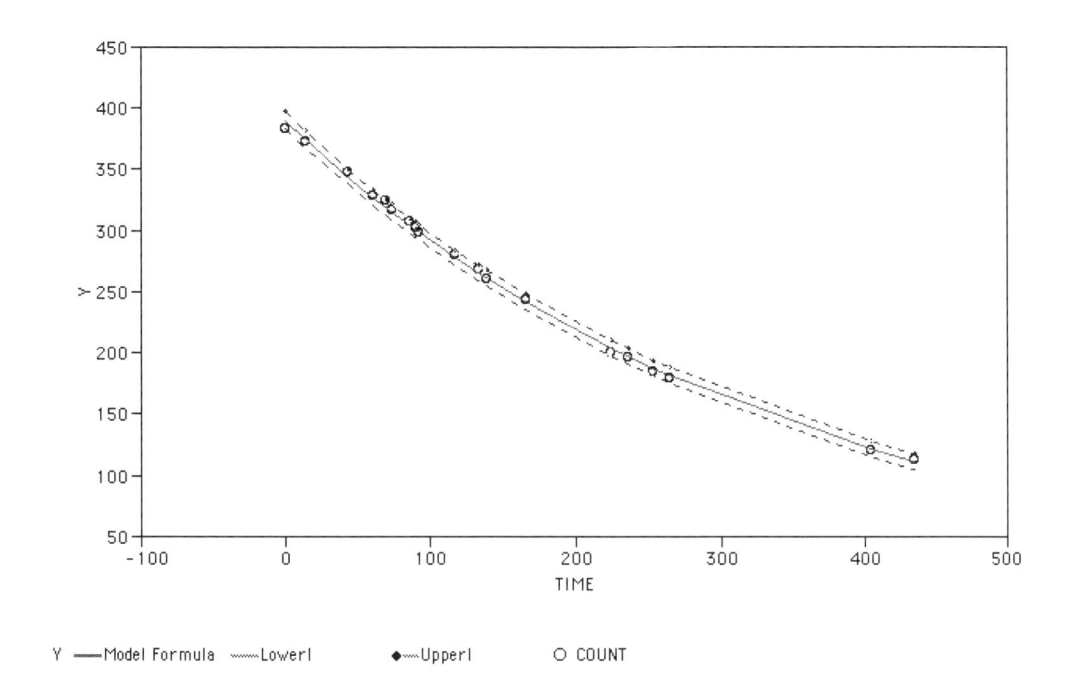

ized versions fitted by linear regression. The above decay model can be linearized by taking logarithms of the dependent variable and performing a linear regression using these values. In this example, the model

$$\log(\text{COUNT}) = \beta + \gamma(\text{TIME}) + \varepsilon$$

fits the decay model, with $e^\beta$ being the estimated initial value and $\gamma$ the decay constant.

This could be accomplished as expected, by creating a new variable in the data table to hold a formula for log(COUNT). Fit Model could then be used to analyze the data. However, since this example is a simple linear regression of a single *x* onto a single *y*, it is a candidate for the Fit Y by X platform, and is used to show the use of the Fit Special command.

- Select **Analyze → Fit Y by X**.
- Specify COUNT as the Y variable and TIME as the X variable.
- Click **OK**.

## 228 Nonlinear Models

When the scatterplot appears,

🖱 Select **Fit Special** from the platform pop-up menu.

The Fit Special dialog (shown in Figure 7.12) appears.

**Figure 7.12**
*Fit Special Dialog*

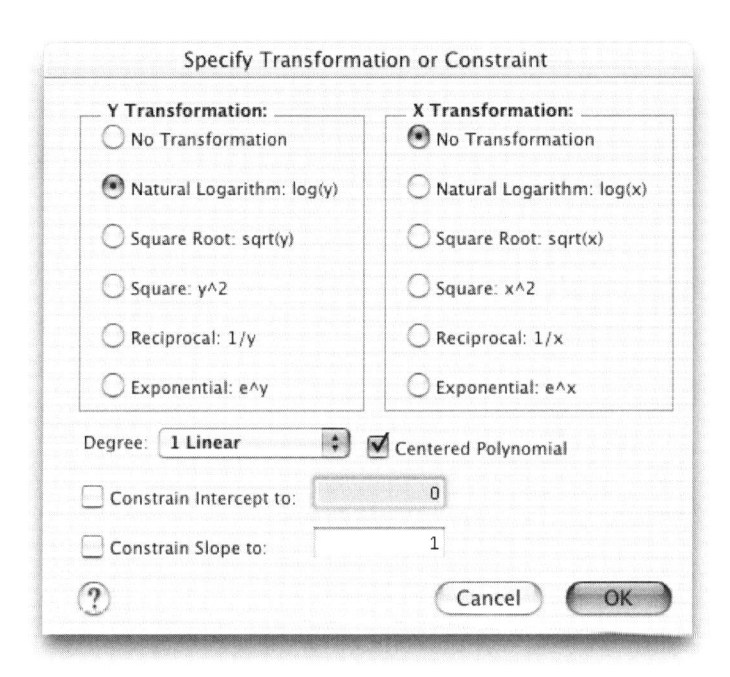

🖱 Select **Natural Logarithm: log (y)** from the **Y Transformation** section.

🖱 Click **OK**.

The results are shown in Figure 7.13.

The result in Figure 7.13 provides estimates of initial value and decay constants of $e^{5.9686}$ and $-0.00291$, which compare favorably with the values 390.3 and $-0.00289$ obtained by Nonlinear Fit in Figure 7.6. The standard error of the linearized model estimate of the decay constant is 0.00002035, compared with the asymptotic standard error of 0.0000297 from Nonlinear Fit. The differences arise primarily in that the linearized estimates are not truly least-squares estimates because the log-linear models account for the standard deviation of residuals being proportional to the mean (see "Introduction" in Chapter 6). Since the residuals do not appear to have this feature (see Figure 7.9 and Figure 7.10), the multiplicative model may not be appropriate.

*Figure 7.13 Fitting a Linearized Nonlinear Model*

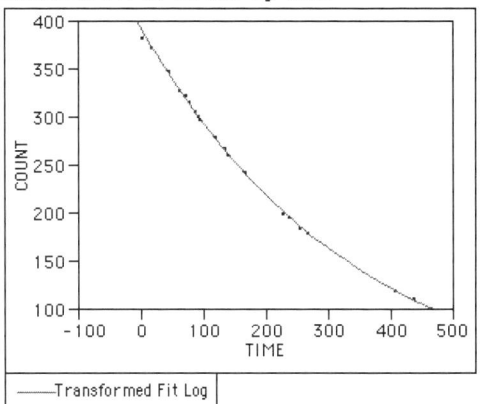

**Bivariate Fit of COUNT By TIME**

―― Transformed Fit Log

**Transformed Fit Log**

Log(COUNT) = 5.9685811 - 0.002906 TIME

**Summary of Fit**

| | |
|---|---|
| RSquare | 0.999167 |
| RSquare Adj | 0.999118 |
| Root Mean Square Error | 0.010521 |
| Mean of Response | 5.525347 |
| Observations (or Sum Wgts) | 19 |

**Analysis of Variance**

| Source | DF | Sum of Squares | Mean Square | F Ratio |
|---|---|---|---|---|
| Model | 1 | 2.2569517 | 2.25695 | 20390.87 |
| Error | 17 | 0.0018816 | 0.00011 | Prob > F |
| C. Total | 18 | 2.2588333 | | <.0001 |

**Parameter Estimates**

| Term | Estimate | Std Error | t Ratio | Prob>|t| |
|---|---|---|---|---|
| Intercept | 5.9685811 | 0.00393193 | 1518 | <.0001 |
| TIME | -0.002906 | 0.00002035 | -142.8 | <.0001 |

**Fit Measured on Original Scale**

| | |
|---|---|
| Sum of Squared Error | 145.26768 |
| Root Mean Square Error | 2.9232102 |
| RSquare | 0.998729 |
| Sum of Residuals | 0.1831994 |

## 7.3 Fitting a Growth Curve with the Nonlinear Platform

A common application of nonlinear regression is fitting growth curves. This application is illustrated with the fish growth data from Chapter 5 using the data for fish stored at 29 degrees. For convenience, the data are shown here in Figure 7.14, with the fish length denoted as the variable **LEN29**.

**Figure 7.14**
*Fish Growth Data for Temperature of 29 Degrees*

| AGE | LEN29 |
|-----|-------|
| 14  | 590   |
| 21  | 910   |
| 28  | 1305  |
| 35  | 1730  |
| 42  | 2140  |
| 49  | 2725  |
| 56  | 2890  |
| 63  | 3685  |
| 70  | 3920  |
| 77  | 4325  |
| 84  | 4410  |
| 91  | 4485  |
| 98  | 4515  |
| 105 | 4480  |
| 112 | 4520  |
| 119 | 4545  |
| 126 | 4525  |
| 133 | 4560  |
| 140 | 4565  |
| 147 | 4626  |
| 154 | 4566  |

The relationship used here is known as the logistic growth curve. The general form of the equation for the logistic growth curve is

$$y = \frac{k}{1 + \left(\frac{k - n_0}{n_0}\right)e^{-rt}} + \varepsilon$$

This model has three parameters: $k$, $n_0$, and $r$. The parameter $n_0$ is the expected value of $y$ at time $t = 0$, $k$ is the height of the horizontal asymptote (the expected value of $y$ for very large $t$), and $r$ is a measure of growth rate. The term $\varepsilon$ is the random error and is assumed to have mean zero and unit variance.

You can fit the logistic model to the fish growth data with the following steps:

- Create a new column **Model Formula** to hold the formula.

- Create new parameters k, n0, and r with initial values 4500, 500, and 1, respectively.

- Double-click the words *no formula* in the Formula Editor to change them into a text box.

This illustrates an alternative, textual way to enter a formula.

- Enter the formula k / (1 + ((k - n0) / n0) * Exp(-r * age)).

- Select **Analyze** → **Nonlinear Fit**.

- Specify LEN29 as Y and Model Formula as X.

- Click **OK**.
- Select **Plot** from the platform pop-up menu.
- Click **Go** to begin the fitting process.

The starting values for the parameters are preliminary guesses based on knowledge of what the parameters stand for. The value $k = 4500$ is selected because the values of **LEN29** for large values of **AGE** are approximately 4500, and the value $n_0 = 500$ is selected because the value of **LEN29** for early ages is around 500. Less is known about the value for $r$. Since growth is positive (the values of **LEN29** increase with age), $r$ should be a small positive number. Because the starting values for $k$ and $n_0$ appear to be quite good, a starting value of 1 should suffice for $r$. The results are shown in Figure 7.15.

The result shows that the iterations failed to converge after many step-halvings. The reason for this is probably bad starting values. The analysis should be repeated, with adjusted starting values.

Notice at the bottom of the report, below the plot of the curve, there are sliders beside each parameter estimate. The starting values for $k$ and $n_0$ were based on the observations and are probably quite good. However, the starting value of 1 for $r$ was quite arbitrary, and it should probably be changed. It is a positive number, but could be anything larger than zero. To use the sliders to examine many values of $r$,

- Change the 0.0325 in the Low text box to 0.
- Similarly, set the High value to 1.5.

This change allows the slider to vary between values of 0 and 1.5.

Note also that the value for n0 has spiraled off to a very large number. Change it back to 500.

- Enter 500 in the Estimate box beside the n0 slider.
- Drag the slider for $r$ to the left, and observe the corresponding change in the plotted curve.
- Move the slider to a point near $r = 0.05$.

This is obviously a better starting value for $r$.

- Click **Reset** to initialize the Nonlinear platform to these new values.
- Click **Go** to begin the iterations with this new value of $r$.

The plot this time converges, as shown in Figure 7.16.

**Figure 7.15** *Nonlinear Fit Output for Logistic Growth Curve Regression*

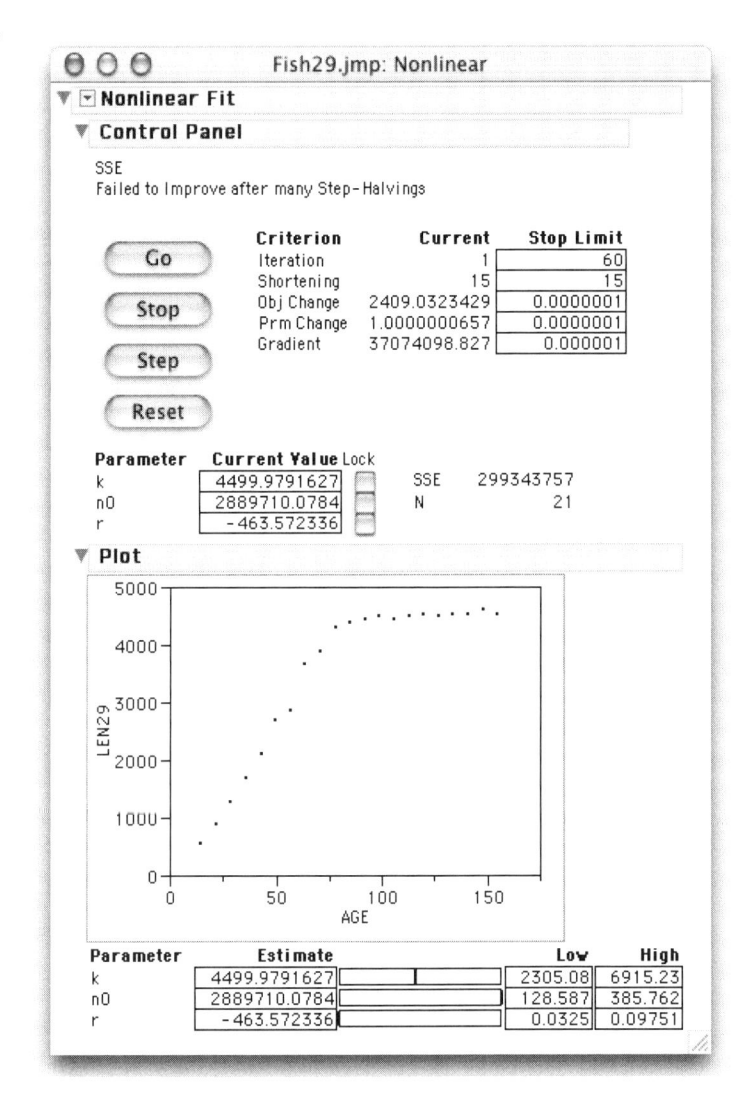

Asymptotic standard errors and corresponding confidence intervals for the parameters show that they are estimated with useful precision. The large negative correlation between $n_0$ and $r$ (shown in the Correlation of Estimates table) indicates the presence of the nonlinear version of collinearity. This correlation could indicate a family of curves with differing values of $r$ and $n_0$ that all fit about as

*Figure 7.16
Converged
Fit*

**Nonlinear Fit**

**Control Panel**

Report
Converged in Objective Function

| Criterion | Current | Stop Limit |
|---|---|---|
| Iteration | 3 | 60 |
| Shortening | 0 | 15 |
| Obj Change | 8.44379e-8 | 0.0000001 |
| Prm Change | 0.000073867 | 0.0000001 |
| Gradient | 0.009349169 | 0.000001 |

| Parameter | Current Value | Lock | | |
|---|---|---|---|---|
| k | 4610.1560452 | | SSE | 177874.23565 |
| n0 | 257.17436567 | | N | 21 |
| r | 0.0650083577 | | | |

Edit Alpha  0.050
Convergence Criterion  0.00001
Goal SSE for CL  221491.70014

**Plot**

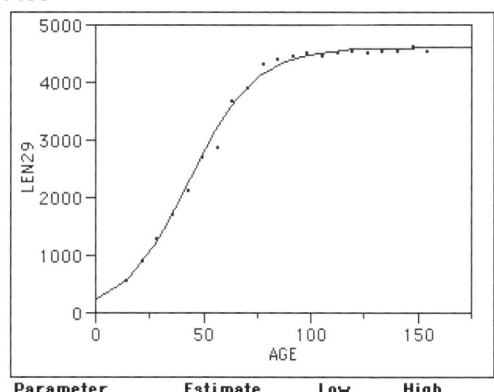

[Growth curve plot: LEN29 vs AGE, sigmoidal curve from ~250 at age 0 rising to ~4600 plateau by age 150]

| Parameter | Estimate | Low | High |
|---|---|---|---|
| k | 4610.1560452 | 2305.08 | 6915.23 |
| n0 | 257.17436567 | 128.587 | 385.762 |
| r | 0.0650083577 | 0 | 1.5 |

**Solution**

| SSE | DFE | MSE | RMSE |
|---|---|---|---|
| 177874.23565 | 18 | 9881.902 | 99.407756 |

| Parameter | Estimate | ApproxStdErr | Lower CL | Upper CL |
|---|---|---|---|---|
| k | 4610.1560452 | 35.1102357 | 4538.49749 | 4683.61644 |
| n0 | 257.17436567 | 28.1791153 | 203.10068 | 319.109767 |
| r | 0.0650083577 | 0.00261453 | 0.05993221 | 0.07053042 |

**Correlation of Estimates**

| | k | n0 | r |
|---|---|---|---|
| k | 1.0000 | 0.3786 | -0.5048 |
| n0 | 0.3786 | 1.0000 | -0.9434 |
| r | -0.5048 | -0.9434 | 1.0000 |

well as each other, meaning that parameter estimates are imprecise. However, the satisfactorily small standard errors indicate this is not the case.

You can examine the residuals from the fitted logistic growth curve as a further check on the fit of the model. As before, a column must be created to hold the residuals.

- Click **Save Estimates** to store the estimates in the data table.

- Create a new column named **Residuals**.

- Right-click (Control-click on the Macintosh) on the new column and select **Formula** from the menu that appears.

- Enter the formula Len29 – Model Formula.

- Click **OK**.

Now, plot the residuals.

- Select **Graph → Overlay Plot**.

- Designate **Residuals** as the Y variable and **AGE** as the X variable.

- Click **OK**.

When the plot appears,

- Double-click on the $y$-axis.

- Click **Add Ref Line** in the dialog that appears to add a reference line at 0.

The residuals appear in Figure 7.17.

There is a large negative residual of about –300 corresponding to an age in the upper 60s, which is an apparent outlier. Also, there is a moderately large residual among a string of six negative residuals from ages 105 to 140. This indicates modest lack of fit in this region.

After saving confidence limits to the data table, you can use the same method as before to show predicted values. Results in Figure 7.18 agree with the residual analysis.

*Figure 7.17*
*Residual Plot for Logistic Growth Curve*

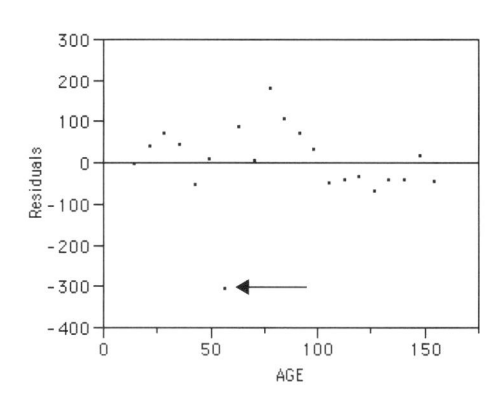

*Figure 7.18*
*Plot of Fitted Values for Logistic Growth Curve*

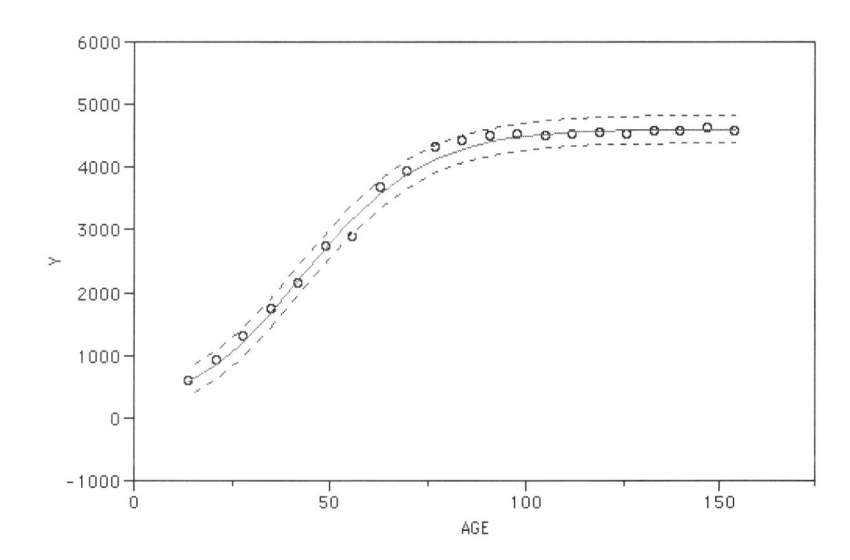

## 7.4 Summary

This chapter has provided some relatively simple examples of how Nonlinear Fit can be used to estimate nonlinear regression models. Additional options for dealing with more complicated models have been briefly noted but not explicitly illustrated.

Fitting nonlinear models is not always an easy task, especially for models containing as few as four or five parameters. Special strategies may need to be considered.

Therefore, if a nonlinear model contains a number of linear parameters, it may be possible to estimate the linear parameters using reasonable values of the nonlinear parameters to get starting values.

As a rule, if you need to fit a rather complicated model and you are not very familiar with nonlinear models in general and the Nonlinear platform in particular, try some simple examples first.

# Chapter 8    Regression with JMP Scripting Language

*8.1   Introduction   237*
*8.2   Performing a Simple Regression   237*
*8.3   Regression Matrices   241*
*8.4   Collinearity Diagnostics   242*
*8.5   Summary   246*

## 8.1 Introduction

JMP provides a flexible array of procedures for performing regression analyses. You could also perform these analyses by direct application of the matrix formulas presented in the previous section using JMP Scripting Language (JSL). JSL is most frequently used for the custom programming of methods too specialized or too new to be packaged into the standard regression procedures. It is also useful as an instructional tool for illustrating linear model and other methodologies.

## 8.2 Performing a Simple Regression

The following example illustrates a regression analysis performed by JSL. This example is not intended to serve as an exhaustive tutorial in the use of JSL, but to serve as an example of how methods in this book can be implemented. If you need more information on JSL, refer to the *JMP Scripting Language Guide*.

The example data for this section is also used in Chapter 2, "Regressions in JMP," to illustrate the Fit Y by X platform; the data set is described, and the data are presented in the section called "Introduction." For this presentation, the variable **Cost** is the dependent variable $y$, and the variables **Use**, **Seats**, **Load**, and **Length** are the independent variables $x_1$, $x_2$, $x_3$, and $x_4$, respectively. Comment statements are used in the JSL script to explain the individual steps in the analysis. The script for this example is named regression.jsl.

```
//let dt point to the data table named "air"
dt=Data Table("air");

//cXXX are pointers to the individual columns
cUse=column("Use");
cSeats=column("Seats");
cLoad=column("Load");
cLength=column("Length");
cCost=column("Cost");

//get appropriate columns into X and Y
X=(cUse<<GetAsMatrix)||(cSeats<<GetAsMatrix)
||(cLoad<<GetAsMatrix)||(cLength<<GetAsMatrix);
Y=cCost<<GetAsMatrix;

//Define the number of observations (N) and the number of
//variables (M) as the number of rows and columns of X.

N=nrow(X); //number of observations
M=ncol(X); //number of variables

//Add a column of ones for the intercept variable to the
//X matrix

X=j(n,1,1)||X;

//Compute c, the inverse of X'X and the vector of
//coefficient estimates bHat.

C=inv(X`*X);
bHat=c*X`*Y;


//Compute residuals, SSE, the residual sum of squares,
//and MSE, the residual mean square (variance estimate).

resid=Y-X*bHat;
SSE=resid`*resid;
dfe=n-m-1;
MSE=SSE/dfe;

//The test for the model can be restated as a test for
//the linear function L where L is the matrix

L=[0 1 0 0 0,
   0 0 1 0 0,
   0 0 0 1 0,
   0 0 0 0 1];
```

```
//Compute SS(model) and MS(model) and the corresponding
//F ratio.

ssModel=(L*bHat)`*inv(L*c*(L`))*(L*bHat);
msModel=ssModel/m;
F=(ssModel/m)/MSE;
probF=1-F Distribution(F, m, dfe);

//Compute standard errors of the bHats, t ratios,
// and p values for the t statistics
seb=sqrt(vecdiag(c)*mse);
t=bHat:/seb;
probt=2*(1-tdistribution(abs(t),dfe));

//Compute
//yHat     predicted values
yHat=x*bHat;

//Create some matrices for formatting results
dfMat=Matrix({m})|/Matrix({dfe});
SSMat=ssModel|/sse;
MSMat=msModel|/mse;

//Create a window containing results
New Window("Regression Results",
TableBox(
    StringColBox("Source", {"Model", "Error"}),
    NumberColBox("DF", dfMat),
    NumberColBox("SS",SSMat),
    NumberColBox("MS",MSMat),
    NumberColBox("F Ratio",F),
    NumberColBox("Prob > F", probF)
  ),
  TableBox(
    StringColBox("Parameter", {"ITL",
      "Use","Seats","Load","Length"}),
    NumberColBox("Estimate", bHat),
    NumberColBox("Std Error",seb),
    NumberColBox("t Ratio",t),
    NumberColBox("Prob>|t|", probt)
  ),
  TableBox(
    NumberColBox("Observed", y),
    NumberColBox("Predicted", yHat),
    NumberColBox("Residual", resid)
  )
)
```

The results of this sample program are shown in Figure 8.1.

## Figure 8.1 Regression Output

```
Regression Results
Source      DF      SS        MS       F Ratio   Prob > F
Model        4    6.57115   1.64279    10.556    0.00002
Error       28    4.35752   0.15563

Parameter   Estimate   Std Error   t Ratio   Prob>|t|
Intercept    8.59553    0.90278    9.52122      0
Use         -0.2128     0.06509   -3.2697    0.00285
Seats       -4.9503     1.21695   -4.0678    0.00035
Load        -7.2114     1.32056   -5.4608     8e-6
Length       0.33277    0.18133    1.83512   0.07713

Observed   Predicted   Residual
 2.258     2.57373    -0.3157
 2.275     2.13616     0.13884
 2.341     3.43985    -1.0988
 2.357     2.42431    -0.0673
 2.363     2.56342    -0.2004
 2.404     2.87937    -0.4754
 2.425     2.28974     0.13526
 2.711     2.76455    -0.0535
 2.743     3.36729    -0.6243
 2.78      2.87305    -0.093
 2.833     2.63593     0.19707
 2.846     3.18301    -0.337
 2.906     3.18978    -0.2838
 2.954     2.93247     0.02153
 2.962     2.97466    -0.0127
 2.971     3.01908    -0.0481
 3.044     3.32383    -0.2798
 3.096     2.75176     0.34424
 3.14      3.09366     0.04634
 3.306     3.56916    -0.2632
 3.306     2.74835     0.55765
 3.311     3.48254    -0.1715
 3.313     3.23736     0.07564
 3.392     3.44268    -0.0507
 3.437     3.52013    -0.0831
 3.462     3.24512     0.21688
 3.527     3.14946     0.37754
 3.689     3.64368     0.04532
 3.76      3.48788     0.27212
 3.856     3.56531     0.29069
 3.959     3.52048     0.43852
 4.024     3.15836     0.86564
 4.737     4.30183     0.43517
```

When you use JSL for these type of analyses, it is convenient to have all results in the form of matrices. Each matrix is identified by its name, and its elements are identified by row and column indices. You may find it necessary to refer to the script to identify specific elements.

The results of this analysis are discussed thoroughly in Chapter 2; therefore, in this section only the results that can be compared with those from Fit Model (shown in Figure 2.6) are identified.

The first section of statistics printed corresponds to overall model statistics produced by Fit Model. Included here are the degrees of freedom, sums of squares, and mean square for the model and for the error. The *F* statistic tests the significance of the entire model, which includes the independent variables Use, Seats, Load, and Length.

The next table contains the information on the parameter estimates. Rows correspond to parameters (intercept and independent variables Use, Seats, Load, and Length, respectively), and columns correspond to the different statistics. The first column contains the coefficient estimates (from matrix bHat), the second contains the standard errors of the estimates (from matrix SEB), and the third contains the *t* statistics (from matrix T). The final column (PROBT) contains the probability associated with the *t* statistic.

The third table contains the information on observations. The rows correspond to the observations. Column one contains the original *y* values (matrix Y), column two contains the predicted values (from matrix YHAT), and column three contains the residuals (from matrix RESID).

The results achieved by using JSL agree with those from Fit Model, as shown in Figure 2.6. JSL is most frequently used for the custom programming of new or specialized methods; the built-in regression procedures are more efficient with respect to both programming time and computing time. For this reason, you should try to use these procedures whenever possible. In addition, the output produced with the standard regression procedures is designed to present analysis results more clearly than the matrices produced with JSL.

## 8.3 Regression Matrices

The matrices used in regression computations—the X matrix and the $(X'X)^{-1}$ matrix—are available through the use of JMP's scripting language. In essence, a model is assigned a reference in the script, then messages are sent to the reference to Get X Matrix and Get XPX Inverse. The following short script accomplishes this for the example in this chapter.

```
//First, fit the model and assign it to "ft"
//The "invisible" option hides the initial report
ft=Fit Model(Y( :Cost), Effects( :Load, :Use, :Length,
:Seats), Personality(Standard Least Squares), Empha-
sis(Minimal Report), Run Model, invisible);

//Send Messages to ft to get matrices
x=ft<<GetXMatrix;
xpxi=ft<<GetXPXInverse;
```

```
//close the invisible report -- necessary for invisible
//platforms to keep them from unknowingly take up memory
ft<<close window;

//draw a window with labels to display the matrices
New Window("Regression Matrices",
    HListBox(
        VListBox(
            Text Box("X Matrix"),
            MatrixBox(x)
        ),
        VListBox(
            Text Box ("X'X Inverse Matrix"),
            MatrixBox(xpxi)
        )
    )
)
```

This script is stored with the data table and can be executed automatically.

- Select the drop-down menu next to the script labeled **Matrices**.

- Select **Run Script** from the menu that appears.

A window appears with the results, as shown in Figure 8.2.

The columns of the X matrix correspond to the variables in the model. The first column, the intercept, corresponds to the dummy variable whose value is 1 for all observations and which is used to estimate the intercept coefficient ($\beta_0$).

## 8.4 Collinearity Diagnostics

In "Detecting Collinearity" on page 107, JMP's Multivariate platform was used to analyze the principal component structure of a data set. Condition numbers and the condition index were introduced. However, these two quantities had to be calculated by hand, since they are not part of JMP's default reports.

In addition, the analysis is only possible on centered and scaled variables. In most cases, this centering and scaling is appropriate. However, there are times when it is appropriate to use unscaled and uncentered variables, and to include the intercept as part of the eigenvalue analysis.

The following script duplicates some of the output shown in the Multivariate report as in Figure 4.8 on page 120. In addition, it allows the option of using uncentered and unscaled variables in the analysis. It is stored in Collinearity.jsl.

## Collinearity Diagnostics 243

*Figure 8.2* Regression Matrices

| X Matrix | | | | | X'X Inverse Matrix | | | | |
|---|---|---|---|---|---|---|---|---|---|
| 1 | 0.591 | 7.87 | 1.79 | 0.1375 | 22.321969 | -25.8633 | -0.471931 | -1.549013 | -40.03468 |
| 1 | 0.488 | 9.5 | 2.515 | 0.3546 | -25.8633 | 48.849416 | 0.2354921 | -6.805531 | 62.78691 |
| 1 | 0.412 | 7.91 | 1.35 | 0.192 | -0.471931 | 0.2354921 | 0.0558129 | -0.055876 | -0.251288 |
| 1 | 0.397 | 13.3 | 3.607 | 0.339 | -1.549013 | -6.805531 | -0.055876 | 7.6155979 | -15.6793 |
| 1 | 0.582 | 8.48 | 1.963 | 0.1381 | -40.03468 | 62.78691 | -0.251288 | -15.6793 | 214.14368 |
| 1 | 0.466 | 9.38 | 1.123 | 0.1481 | | | | | |
| 1 | 0.535 | 10.8 | 1.576 | 0.1361 | | | | | |
| 1 | 0.434 | 8.36 | 1.912 | 0.3148 | | | | | |
| 1 | 0.439 | 8.43 | 1.584 | 0.1607 | | | | | |
| 1 | 0.417 | 8.83 | 2.377 | 0.3287 | | | | | |
| 1 | 0.4 | 8.42 | 1.495 | 0.3597 | | | | | |
| 1 | 0.41 | 9.62 | 0.84 | 0.139 | | | | | |
| 1 | 0.478 | 8.71 | 1.392 | 0.1148 | | | | | |
| 1 | 0.495 | 8.44 | 0.871 | 0.1186 | | | | | |
| 1 | 0.476 | 8.91 | 0.961 | 0.1236 | | | | | |
| 1 | 0.539 | 6.84 | 1.008 | 0.115 | | | | | |
| 1 | 0.409 | 9 | 0.845 | 0.139 | | | | | |
| 1 | 0.381 | 10.2 | 1.692 | 0.3007 | | | | | |
| 1 | 0.486 | 8.29 | 0.877 | 0.106 | | | | | |
| 1 | 0.287 | 8.09 | 1.528 | 0.3522 | | | | | |
| 1 | 0.504 | 9.47 | 1.408 | 0.1345 | | | | | |
| 1 | 0.455 | 7.7 | 1.236 | 0.1221 | | | | | |
| 1 | 0.405 | 9.57 | 0.863 | 0.139 | | | | | |
| 1 | 0.422 | 8.35 | 1.031 | 0.1365 | | | | | |
| 1 | 0.476 | 7.27 | 1.416 | 0.1145 | | | | | |
| 1 | 0.426 | 7.52 | 0.975 | 0.2025 | | | | | |
| 1 | 0.349 | 9.56 | 2.189 | 0.3279 | | | | | |
| 1 | 0.394 | 7.94 | 0.949 | 0.1488 | | | | | |
| 1 | 0.452 | 7.55 | 1.164 | 0.127 | | | | | |
| 1 | 0.425 | 10.6 | 2.78 | 0.1282 | | | | | |
| 1 | 0.362 | 10.8 | 1.518 | 0.1356 | | | | | |
| 1 | 0.541 | 6.31 | 0.823 | 0.0943 | | | | | |
| 1 | 0.378 | 5.65 | 0.821 | 0.129 | | | | | |

```
//get a reference to the current data table
dt=current data table();

//fit a model
fm=
//replace the following with a call to your own analysis
Fit Model(Y( :Std MANH), Effects( :Std OCCUP,  :Std
CHECKIN,  :Std HOURS,  :Std COMMON,  :Std WINGS,  :Std
CAP,  :Std ROOMS), Personality(Standard Least Squares),
Emphasis(Minimal Report), Run Model, Invisible);

//get the list of effects from the platform
effectslist=fm<<Get Parameter Names;

//get the design matrix from the platform
x=fm<<get X matrix;

//create a dialog to ask if the intercept should be
//included
dlg=Dialog(
"Include Intercept?",
 choice=Radio Buttons("Exclude", "Include"),
```

# 244 Regression with JMP Scripting Language

```
 Button("OK"), Button("Cancel")
);

//if the intercept is not included, delete the first
//column of the design matrix and the Intercept
//label from the list of effects
if(dlg["choice"]==1,
    x[0,1]=[];
    RemoveFrom(effectsList, 1);
);

//Compute X'X
xpx=x`*x;

//Get X'X inverse from the platform
xpxi = fm<<Get XPX Inverse;

//close the report, since we're through with it
fm<<Close Window;

//Compute Eigenvectors, Variance Components, Condition
Numbers
stdx = sqrt(vecdiag(xpx));
s=diag(1/stdx);
corrx = s*xpx*s;
corrxi = inv(corrx);
f=diag(corrxi);
g=inv(f);
{evals,evec}=eigen(corrx);
a = diag(evals);
b=inv(a);
c=evec`:*evec`;
d = b*c;
varprop = d*g;
cond=vecdiag(sqrt(max(a)*b));

//create a matrix to hold 1, 2, 3,
//...to the number of effects
//used in the report below for 'Dimensions' column
numberEffects=1::nItems(effectsList);

//Create a new window for results
New Window ("Collinearity Diagnostics",

//First Outline Box holds Eigenvalues and Cond Numbers
OutlineBox("Eigenvalues and Condition Numbers",
HListBox(
 Number Col Box("Dimension", numberEffects),
 Number Col Box("Eigenvalue", evals),
```

```
    Number Col Box("Condition Number",cond)
    )
  ),

  //second Outline box will hold the Variance Proportions
  //but isn't populated yet
  Outline Box ("Variance Proportions",
  hb = HListBox(
    Number Col Box("Dimension", numberEffects)
      )
  )
  );

  //This for loop adds a column for each effect
  for(i=1, i<=NItems(effectsList), i++,
      hb << append(Number Col Box(effectslist[i],
  varprop[0,i]))
  );
```

Note that this script requires some customization before its use. The first line of the script shows that the current data table (in most cases, the front-most data table) is used. Also, the second section (beginning with fm=Fit Model) holds the script that is obtained from an existing Fit Model report. To obtain this portion of the script for your data,

- Run a Fit Model report with your data using JMP's interactive methods.

- When the report appears, select **Script → Save Script to Script Window**.

This produces a text window containing the proper JSL to reproduce the analysis.

- Cut and paste the resulting script from the script journal into the Collinearity script, replacing the existing text.

The script can then be run. In this example, it is set up to use with the BOQ.JMP data table. Initially, it presents a dialog to ask if the intercept should be included or excluded (Figure 8.3). If the intercept is included, the raw data is used in the analysis. If the intercept is excluded, the data is first centered and scaled, and the intercept is removed from the analysis.

Centered and scaled output for this script using the BOQ.jmp data (excluding observation 25) is shown in Figure 8.4.

**Figure 8.3**
*Dialog from* Collinearity.jsl

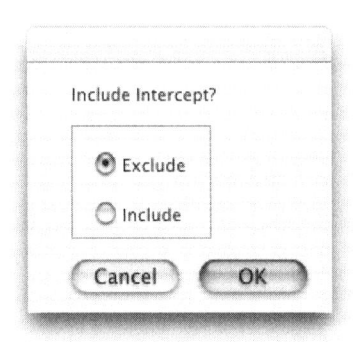

**Figure 8.4** *Collinearity Diagnostics*

**Collinearity Diagnostics**

**Eigenvalues and Condition Numbers**

| Dimension | Eigenvalue | Condition Number |
|---|---|---|
| 1 | 5.04674 | 1 |
| 2 | 0.72303 | 2.64197 |
| 3 | 0.69939 | 2.68624 |
| 4 | 0.31781 | 3.98494 |
| 5 | 0.15871 | 5.63909 |
| 6 | 0.05049 | 9.99779 |
| 7 | 0.00384 | 36.254 |

**Variance Proportions**

| Dimension | Std OCCUP | Std CHECKIN | Std HOURS | Std COMMON | Std WINGS | Std CAP | Std ROOMS |
|---|---|---|---|---|---|---|---|
| 1 | 0.00083 | 0.00649 | 0.0097 | 0.00505 | 0.00686 | 0.00062 | 0.00021 |
| 2 | 8e-6 | 0.00948 | 0.70454 | 0.04625 | 0.04961 | 3e-7 | 0.00003 |
| 3 | 0.00164 | 0.05107 | 0.23867 | 0.13255 | 0.03443 | 0.00167 | 0.00021 |
| 4 | 0.00262 | 0.05098 | 0.02636 | 0.28025 | 0.41437 | 0.00085 | 0.00002 |
| 5 | 0.00165 | 0.77761 | 0.00643 | 0.0049 | 0.1162 | 0.02905 | 0.00326 |
| 6 | 0.2717 | 0.10408 | 0.00341 | 0.0586 | 0.36479 | 0.10251 | 0.00026 |
| 7 | 0.72155 | 0.00029 | 0.01088 | 0.4724 | 0.01376 | 0.8653 | 0.996 |

## 8.5 Summary

This chapter illustrated JMP's scripting language. Three scripts show how simple programs can be used to

- ❑ extend JMP's capabilities
- ❑ produce custom reports
- ❑ illustrate statistical concepts.

A complete reference on JSL is found in the *JMP Scripting Language* guide.

# References

Allen, D.M. (1970), "Mean Square Error of Prediction as a Criterion for Selecting Variables," *Technometrics*, 13, 469–475.

Belsley, D.A. (1984), "Demeaning Conditions Through Centering," followed by comments by R.D. Cook et al., *The American Statistician*, 38, 73–93.

Belsley, D.A., Kuh, E., and Welsch, R.E. (1980), *Regression Diagnostics*, New York: John Wiley & Sons, Inc.

Berk, K.N. (1977), "Tolerance and Condition in Regression Computations," *Journal of the American Statistical Association*, 72, 863–866.

Brocklebank, J.C. and Dickey, D.A. (1986), *SAS System for Forecasting Time Series*, Cary, NC: SAS Institute Inc.

Dickens, J.W. and Mason, D.D. (1962), "A Peanut Sheller for Grading Samples: An Application in Statistical Design," *Transactions of the ASAE*, Volume 5, Number 1, 42–45.

Draper, N.L. and Smith, H. (1998), *Applied Regression Analysis*, Third Edition, New York: John Wiley & Sons, Inc.

Freund, R.J., Littell, R.C., and Spector, P.C. (1991), *SAS System for Linear Models, Third Edition*, Cary, NC: SAS Institute Inc.

Freund, R.J. and Minton, P.D. (1979), *Regression Methods*, New York: Marcel Dekker, Inc.

Freund, R.J. and Wilson, W. J. (1998), *Regression Analysis*, San Diego: Academic Press.

Fuller, W.A. (1978), *Introduction to Statistical Time Series*, New York: John Wiley & Sons, Inc.

Graybill, F. (1976), *Theory and Application of the Linear Model*, Boston: PWS and Kent Publishing Company, Inc.

Johnson, R.A. and Wichern, D.W. (1982), *Applied Multivariate Statistical Analysis*, Englewood Cliffs, NJ: Prentice Hall.

Kvalseth, T.O. (1985), "Cautionary Note about R2," *The American Statistician*, 39, 279–286.

Mallows, C.P. (1973), "Some Comments on C(p)," *Technometrics*, 15, 661–675.

Montgomery, D.C. and Peck, E.A. (1982), *Introduction to Linear Regression Analysis*, New York: John Wiley & Sons, Inc.

Morrison, D.F. (1976), *Multivariate Statistical Methods, Second Edition*, New York: McGraw-Hill Book Co.

Myers, R.H. (1976), *Response Surface Methodology*, Blacksburg, VA: Virginia Polytechnic Institute and State University.

Myers, R.H. (1990), *Classical and Modern Regression with Applications*, Second Edition, Boston: PWS and Kent Publishing Company, Inc.

Neter, J., Wasserman, W., and Kutner, M.H. (1989), *Applied Linear Regression Models, Second Edition*, Homewood, IL: Richard D. Irwin Inc.

Rawlings, J.O. (1988), *Applied Regression Analysis: A Research Tool*, Pacific Grove, CA: Wadsworth & Brooks/Cole.

Ryan, T.P. (1997), *Modern Regression Methods*, New York: John Wiley & Sons, Inc.

Sall, J.P. (1990), "Leverage Plots for General Linear Hypotheses," *American Statistician*, Volume 44, Number 4:303–315.

Sall, J., Lehman, A., and Creighton, L. (2001) *JMP Start Statistics*. John Wiley & Sons.

SAS Institute Inc. (1988), *SAS/ETS User's Guide*, Version 8, First Edition, Cary, NC: SAS Institute Inc.

SAS Institute Inc. (1990), *SAS/IML Software: Usage and Reference*, Version 8, First Edition, Cary, NC: SAS Institute Inc.

SAS Institute Inc. (1990), *SAS Language and Procedures: Usage*, Version 8, First Edition, Cary, NC: SAS Institute Inc.

SAS Institute Inc. (1990), *SAS Language: Reference*, Version 8, First Edition, Cary, NC: SAS Institute Inc.

SAS Institute Inc. (1990), *SAS Procedures Guide*, Version 8, Third Edition, Cary, NC: SAS Institute Inc.

SAS Institute Inc. (1990), *SAS/STAT User's Guide*, Version 8, Fourth Edition, Volume 2, Cary, NC: SAS Institute Inc.

SAS Institute Inc. (2000), *JMP Scripting Guide*, Version 4, Cary, NC: SAS Institute Inc.

SAS Institute Inc. (2000), *JMP Statistics and Graphics Guide*, Version 4, Cary, NC: SAS Institute Inc.

Searle, S.R. (1971), *Linear Models*, New York: John Wiley & Sons, Inc.

Smith, P.L. (1979), "Splines as a Useful and Convenient Statistical Tool," *The American Statistician*, 33, 57–62.

Steel, R.G.B. and Torrie, J. H. (1980), *Principles and Procedures of Statistics*, Second Edition, New York: McGraw-Hill Book Co.

# Index

## A

Add Graphics Script option  127
Add Ref Line button  61
adjusted $R^2$, airline cost data (example)  35
airline cost data (example)  26–27
   adjusted $R^2$  35
   corrected total sum of squares  30
   Effect Leverage emphasis  34
   Effect Screening emphasis  34
   exact collinearity  67–70
   $F$ statistic  30
   Fit Model platform  34–36
   Fit Y by X platform  28–31
   indicator variables  196–203
   Mean of Response  30
   Minimal Report emphasis  34
   one independent variable  27–31
   pairwise correlations  32–34
   predicting to different sets of data  63–67
   Root Mean Square Error  30
   Rsquare  30, 34
   several independent variables  32–36
   simple regression analysis with JSL  237–241
   $t$ statistic  31, 36
All Possible Models option  126–131, 136
analysis of structure
   *See* principal components analysis
analysis of variance  34

## B

Bachelor Officers Quarters operation
   *See* U.S. Navy Bachelor Officers Quarters operation (example)
backward elimination  133
Barbados exports (example)  167
   moving average  167–169
   splines  172
   time series analysis  170–171
Bernoulli variables  203–214
binary response variables  203–214
binomial (logistic) regression  203–214
bivariate investigation for outliers  76–80

## C

carriers of muscular dystrophy (example)  204–214
categorical (indicator) variables  195–203
Centered Polynomials options  143, 198, 201
child and parent height data (example)  176–181
Clear Current Selection option  58–60
coefficients
   correlation coefficient  10
   standardized regression coefficients  43–44
collinearity  105–137
   avoiding with model building  107
   detecting  107–115
   diagnostics, JSL for  242–246
   exact  67–70
   leverage plots  93–95, 108–111
   principal components analysis  111–115
   VIF (variance inflation factors)  108–110, 122–123
color  55, 56
Color or Mark by Column option  55
complete (unrestricted) models  17
components
   *See* principal components analysis
condition number  115, 242
Confid Curves Fit option  103
Confid Curves Indiv option  99
confidence intervals  19, 37–41
Confidence Limits option  220–221
Constraining Intercept To option  48

contour plots 156–158
   peanut shelling data (example) 158–166
Contour Profiler option 156–158, 161–163
Cook's D Influence option 82, 86
corrected total sum of squares 16
   airline cost data (example) 30
correction for the mean 42
correlation coefficient 10
Correlation of Estimates table 224
correlations 9–13
   among errors 74
   eigenvalues and eigenvectors of 112–115
covariance matrix, eigenvalues and eigenvectors of 112–115
COVRATIO statistic 88
$C_p$ statistic 126, 130–131
curve fitting 139, 167–173
   moving average 167–169
   splines 172
   Time Series platform 169–171
curves
   Confid Curves Fit option 103
   Confid Curves Indiv option 99
   growth curves 140–141, 229–235
   one-variable polynomial curves 139–151
Custom Test command 51–53, 187

## D

data dredging 107
data smoothing 139, 167–173
   moving average 167–169
   simple exponential smoothing 170–171
   splines 172
   Time Series platform 169–171
Data Tables 127
degree of the model 140
deleted observations, regression with 58–60, 90–91
deleting effects from plots 60–63
Density Ellipse option 180
Desirability Functions option 163–166

desirability profiles 163–166
detecting collinearity 107–115
detecting outliers
   *See* outlier detection
DFFITS statistic 88
diamond price data (example) 97–103
Direction options 132–133
distribution, error 74
Distribution platform 2, 23
dredging data 107
dummy (indicator) variables 195–203

## E

Effect Leverage emphasis 108
   airline cost data (example) 34
   irrigation effects (example) 95
Effect Screening emphasis, airline cost data (example) 34
eigenvalues and eigenvectors 112–115
elasticities 181
eliminating observations 90–91
equal variance assumption, violations to 96–103
Equal Variances option 179–180
error sum of squares
   *See* residual sum of squares
errors 73–74
   *See also* observations
   eliminating observations 90–91
   in independent variables (orthogonal regression) 173–181
   nonlinear regression 224–229
   Root Mean Square Error 30
   specification errors 74, 91–96
estimable functions 22
exact collinearity 67–70
Exclude option 59–60, 91
excluding observations from regression analysis 58–60, 90–91
exponential growth/decay model 14, 215–229
   sum of squares surface 223–224

exponential smoothing, simple   170–171
exports
   *See* Barbados exports (example)

# F

*F* statistic   18
   airline cost data (example)   30
   No Intercept option   44–50
fingerling fish population growth (example)   140–141
   fitting growth curves with nonlinear models   229–235
   polynomial centering   141–144
   polynomial regression, multivariate, Fit Model analysis   152–156
   polynomial regression, one-variable, Fit Model analysis   148–151
   polynomial regression, one-variable, Fit Y by X analysis   145–148
   spline models   192–195
first principal component   178
Fit Model platform   23
   airline cost data (example)   34–36
   changing the model   53–54
   exact collinearity   69–70
   indicator variables   196–203
   Nonlinear platform vs.   220
   plotting observations   54–63
   polynomial curves, one variable   148–151
   polynomial curves, several variables   152–156
   predicted values and confidence intervals   37–41
   predicting to different sets of data   63–67
   regression through the origin   44–50
   response surface and contour plots   156–158
   Save Probability Formula option   211
   sequential and partial sums of squares   41–43
   standardized regression coefficients   43–44
   Stepwise personality   126, 212
   tests for subsets and linear functions of parameters   50–53
Fit Orthogonal option   179–181
Fit Polynomial option   97–100
Fit Special command   47, 228
Fit Spline option   172
Fit Y by X platform   23
   airline cost data (example)   28–31
   binomial regression   204–214
   height and weight data (example)   3
   intercepts   47–49
   one-variable polynomial curves   145–148
   plotting observations   54–63
forward selection   132
functions
   Desirability Functions option   163–166
   estimable   22
   lag function   168–169
   linear functions of parameters, tests for   50–53
   logit link function   208
   Maximum function   192
   Mean function   168

# G

Galton, Frances   176–177
generalized inverse   21–22, 67–70
generalized variance   88
graphics script   127
growth curves   140–141
   *See also* polynomial models
   fitting with nonlinear models   229–235
growth/decay model, exponential   14, 215–229
   sum of squares surface   223–224

# H

hat diagonal   85
Hats option   86

## 252  Index

height and weight data (examples)   3, 176–181
heterogeneous variances   96–103
   weighted least squares   100–103
heteroscedasticity   74
hypothesis testing   18–20

## I

independent variables
   airline cost data (example)   27–36
   error in   173–181
   polynomial models   139–156
   regression   7–9, 27–36
indicator variables   195–203
Indiv Confidence Interval option   39–40
inference, simultaneous   19
influence statistics   85–91
   leverage plots   93–95, 108–111
   leverages   85
intercepts
   Constraining Intercept To option   48
   Fit Y by X platform   47–49
   No Intercept option   44–50
inverse, generalized   21–22, 67–70
investment grade diamonds (example)   97–103
irrigation effects (example)   91–96

## J

Jackknife Distances option   78
JMP platforms for regression analysis   23
JSL (JMP Scripting Language)   237–246
   collinearity diagnostics   242–246
   regression matrices   241–242
   simple regression analysis   237–241

## K

knots, spline   172, 191–195

## L

lag function   168–169
least-squares regressions   5–7, 13
   partial least squares   23
   physical model   7–9
   weighted least squares   100–103
leverage plots   93–95, 108–111
leverages of observations   85
line of best fit   6
linear-by-linear interaction   152
linear dependency   67–70
linear functions of parameters, tests for   50–53
linear regression models
   binary response variables (logistic regression)   203–214
   indicator variables   195–203
   multiplicative models   181–191
   orthogonal regression   173–181
   simple linear regression   27–31
   spline models   191–195
logistic (binary) regression   203–214
logit link function   208
lumber weight data (example)   182–191

## M

Mahalanobis distances   78
Make into Data Table option   127
Mallows' $C_p$ statistic   126, 130–131
matrix notation   15
Maximize Desirability option   165
Maximum function   192
maximum likelihood estimation (MLE)   208
Mean Confidence Interval option   38–40
Mean function   168
Mean of Response, airline cost data (example)   30
mean square error (MSE)   17
Minimal Report emphasis
   airline cost data (example)   34

exact collinearity  69–70
No Intercept option  44–50
mixed selection  133
MLE (maximum likelihood estimation)  208
model, degree of the  140
model building, to avoid collinearity  107
model restructuring  115–125
model selection
    *See* variable selection
model specification errors  74, 91–96
model sum of squares
    *See* residual sum of squares
More Moments option  47
moving average  167–169
MSE (mean square error)  17
multidimensional polynomial regressions  151–156
multiple linear regression  7–9, 32–36
    *See also* regressions
multiplicative models  181–191
multivariate analysis  112
    principal component regression  115, 117–125
    principal components analysis  111–115
multivariate investigation for outliers  77–80
Multivariate platform  23
    airline cost data (example)  32–36
multivariate structure analysis,  117–125
muscular dystrophy carriers data (example)  204–214

# N

Natural Logarithm option  228
Navy Bachelor Officers Quarters operation
    *See* U.S. Navy Bachelor Officers Quarters operation (example)
Neural Net platform  23
No Intercept option  44–50
Nonlinear Fit option  230–235
Nonlinear platform  23, 215–236
    exponential growth/decay model  215–229
    Fit Model platform vs.  220
    fitting growth curves  229–235
nonlinear regression  215–236
    estimates and standard errors  224–229
    exponential growth/decay model  215–229
    fitting growth curves  229–235
    sum of squares surface  223–224

# O

observations  73–104
    *See also* errors
    *See also* plotting observations
    deleted, regression with  58–60
    eliminating  90–91
    excluding from regression analysis  58–60, 90–91
    heterogeneous variances  96–103
    influence statistics  85–91
    leverage plots  93–95, 108–111
    leverages of  85
    outlier detection  73–91
    specification errors  91–96
odds ratio  211
Officers Quarters operation
    *See* U.S. Navy Bachelor Officers Quarters operation (example)
one-variable polynomial curves  139–151
    Fit Model platform  148–151
    Fit Y by X analysis  145–148
    polynomial centering  141–144, 198, 201
operating costs of airlines
    *See* airline cost data (example)
optimum estimated response  154
origin, regression through  44–50
orthogonal regression  173–181
Outlier Analysis option  78
outlier detection  73–91
    bivariate investigation  76–80
    influence statistics  85–91
    multivariate investigation  77–80
    Plot Residual by Predicted option  80–84

outlier detection (*continued*)
   Plot Residual by Row option 80–84
   Prediction Formula option 82
   residuals and studentized residuals 80–84, 87
   specification errors 74, 91–96
   univariate investigation 76–80
Overlay Plot option 57, 60–63
overspecified models 131

# P

pairwise correlations, airline cost data (example) 32–34
Pairwise Correlations option 121
parameter estimates 67–70
parameters, linear functions and subsets of 50–53
parent and child height data (example) 176–181
partial least squares 23
partial regression residual plots
   *See* leverage plots
partial sums of squares 41–43
partitioning sums of squares 16–18
peanut shelling data (example) 158–166
physical model 7–9
pine lumber weight data (example) 182–191
Plot Effect Leverage option 95
Plot Residual by Predicted option 40–41, 54–63
   outlier detection 80–84
   specification errors 93
Plot Residual by Row option 54–63
   outlier detection 80–84
Plot Residuals option 54–63
plotting observations 54–63
   deleting effects from plots 60–63
   leverage plots 93–95, 108–111
   Overlay Plot option 57, 60–63
   Range Plot option 61–62
   residuals 40–41

response surface and contour plots 156–158
scatter plots 54–63
smoothing data 139, 167–173
PLS platform 23
polynomial centering 141–144, 198, 201
Polynomial Fit Degree option 99
polynomial models
   Fit Model platform (one variable) 148–151
   Fit Polynomial option 97–100
   Fit Y by X analysis (one variable) 145–148
   multidimensional polynomial regression 151–156
   one independent variable 139–151
   polynomial centering 141–144, 198, 201
   response surface plots 156–158
   response surface plots, three-factor (example) 158–166
   several independent variables 151–156
Polynomial to Degree option 148
population growth
   *See* fingerling fish population growth (example)
predicted values 37–41
predicting to different sets of data 63–67
Prediction Formula option 37, 66–67
   outlier detection 82
Press option 89
PRESS statistic 89
pricing diamonds (example) 97–103
Prin Comp option, Univariate Variances 179–180
principal component regression 115, 117–125
principal components analysis 111–115
Principal Components option 114
Prob to Enter option 133–134
Prob to Leave option 133–134
probabilities, stepwise 133–135, 212

## Q

quadratic response surface models   152–156
qualitative (indicator) variables   195–203

## R

radioactive decay data (example)   215–229
   estimates and standard errors   224–229
   sum of squares surface   223–224
random variation   30
Range Plot option   61–62
redefining variables   116–117
Redo Analysis option   53–54
reduced (restricted) models   17
reduction notation   43
reference line, adding   61
regression matrices   241–242
regression sum of squares   16
regressions
   *See also* collinearity
   *See also* least-squares regressions
   *See also* linear regression models
   *See also* nonlinear regression
   deleted observations   58–60, 90–91
   hypothesis testing   18–20
   indicator variables   195–203
   JMP platforms   23
   JSL for   237–241
   logistic (binary) regression   203–214
   multiple linear regression   7–9, 32–36
   one independent variable   27–31
   orthogonal regression   173–181
   physical model   7–9
   polynomial models, one independent variable   139–151
   polynomial models, several independent variable   151–156
   principal component regression   115, 117–125
   several independent variables   7–9, 32–36
   simple regression analysis   237–241
   standardized regression coefficients   43–44
   statistical background   13–14
   through the origin   44–50
   visualizing   1–7
relationships between variables (correlations)   9–13
   among errors   74
   eigenvalues and eigenvectors of   112–115
Remove Fit option   146
replicates   101
residual sum of squares   13, 16–17
   generalized inverse   21
   minimizing through variable selection   125–136
   No Intercept option   45–46
residuals   4, 40
   outlier detection   80–84, 87
   Plot Residual by Predicted option   40–41, 54–63, 80–84, 93
   Plot Residuals option   54–63
   plotting observations   40–41
   specification errors   74, 91–96
   Std Error of Residual option   82
   studentized   80–84, 87
Residuals option   40, 82
response surface plots   156–158
   three-factor (peanut shelling example)   158–166
restricted (reduced) models   17
Root Mean Square Error, airline cost data (example)   30
rows, excluding from regression analysis   58–60, 90–91
RSquare, airline cost data (example)   30, 34
RSTUDENT statistic   87

## S

Save Predicteds option 101
Save Principal Components option 120
Save Probability Formula option 211
scaling factor 181
scatter plots 54–63
selecting variables 125–136
    All Possible Models option 126–131, 136
    step-type procedures 132–133
Separate Axes option 57
sequential sums of squares 41–43
    one-variable polynomial curves 149
Sequential Tests option 41, 148
Set Color by Value option 56
Set Marker by Value option 56
several-variable polynomial regressions 151–156
shelling peanuts (example) 158–166
simple exponential smoothing 170–171
simple linear regression 27–31
simple regression analysis 237–241
simultaneous inference 19
slope shift 197
smoothing data 139, 167–173
    moving average 167–169
    simple exponential smoothing 170–171
    splines 172
    Time Series platform 169–171
specification errors 74, 91–96
Specified Variance Ratio option 179
Specify Grid Of Contour Values dialog 158
splines 172, 191–195
SS (sums of squares)
    *See* sums of squares
SSE Grid option 223–224
standardized regression coefficients 43–44
statistical background 13–14
Std Beta option 44
Std Error of Predicted option 39
Std Error of Residual option 82
step-type model selection procedures 132–133
    stepwise probabilities 133–135

Stepwise personality 126, 212
    Direction options 132–133
stepwise probabilities 133–135, 212
structural analysis
    *See* principal components analysis
studentized residuals for outlier detection 80–84, 87
Studentized Residuals option 81
subsets of parameters, tests for 50–53
sums of squares
    *See also* residual sum of squares
    partial 41–43
    partitioning 16–18
    regression sum of squares 16
    sequential 41–43, 149
    sum of squares surface, nonlinear regression 223–224
    total 16, 30, 44–50
    Type I 41–43
    Type III 41–43, 149
    weighted least squares 100–103
Survival platform 23

## T

$t$ statistics 18
    airline cost data (example) 31, 36
    tests for subsets and linear functions of parameters 50–53
three-factor response surface experiment (example) 158–166
Time Series platform 169–171
total sums of squares 44–50
    corrected 16, 30
Type I sums of squares 41–43
Type III sums of squares 41–43, 149

## U

U.S. Navy Bachelor Officers Quarters operation (example) 75
    detecting collinearity 107–115

eliminating observations 90–91
outlier detection 73–91
principal component regression 117–125
variable redefinition 116
variable selection 125–136
univariate investigation for outliers 76–80
Univariate Variances, Prin Comp option 179–180
unrestricted (complete) models 17

# V

variable correlations 9–13
    among errors 74
    eigenvalues and eigenvectors of 112–115
variable selection 125–136
    All Possible Models option 126–131, 136
    step-type procedures 132–133
variables
    *See also* independent variables
    *See also* variable correlations
    *See also* variable selection
    binary (Bernoulli) response variables 203–214
    categorical variables 195–203
    collinearity 105–137, 242–246
    dummy variables 195–203
    error in independent variables 173–181
    indicator variables 195–203
    leverage plots 93–95, 108–111
    principal component regression 115, 117–125
    principal components analysis 111–115
    qualitative variables 195–203
    redefining 116–117
    VIF (variance inflation factors) 108–110, 122–123
variances
    Equal Variances option 179–180
    generalized 88
    heterogeneous 96–103
    Specified Variance Ratio option 179

Univariate Variances, Prin Comp option 179–180
VIF (variance inflation factors) 108–110
    principal component regression 122–123
VIF option 108, 122
visualizing regression 1–7

# W

weight of pine lumber data (example) 182–191
weighted least squares 100–103

# Y

Y by X platform
    *See* Fit Y by X platform

# Books from SAS Institute's Books by Users Press

*Advanced Log-Linear Models Using SAS®*
by **Daniel Zelterman**

*Annotate: Simply the Basics*
by **Art Carpenter**

*Applied Multivariate Statistics with SAS® Software, Second Edition*
by **Ravindra Khattree**
and **Dayanand N. Naik**

*Applied Statistics and the SAS® Programming Language, Fourth Edition*
by **Ronald P. Cody**
and **Jeffrey K. Smith**

*An Array of Challenges — Test Your SAS® Skills*
by **Robert Virgile**

*Beyond the Obvious with SAS® Screen Control Language*
by **Don Stanley**

*Carpenter's Complete Guide to the SAS® Macro Language*
by **Art Carpenter**

*The Cartoon Guide to Statistics*
by **Larry Gonick**
and **Woollcott Smith**

*Categorical Data Analysis Using the SAS® System, Second Edition*
by **Maura E. Stokes, Charles S. Davis,**
and **Gary G. Koch**

*Cody's Data Cleaning Techniques Using SAS® Software*
by **Ron Cody**

*Common Statistical Methods for Clinical Research with SAS® Examples, Second Edition*
by **Glenn A. Walker**

*Concepts and Case Studies in Data Management*
by **William S. Calvert**
and **J. Meimei Ma**

*Debugging SAS® Programs: A Handbook of Tools and Techniques*
by **Michele M. Burlew**

*Efficiency: Improving the Performance of Your SAS® Applications*
by **Robert Virgile**

*A Handbook of Statistical Analyses Using SAS®, Second Edition*
by **B.S. Everitt**
and **G. Der**

*Health Care Data and the SAS® System*
by **Marge Scerbo, Craig Dickstein,**
and **Alan Wilson**

*The How-To Book for SAS/GRAPH® Software*
by **Thomas Miron**

*In the Know... SAS® Tips and Techniques From Around the Globe*
by **Phil Mason**

support.sas.com/pubs

*Integrating Results through Meta-Analytic Review Using SAS® Software*
by **Morgan C. Wang**
and **Brad J. Bushman**

*Learning SAS® in the Computer Lab, Second Edition*
by **Rebecca J. Elliott**

*The Little SAS® Book: A Primer*
by **Lora D. Delwiche**
and **Susan J. Slaughter**

*The Little SAS® Book: A Primer, Second Edition*
by **Lora D. Delwiche**
and **Susan J. Slaughter**
(updated to include Version 7 features)

*Logistic Regression Using the SAS® System: Theory and Application*
by **Paul D. Allison**

*Longitudinal Data and SAS®: A Programmer's Guide*
by **Ron Cody**

*Maps Made Easy Using SAS®*
by **Mike Zdeb**

*Models for Discrete Date*
by **Daniel Zelterman**

*Multiple Comparisons and Multiple Tests Using SAS® Text and Workbook Set*
(books in this set also sold separately)
by **Peter H. Westfall, Randall D. Tobias, Dror Rom, Russell D. Wolfinger**
and **Yosef Hochberg**

*Multiple-Plot Displays: Simplified with Macros*
by **Perry Watts**

*Multivariate Data Reduction and Discrimination with SAS® Software*
by **Ravindra Khattree,**
and **Dayanand N. Naik**

*The Next Step: Integrating the Software Life Cycle with SAS® Programming*
by **Paul Gill**

*Output Delivery System: The Basics*
by **Lauren E. Haworth**

*Painless Windows: A Handbook for SAS® Users*
by **Jodie Gilmore**
(for Windows NT and Windows 95)

*Painless Windows: A Handbook for SAS® Users, Second Edition*
by **Jodie Gilmore**
(updated to include Version 7 features)

*PROC TABULATE by Example*
by **Lauren E. Haworth**

*Professional SAS® Programmer's Pocket Reference, Fourth Edition*
by **Rick Aster**

*Professional SAS® Programmer's Pocket Reference, Second Edition*
by **Rick Aster**

*Professional SAS® Programming Shortcuts*
by **Rick Aster**

*Programming Techniques for Object-Based Statistical Analysis with SAS® Software*
by **Tanya Kolosova**
and **Samuel Berestizhevsky**

*Quick Results with SAS/GRAPH® Software*
by **Arthur L. Carpenter**
and **Charles E. Shipp**

*Quick Results with the Output Delivery System*
by **Sunil Gupta**

*Quick Start to Data Analysis with SAS®*
by **Frank C. Dilorio**
and **Kenneth A. Hardy**

*Reading External Data Files Using SAS®: Examples Handbook*
by **Michele M. Burlew**

**support.sas.com/pubs**

*Regression and ANOVA: An Integrated Approach Using SAS® Software*
by **Keith E. Muller**
and **Bethel A. Fetterman**

*Reporting from the Field: SAS® Software Experts Present Real-World Report-Writing Applications*

*SAS®Applications Programming: A Gentle Introduction*
by **Frank C. Dilorio**

*SAS® for Forecasting Time Series, Second Edition*
by **John C. Brocklebank**
and **David A. Dickey**

*SAS® for Linear Models, Fourth Edition*
by **Ramon C. Littell, Walter W. Stroup,**
and **Rudolf Freund**

*SAS® for Monte Carlo Studies: A Guide for Quantitative Researchers*
by **Xitao Fan, Ákos Felsőválya, Stephen A. Sivo,**
and **Sean C. Keenan**

*SAS® Macro Programming Made Easy*
by **Michele M. Burlew**

*SAS® Programming by Example*
by **Ron Cody**
and **Ray Pass**

*SAS® Programming for Researchers and Social Scientists, Second Edition*
by **Paul E. Spector**

*SAS® Software Roadmaps: Your Guide to Discovering the SAS® System*
by **Laurie Burch**
and **SherriJoyce King**

*SAS® Software Solutions: Basic Data Processing*
by **Thomas Miron**

*SAS® Survival Analysis Techniques for Medical Research, Second Edition*
by **Alan B. Cantor**

*SAS® System for Elementary Statistical Analysis, Second Edition*
by **Sandra D. Schlotzhauer**
and **Ramon C. Littell**

*SAS® System for Forecasting Time Series, 1986 Edition*
by **John C. Brocklebank**
and **David A. Dickey**

*SAS® System for Mixed Models*
by **Ramon C. Littell, George A. Milliken, Walter W. Stroup,** and **Russell D. Wolfinger**

*SAS® System for Regression, Second Edition*
by **Rudolf J. Freund**
and **Ramon C. Littell**

*SAS® System for Statistical Graphics, First Edition*
by **Michael Friendly**

*The SAS® Workbook* and *Solutions* Set
(books in this set also sold separately)
by **Ron Cody**

*Selecting Statistical Techniques for Social Science Data: A Guide for SAS® Users*
by **Frank M. Andrews, Laura Klem, Patrick M. O'Malley, Willard L. Rodgers, Kathleen B. Welch,** and **Terrence N. Davidson**

*Solutions for Your GUI Applications Development Using SAS/AF® FRAME Technology*
by **Don Stanley**

*Statistical Quality Control Using the SAS® System*
by **Dennis W. King**

*A Step-by-Step Approach to Using the SAS® System for Factor Analysis and Structural Equation Modeling*
by **Larry Hatcher**

*A Step-by-Step Approach to Using the SAS® System for Univariate and Multivariate Statistics*
by **Larry Hatcher**
and **Edward Stepanski**

**support.sas.com/pubs**

*Step-by-Step Basic Statistics Using SAS®: Student Guide* and *Exercises*
(books in this set also sold separately)
by **Larry Hatcher**

*Strategic Data Warehousing Principles Using SAS® Software*
by **Peter R. Welbrock**

*Survival Analysis Using the SAS® System: A Practical Guide*
by **Paul D. Allison**

*Table-Driven Strategies for Rapid SAS® Applications Development*
by **Tanya Kolosova**
and **Samuel Berestizhevsky**

*Tuning SAS® Applications in the MVS Environment*
by **Michael A. Raithel**

*Univariate and Multivariate General Linear Models: Theory and Applications Using SAS® Software*
by **Neil H. Timm**
and **Tammy A. Mieczkowski**

*Using SAS® in Financial Research*
by **Ekkehart Boehmer, John Paul Broussard,**
and **Juha-Pekka Kallunki**

*Using the SAS® Windowing Environment: A Quike Tutorial*
by **Larry Hatcher**

*Visualizing Categorical Data*
by **Michael Friendly**

*Working with the SAS® System*
by **Erik W. Tilanus**

*Your Guide to Survey Research Using the SAS® System*
by **Archer Gravely**

**JMP® Books**

*Basic Business Statistics: A Casebook*
by **Dean P. Foster, Robert A. Stine,**
and **Richard P. Waterman**

*Business Analysis Using Regression: A Casebook*
by **Dean P. Foster, Robert A. Stine,**
and **Richard P. Waterman**

*JMP® Start Statistics, Second Edition*
by **John Sall, Ann Lehman,**
and **Lee Creighton**

*Regression Using JMP®*
by **Rudolf J. Freund, Ramon C. Littell,**
and **Lee Creighton**

**support.sas.com/pubs**

WILEY SERIES IN PROBABILITY AND STATISTICS

Established by WALTER A. SHEWHART and SAMUEL S. WILKS

Editors: *David J. Balding, Noel A. C. Cressie, Nicholas I. Fisher, Iain M. Johnstone, J. B. Kadane, Louise M. Ryan, David W. Scott, Adrian F. M. Smith, Jozef L. Teugels*
Editors Emeriti: *Vic Barnett, J. Stuart Hunter, David G. Kendall*

A complete list of the titles in this series appears at the end of this volume.

# WILEY SERIES IN PROBABILITY AND STATISTICS

ESTABLISHED BY WALTER A. SHEWHART AND SAMUEL S. WILKS

Editors: *David J. Balding, Noel A. C. Cressie, Nicholas I. Fisher, Iain M. Johnstone, J. B. Kadane, Louise M. Ryan, David W. Scott, Adrian F. M. Smith, Jozef L. Teugels*
Editors Emeriti: *Vic Barnett, J. Stuart Hunter, David G. Kendall*

The **Wiley Series in Probability and Statistics** is well established and authoritative. It covers many topics of current research interest in both pure and applied statistics and probability theory. Written by leading statisticians and institutions, the titles span both state-of-the-art developments in the field and classical methods.

Reflecting the wide range of current research in statistics, the series encompasses applied, methodological and theoretical statistics, ranging from applications and new techniques made possible by advances in computerized practice to rigorous treatment of theoretical approaches.

This series provides essential and invaluable reading for all statisticians, whether in academia, industry, government, or research.

ABRAHAM and LEDOLTER · Statistical Methods for Forecasting
AGRESTI · Analysis of Ordinal Categorical Data
AGRESTI · An Introduction to Categorical Data Analysis
AGRESTI · Categorical Data Analysis, *Second Edition*
ANDĚL · Mathematics of Chance
ANDERSON · An Introduction to Multivariate Statistical Analysis, *Third Edition*
*ANDERSON · The Statistical Analysis of Time Series
ANDERSON, AUQUIER, HAUCK, OAKES, VANDAELE, and WEISBERG · Statistical Methods for Comparative Studies
ANDERSON and LOYNES · The Teaching of Practical Statistics
ARMITAGE and DAVID (editors) · Advances in Biometry
ARNOLD, BALAKRISHNAN, and NAGARAJA · Records
*ARTHANARI and DODGE · Mathematical Programming in Statistics
*BAILEY · The Elements of Stochastic Processes with Applications to the Natural Sciences
BALAKRISHNAN and KOUTRAS · Runs and Scans with Applications
BARNETT · Comparative Statistical Inference, *Third Edition*
BARNETT and LEWIS · Outliers in Statistical Data, *Third Edition*
BARTOSZYNSKI and NIEWIADOMSKA-BUGAJ · Probability and Statistical Inference
BASILEVSKY · Statistical Factor Analysis and Related Methods: Theory and Applications
BASU and RIGDON · Statistical Methods for the Reliability of Repairable Systems
BATES and WATTS · Nonlinear Regression Analysis and Its Applications
BECHHOFER, SANTNER, and GOLDSMAN · Design and Analysis of Experiments for Statistical Selection, Screening, and Multiple Comparisons
BELSLEY · Conditioning Diagnostics: Collinearity and Weak Data in Regression
BELSLEY, KUH, and WELSCH · Regression Diagnostics: Identifying Influential Data and Sources of Collinearity
BENDAT and PIERSOL · Random Data: Analysis and Measurement Procedures, *Third Edition*
BERRY, CHALONER, and GEWEKE · Bayesian Analysis in Statistics and Econometrics: Essays in Honor of Arnold Zellner
BERNARDO and SMITH · Bayesian Theory
BHAT and MILLER · Elements of Applied Stochastic Processes, *Third Edition*
BHATTACHARYA and JOHNSON · Statistical Concepts and Methods

*Now available in a lower priced paperback edition in the Wiley Classics Library.

BHATTACHARYA and WAYMIRE · Stochastic Processes with Applications
BILLINGSLEY · Convergence of Probability Measures, *Second Edition*
BILLINGSLEY · Probability and Measure, *Third Edition*
BIRKES and DODGE · Alternative Methods of Regression
BLISCHKE AND MURTHY (editors) · Case Studies in Reliability and Maintenance
BLISCHKE AND MURTHY · Reliability: Modeling, Prediction, and Optimization
BLOOMFIELD · Fourier Analysis of Time Series: An Introduction, *Second Edition*
BOLLEN · Structural Equations with Latent Variables
BOROVKOV · Ergodicity and Stability of Stochastic Processes
BOULEAU · Numerical Methods for Stochastic Processes
BOX · Bayesian Inference in Statistical Analysis
BOX · R. A. Fisher, the Life of a Scientist
BOX and DRAPER · Empirical Model-Building and Response Surfaces
*BOX and DRAPER · Evolutionary Operation: A Statistical Method for Process Improvement
BOX, HUNTER, and HUNTER · Statistics for Experimenters: An Introduction to Design, Data Analysis, and Model Building
BOX and LUCEÑO · Statistical Control by Monitoring and Feedback Adjustment
BRANDIMARTE · Numerical Methods in Finance: A MATLAB-Based Introduction
BROWN and HOLLANDER · Statistics: A Biomedical Introduction
BRUNNER, DOMHOF, and LANGER · Nonparametric Analysis of Longitudinal Data in Factorial Experiments
BUCKLEW · Large Deviation Techniques in Decision, Simulation, and Estimation
CAIROLI and DALANG · Sequential Stochastic Optimization
CHAN · Time Series: Applications to Finance
CHATTERJEE and HADI · Sensitivity Analysis in Linear Regression
CHATTERJEE and PRICE · Regression Analysis by Example, *Third Edition*
CHERNICK · Bootstrap Methods: A Practitioner's Guide
CHERNICK and FRIIS · Introductory Biostatistics for the Health Sciences
CHILÈS and DELFINER · Geostatistics: Modeling Spatial Uncertainty
CHOW and LIU · Design and Analysis of Clinical Trials: Concepts and Methodologies
CLARKE and DISNEY · Probability and Random Processes: A First Course with Applications, *Second Edition*
*COCHRAN and COX · Experimental Designs, *Second Edition*
CONGDON · Bayesian Statistical Modelling
CONOVER · Practical Nonparametric Statistics, *Second Edition*
COOK · Regression Graphics
COOK and WEISBERG · Applied Regression Including Computing and Graphics
COOK and WEISBERG · An Introduction to Regression Graphics
CORNELL · Experiments with Mixtures, Designs, Models, and the Analysis of Mixture Data, *Third Edition*
COVER and THOMAS · Elements of Information Theory
COX · A Handbook of Introductory Statistical Methods
*COX · Planning of Experiments
CRESSIE · Statistics for Spatial Data, *Revised Edition*
CSÖRGŐ and HORVÁTH · Limit Theorems in Change Point Analysis
DANIEL · Applications of Statistics to Industrial Experimentation
DANIEL · Biostatistics: A Foundation for Analysis in the Health Sciences, *Sixth Edition*
*DANIEL · Fitting Equations to Data: Computer Analysis of Multifactor Data, *Second Edition*
DASU and JOHNSON · Exploratory Data Mining and Data Cleaning
DAVID and NAGARAJA · Order Statistics, *Third Edition*
*DEGROOT, FIENBERG, and KADANE · Statistics and the Law
DEL CASTILLO · Statistical Process Adjustment for Quality Control
DETTE and STUDDEN · The Theory of Canonical Moments with Applications in Statistics, Probability, and Analysis

*Now available in a lower priced paperback edition in the Wiley Classics Library.

DEY and MUKERJEE · Fractional Factorial Plans
DILLON and GOLDSTEIN · Multivariate Analysis: Methods and Applications
DODGE · Alternative Methods of Regression
*DODGE and ROMIG · Sampling Inspection Tables, *Second Edition*
*DOOB · Stochastic Processes
DOWDY and WEARDEN · Statistics for Research, *Second Edition*
DRAPER and SMITH · Applied Regression Analysis, *Third Edition*
DRYDEN and MARDIA · Statistical Shape Analysis
DUDEWICZ and MISHRA · Modern Mathematical Statistics
DUNN and CLARK · Applied Statistics: Analysis of Variance and Regression, *Second Edition*
DUNN and CLARK · Basic Statistics: A Primer for the Biomedical Sciences, *Third Edition*
DUPUIS and ELLIS · A Weak Convergence Approach to the Theory of Large Deviations
*ELANDT-JOHNSON and JOHNSON · Survival Models and Data Analysis
ENDERS · Applied Econometric Time Series
ETHIER and KURTZ · Markov Processes: Characterization and Convergence
EVANS, HASTINGS, and PEACOCK · Statistical Distributions, *Third Edition*
FELLER · An Introduction to Probability Theory and Its Applications, Volume I, *Third Edition,* Revised; Volume II, *Second Edition*
FISHER and VAN BELLE · Biostatistics: A Methodology for the Health Sciences
*FLEISS · The Design and Analysis of Clinical Experiments
FLEISS · Statistical Methods for Rates and Proportions, *Second Edition*
FLEMING and HARRINGTON · Counting Processes and Survival Analysis
FULLER · Introduction to Statistical Time Series, *Second Edition*
FULLER · Measurement Error Models
GALLANT · Nonlinear Statistical Models
GHOSH, MUKHOPADHYAY, and SEN · Sequential Estimation
GIFI · Nonlinear Multivariate Analysis
GLASSERMAN and YAO · Monotone Structure in Discrete-Event Systems
GNANADESIKAN · Methods for Statistical Data Analysis of Multivariate Observations, *Second Edition*
GOLDSTEIN and LEWIS · Assessment: Problems, Development, and Statistical Issues
GREENWOOD and NIKULIN · A Guide to Chi-Squared Testing
GROSS and HARRIS · Fundamentals of Queueing Theory, *Third Edition*
*HAHN and SHAPIRO · Statistical Models in Engineering
HAHN and MEEKER · Statistical Intervals: A Guide for Practitioners
HALD · A History of Probability and Statistics and their Applications Before 1750
HALD · A History of Mathematical Statistics from 1750 to 1930
HAMPEL · Robust Statistics: The Approach Based on Influence Functions
HANNAN and DEISTLER · The Statistical Theory of Linear Systems
HEIBERGER · Computation for the Analysis of Designed Experiments
HEDAYAT and SINHA · Design and Inference in Finite Population Sampling
HELLER · MACSYMA for Statisticians
HINKELMAN and KEMPTHORNE: · Design and Analysis of Experiments, Volume 1: Introduction to Experimental Design
HOAGLIN, MOSTELLER, and TUKEY · Exploratory Approach to Analysis of Variance
HOAGLIN, MOSTELLER, and TUKEY · Exploring Data Tables, Trends and Shapes
*HOAGLIN, MOSTELLER, and TUKEY · Understanding Robust and Exploratory Data Analysis
HOCHBERG and TAMHANE · Multiple Comparison Procedures
HOCKING · Methods and Applications of Linear Models: Regression and the Analysis of Variance, *Second Edition*
HOEL · Introduction to Mathematical Statistics, *Fifth Edition*
HOGG and KLUGMAN · Loss Distributions
HOLLANDER and WOLFE · Nonparametric Statistical Methods, *Second Edition*

*Now available in a lower priced paperback edition in the Wiley Classics Library.

HOSMER and LEMESHOW · Applied Logistic Regression, *Second Edition*
HOSMER and LEMESHOW · Applied Survival Analysis: Regression Modeling of Time to Event Data
HØYLAND and RAUSAND · System Reliability Theory: Models and Statistical Methods
HUBER · Robust Statistics
HUBERTY · Applied Discriminant Analysis
HUNT and KENNEDY · Financial Derivatives in Theory and Practice
HUSKOVA, BERAN, and DUPAC · Collected Works of Jaroslav Hajek—with Commentary
IMAN and CONOVER · A Modern Approach to Statistics
JACKSON · A User's Guide to Principle Components
JOHN · Statistical Methods in Engineering and Quality Assurance
JOHNSON · Multivariate Statistical Simulation
JOHNSON and BALAKRISHNAN · Advances in the Theory and Practice of Statistics: A Volume in Honor of Samuel Kotz
JUDGE, GRIFFITHS, HILL, LÜTKEPOHL, and LEE · The Theory and Practice of Econometrics, *Second Edition*
JOHNSON and KOTZ · Distributions in Statistics
JOHNSON and KOTZ (editors) · Leading Personalities in Statistical Sciences: From the Seventeenth Century to the Present
JOHNSON, KOTZ, and BALAKRISHNAN · Continuous Univariate Distributions, Volume 1, *Second Edition*
JOHNSON, KOTZ, and BALAKRISHNAN · Continuous Univariate Distributions, Volume 2, *Second Edition*
JOHNSON, KOTZ, and BALAKRISHNAN · Discrete Multivariate Distributions
JOHNSON, KOTZ, and KEMP · Univariate Discrete Distributions, *Second Edition*
JUREČKOVÁ and SEN · Robust Statistical Procedures: Aymptotics and Interrelations
JUREK and MASON · Operator-Limit Distributions in Probability Theory
KADANE · Bayesian Methods and Ethics in a Clinical Trial Design
KADANE AND SCHUM · A Probabilistic Analysis of the Sacco and Vanzetti Evidence
KALBFLEISCH and PRENTICE · The Statistical Analysis of Failure Time Data, *Second Edition*
KASS and VOS · Geometrical Foundations of Asymptotic Inference
KAUFMAN and ROUSSEEUW · Finding Groups in Data: An Introduction to Cluster Analysis
KEDEM and FOKIANOS · Regression Models for Time Series Analysis
KENDALL, BARDEN, CARNE, and LE · Shape and Shape Theory
KHURI · Advanced Calculus with Applications in Statistics, *Second Edition*
KHURI, MATHEW, and SINHA · Statistical Tests for Mixed Linear Models
KLEIBER and KOTZ · Statistical Size Distributions in Economics and Actuarial Sciences
KLUGMAN, PANJER, and WILLMOT · Loss Models: From Data to Decisions
KLUGMAN, PANJER, and WILLMOT · Solutions Manual to Accompany Loss Models: From Data to Decisions
KOTZ, BALAKRISHNAN, and JOHNSON · Continuous Multivariate Distributions, Volume 1, *Second Edition*
KOTZ and JOHNSON (editors) · Encyclopedia of Statistical Sciences: Volumes 1 to 9 with Index
KOTZ and JOHNSON (editors) · Encyclopedia of Statistical Sciences: Supplement Volume
KOTZ, READ, and BANKS (editors) · Encyclopedia of Statistical Sciences: Update Volume 1
KOTZ, READ, and BANKS (editors) · Encyclopedia of Statistical Sciences: Update Volume 2
KOVALENKO, KUZNETZOV, and PEGG · Mathematical Theory of Reliability of Time-Dependent Systems with Practical Applications
LACHIN · Biostatistical Methods: The Assessment of Relative Risks
LAD · Operational Subjective Statistical Methods: A Mathematical, Philosophical, and Historical Introduction
LAMPERTI · Probability: A Survey of the Mathematical Theory, *Second Edition*
LANGE, RYAN, BILLARD, BRILLINGER, CONQUEST, and GREENHOUSE · Case Studies in Biometry
LARSON · Introduction to Probability Theory and Statistical Inference, *Third Edition*
LAWLESS · Statistical Models and Methods for Lifetime Data, *Second Edition*
LAWSON · Statistical Methods in Spatial Epidemiology
LE · Applied Categorical Data Analysis
LE · Applied Survival Analysis

*Now available in a lower priced paperback edition in the Wiley Classics Library.

LEE and WANG · Statistical Methods for Survival Data Analysis, *Third Edition*
LePAGE and BILLARD · Exploring the Limits of Bootstrap
LEYLAND and GOLDSTEIN (editors) · Multilevel Modelling of Health Statistics
LIAO · Statistical Group Comparison
LINDVALL · Lectures on the Coupling Method
LINHART and ZUCCHINI · Model Selection
LITTLE and RUBIN · Statistical Analysis with Missing Data, *Second Edition*
LLOYD · The Statistical Analysis of Categorical Data
MAGNUS and NEUDECKER · Matrix Differential Calculus with Applications in Statistics and Econometrics, *Revised Edition*
MALLER and ZHOU · Survival Analysis with Long Term Survivors
MALLOWS · Design, Data, and Analysis by Some Friends of Cuthbert Daniel
MANN, SCHAFER, and SINGPURWALLA · Methods for Statistical Analysis of Reliability and Life Data
MANTON, WOODBURY, and TOLLEY · Statistical Applications Using Fuzzy Sets
MARDIA and JUPP · Directional Statistics
MASON, GUNST, and HESS · Statistical Design and Analysis of Experiments with Applications to Engineering and Science, *Second Edition*
McCULLOCH and SEARLE · Generalized, Linear, and Mixed Models
McFADDEN · Management of Data in Clinical Trials
McLACHLAN · Discriminant Analysis and Statistical Pattern Recognition
McLACHLAN and KRISHNAN · The EM Algorithm and Extensions
McLACHLAN and PEEL · Finite Mixture Models
McNEIL · Epidemiological Research Methods
MEEKER and ESCOBAR · Statistical Methods for Reliability Data
MEERSCHAERT and SCHEFFLER · Limit Distributions for Sums of Independent Random Vectors: Heavy Tails in Theory and Practice
*MILLER · Survival Analysis, *Second Edition*
MONTGOMERY, PECK, and VINING · Introduction to Linear Regression Analysis, *Third Edition*
MORGENTHALER and TUKEY · Configural Polysampling: A Route to Practical Robustness
MUIRHEAD · Aspects of Multivariate Statistical Theory
MURRAY · X-STAT 2.0 Statistical Experimentation, Design Data Analysis, and Nonlinear Optimization
MYERS and MONTGOMERY · Response Surface Methodology: Process and Product Optimization Using Designed Experiments, *Second Edition*
MYERS, MONTGOMERY, and VINING · Generalized Linear Models. With Applications in Engineering and the Sciences
NELSON · Accelerated Testing, Statistical Models, Test Plans, and Data Analyses
NELSON · Applied Life Data Analysis
NEWMAN · Biostatistical Methods in Epidemiology
OCHI · Applied Probability and Stochastic Processes in Engineering and Physical Sciences
OKABE, BOOTS, SUGIHARA, and CHIU · Spatial Tesselations: Concepts and Applications of Voronoi Diagrams, *Second Edition*
OLIVER and SMITH · Influence Diagrams, Belief Nets and Decision Analysis
PANKRATZ · Forecasting with Dynamic Regression Models
PANKRATZ · Forecasting with Univariate Box-Jenkins Models: Concepts and Cases
*PARZEN · Modern Probability Theory and Its Applications
PEÑA, TIAO, and TSAY · A Course in Time Series Analysis
PIANTADOSI · Clinical Trials: A Methodologic Perspective
PORT · Theoretical Probability for Applications
POURAHMADI · Foundations of Time Series Analysis and Prediction Theory
PRESS · Bayesian Statistics: Principles, Models, and Applications
PRESS · Subjective and Objective Bayesian Statistics, *Second Edition*
PRESS and TANUR · The Subjectivity of Scientists and the Bayesian Approach

*Now available in a lower priced paperback edition in the Wiley Classics Library.

PUKELSHEIM · Optimal Experimental Design
PURI, VILAPLANA, and WERTZ · New Perspectives in Theoretical and Applied Statistics
PUTERMAN · Markov Decision Processes: Discrete Stochastic Dynamic Programming
*RAO · Linear Statistical Inference and Its Applications, *Second Edition*
RENCHER · Linear Models in Statistics
RENCHER · Methods of Multivariate Analysis, *Second Edition*
RENCHER · Multivariate Statistical Inference with Applications
RIPLEY · Spatial Statistics
RIPLEY · Stochastic Simulation
ROBINSON · Practical Strategies for Experimenting
ROHATGI and SALEH · An Introduction to Probability and Statistics, *Second Edition*
ROLSKI, SCHMIDLI, SCHMIDT, and TEUGELS · Stochastic Processes for Insurance and Finance
ROSENBERGER and LACHIN · Randomization in Clinical Trials: Theory and Practice
ROSS · Introduction to Probability and Statistics for Engineers and Scientists
ROUSSEEUW and LEROY · Robust Regression and Outlier Detection
RUBIN · Multiple Imputation for Nonresponse in Surveys
RUBINSTEIN · Simulation and the Monte Carlo Method
RUBINSTEIN and MELAMED · Modern Simulation and Modeling
RYAN · Modern Regression Methods
RYAN · Statistical Methods for Quality Improvement, *Second Edition*
SALTELLI, CHAN, and SCOTT (editors) · Sensitivity Analysis
*SCHEFFE · The Analysis of Variance
SCHIMEK · Smoothing and Regression: Approaches, Computation, and Application
SCHOTT · Matrix Analysis for Statistics
SCHUSS · Theory and Applications of Stochastic Differential Equations
SCOTT · Multivariate Density Estimation: Theory, Practice, and Visualization
*SEARLE · Linear Models
SEARLE · Linear Models for Unbalanced Data
SEARLE · Matrix Algebra Useful for Statistics
SEARLE, CASELLA, and McCULLOCH · Variance Components
SEARLE and WILLETT · Matrix Algebra for Applied Economics
SEBER and LEE · Linear Regression Analysis, *Second Edition*
SEBER · Multivariate Observations
SEBER and WILD · Nonlinear Regression
SENNOTT · Stochastic Dynamic Programming and the Control of Queueing Systems
*SERFLING · Approximation Theorems of Mathematical Statistics
SHAFER and VOVK · Probability and Finance: It's Only a Game!
SMALL and McLEISH · Hilbert Space Methods in Probability and Statistical Inference
SRIVASTAVA · Methods of Multivariate Statistics
STAPLETON · Linear Statistical Models
STAUDTE and SHEATHER · Robust Estimation and Testing
STOYAN, KENDALL, and MECKE · Stochastic Geometry and Its Applications, *Second Edition*
STOYAN and STOYAN · Fractals, Random Shapes and Point Fields: Methods of Geometrical Statistics
STYAN · The Collected Papers of T. W. Anderson: 1943–1985
SUTTON, ABRAMS, JONES, SHELDON, and SONG · Methods for Meta-Analysis in Medical Research
TANAKA · Time Series Analysis: Nonstationary and Noninvertible Distribution Theory
THOMPSON · Empirical Model Building
THOMPSON · Sampling, *Second Edition*
THOMPSON · Simulation: A Modeler's Approach
THOMPSON and SEBER · Adaptive Sampling
THOMPSON, WILLIAMS, and FINDLAY · Models for Investors in Real World Markets

*Now available in a lower priced paperback edition in the Wiley Classics Library.

TIAO, BISGAARD, HILL, PEÑA, and STIGLER (editors) · Box on Quality and Discovery: with Design, Control, and Robustness
TIERNEY · LISP-STAT: An Object-Oriented Environment for Statistical Computing and Dynamic Graphics
TSAY · Analysis of Financial Time Series
UPTON and FINGLETON · Spatial Data Analysis by Example, Volume II: Categorical and Directional Data
VAN BELLE · Statistical Rules of Thumb
VIDAKOVIC · Statistical Modeling by Wavelets
WEISBERG · Applied Linear Regression, *Second Edition*
WELSH · Aspects of Statistical Inference
WESTFALL and YOUNG · Resampling-Based Multiple Testing: Examples and Methods for *p*-Value Adjustment
WHITTAKER · Graphical Models in Applied Multivariate Statistics
WINKER · Optimization Heuristics in Economics: Applications of Threshold Accepting
WONNACOTT and WONNACOTT · Econometrics, *Second Edition*
WOODING · Planning Pharmaceutical Clinical Trials: Basic Statistical Principles
WOOLSON and CLARKE · Statistical Methods for the Analysis of Biomedical Data, *Second Edition*
WU and HAMADA · Experiments: Planning, Analysis, and Parameter Design Optimization
YANG · The Construction Theory of Denumerable Markov Processes
\*ZELLNER · An Introduction to Bayesian Inference in Econometrics
ZHOU, OBUCHOWSKI, and McCLISH · Statistical Methods in Diagnostic Medicine

\*Now available in a lower priced paperback edition in the Wiley Classics Library.